BUCK ROGERS®

VOLUME 2: FROM THE EARTH TO THE MOON

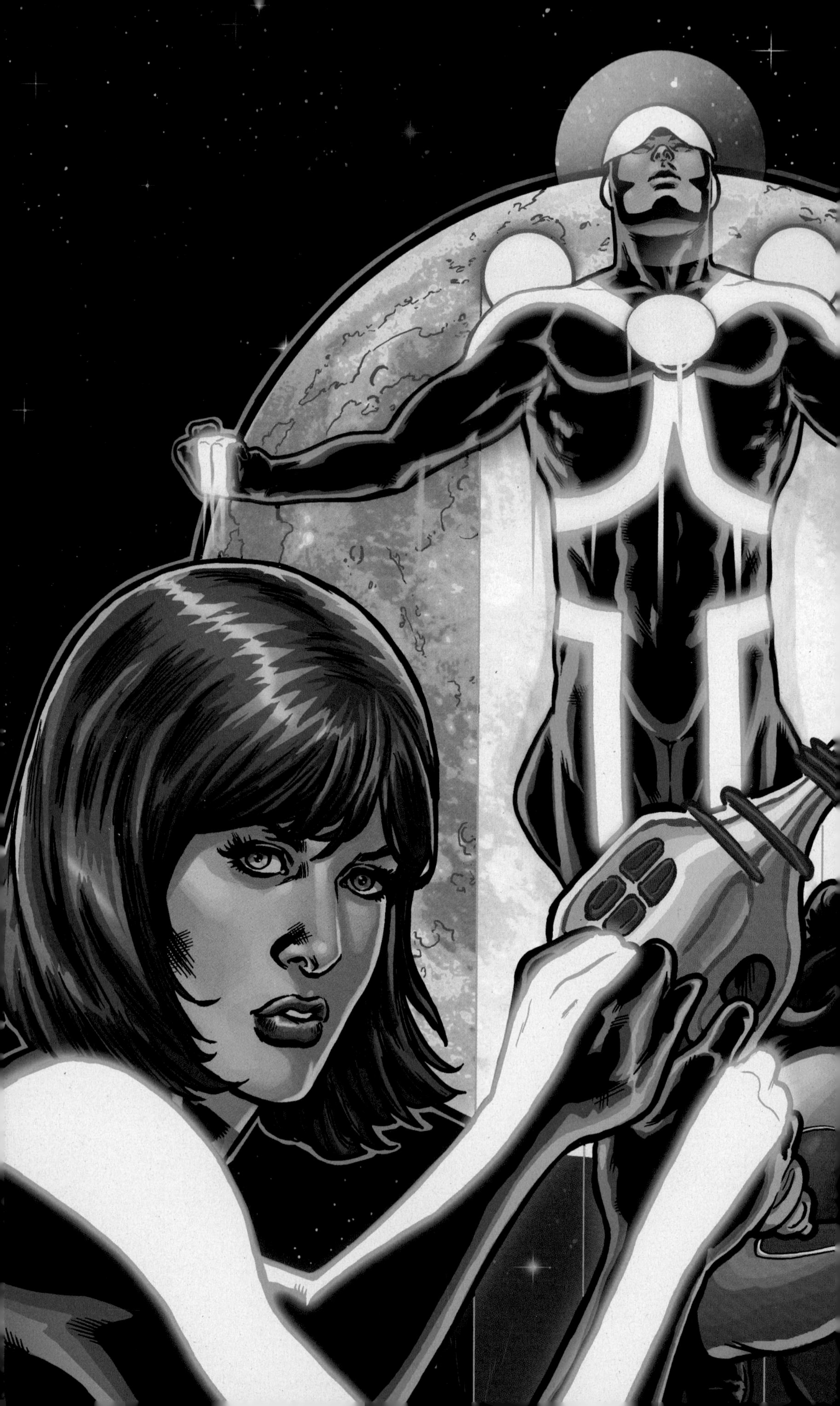

Written by

SCOTT BEATTY

Illustrated by

CARLOS RAFAEL (Issues 7-12)

and **CARLOS PAUL** (Issue 6)

Colored by

CARLOS LOPEZ

Lettered by

SIMON BOWLAND

Cover by

CARLOS RAFAEL

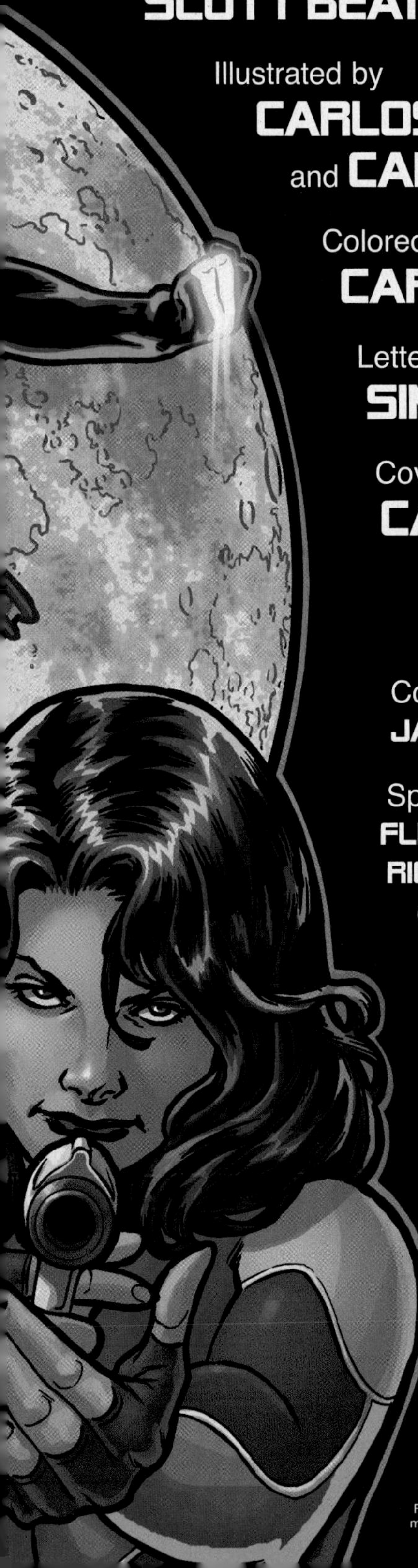

Collection design by

JASON ULLMEYER

Special thanks to

FLINT DILLE of the Dille Family Trust,

RICHARD LEIBOWITZ and **HOWARD BLISS**

of Union Entertainment

HARRIS MILLER II, SCOTT CHERRIN

and **LESLIE LEVINE**

DYNAMITE ENTERTAINMENT

DYNAMITEENTERTAINMENT.COM

NICK BARRUCCI • PRESIDENT
JUAN COLLADO • CHIEF OPERATING OFFICER
JOSEPH RYBANDT • EDITOR
JOSH JOHNSON • CREATIVE DIRECTOR
RICH YOUNG • BUSINESS DEVELOPMENT
JASON ULLMEYER • GRAPHIC DESIGNER

ISBN-10: 1-60690-152-4 ISBN-13: 978-1-60690-152-6 First Printing 10 9 8 7 6 5 4 3 2 1

For information regarding press, media rights, foreign rights, licensing, promotions, and advertising e-mail: marketing@dynamiteentertainment.com

THE FUTURE IS NOW!

For Anthony "Buck" Rogers, the leap forward 500 years to the 25th century occurred in the blink of an eye. He is now a stranger in not-so-strange lands, an Earth both familiar and radically altered in five tumultuous centuries since his quantum acceleration forward in time, the result of an accident involving Buck's untested gravity drive, a device he had hoped would make space travel fast and easy for all mankind. Unfortunately, he was half right.

While attempting to retrieve a wayward space probe loaded with genetic specimens of various Terran life-forms, Buck most definitely overshot his mark. The probe was ultimately found by The Pack, voracious aliens from beyond our solar system who measured the galaxy on a caloric standard. Bio-engineering the Terran gene-samples into its own army of hunting scouts, The Pack sent the animals home to prey upon an Earth still struggling to rebuild after wars and calamity had laid waste to large portions of the planet. Buck Rogers himself brought the story full-circle when he--along with Colonel Wilma Deering, a beautiful officer in Earth's Unified Orgs defense forces--found themselves in The Pack's hungry clutches. A man out of time with nothing left to lose and everything to win, Buck led the do-or-die mission to scuttle The Pack's abattoir ship, thus forcing the aliens to return to deep space without their spoils of war.

Hailed as a hero on Earth by human citizens grateful to escape The Pack's slaughter-ships, Buck was less than successful in convincing the Unified Orgs leadership that he was indeed a bona fide time-traveler. As the UO ponders his fate, Buck set out to explore the brave new world that was once his home a half-millennium ago. With the genius Dr. Huer and Wilma Deering's kid brother Buddy in tow, it isn't long before Buck finds Earth's future troubled by new threats from both within and without.

Underground, in the air, and to the Moon, the story of Buck Rogers in the 25th century is far from over!

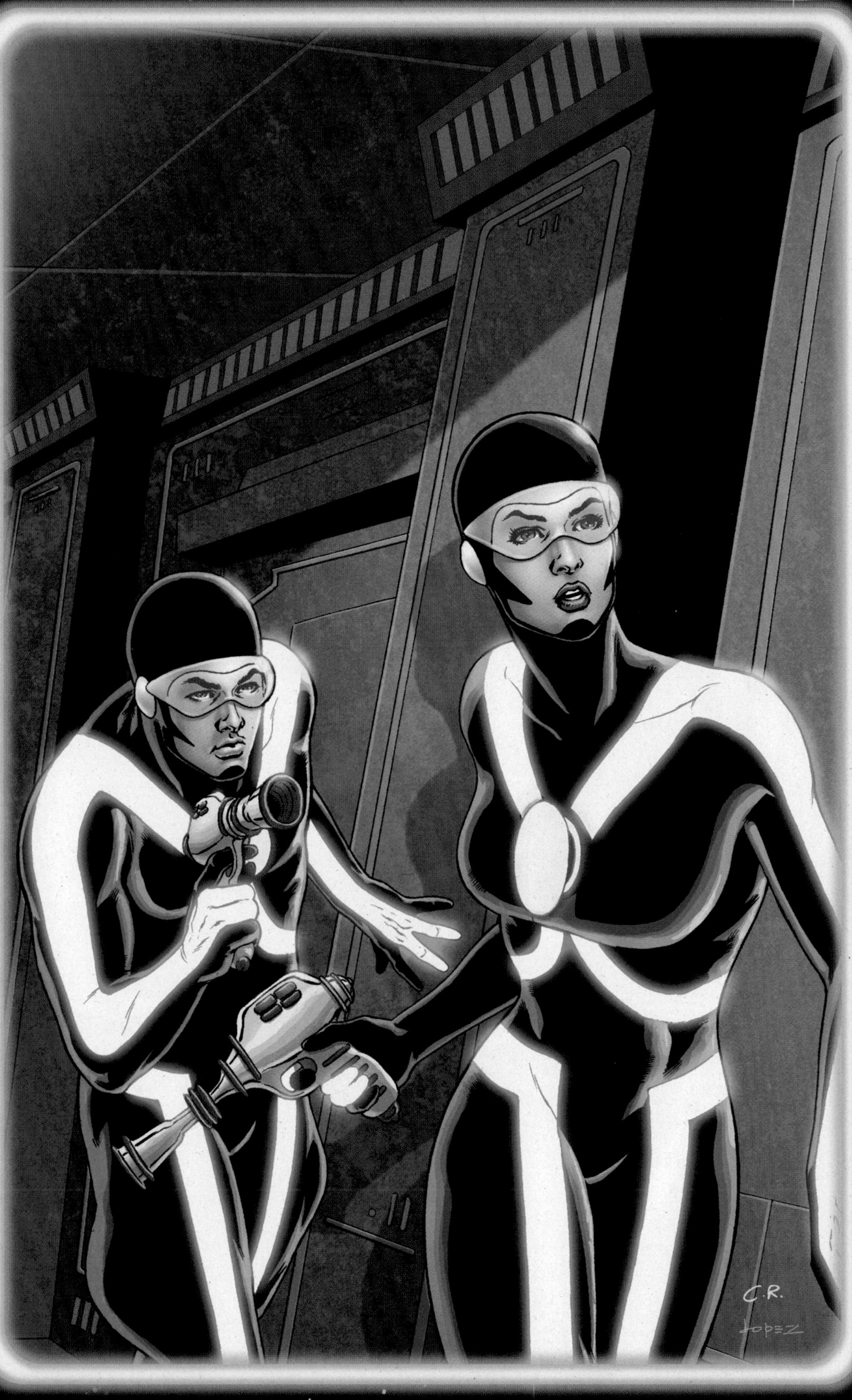

FUTURE SHOCK EPILOGUE: Never Mind What You Leave Behind

ISSUE SIX COVER BY CARLOS RAFAEL

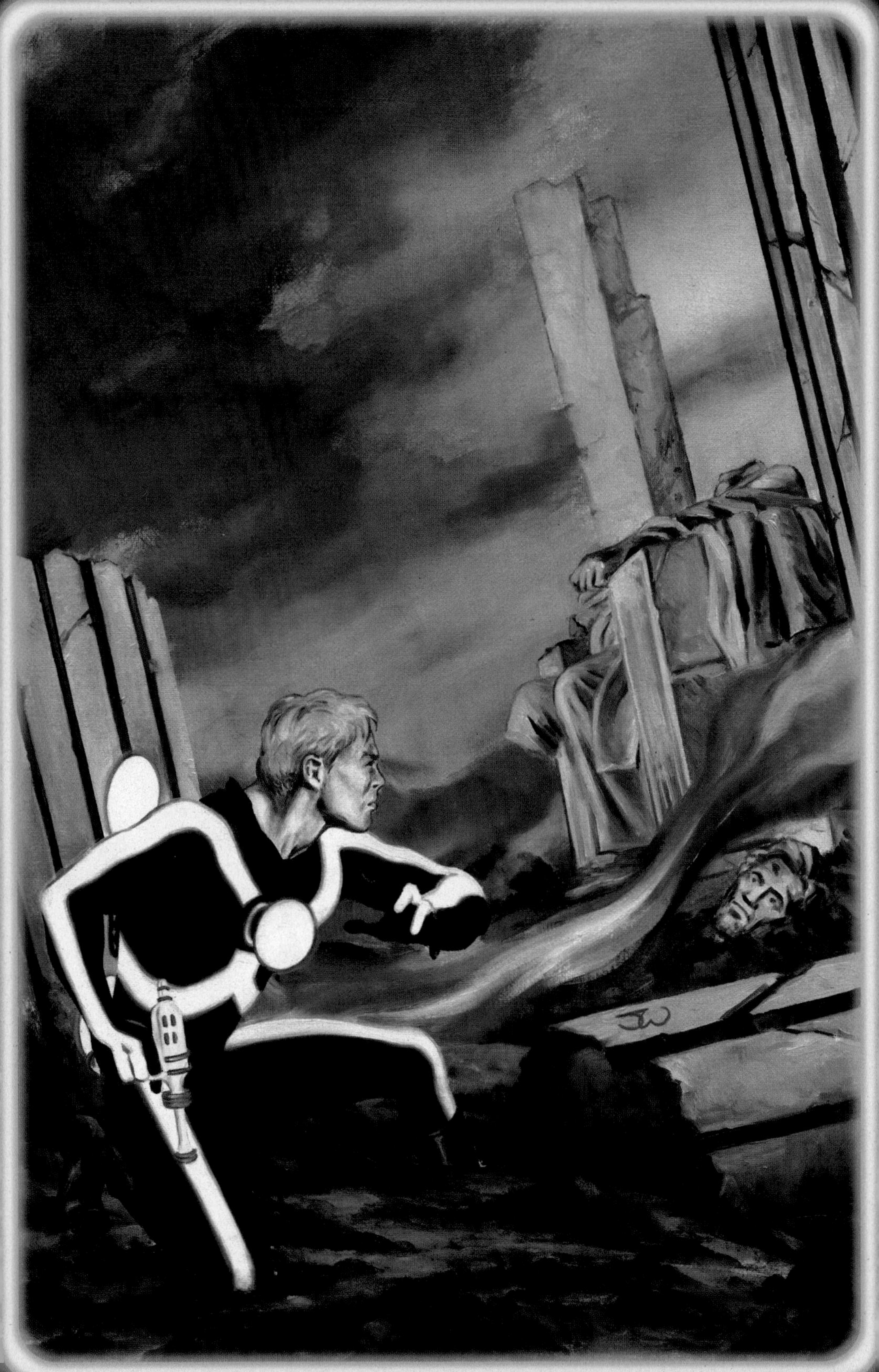
JW

ALTERNATE COVER BY JOHN WATSON

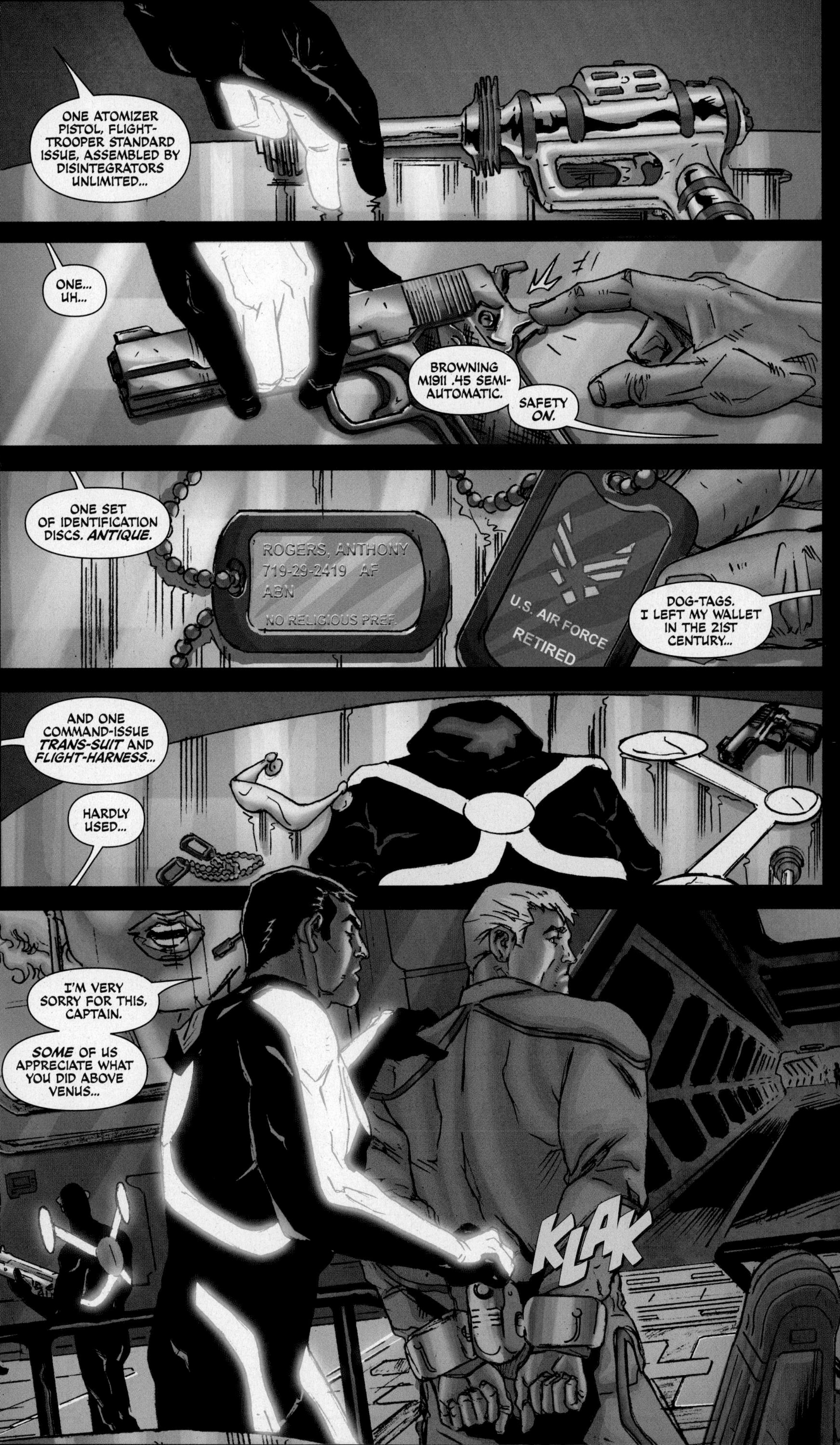
ONE ATOMIZER PISTOL, FLIGHT-TROOPER STANDARD ISSUE, ASSEMBLED BY DISINTEGRATORS UNLIMITED...
ONE... UH...
BROWNING M1911 .45 SEMI-AUTOMATIC.
SAFETY ON.
ONE SET OF IDENTIFICATION DISCS. ANTIQUE.
ROGERS, ANTHONY
719-29-2419 AF
ABN
NO RELIGIOUS PREF.
U.S. AIR FORCE
RETIRED
DOG-TAGS. I LEFT MY WALLET IN THE 21ST CENTURY...
AND ONE COMMAND-ISSUE TRANS-SUIT AND FLIGHT-HARNESS...
HARDLY USED...
I'M VERY SORRY FOR THIS, CAPTAIN.
SOME OF US APPRECIATE WHAT YOU DID ABOVE VENUS...
KLAK

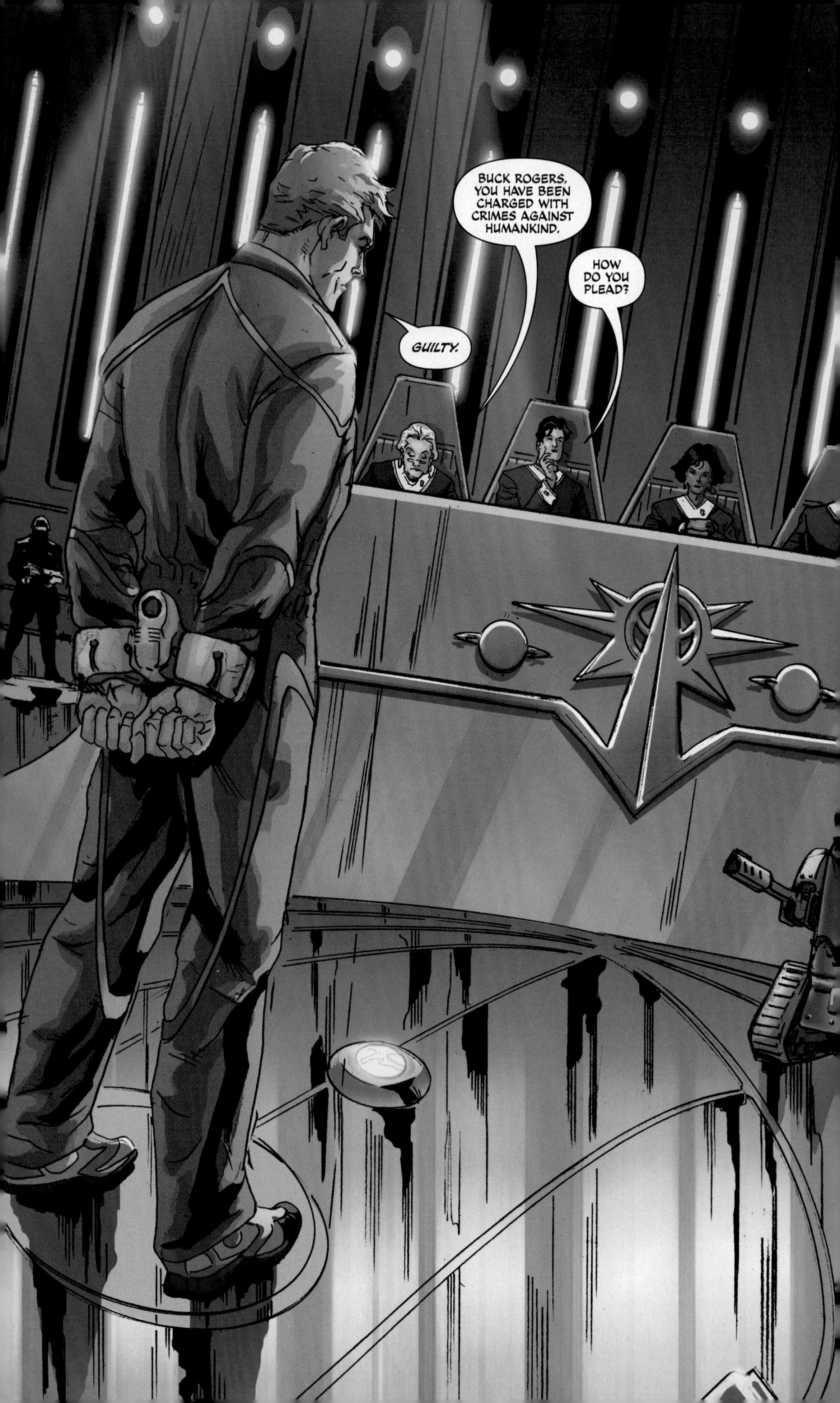
BUCK ROGERS, YOU HAVE BEEN CHARGED WITH CRIMES AGAINST HUMANKIND.
HOW DO YOU PLEAD?
GUILTY.

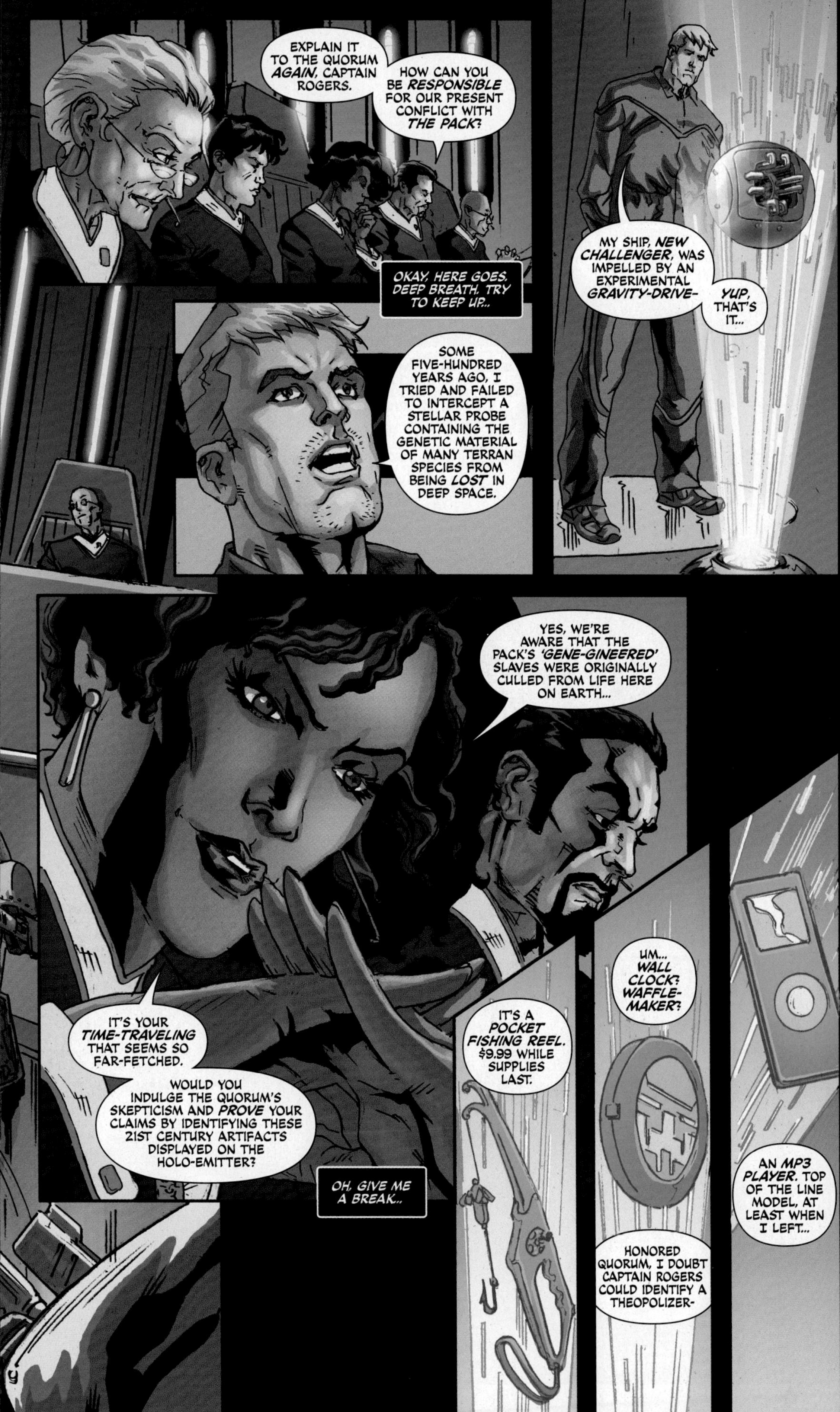
EXPLAIN IT TO THE QUORUM *AGAIN*, CAPTAIN ROGERS.
HOW CAN YOU BE *RESPONSIBLE* FOR OUR PRESENT CONFLICT WITH *THE PACK*?
OKAY, HERE GOES. DEEP BREATH. TRY TO KEEP UP...
SOME FIVE-HUNDRED YEARS AGO, I TRIED AND FAILED TO INTERCEPT A STELLAR PROBE CONTAINING THE GENETIC MATERIAL OF MANY TERRAN SPECIES FROM BEING *LOST* IN DEEP SPACE.
MY SHIP, *NEW CHALLENGER*, WAS IMPELLED BY AN EXPERIMENTAL *GRAVITY-DRIVE*-
YUP, THAT'S IT...
YES, WE'RE AWARE THAT THE PACK'S *'GENE-GINEERED'* SLAVES WERE ORIGINALLY CULLED FROM LIFE HERE ON EARTH...
IT'S YOUR *TIME-TRAVELING* THAT SEEMS SO FAR-FETCHED.
WOULD YOU INDULGE THE QUORUM'S SKEPTICISM AND *PROVE* YOUR CLAIMS BY IDENTIFYING THESE 21ST CENTURY ARTIFACTS DISPLAYED ON THE HOLO-EMITTER?
OH, GIVE ME A BREAK...
IT'S A *POCKET FISHING REEL*. $9.99 WHILE SUPPLIES LAST.
UM... *WALL CLOCK*? *WAFFLE-MAKER*?
HONORED QUORUM, I DOUBT CAPTAIN ROGERS COULD IDENTIFY A THEOPOLIZER-
AN *MP3 PLAYER*. TOP OF THE LINE MODEL, AT LEAST WHEN I LEFT...

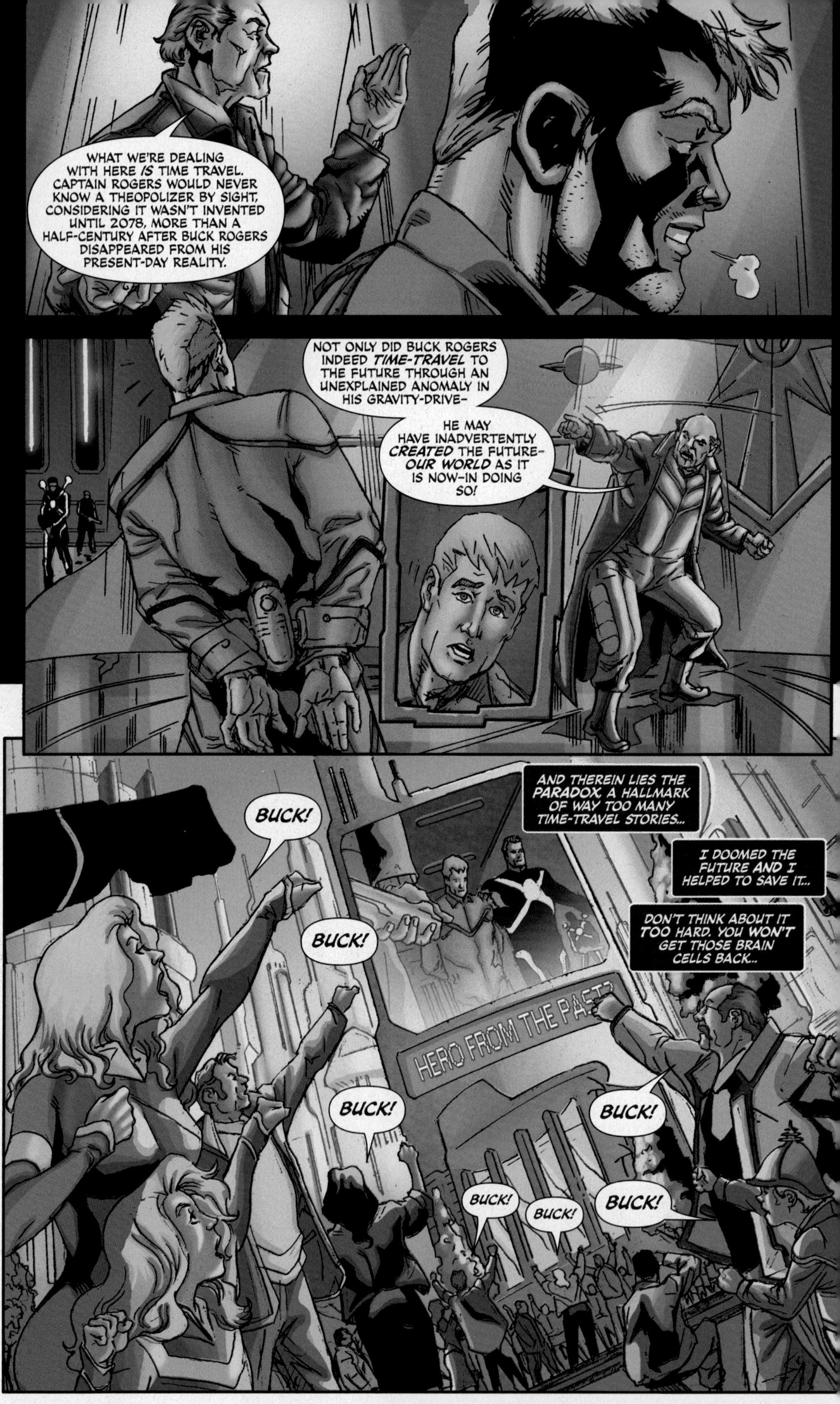
WHAT WE'RE DEALING WITH HERE *IS* TIME TRAVEL. CAPTAIN ROGERS WOULD NEVER KNOW A THEOPOLIZER BY SIGHT, CONSIDERING IT WASN'T INVENTED UNTIL 2078, MORE THAN A HALF-CENTURY AFTER BUCK ROGERS DISAPPEARED FROM HIS PRESENT-DAY REALITY.
NOT ONLY DID BUCK ROGERS INDEED *TIME-TRAVEL* TO THE FUTURE THROUGH AN UNEXPLAINED ANOMALY IN HIS GRAVITY-DRIVE–
HE MAY HAVE INADVERTENTLY *CREATED* THE FUTURE– *OUR WORLD* AS IT IS NOW–IN DOING SO!
AND THEREIN LIES THE *PARADOX*, A HALLMARK OF WAY TOO MANY TIME-TRAVEL STORIES...
BUCK!
I DOOMED THE FUTURE AND I HELPED TO SAVE IT...
DON'T THINK ABOUT IT TOO HARD. YOU *WON'T* GET THOSE BRAIN CELLS BACK...
BUCK!
HERO FROM THE PAST
BUCK!
BUCK!
BUCK!
BUCK!
BUCK!

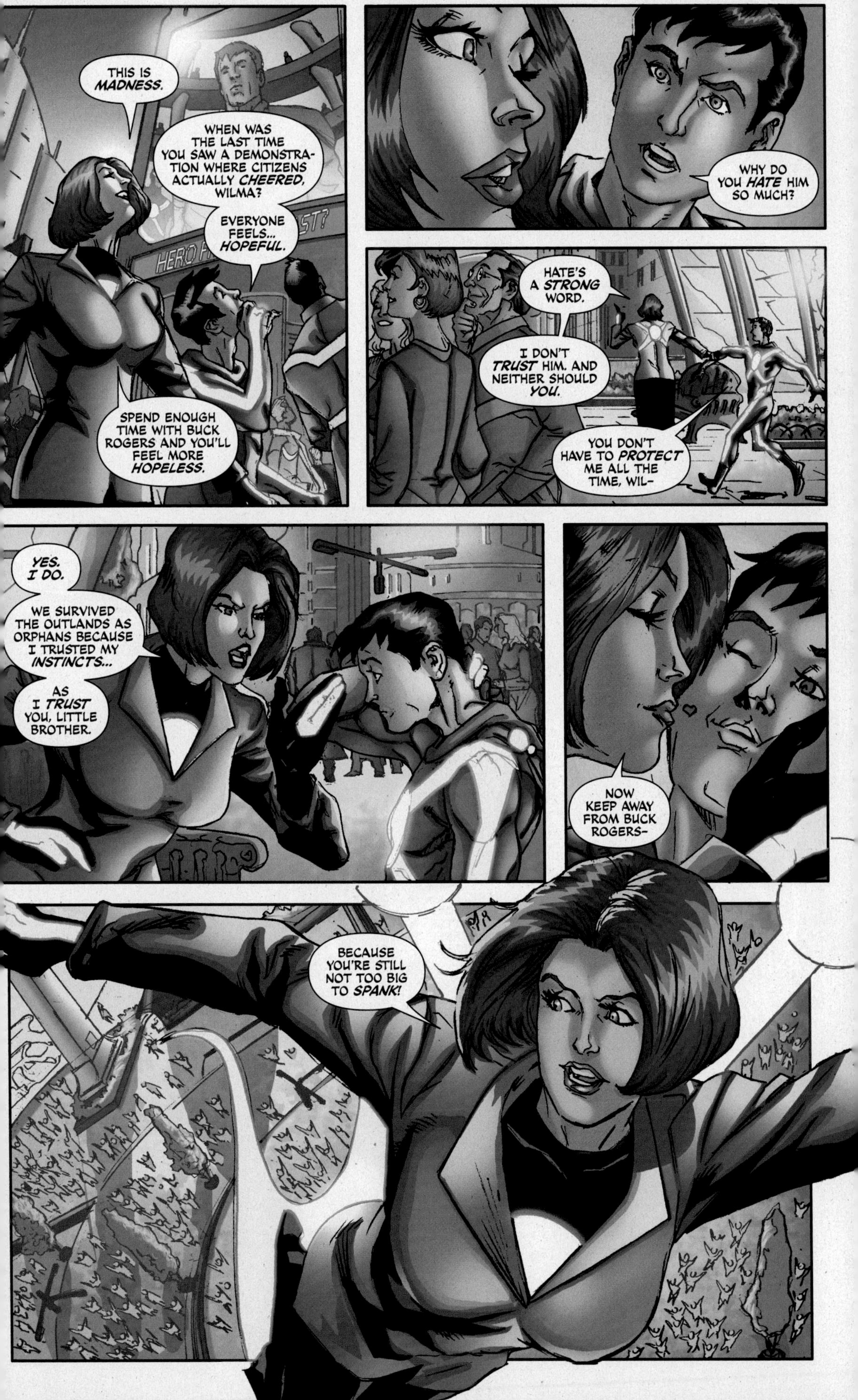
THIS IS MADNESS.
WHEN WAS THE LAST TIME YOU SAW A DEMONSTRATION WHERE CITIZENS ACTUALLY CHEERED, WILMA?
EVERYONE FEELS... HOPEFUL.
SPEND ENOUGH TIME WITH BUCK ROGERS AND YOU'LL FEEL MORE HOPELESS.
HERO
WHY DO YOU HATE HIM SO MUCH?
HATE'S A STRONG WORD.
I DON'T TRUST HIM. AND NEITHER SHOULD YOU.
YOU DON'T HAVE TO PROTECT ME ALL THE TIME, WIL-
YES. I DO.
WE SURVIVED THE OUTLANDS AS ORPHANS BECAUSE I TRUSTED MY INSTINCTS...
AS I TRUST YOU, LITTLE BROTHER.
NOW KEEP AWAY FROM BUCK ROGERS-
BECAUSE YOU'RE STILL NOT TOO BIG TO SPANK!

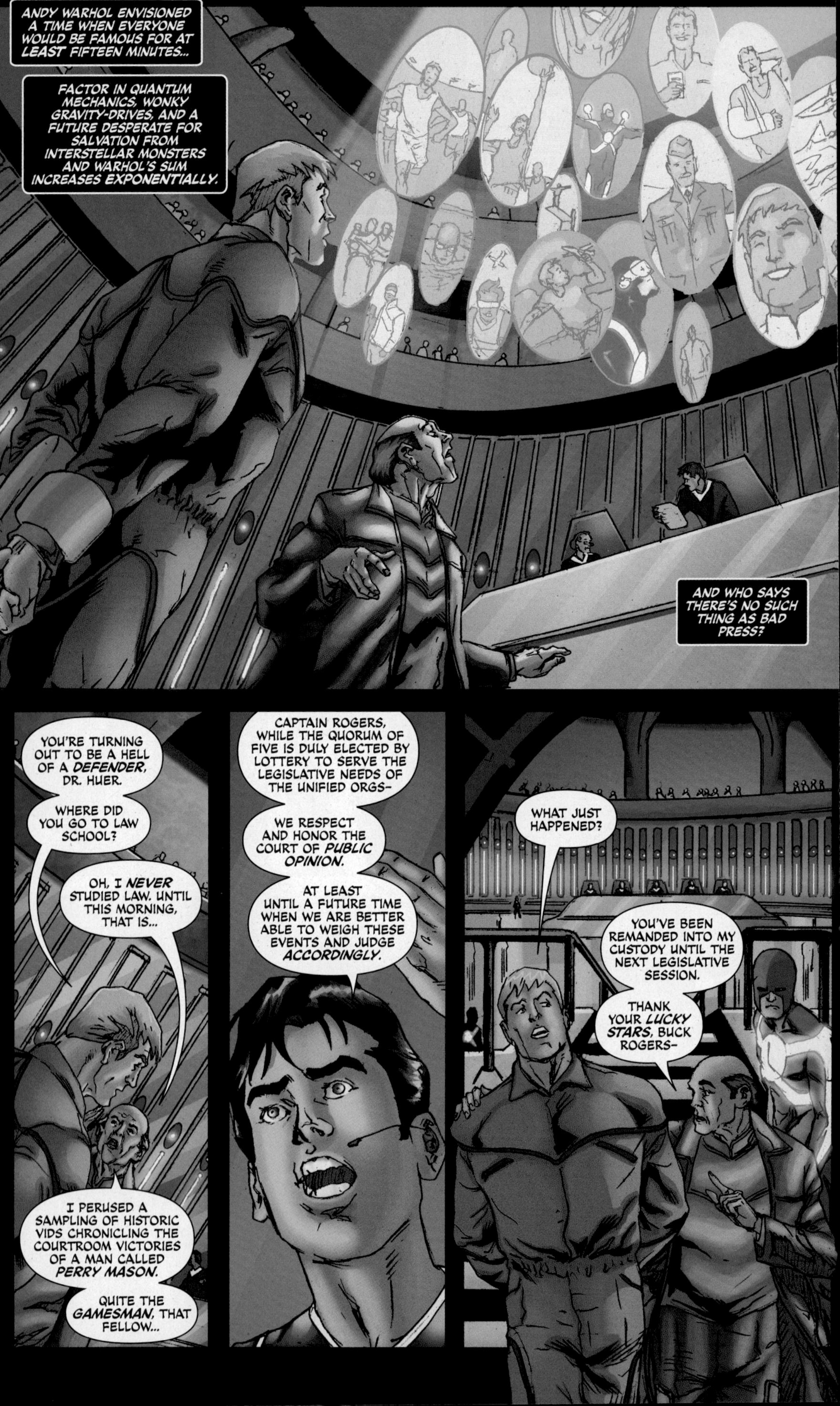

ANDY WARHOL ENVISIONED A TIME WHEN EVERYONE WOULD BE FAMOUS FOR AT LEAST FIFTEEN MINUTES...
FACTOR IN QUANTUM MECHANICS, WONKY GRAVITY-DRIVES, AND A FUTURE DESPERATE FOR SALVATION FROM INTERSTELLAR MONSTERS AND WARHOL'S SUM INCREASES EXPONENTIALLY.
AND WHO SAYS THERE'S NO SUCH THING AS BAD PRESS?
YOU'RE TURNING OUT TO BE A HELL OF A DEFENDER, DR. HUER.
WHERE DID YOU GO TO LAW SCHOOL?
OH, I NEVER STUDIED LAW. UNTIL THIS MORNING, THAT IS...
I PERUSED A SAMPLING OF HISTORIC VIDS CHRONICLING THE COURTROOM VICTORIES OF A MAN CALLED PERRY MASON.
QUITE THE GAMESMAN, THAT FELLOW...
CAPTAIN ROGERS, WHILE THE QUORUM OF FIVE IS DULY ELECTED BY LOTTERY TO SERVE THE LEGISLATIVE NEEDS OF THE UNIFIED ORGS-
WE RESPECT AND HONOR THE COURT OF PUBLIC OPINION.
AT LEAST UNTIL A FUTURE TIME WHEN WE ARE BETTER ABLE TO WEIGH THESE EVENTS AND JUDGE ACCORDINGLY.
WHAT JUST HAPPENED?
YOU'VE BEEN REMANDED INTO MY CUSTODY UNTIL THE NEXT LEGISLATIVE SESSION.
THANK YOUR LUCKY STARS, BUCK ROGERS-

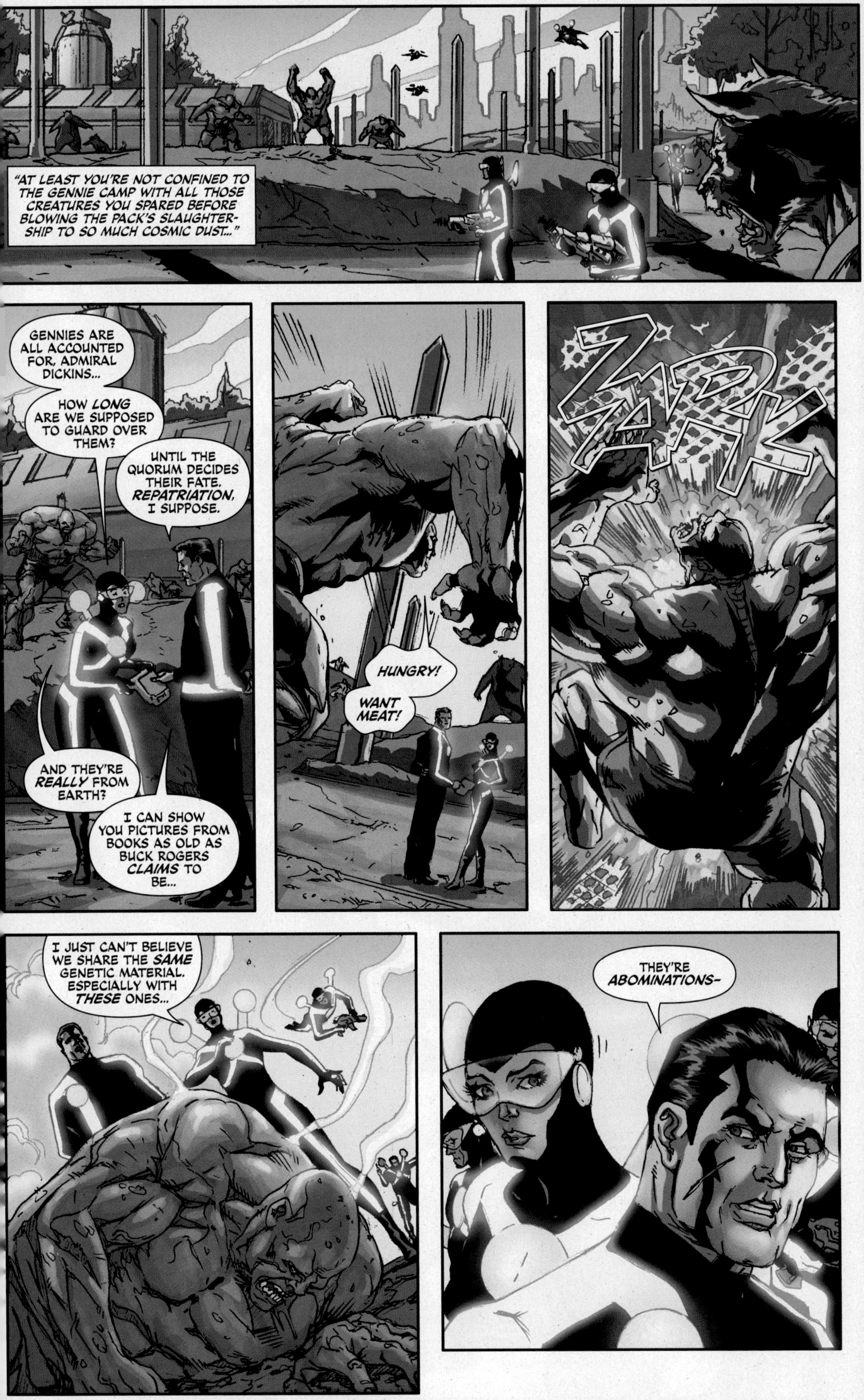
"AT LEAST YOU'RE NOT CONFINED TO THE GENNIE CAMP WITH ALL THOSE CREATURES YOU SPARED BEFORE BLOWING THE PACK'S SLAUGHTER-SHIP TO SO MUCH COSMIC DUST..."
GENNIES ARE ALL ACCOUNTED FOR, ADMIRAL DICKINS...
HOW *LONG* ARE WE SUPPOSED TO GUARD OVER THEM?
UNTIL THE QUORUM DECIDES THEIR FATE. *REPATRIATION*, I SUPPOSE.
AND THEY'RE *REALLY* FROM EARTH?
I CAN SHOW YOU PICTURES FROM BOOKS AS OLD AS BUCK ROGERS *CLAIMS* TO BE...
HUNGRY!
WANT MEAT!
ZARK
I JUST CAN'T BELIEVE WE SHARE THE *SAME* GENETIC MATERIAL. ESPECIALLY WITH *THESE* ONES...
THEY'RE *ABOMINATIONS*-

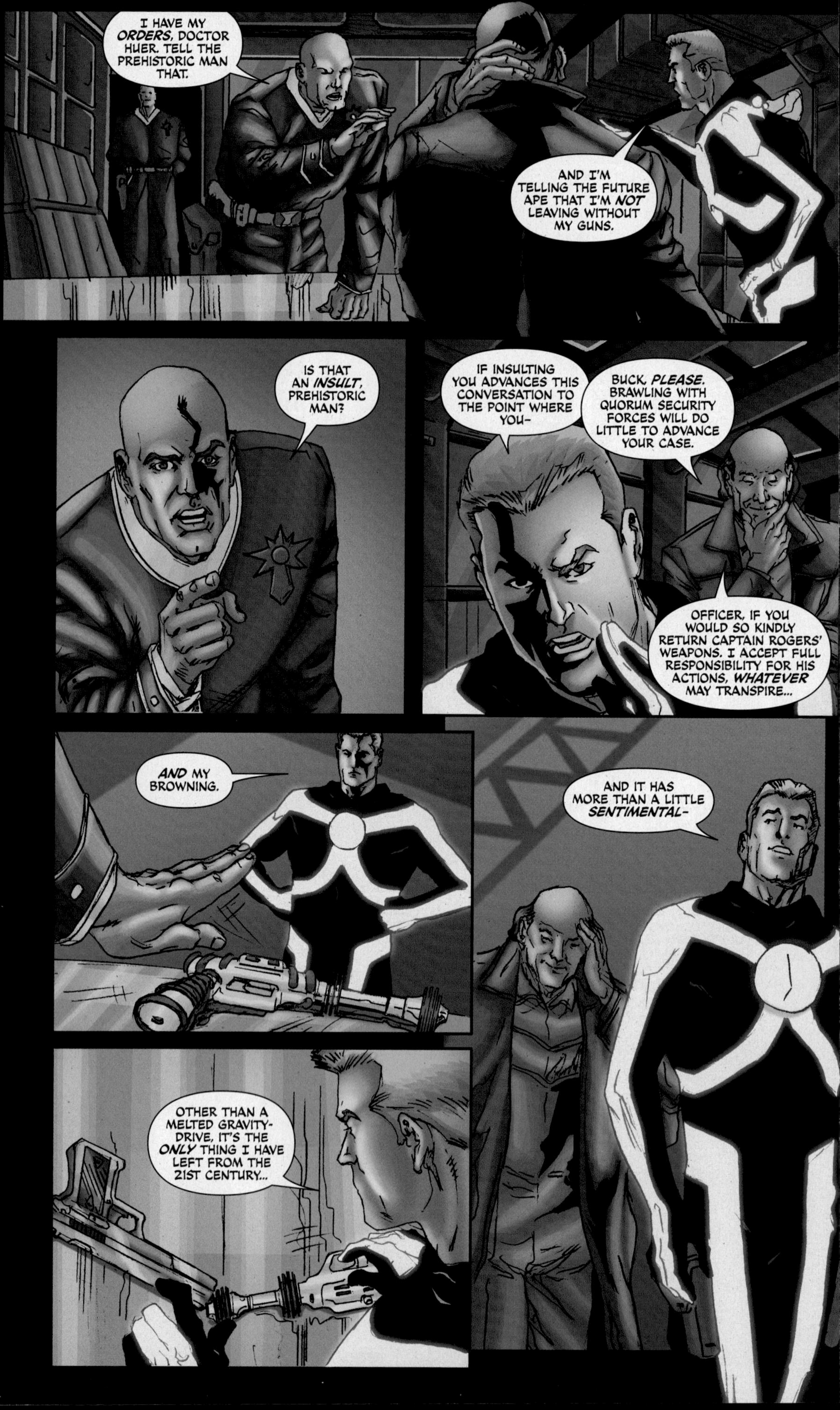
I HAVE MY ORDERS, DOCTOR HUER. TELL THE PREHISTORIC MAN THAT.
AND I'M TELLING THE FUTURE APE THAT I'M NOT LEAVING WITHOUT MY GUNS.
IS THAT AN INSULT, PREHISTORIC MAN?
IF INSULTING YOU ADVANCES THIS CONVERSATION TO THE POINT WHERE YOU-
BUCK, PLEASE. BRAWLING WITH QUORUM SECURITY FORCES WILL DO LITTLE TO ADVANCE YOUR CASE.
OFFICER, IF YOU WOULD SO KINDLY RETURN CAPTAIN ROGERS' WEAPONS. I ACCEPT FULL RESPONSIBILITY FOR HIS ACTIONS, WHATEVER MAY TRANSPIRE...
AND MY BROWNING.
AND IT HAS MORE THAN A LITTLE SENTIMENTAL-
OTHER THAN A MELTED GRAVITY-DRIVE, IT'S THE ONLY THING I HAVE LEFT FROM THE 21ST CENTURY...

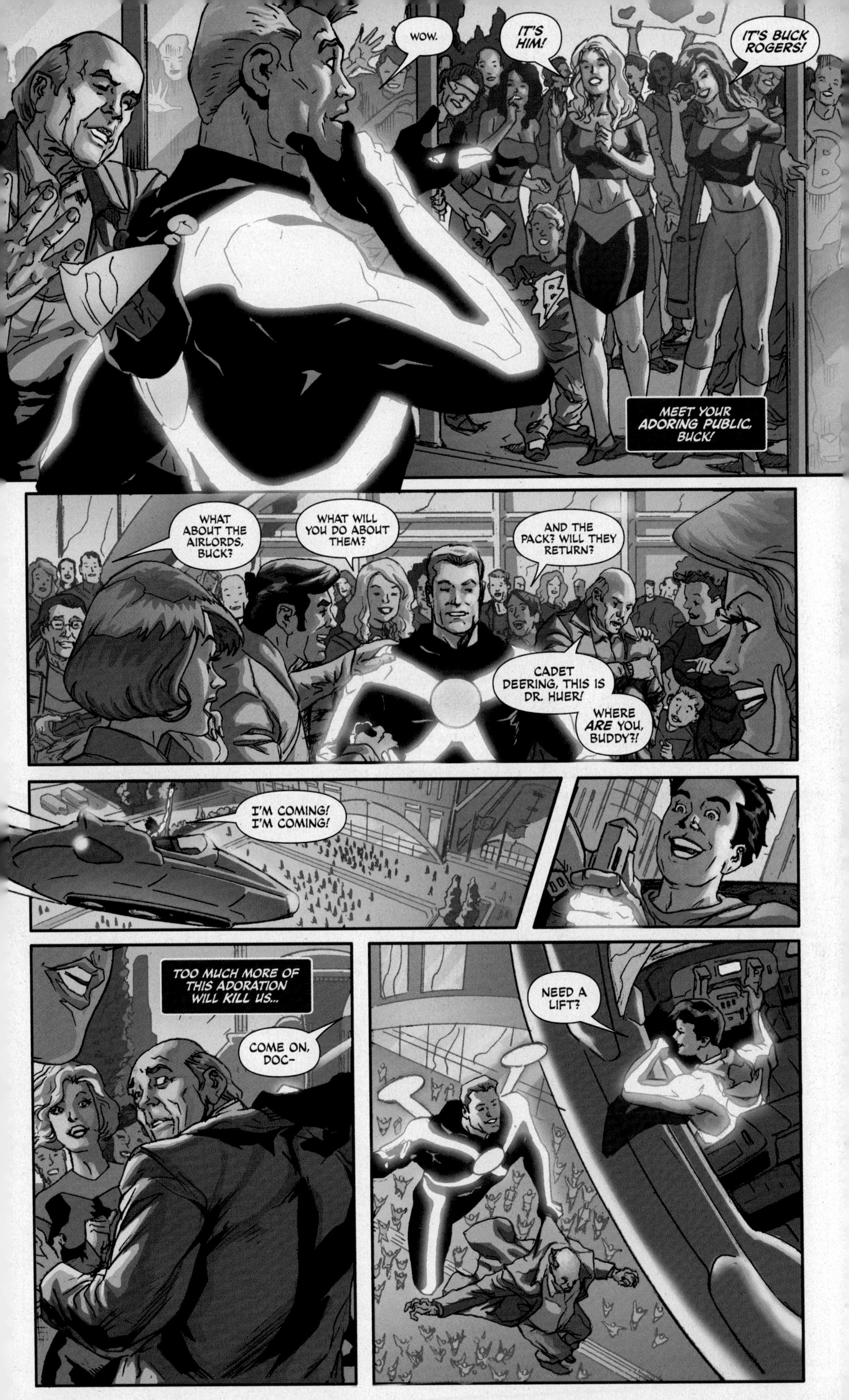
WOW.
IT'S HIM!
IT'S BUCK ROGERS!
MEET YOUR ADORING PUBLIC, BUCK!
WHAT ABOUT THE AIRLORDS, BUCK?
WHAT WILL YOU DO ABOUT THEM?
AND THE PACK? WILL THEY RETURN?
CADET DEERING, THIS IS DR. HUER!
WHERE ARE YOU, BUDDY?!
I'M COMING! I'M COMING!
TOO MUCH MORE OF THIS ADORATION WILL KILL US...
COME ON, DOC-
NEED A LIFT?

SO, WHERE TO?

WILMA'S ON A DIPLOMATIC MISSION TO *HAN* AND I FINISHED ALL MY ACADEMY STUDIES FOR THE-

BUDDY!

WATCH WHERE YOU'RE GOING!

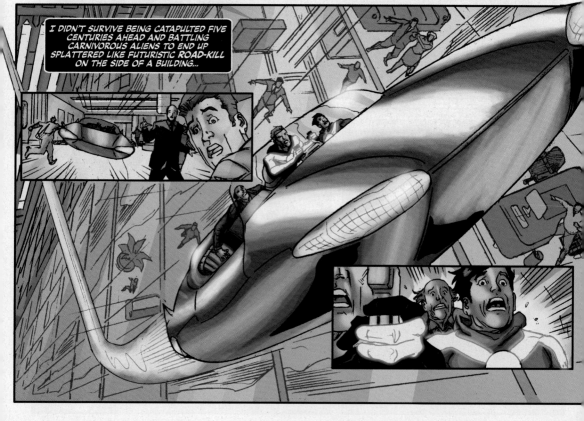

I DIDN'T SURVIVE BEING CATAPULTED FIVE CENTURIES AHEAD AND BATTLING CARNIVOROUS ALIENS TO END UP SPLATTERED LIKE FUTURISTIC ROAD-KILL ON THE SIDE OF A BUILDING...

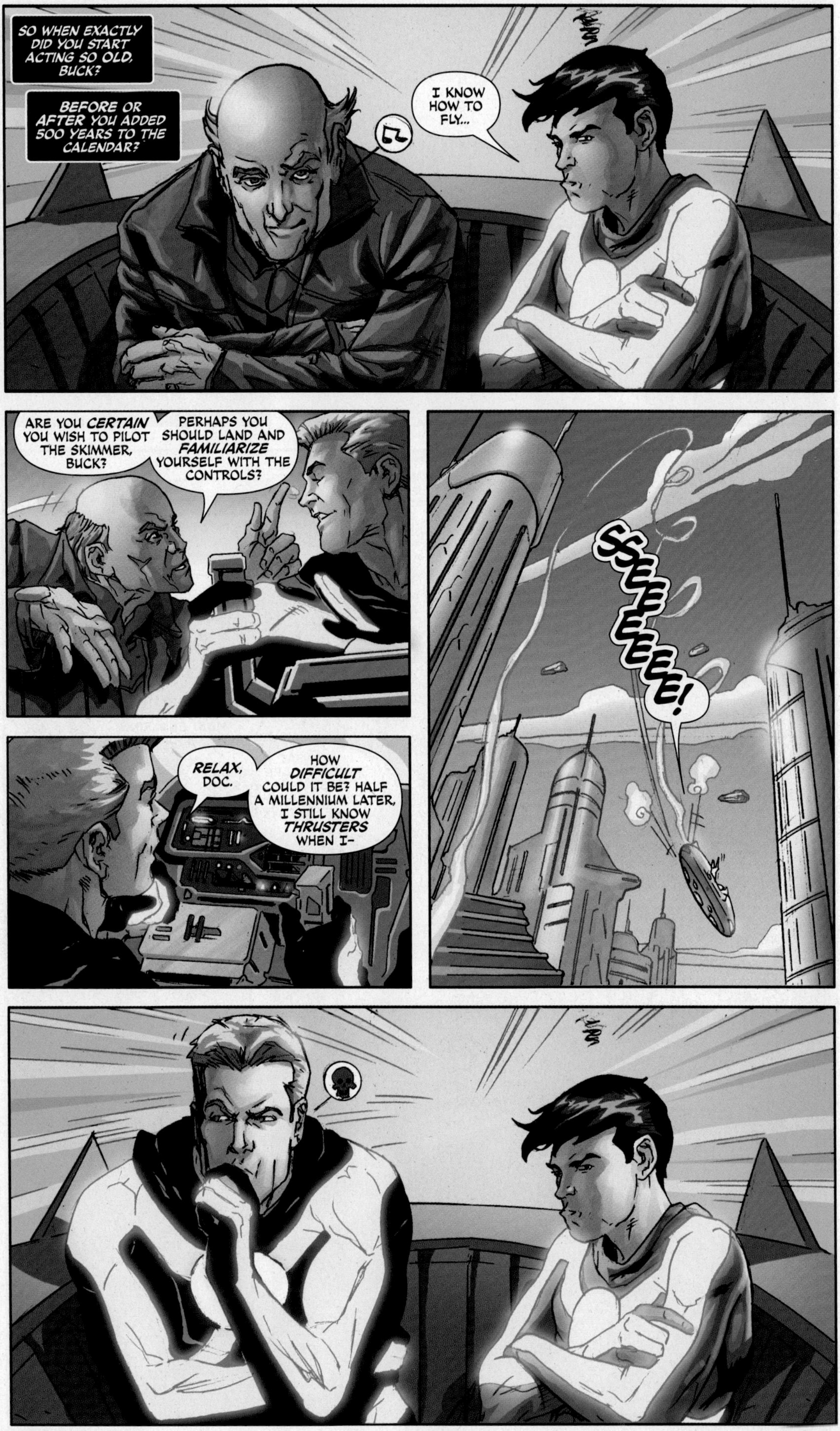
SO WHEN EXACTLY DID YOU START ACTING SO OLD, BUCK?
BEFORE OR AFTER YOU ADDED 500 YEARS TO THE CALENDAR?
I KNOW HOW TO FLY...
ARE YOU CERTAIN YOU WISH TO PILOT THE SKIMMER, BUCK?
PERHAPS YOU SHOULD LAND AND FAMILIARIZE YOURSELF WITH THE CONTROLS?
RELAX, DOC.
HOW DIFFICULT COULD IT BE? HALF A MILLENNIUM LATER, I STILL KNOW THRUSTERS WHEN I-
SSEEEEEEE!

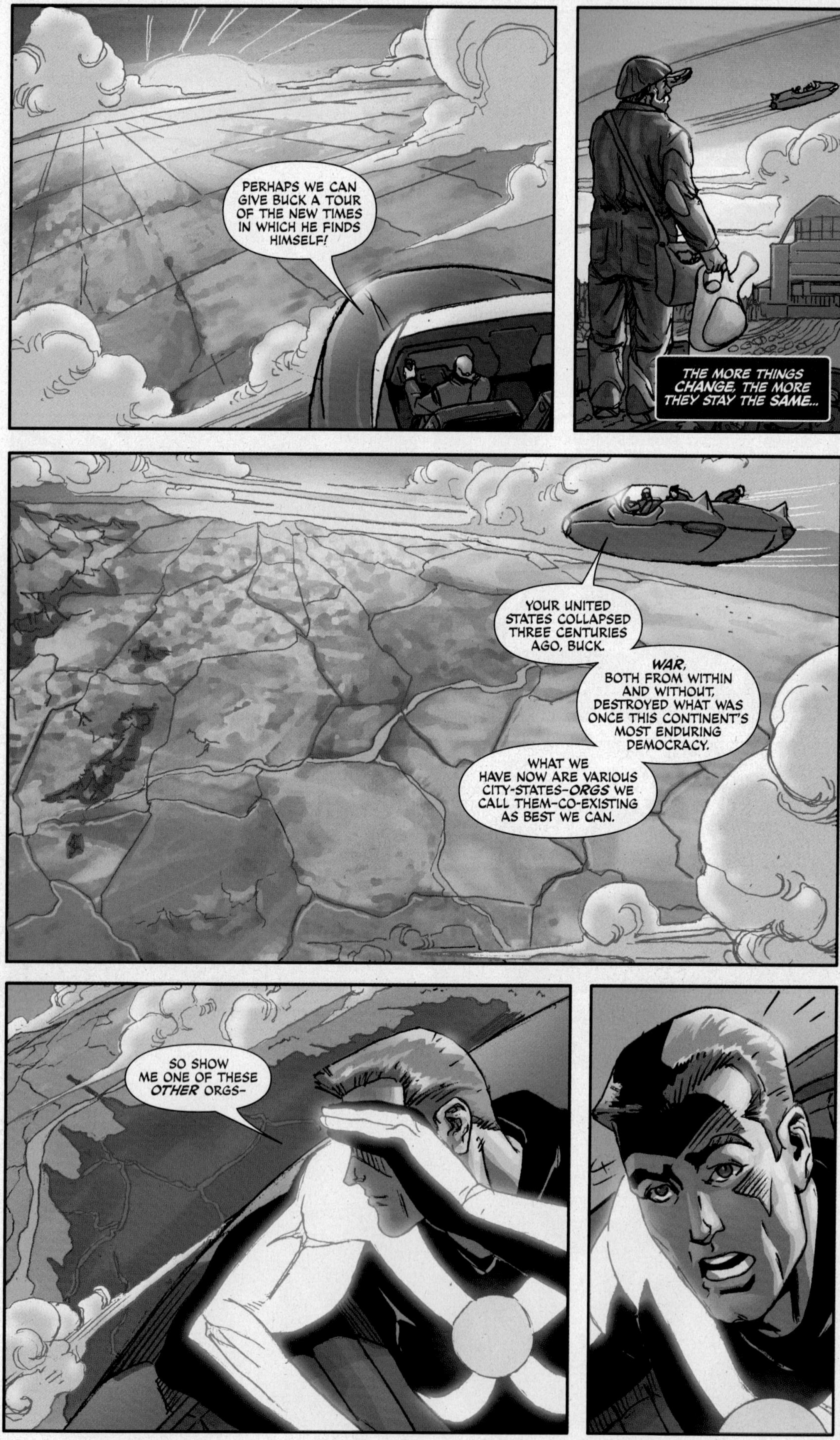
PERHAPS WE CAN GIVE BUCK A TOUR OF THE NEW TIMES IN WHICH HE FINDS HIMSELF!
THE MORE THINGS CHANGE, THE MORE THEY STAY THE SAME...
YOUR UNITED STATES COLLAPSED THREE CENTURIES AGO, BUCK.
WAR, BOTH FROM WITHIN AND WITHOUT, DESTROYED WHAT WAS ONCE THIS CONTINENT'S MOST ENDURING DEMOCRACY.
WHAT WE HAVE NOW ARE VARIOUS CITY-STATES-ORGS WE CALL THEM-CO-EXISTING AS BEST WE CAN.
SO SHOW ME ONE OF THESE OTHER ORGS-

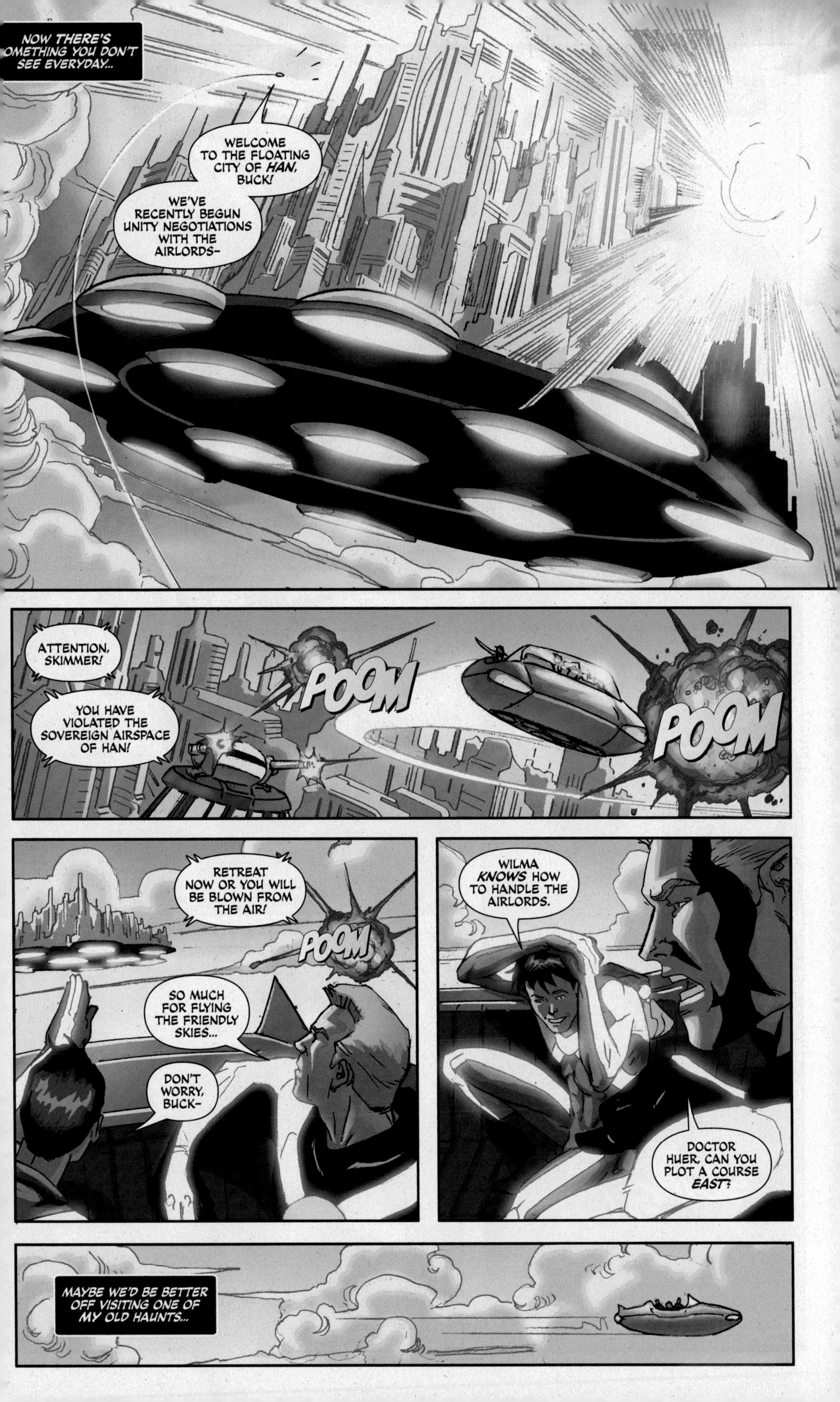
NOW THERE'S OMETHING YOU DON'T SEE EVERYDAY...
WELCOME TO THE FLOATING CITY OF HAN, BUCK!
WE'VE RECENTLY BEGUN UNITY NEGOTIATIONS WITH THE AIRLORDS-
ATTENTION, SKIMMER!
YOU HAVE VIOLATED THE SOVEREIGN AIRSPACE OF HAN!
POOM
POOM
RETREAT NOW OR YOU WILL BE BLOWN FROM THE AIR!
POOM
SO MUCH FOR FLYING THE FRIENDLY SKIES...
DON'T WORRY, BUCK-
WILMA KNOWS HOW TO HANDLE THE AIRLORDS.
DOCTOR HUER, CAN YOU PLOT A COURSE EAST?
MAYBE WE'D BE BETTER OFF VISITING ONE OF MY OLD HAUNTS...

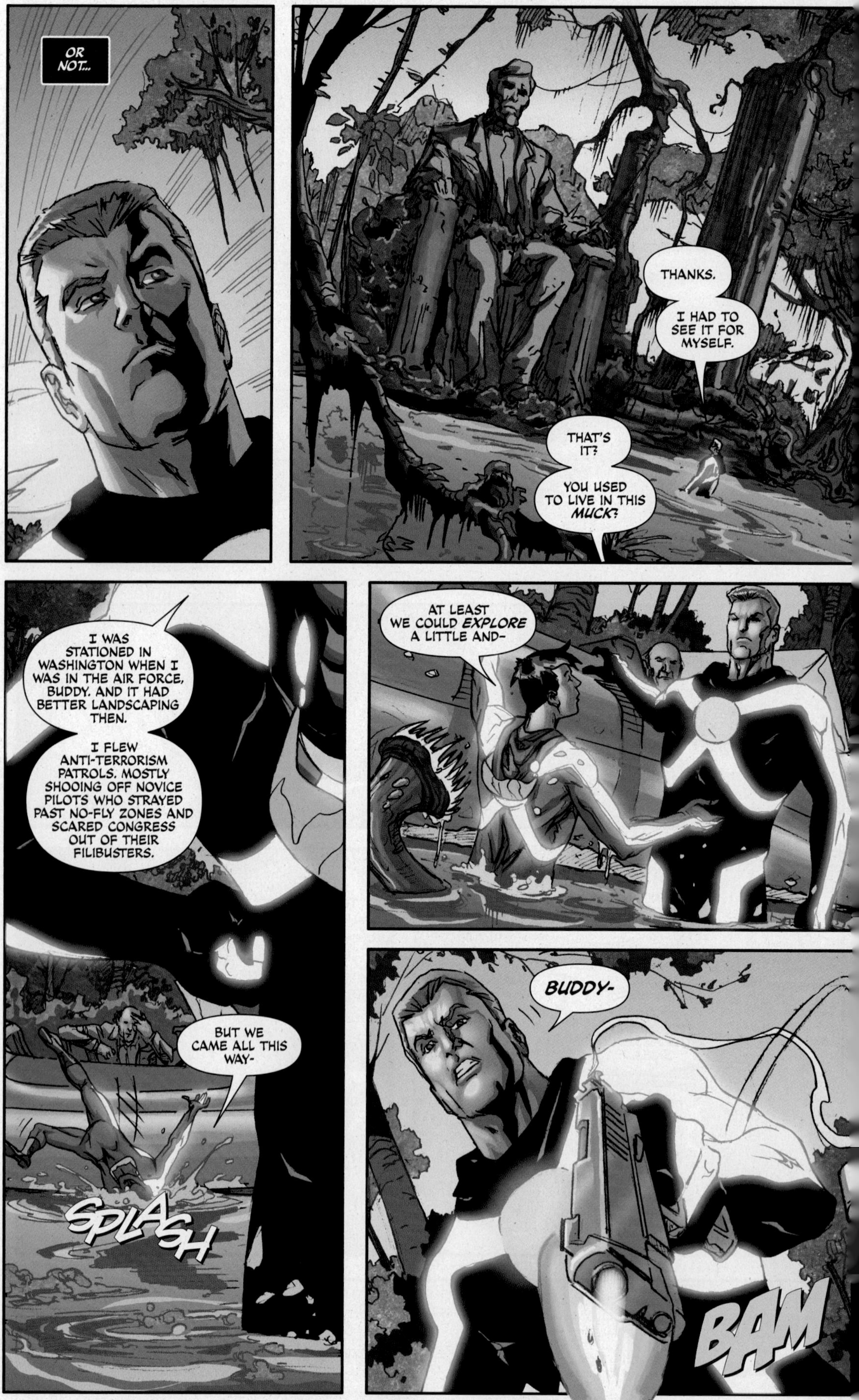
OR NOT...
THANKS.
I HAD TO SEE IT FOR MYSELF.
THAT'S IT?
YOU USED TO LIVE IN THIS MUCK?
I WAS STATIONED IN WASHINGTON WHEN I WAS IN THE AIR FORCE, BUDDY. AND IT HAD BETTER LANDSCAPING THEN.
I FLEW ANTI-TERRORISM PATROLS. MOSTLY SHOOING OFF NOVICE PILOTS WHO STRAYED PAST NO-FLY ZONES AND SCARED CONGRESS OUT OF THEIR FILIBUSTERS.
BUT WE CAME ALL THIS WAY-
SPLASH
AT LEAST WE COULD EXPLORE A LITTLE AND-
BUDDY-
BAM

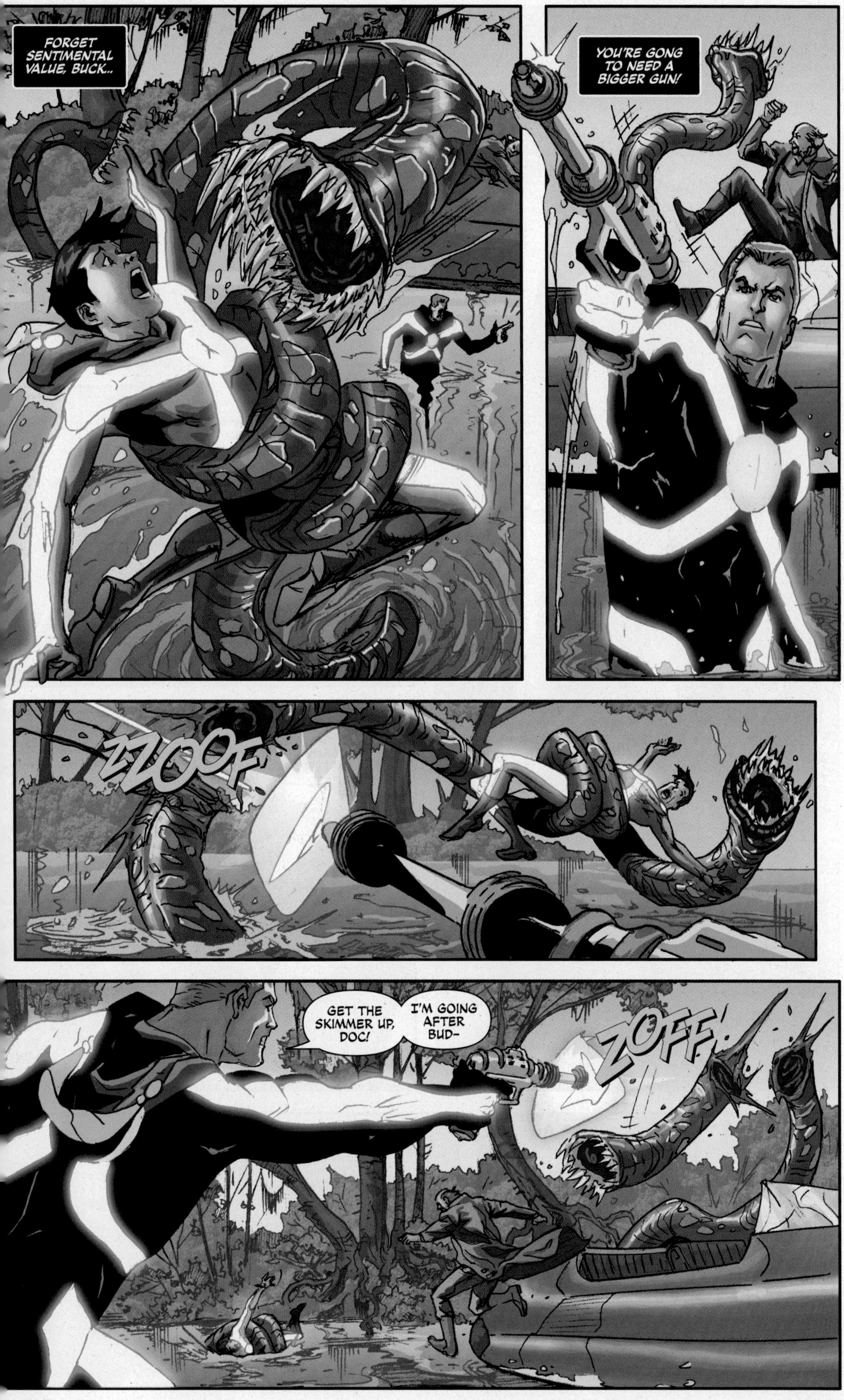
FORGET SENTIMENTAL VALUE, BUCK...
YOU'RE GONG TO NEED A BIGGER GUN!
ZZOOF
GET THE SKIMMER UP, DOC!
I'M GOING AFTER BUD-
ZOFF

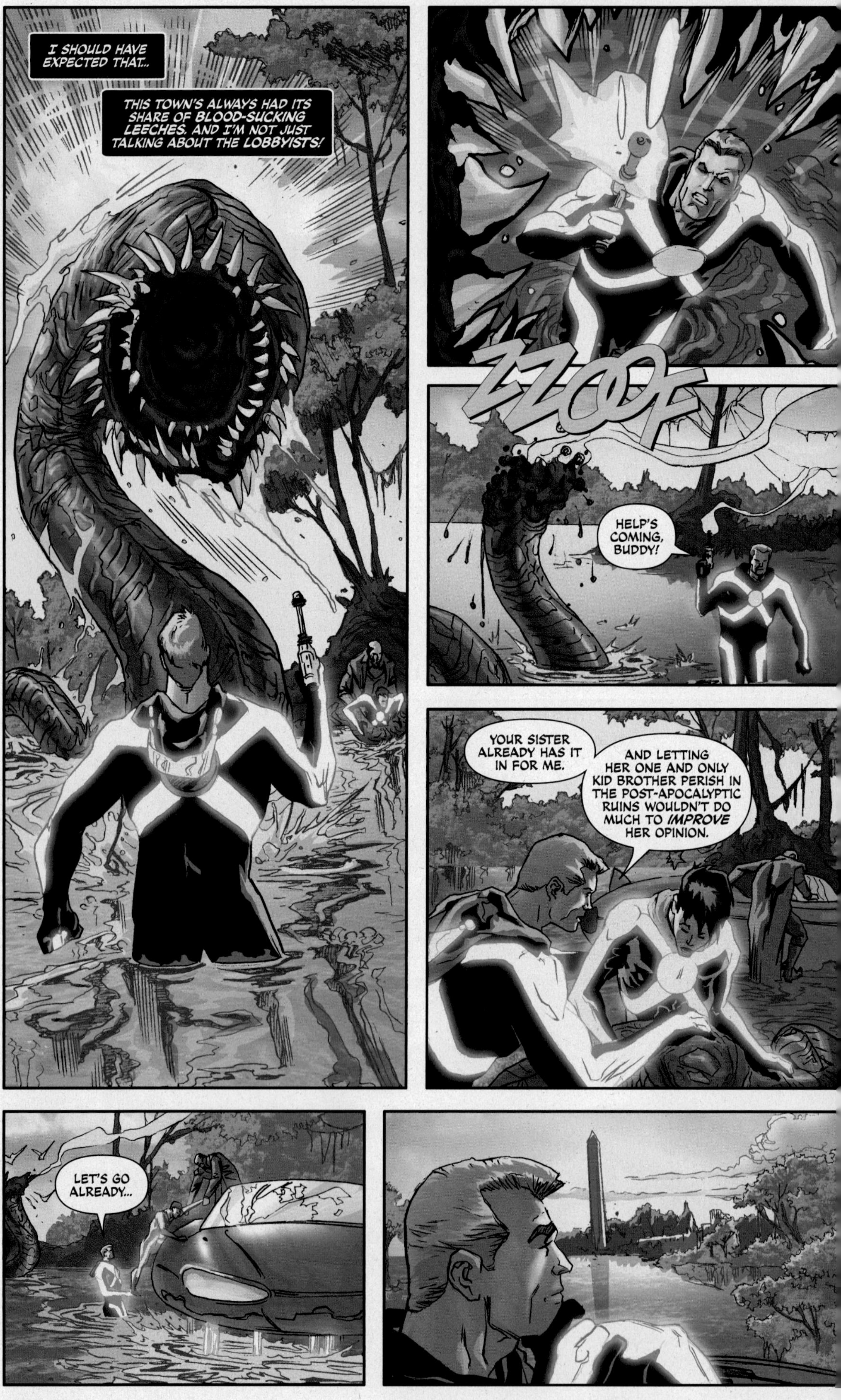

I SHOULD HAVE EXPECTED THAT...
THIS TOWN'S ALWAYS HAD ITS SHARE OF BLOOD-SUCKING LEECHES. AND I'M NOT JUST TALKING ABOUT THE LOBBYISTS!
ZZOOF
HELP'S COMING, BUDDY!
YOUR SISTER ALREADY HAS IT IN FOR ME.
AND LETTING HER ONE AND ONLY KID BROTHER PERISH IN THE POST-APOCALYPTIC RUINS WOULDN'T DO MUCH TO IMPROVE HER OPINION.
LET'S GO ALREADY...

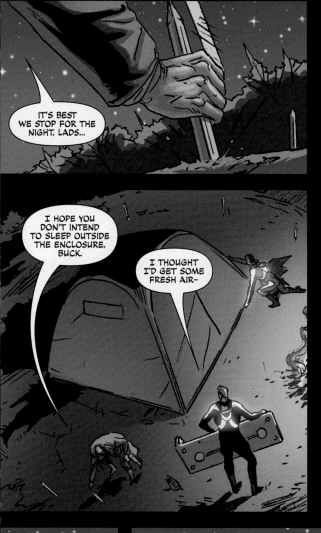

IT'S BEST WE STOP FOR THE NIGHT, LADS...

I HOPE YOU DON'T INTEND TO SLEEP OUTSIDE THE ENCLOSURE, BUCK.

I THOUGHT I'D GET SOME FRESH AIR–

MAYBE GAZE UP AT THOSE LUCKY STARS YOU MENTIONED.

THEY'RE THE ONLY CONSTANT IN ALL OF THIS, STILL ROUGHLY IN THE SAME RELATIVE POSITIONS FIVE CENTURIES LATER.

I SHOULD WARN YOU–

THE FALLOUT THAT MUTATED THOSE TENTACLED BEASTIES BACK IN WASHINGTON MAY HAVE DRIFTED TO THESE PARTS AS WELL...

MEEP

ZARK

HMPH.

PERHAPS I OVERESTIMATED THE EFFECTS OF AMBIENT BACKGROUND RADIATION ON ENDEMIC SPECIES...

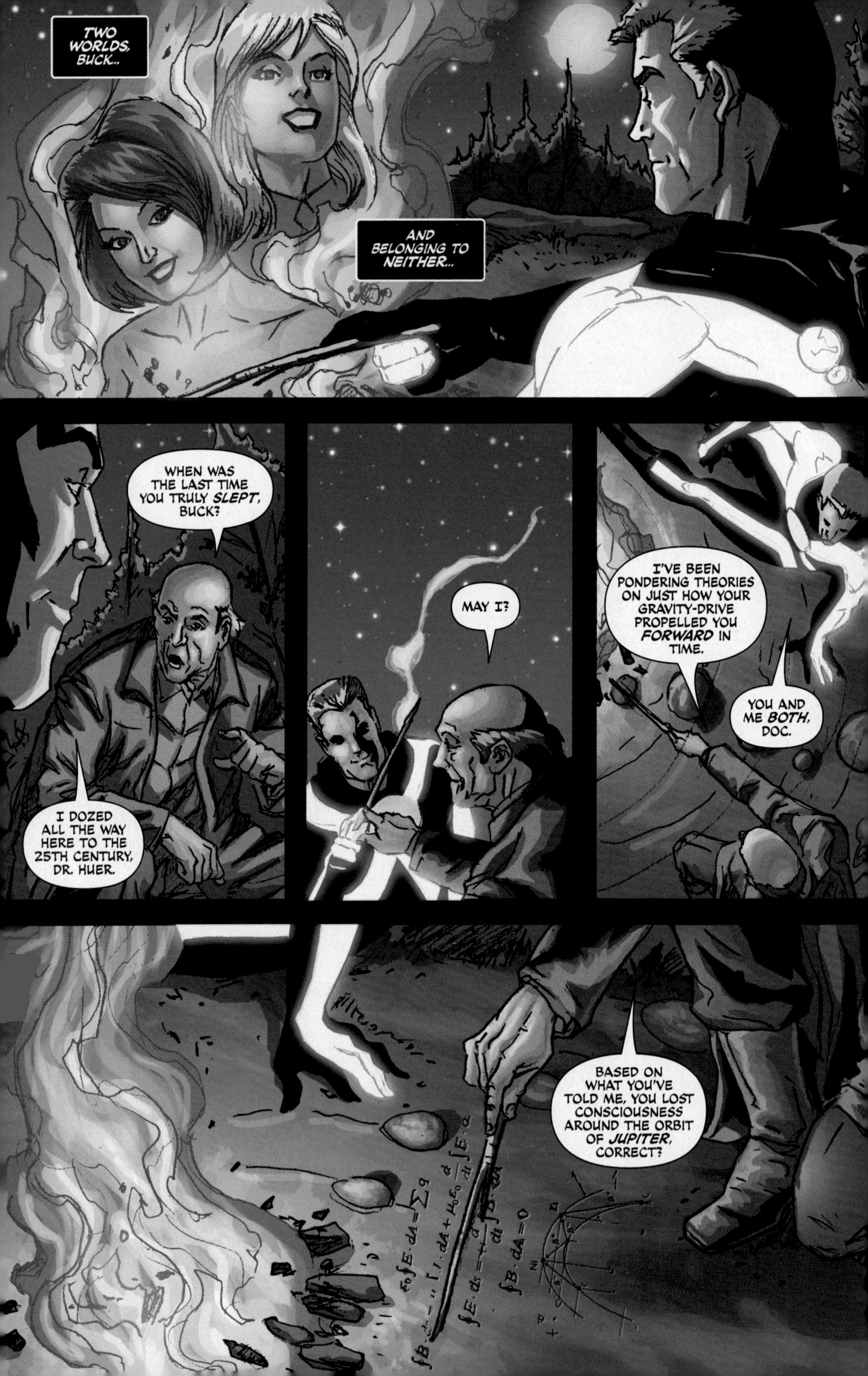

TWO WORLDS, BUCK...
AND BELONGING TO NEITHER...
WHEN WAS THE LAST TIME YOU TRULY SLEPT, BUCK?
I DOZED ALL THE WAY HERE TO THE 25TH CENTURY, DR. HUER.
MAY I?
I'VE BEEN PONDERING THEORIES ON JUST HOW YOUR GRAVITY-DRIVE PROPELLED YOU FORWARD IN TIME.
YOU AND ME BOTH, DOC.
BASED ON WHAT YOU'VE TOLD ME, YOU LOST CONSCIOUSNESS AROUND THE ORBIT OF JUPITER, CORRECT?

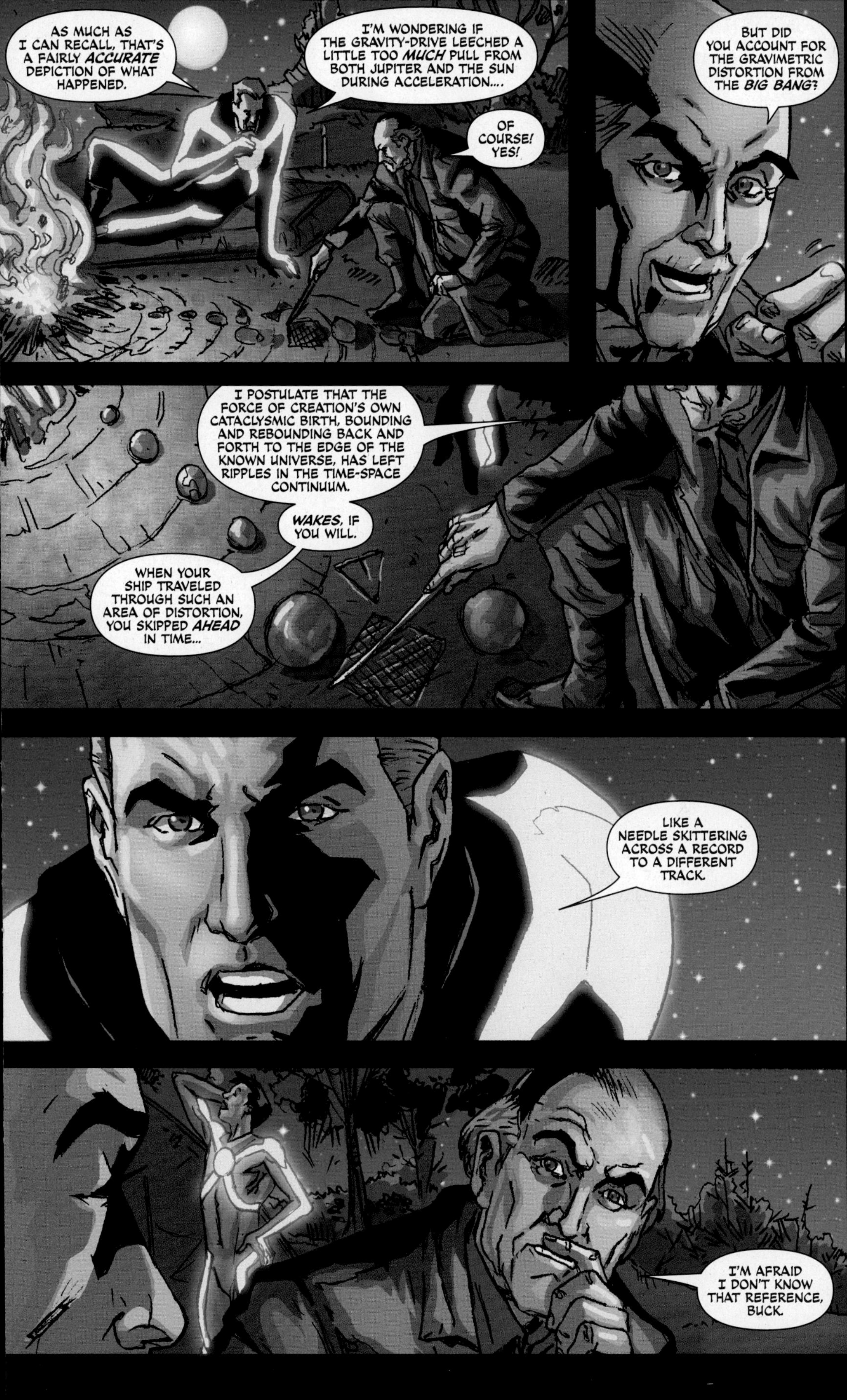
AS MUCH AS I CAN RECALL, THAT'S A FAIRLY *ACCURATE* DEPICTION OF WHAT HAPPENED.
I'M WONDERING IF THE GRAVITY-DRIVE LEECHED A LITTLE TOO *MUCH* PULL FROM BOTH JUPITER AND THE SUN DURING ACCELERATION....
OF COURSE! YES!
BUT DID YOU ACCOUNT FOR THE GRAVIMETRIC DISTORTION FROM THE *BIG BANG*?
I POSTULATE THAT THE FORCE OF CREATION'S OWN CATACLYSMIC BIRTH, BOUNDING AND REBOUNDING BACK AND FORTH TO THE EDGE OF THE KNOWN UNIVERSE, HAS LEFT RIPPLES IN THE TIME-SPACE CONTINUUM.
WAKES, IF YOU WILL.
WHEN YOUR SHIP TRAVELED THROUGH SUCH AN AREA OF DISTORTION, YOU SKIPPED *AHEAD* IN TIME...
LIKE A NEEDLE SKITTERING ACROSS A RECORD TO A DIFFERENT TRACK.
I'M AFRAID I DON'T KNOW THAT REFERENCE, BUCK.

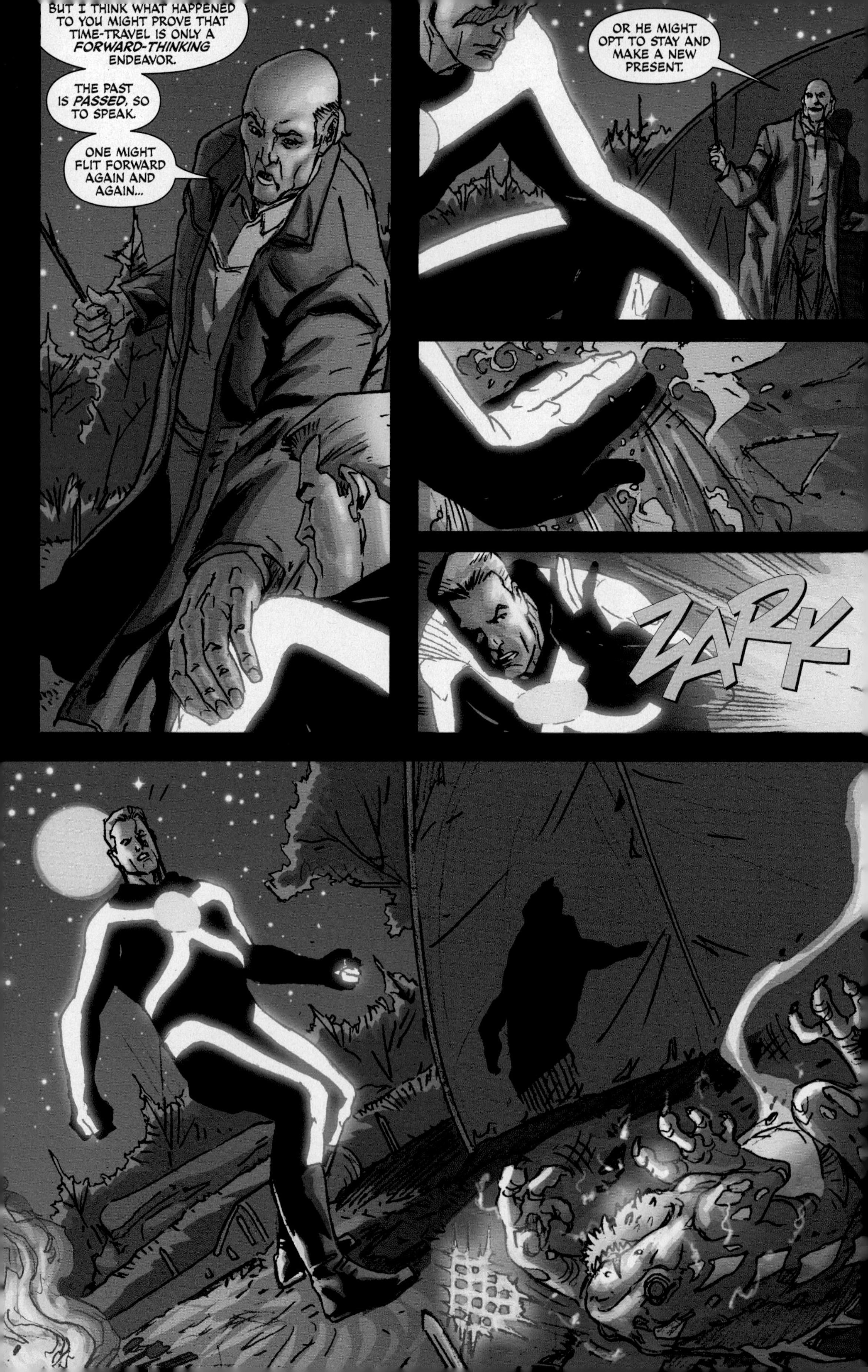
BUT I THINK WHAT HAPPENED TO YOU MIGHT PROVE THAT TIME-TRAVEL IS ONLY A *FORWARD-THINKING* ENDEAVOR.
THE PAST IS *PASSED*, SO TO SPEAK.
ONE MIGHT FLIT FORWARD AGAIN AND AGAIN...
OR HE MIGHT OPT TO STAY AND MAKE A NEW PRESENT.
ZARK

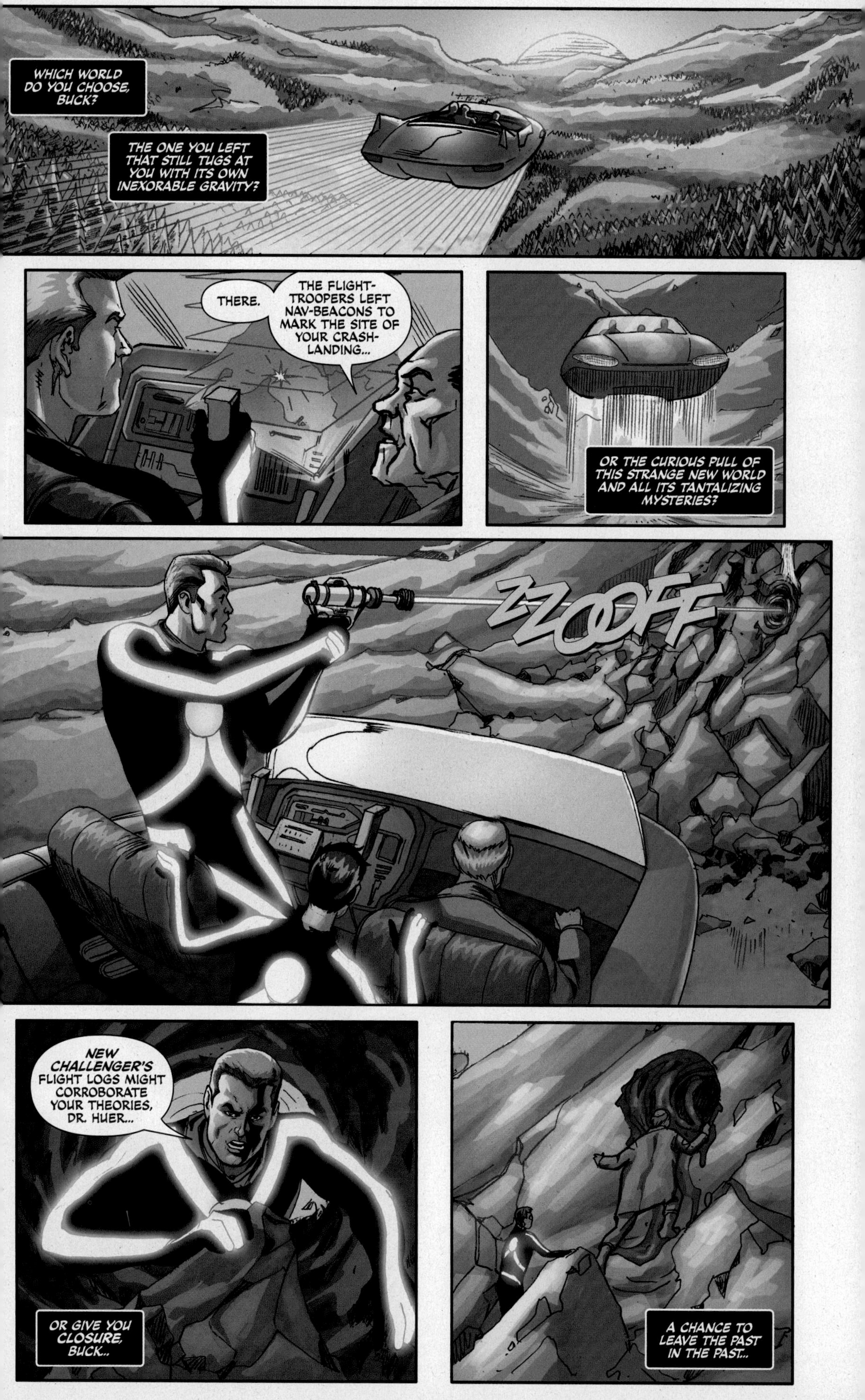
WHICH WORLD DO YOU CHOOSE, BUCK?
THE ONE YOU LEFT THAT STILL TUGS AT YOU WITH ITS OWN INEXORABLE GRAVITY?
THERE.
THE FLIGHT-TROOPERS LEFT NAV-BEACONS TO MARK THE SITE OF YOUR CRASH-LANDING...
OR THE CURIOUS PULL OF THIS STRANGE NEW WORLD AND ALL ITS TANTALIZING MYSTERIES?
ZZOOFF
NEW CHALLENGER'S FLIGHT LOGS MIGHT CORROBORATE YOUR THEORIES, DR. HUER...
OR GIVE YOU CLOSURE, BUCK...
A CHANCE TO LEAVE THE PAST IN THE PAST...

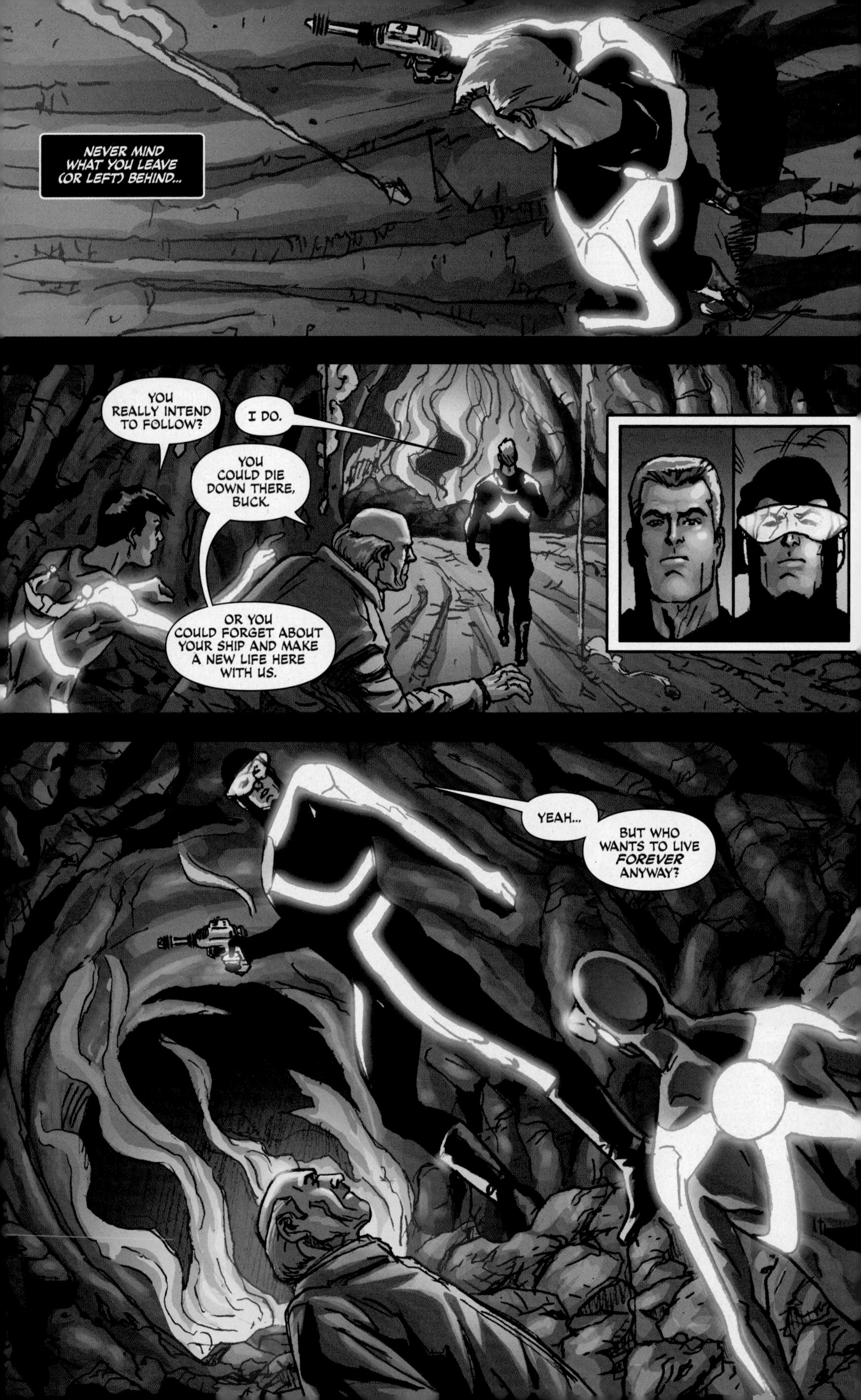
NEVER MIND
WHAT YOU LEAVE
(OR LEFT) BEHIND...
YOU REALLY INTEND TO FOLLOW?
I DO.
YOU COULD DIE DOWN THERE, BUCK.
OR YOU COULD FORGET ABOUT YOUR SHIP AND MAKE A NEW LIFE HERE WITH US.
YEAH...
BUT WHO WANTS TO LIVE *FOREVER* ANYWAY?

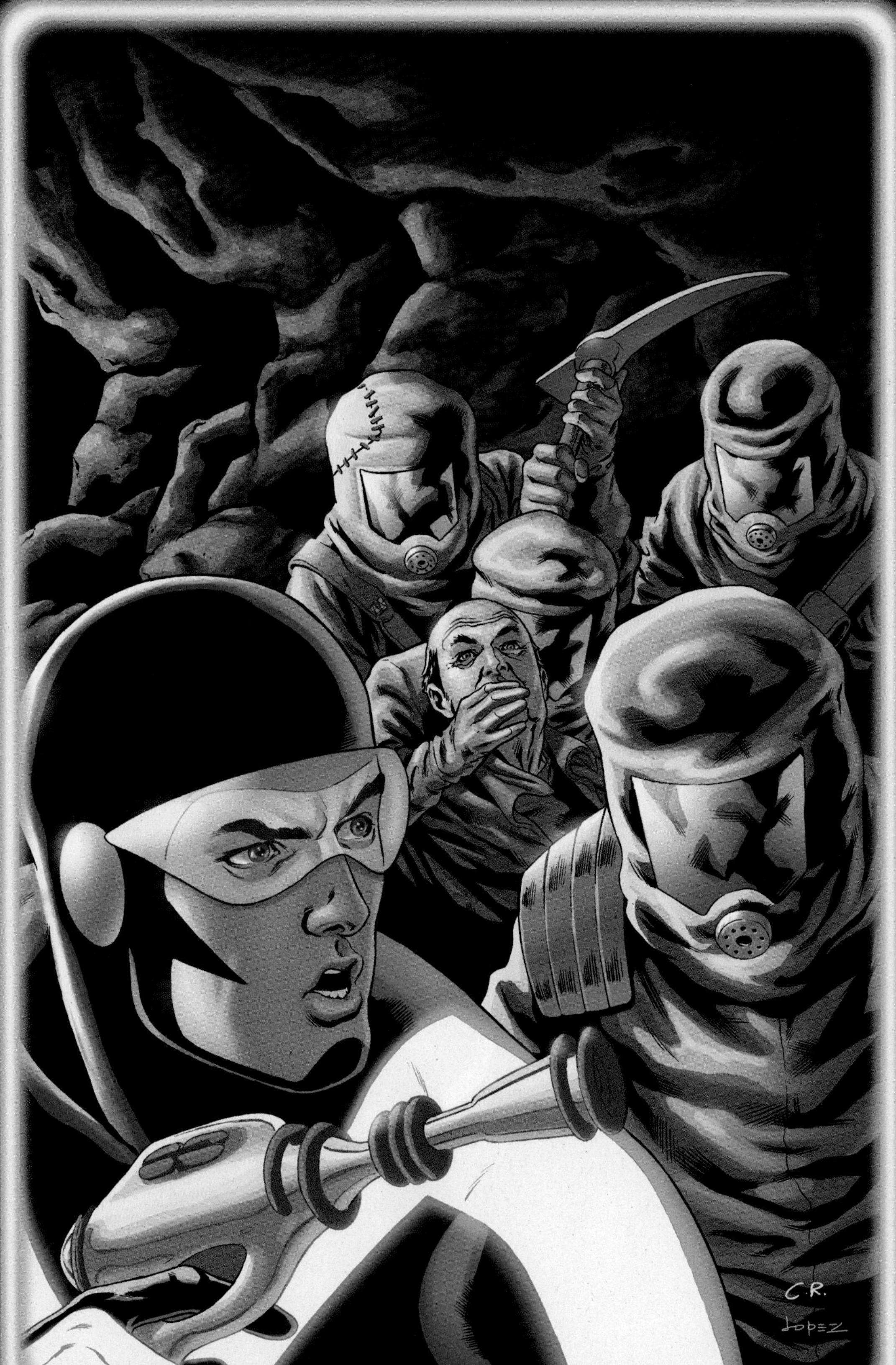
C.R.
LOPEZ

THE SPACE BENEATH PART ONE: Buried Alive

ISSUE SEVEN COVER BY CARLOS RAFAEL

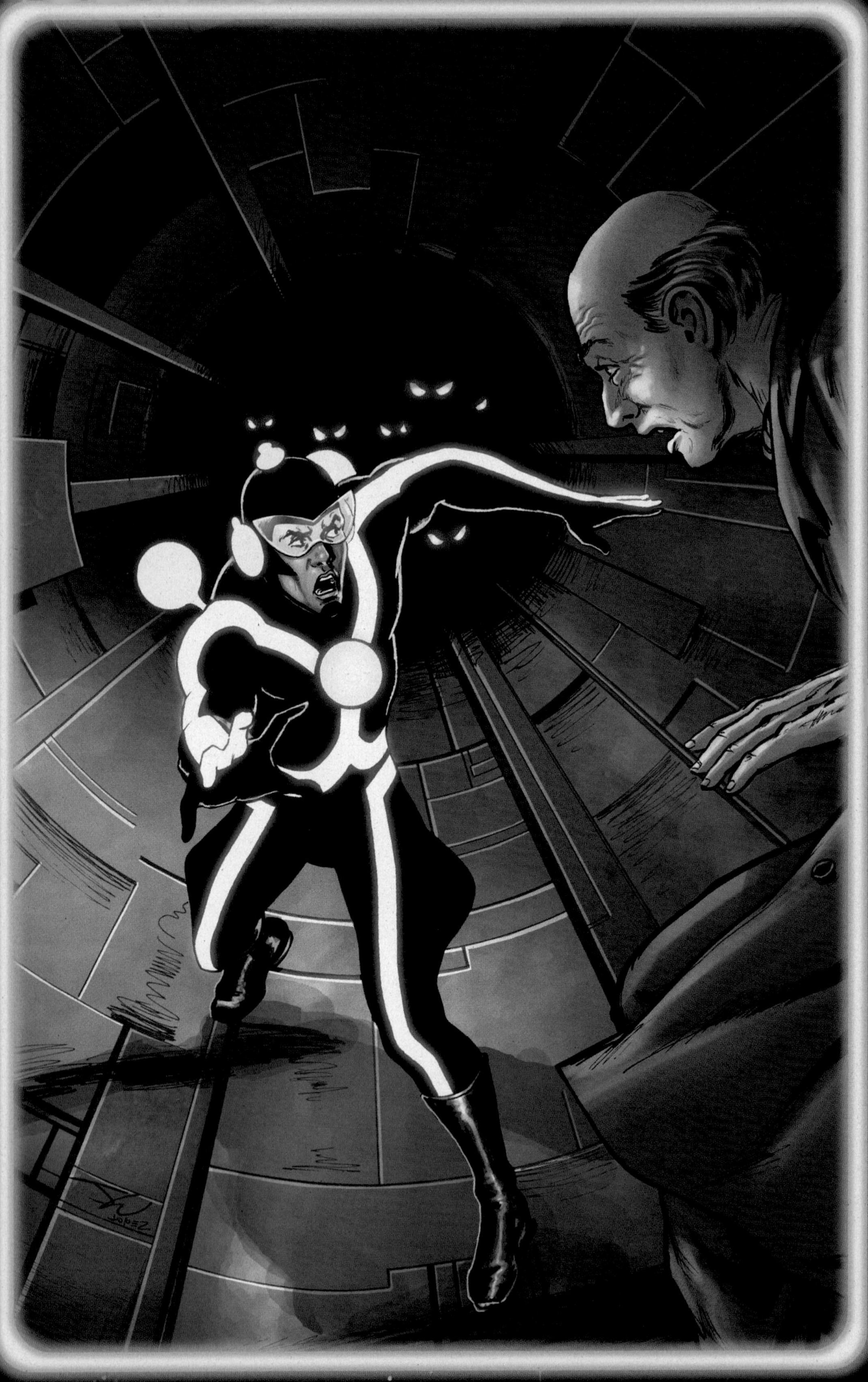

ALTERNATE COVER BY JOHN WATSON

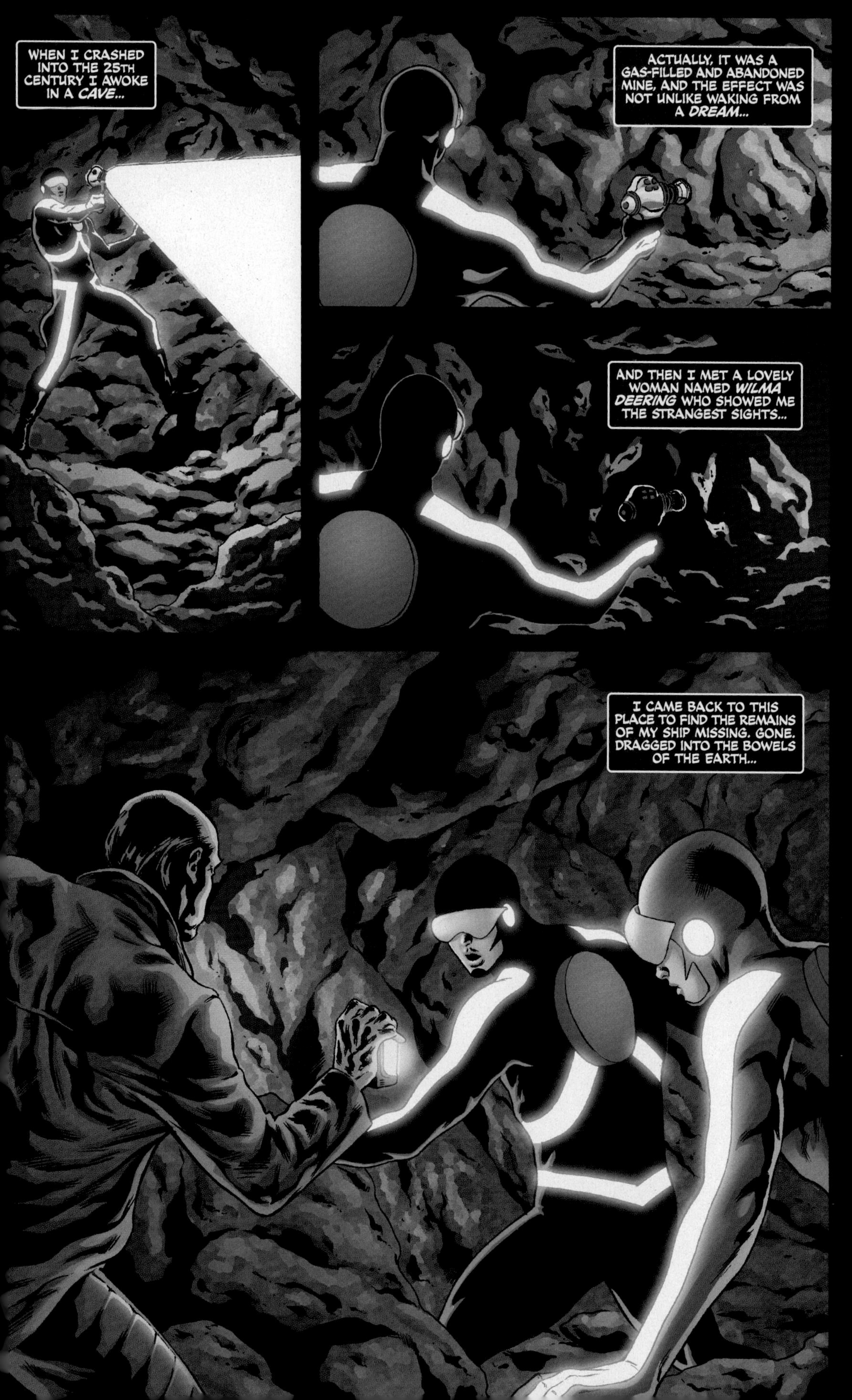
WHEN I CRASHED INTO THE 25TH CENTURY I AWOKE IN A CAVE...
ACTUALLY, IT WAS A GAS-FILLED AND ABANDONED MINE, AND THE EFFECT WAS NOT UNLIKE WAKING FROM A DREAM...
AND THEN I MET A LOVELY WOMAN NAMED WILMA DEERING WHO SHOWED ME THE STRANGEST SIGHTS...
I CAME BACK TO THIS PLACE TO FIND THE REMAINS OF MY SHIP MISSING. GONE. DRAGGED INTO THE BOWELS OF THE EARTH...

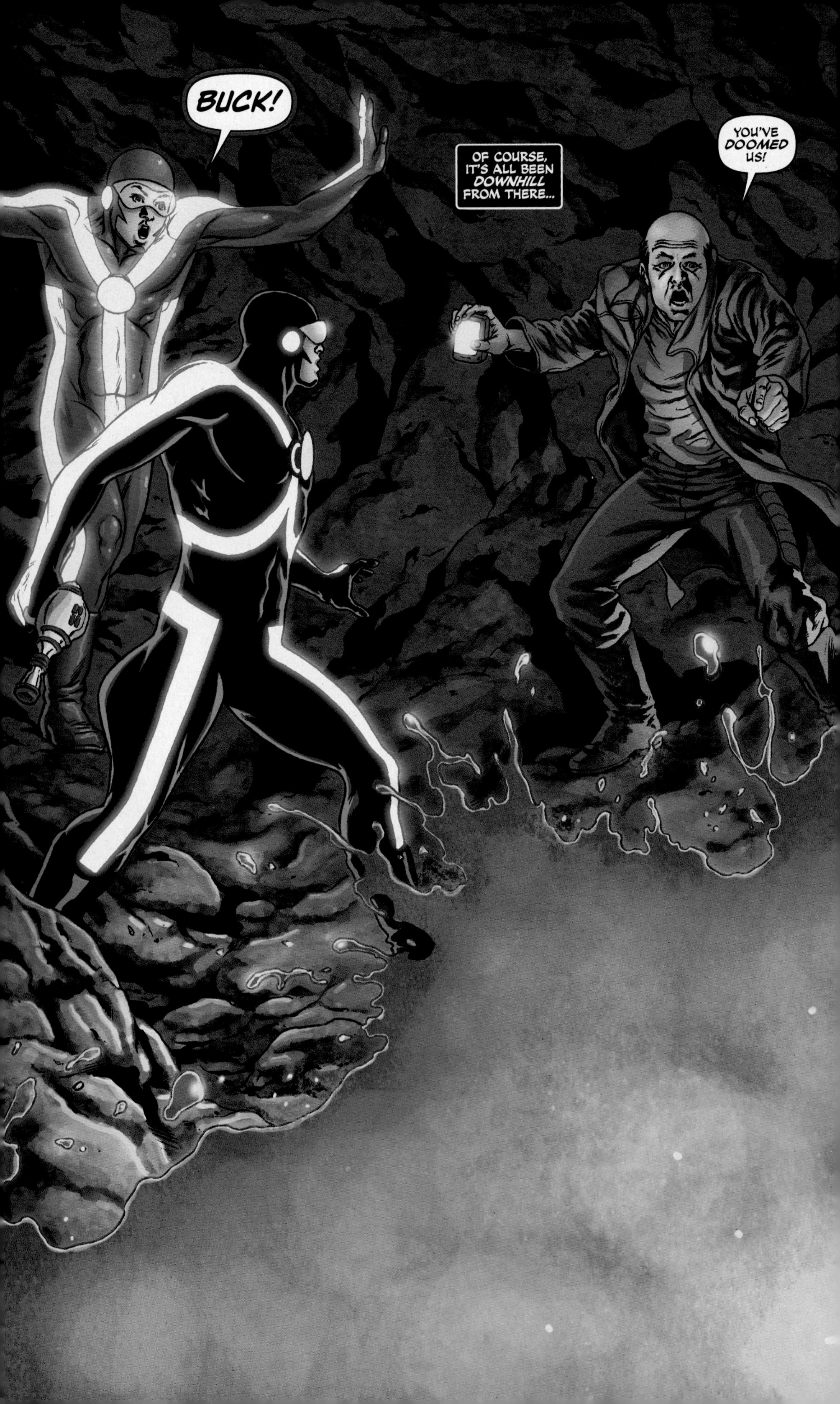
BUCK!
OF COURSE, IT'S ALL BEEN DOWNHILL FROM THERE...
YOU'VE DOOMED US!

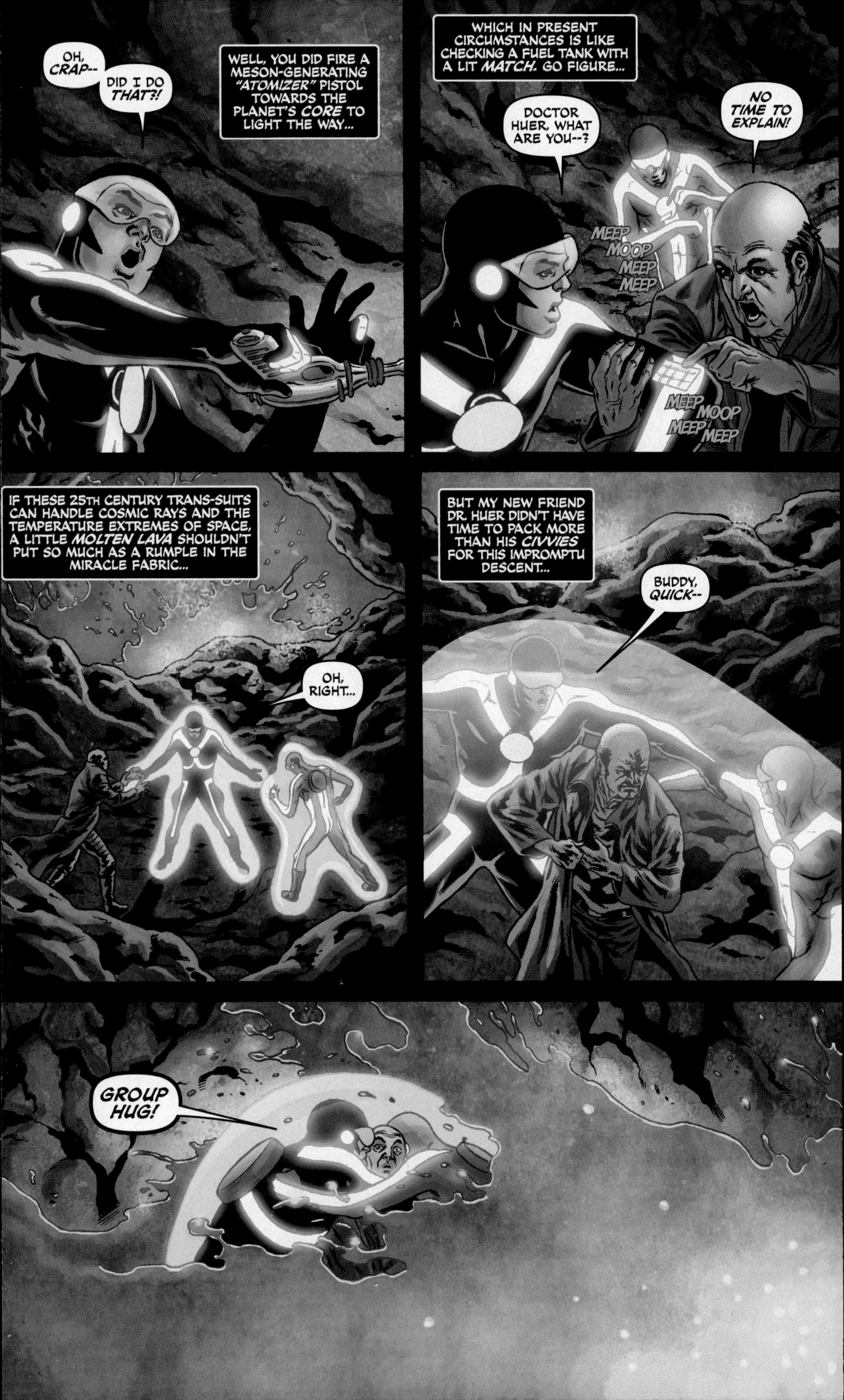

OH, CRAP--
DID I DO THAT?!
WELL, YOU DID FIRE A MESON-GENERATING "ATOMIZER" PISTOL TOWARDS THE PLANET'S CORE TO LIGHT THE WAY...
WHICH IN PRESENT CIRCUMSTANCES IS LIKE CHECKING A FUEL TANK WITH A LIT MATCH. GO FIGURE...
DOCTOR HUER, WHAT ARE YOU--?
NO TIME TO EXPLAIN!
MEEP MOOP MEEP MEEP
MEEP MOOP MEEP MEEP
IF THESE 25TH CENTURY TRANS-SUITS CAN HANDLE COSMIC RAYS AND THE TEMPERATURE EXTREMES OF SPACE, A LITTLE MOLTEN LAVA SHOULDN'T PUT SO MUCH AS A RUMPLE IN THE MIRACLE FABRIC...
OH, RIGHT...
BUT MY NEW FRIEND DR. HUER DIDN'T HAVE TIME TO PACK MORE THAN HIS CIVVIES FOR THIS IMPROMPTU DESCENT...
BUDDY, QUICK--
GROUP HUG!

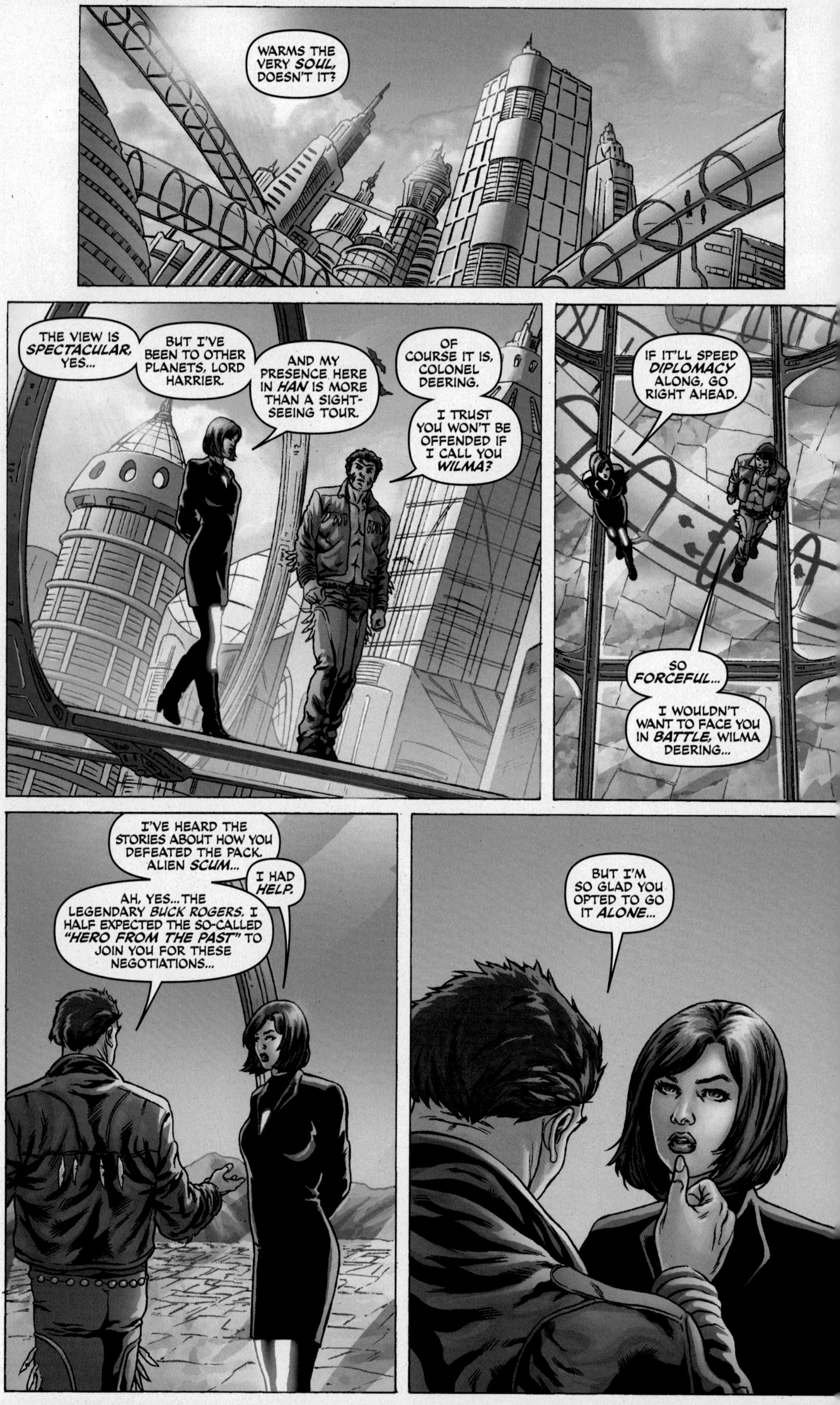
WARMS THE VERY SOUL, DOESN'T IT?
THE VIEW IS SPECTACULAR, YES...
BUT I'VE BEEN TO OTHER PLANETS, LORD HARRIER.
AND MY PRESENCE HERE IN HAN IS MORE THAN A SIGHT-SEEING TOUR.
OF COURSE IT IS, COLONEL DEERING.
I TRUST YOU WON'T BE OFFENDED IF I CALL YOU WILMA?
IF IT'LL SPEED DIPLOMACY ALONG, GO RIGHT AHEAD.
SO FORCEFUL...
I WOULDN'T WANT TO FACE YOU IN BATTLE, WILMA DEERING...
I'VE HEARD THE STORIES ABOUT HOW YOU DEFEATED THE PACK. ALIEN SCUM...
I HAD HELP.
AH, YES... THE LEGENDARY BUCK ROGERS. I HALF EXPECTED THE SO-CALLED "HERO FROM THE PAST" TO JOIN YOU FOR THESE NEGOTIATIONS...
BUT I'M SO GLAD YOU OPTED TO GO IT ALONE...

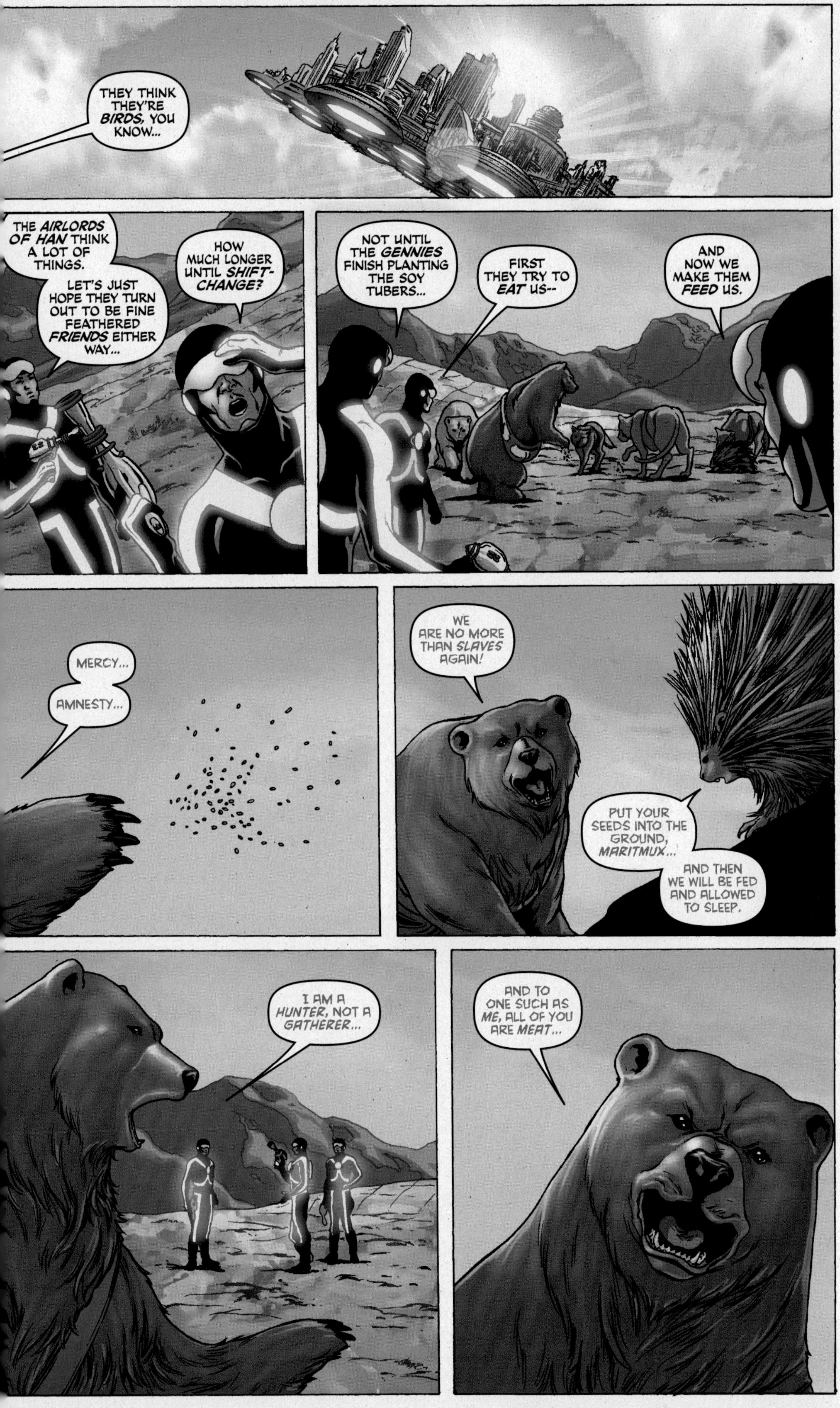
THEY THINK THEY'RE BIRDS, YOU KNOW...
THE AIRLORDS OF HAN THINK A LOT OF THINGS.
LET'S JUST HOPE THEY TURN OUT TO BE FINE FEATHERED FRIENDS EITHER WAY...
HOW MUCH LONGER UNTIL SHIFT-CHANGE?
NOT UNTIL THE GENNIES FINISH PLANTING THE SOY TUBERS...
FIRST THEY TRY TO EAT US--
AND NOW WE MAKE THEM FEED US.
MERCY...
AMNESTY...
WE ARE NO MORE THAN SLAVES AGAIN!
PUT YOUR SEEDS INTO THE GROUND, MARITMUX...
AND THEN WE WILL BE FED AND ALLOWED TO SLEEP.
I AM A HUNTER, NOT A GATHERER...
AND TO ONE SUCH AS ME, ALL OF YOU ARE MEAT...

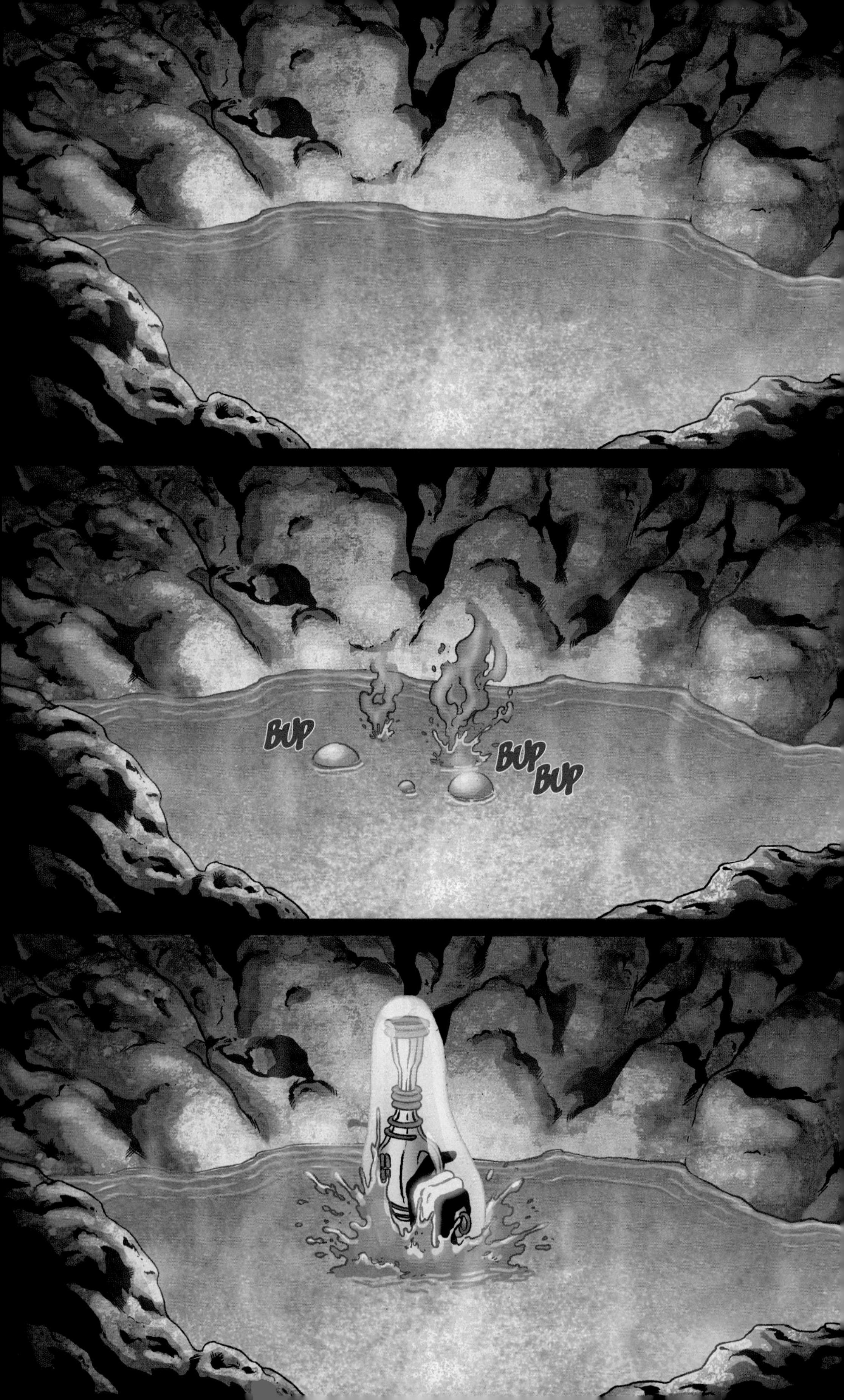
BUP
BUP
BUP

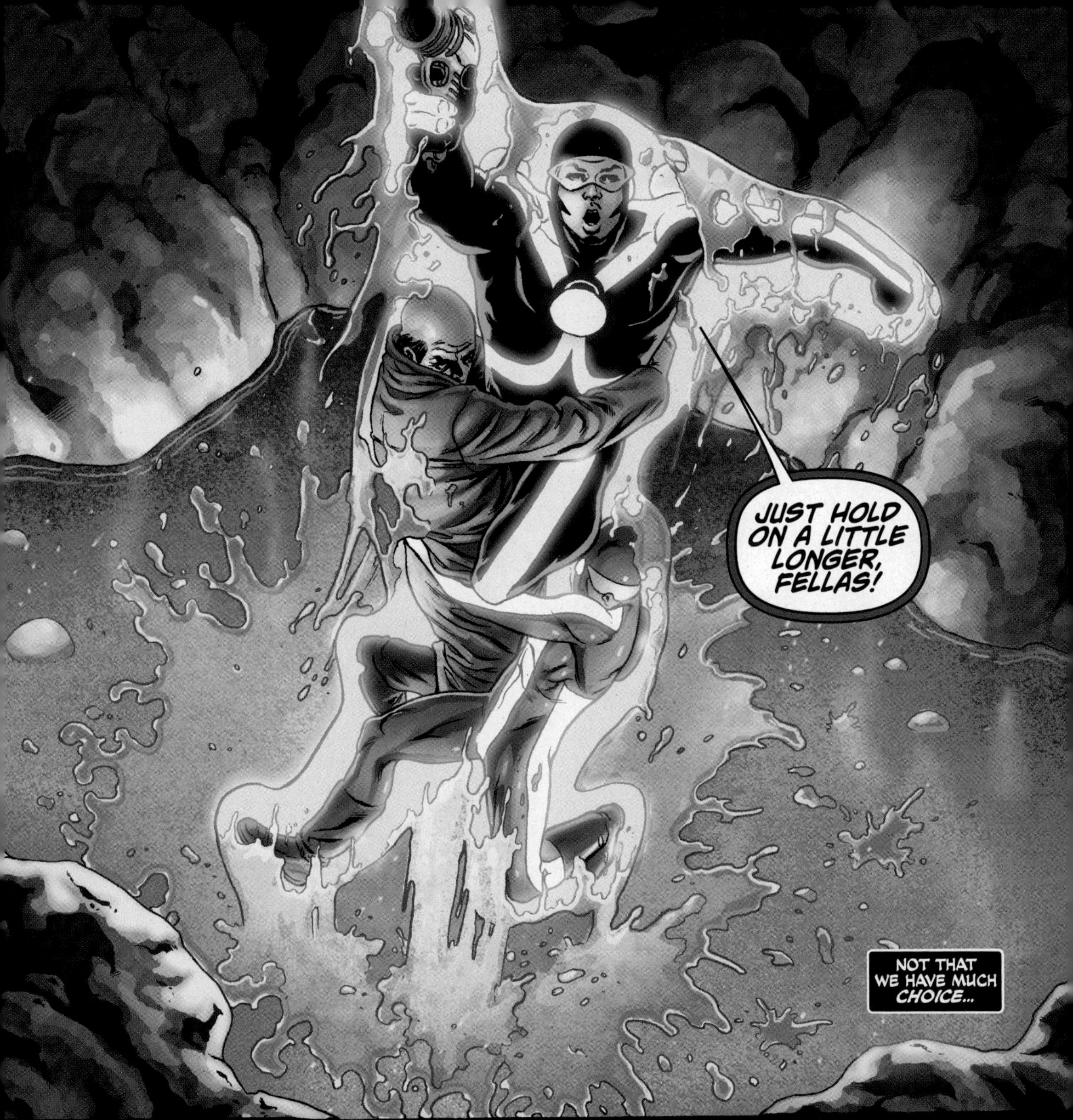
JUST HOLD ON A LITTLE LONGER, FELLAS!
NOT THAT WE HAVE MUCH *CHOICE*...

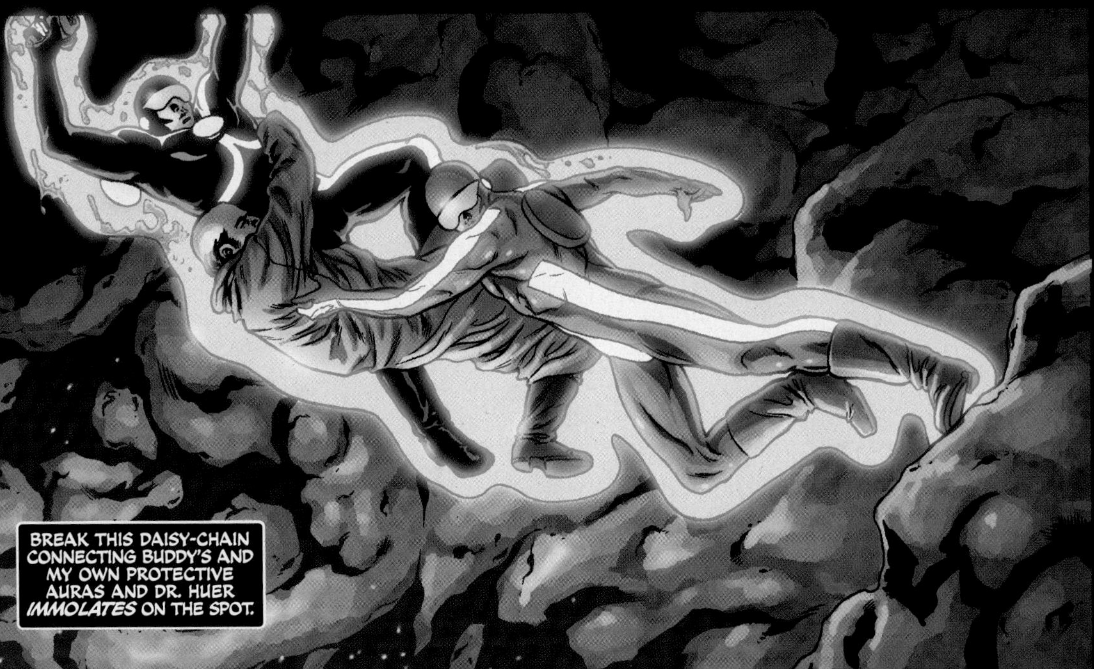
BREAK THIS DAISY-CHAIN CONNECTING BUDDY'S AND MY OWN PROTECTIVE AURAS AND DR. HUER *IMMOLATES* ON THE SPOT.

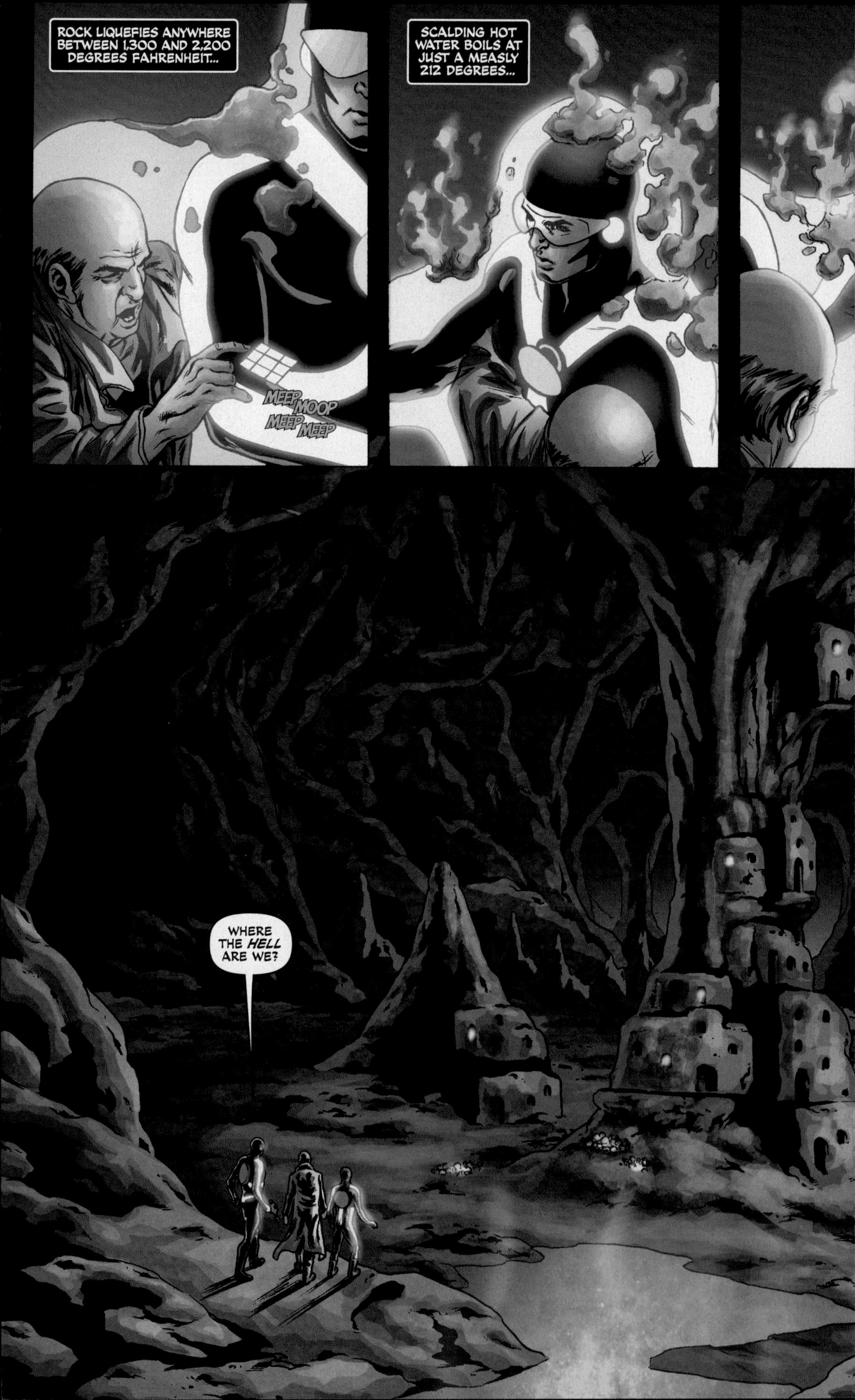
ROCK LIQUEFIES ANYWHERE BETWEEN 1,300 AND 2,200 DEGREES FAHRENHEIT...
MEEP MOOP MEEP MEEP
SCALDING HOT WATER BOILS AT JUST A MEASLY 212 DEGREES...
WHERE THE HELL ARE WE?

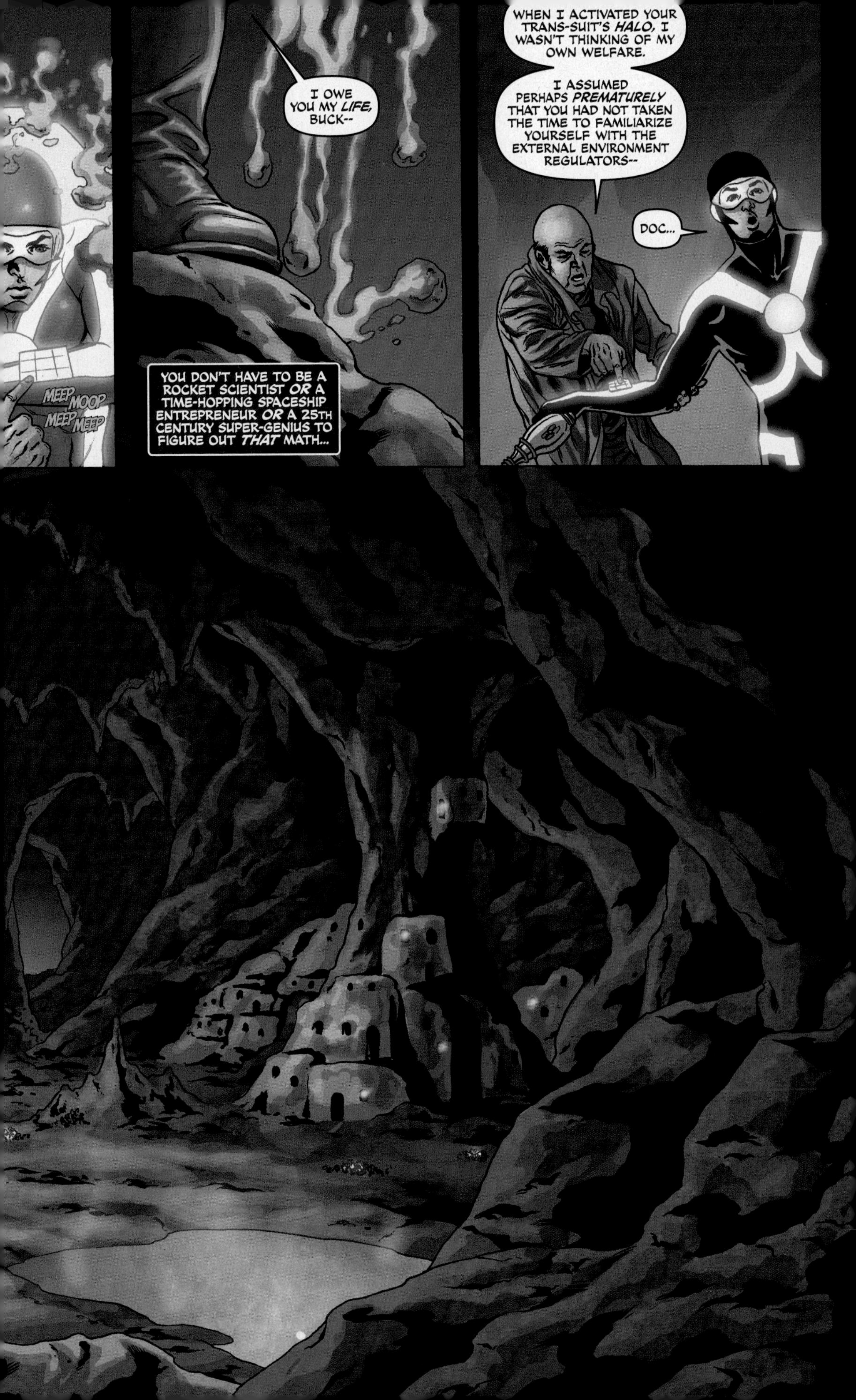
MEEP MOOP
MEEP MEEP
I OWE YOU MY LIFE, BUCK--
YOU DON'T HAVE TO BE A ROCKET SCIENTIST OR A TIME-HOPPING SPACESHIP ENTREPRENEUR OR A 25TH CENTURY SUPER-GENIUS TO FIGURE OUT THAT MATH...
WHEN I ACTIVATED YOUR TRANS-SUIT'S HALO, I WASN'T THINKING OF MY OWN WELFARE.
I ASSUMED PERHAPS PREMATURELY THAT YOU HAD NOT TAKEN THE TIME TO FAMILIARIZE YOURSELF WITH THE EXTERNAL ENVIRONMENT REGULATORS--
DOC...

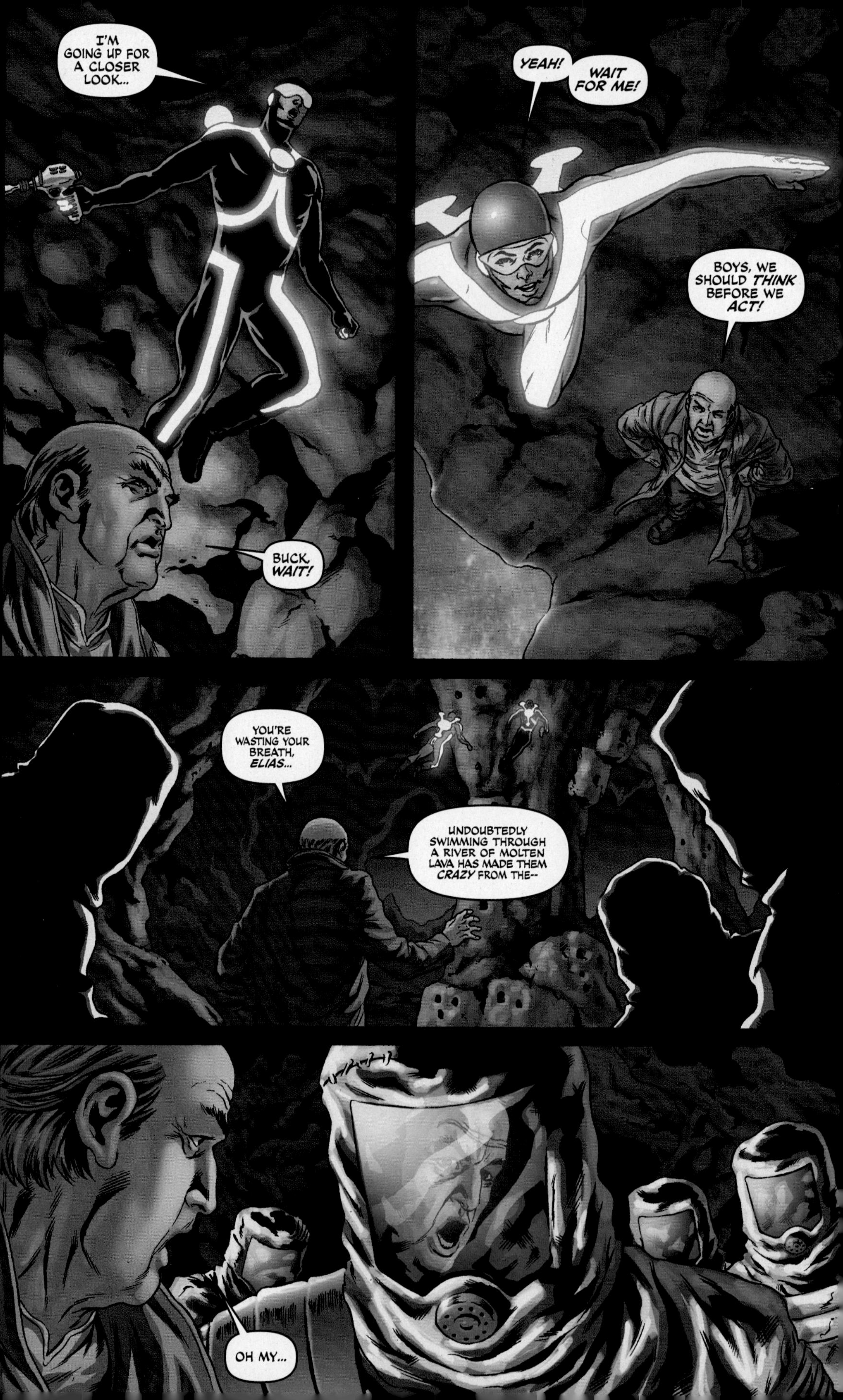

I'M GOING UP FOR A CLOSER LOOK...
BUCK, WAIT!
YEAH!
WAIT FOR ME!
BOYS, WE SHOULD THINK BEFORE WE ACT!
YOU'RE WASTING YOUR BREATH, ELIAS...
UNDOUBTEDLY SWIMMING THROUGH A RIVER OF MOLTEN LAVA HAS MADE THEM CRAZY FROM THE--
OH MY...

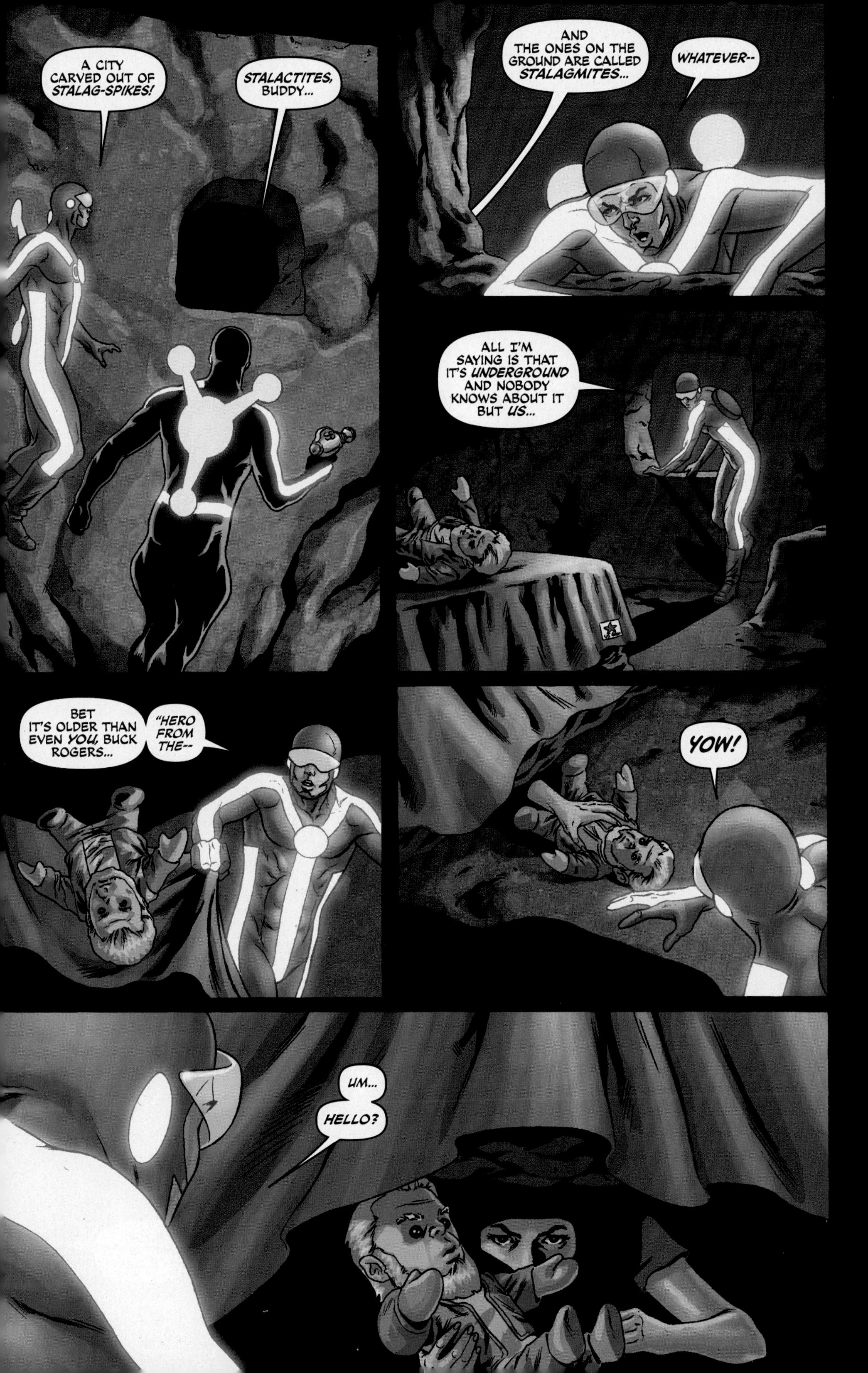
A CITY CARVED OUT OF STALAG-SPIKES!
STALACTITES, BUDDY...
AND THE ONES ON THE GROUND ARE CALLED STALAGMITES...
WHATEVER--
ALL I'M SAYING IS THAT IT'S UNDERGROUND AND NOBODY KNOWS ABOUT IT BUT US...
BET IT'S OLDER THAN EVEN YOU, BUCK ROGERS...
"HERO FROM THE--
YOW!
UM...
HELLO?

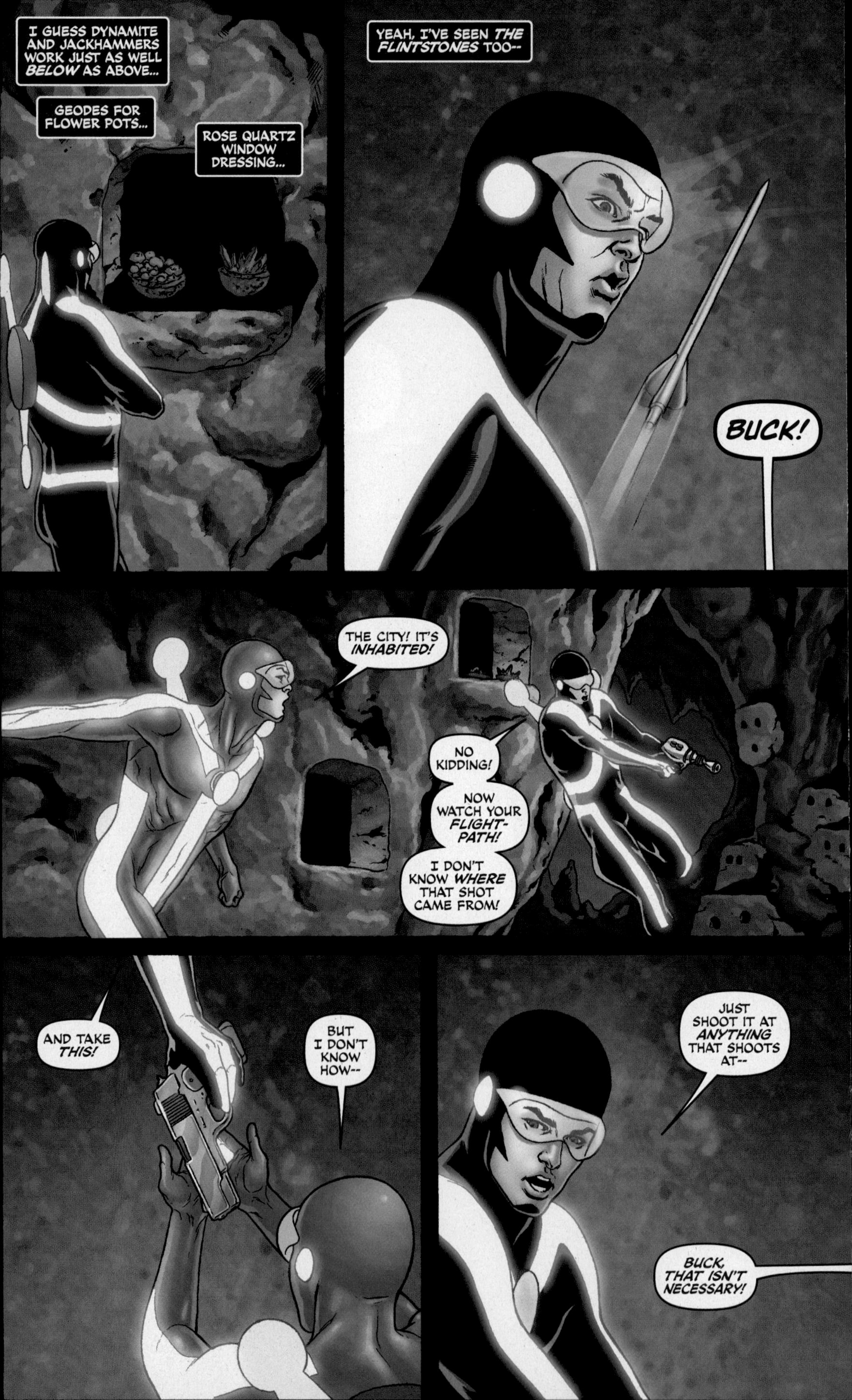
I GUESS DYNAMITE AND JACKHAMMERS WORK JUST AS WELL *BELOW* AS ABOVE...
GEODES FOR FLOWER POTS...
ROSE QUARTZ WINDOW DRESSING...
YEAH, I'VE SEEN *THE FLINTSTONES* TOO--
BUCK!
THE CITY! IT'S *INHABITED!*
NO KIDDING!
NOW WATCH YOUR *FLIGHT-PATH!*
I DON'T KNOW *WHERE* THAT SHOT CAME FROM!
AND TAKE *THIS!*
BUT I DON'T KNOW HOW--
JUST SHOOT IT AT *ANYTHING* THAT SHOOTS AT--
BUCK, THAT ISN'T NECESSARY!

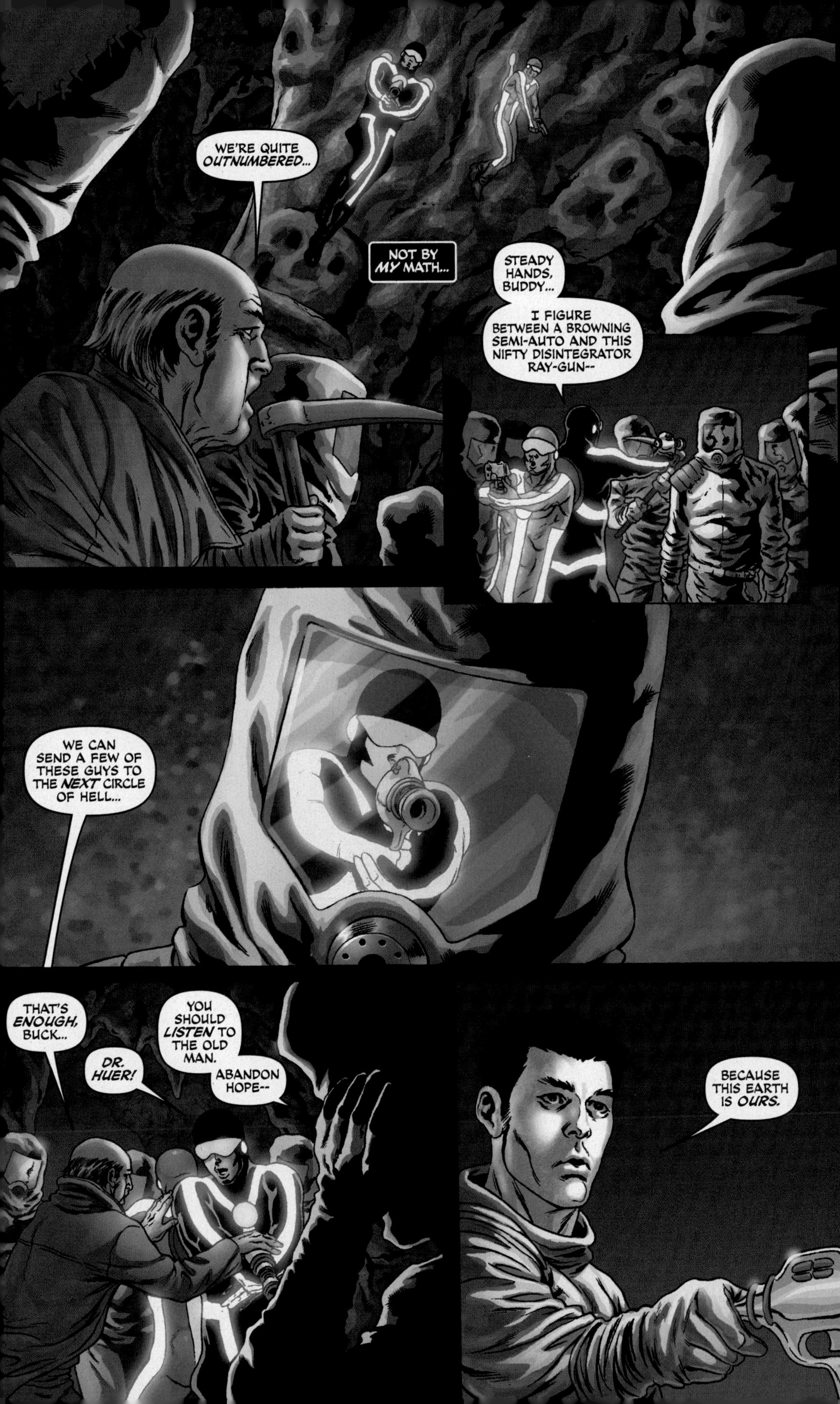
WE'RE QUITE OUTNUMBERED...
NOT BY MY MATH...
STEADY HANDS, BUDDY...
I FIGURE BETWEEN A BROWNING SEMI-AUTO AND THIS NIFTY DISINTEGRATOR RAY-GUN--
WE CAN SEND A FEW OF THESE GUYS TO THE NEXT CIRCLE OF HELL...
THAT'S ENOUGH, BUCK...
DR. HUER!
YOU SHOULD LISTEN TO THE OLD MAN. ABANDON HOPE--
BECAUSE THIS EARTH IS OURS.

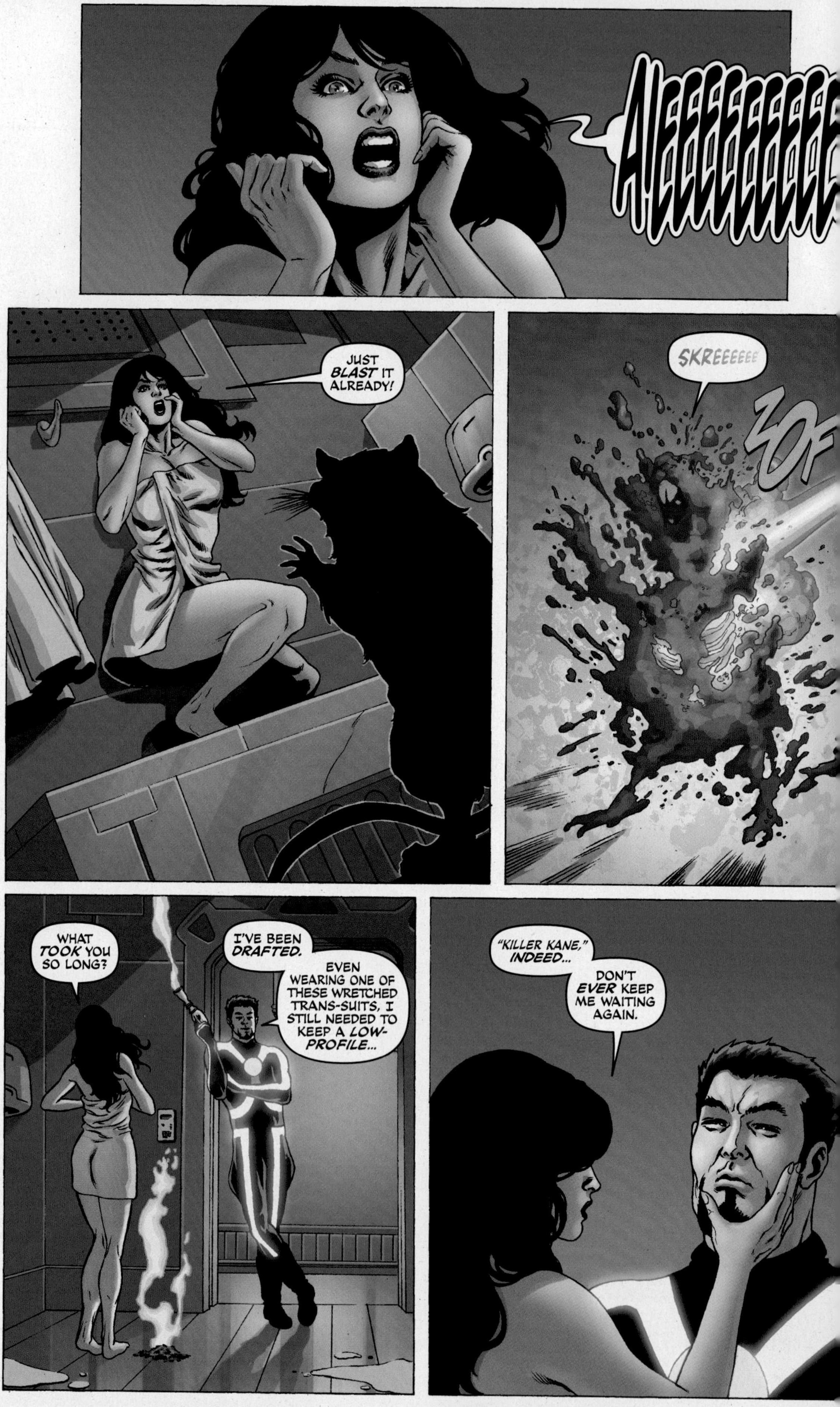
AIEEEEEEEEEE
JUST BLAST IT ALREADY!
SKREEEEEE
ZOF
WHAT TOOK YOU SO LONG?
I'VE BEEN DRAFTED.
EVEN WEARING ONE OF THESE WRETCHED TRANS-SUITS, I STILL NEEDED TO KEEP A LOW-PROFILE...
"KILLER KANE," INDEED...
DON'T EVER KEEP ME WAITING AGAIN.

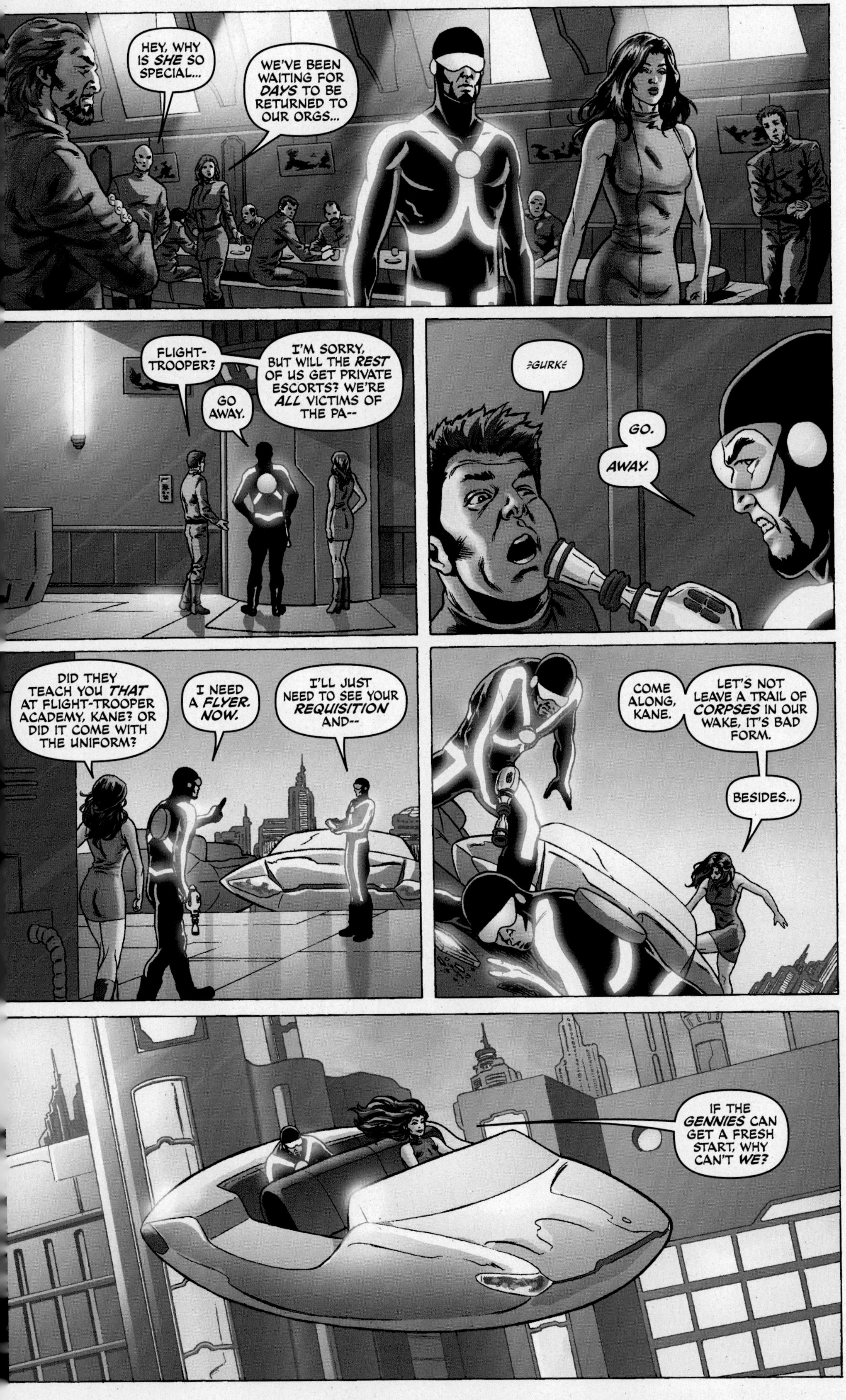
HEY, WHY IS SHE SO SPECIAL...
WE'VE BEEN WAITING FOR DAYS TO BE RETURNED TO OUR ORGS...
FLIGHT-TROOPER?
I'M SORRY, BUT WILL THE REST OF US GET PRIVATE ESCORTS? WE'RE ALL VICTIMS OF THE PA--
GO AWAY.
GURK
GO. AWAY.
DID THEY TEACH YOU THAT AT FLIGHT-TROOPER ACADEMY, KANE? OR DID IT COME WITH THE UNIFORM?
I NEED A FLYER. NOW.
I'LL JUST NEED TO SEE YOUR REQUISITION AND--
COME ALONG, KANE.
LET'S NOT LEAVE A TRAIL OF CORPSES IN OUR WAKE, IT'S BAD FORM.
BESIDES...
IF THE GENNIES CAN GET A FRESH START, WHY CAN'T WE?

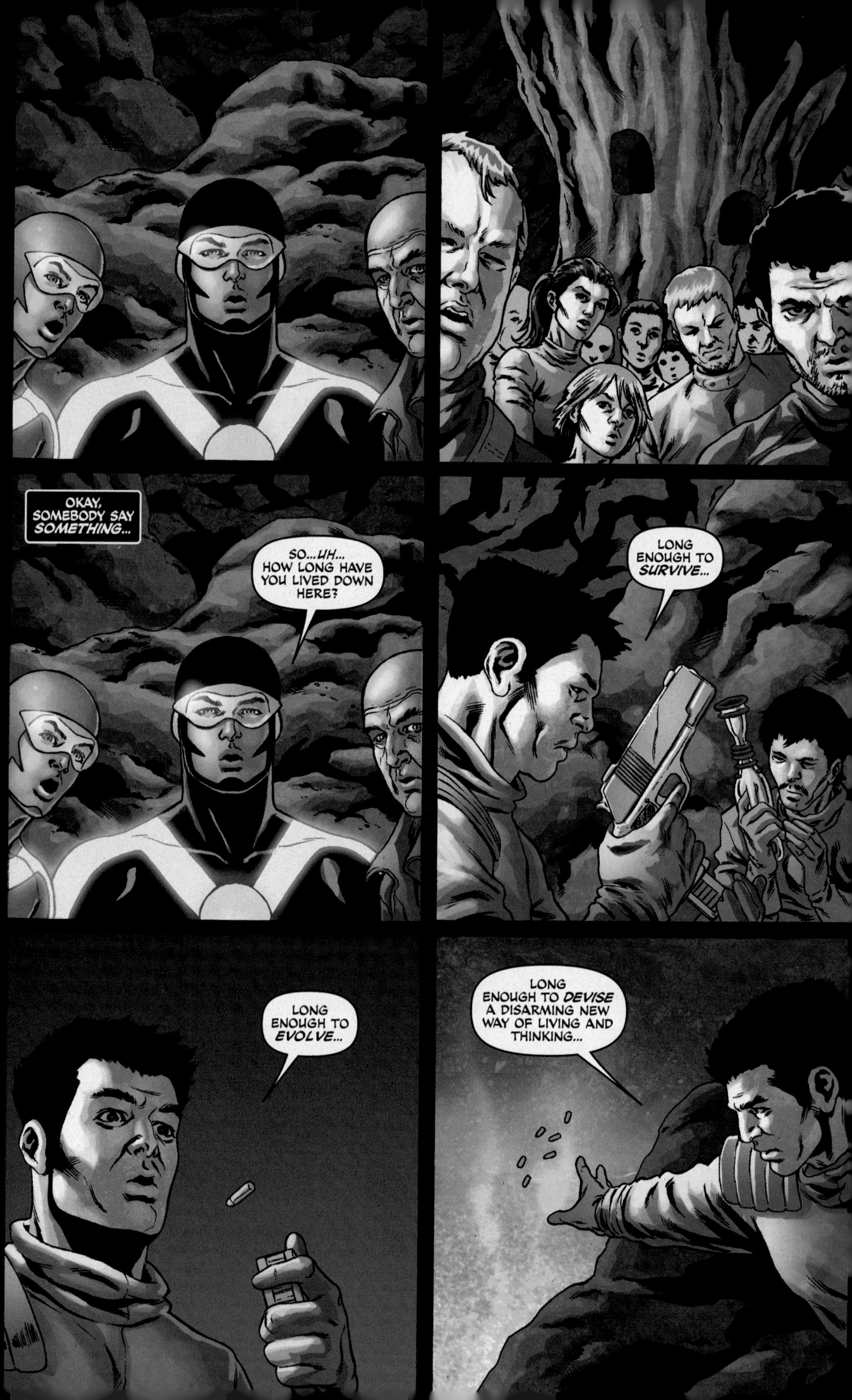
OKAY, SOMEBODY SAY *SOMETHING*...
SO...*UH*... HOW LONG HAVE YOU LIVED DOWN HERE?
LONG ENOUGH TO *SURVIVE*...
LONG ENOUGH TO *EVOLVE*...
LONG ENOUGH TO *DEVISE* A DISARMING NEW WAY OF LIVING AND THINKING...

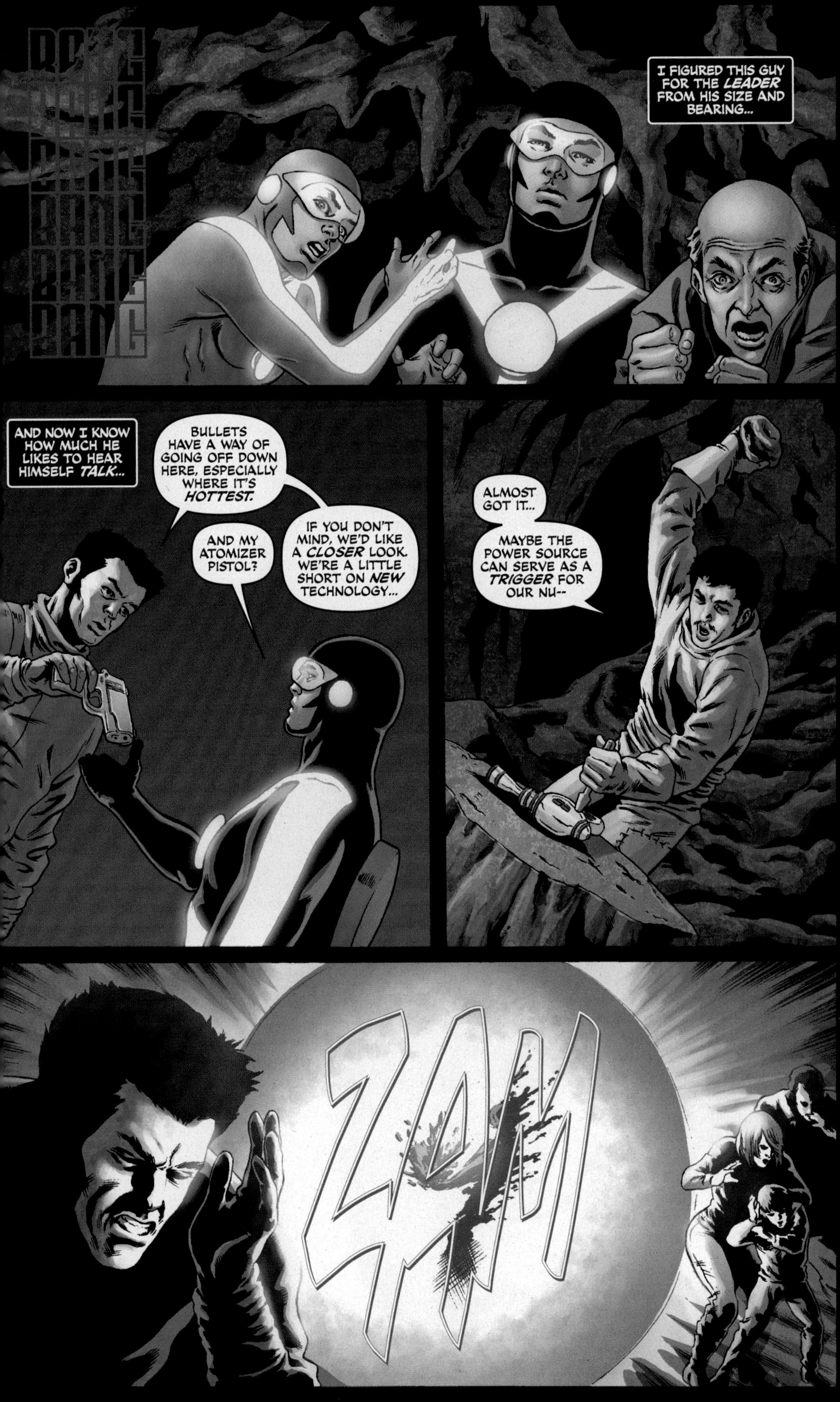
BANG
BANG
BANG
I FIGURED THIS GUY FOR THE *LEADER* FROM HIS SIZE AND BEARING...
AND NOW I KNOW HOW MUCH HE LIKES TO HEAR HIMSELF *TALK*...
BULLETS HAVE A WAY OF GOING OFF DOWN HERE, ESPECIALLY WHERE IT'S *HOTTEST.*
AND MY ATOMIZER PISTOL?
IF YOU DON'T MIND, WE'D LIKE A *CLOSER* LOOK. WE'RE A LITTLE SHORT ON *NEW* TECHNOLOGY...
ALMOST GOT IT...
MAYBE THE POWER SOURCE CAN SERVE AS A *TRIGGER* FOR OUR NU--
ZAM

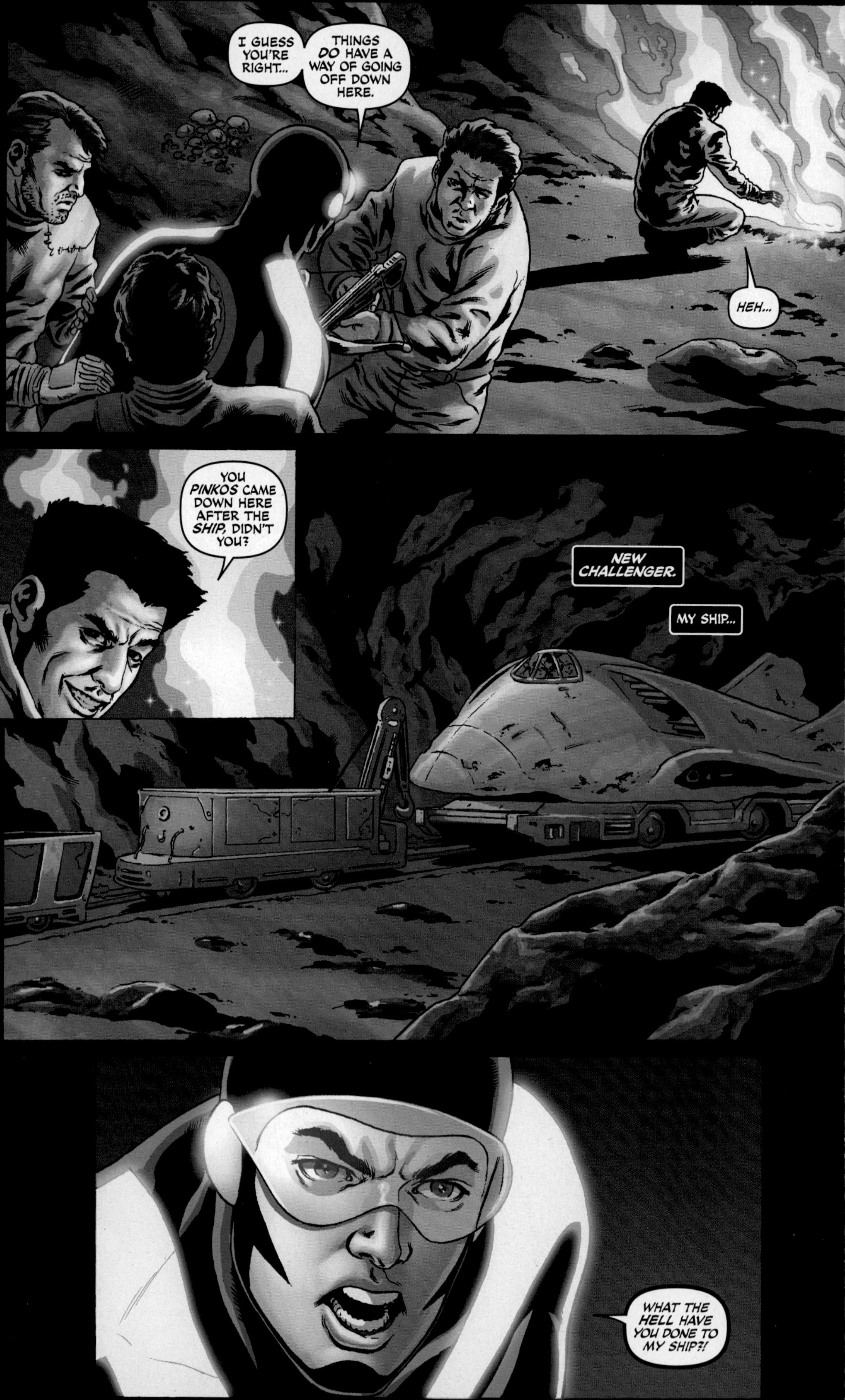
I GUESS YOU'RE RIGHT...
THINGS DO HAVE A WAY OF GOING OFF DOWN HERE.
HEH...
YOU PINKOS CAME DOWN HERE AFTER THE SHIP, DIDN'T YOU?
NEW CHALLENGER.
MY SHIP...
WHAT THE HELL HAVE YOU DONE TO MY SHIP?!

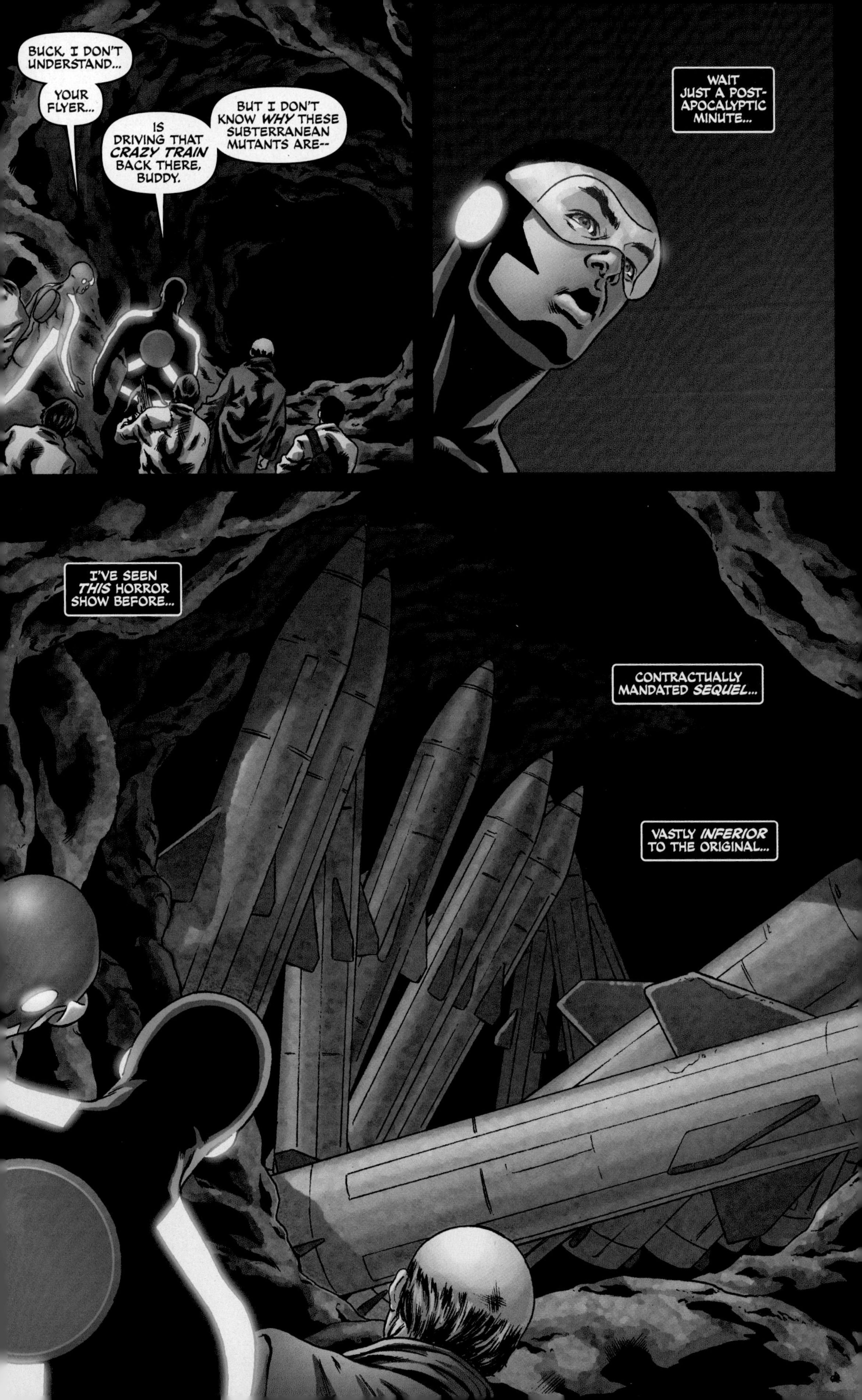

BUCK, I DON'T UNDERSTAND...
YOUR FLYER...
IS DRIVING THAT CRAZY TRAIN BACK THERE, BUDDY.
BUT I DON'T KNOW WHY THESE SUBTERRANEAN MUTANTS ARE--
WAIT JUST A POST-APOCALYPTIC MINUTE...
I'VE SEEN THIS HORROR SHOW BEFORE...
CONTRACTUALLY MANDATED SEQUEL...
VASTLY INFERIOR TO THE ORIGINAL...

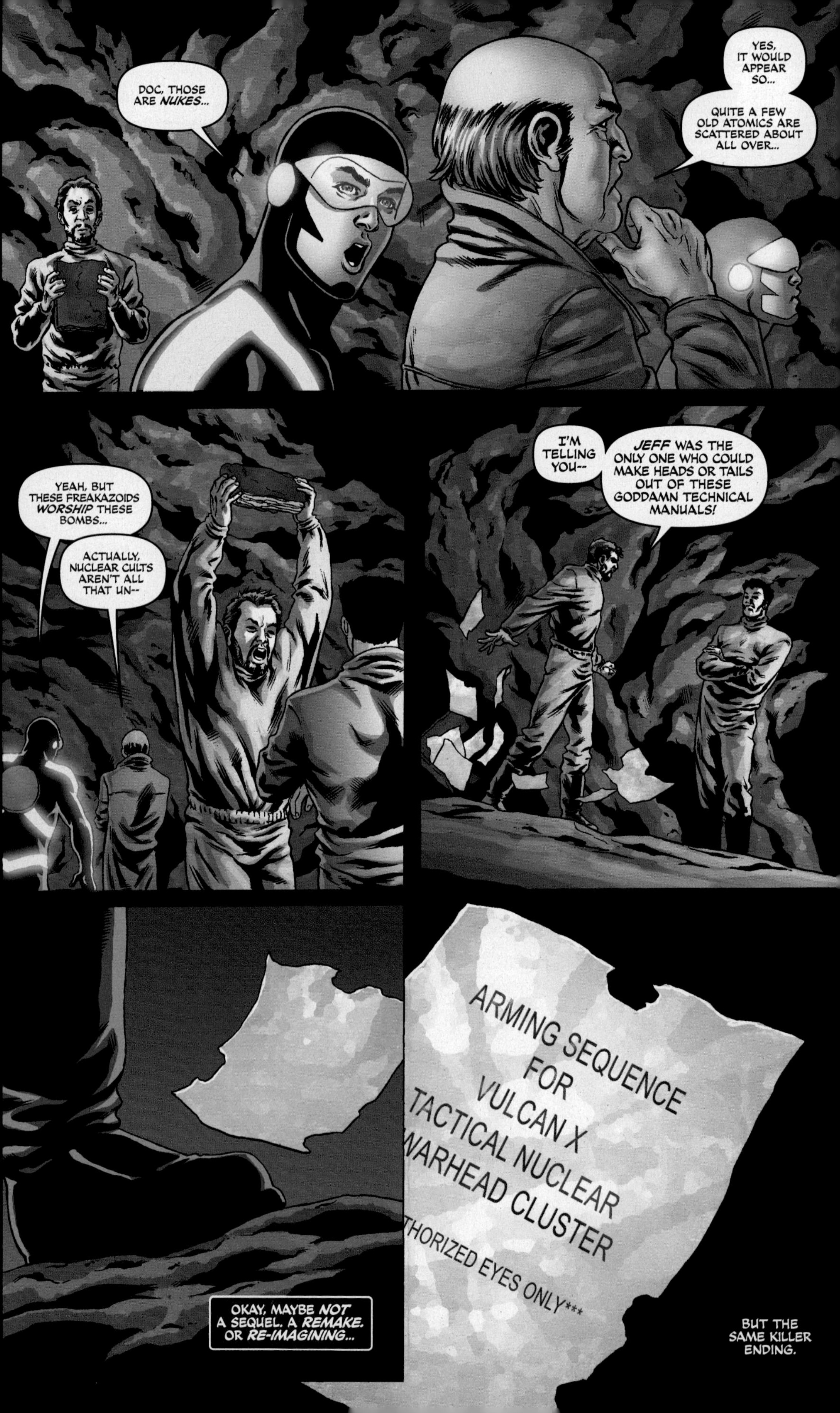
DOC, THOSE ARE *NUKES*...
YES, IT WOULD APPEAR SO...
QUITE A FEW OLD ATOMICS ARE SCATTERED ABOUT ALL OVER...
YEAH, BUT THESE FREAKAZOIDS *WORSHIP* THESE BOMBS...
ACTUALLY, NUCLEAR CULTS AREN'T ALL THAT UN--
I'M TELLING YOU--
JEFF WAS THE ONLY ONE WHO COULD MAKE HEADS OR TAILS OUT OF THESE GODDAMN TECHNICAL MANUALS!
ARMING SEQUENCE FOR VULCAN X TACTICAL NUCLEAR WARHEAD CLUSTER
THORIZED EYES ONLY***
OKAY, MAYBE *NOT* A SEQUEL. A *REMAKE*. OR *RE-IMAGINING*...
BUT THE SAME KILLER ENDING.

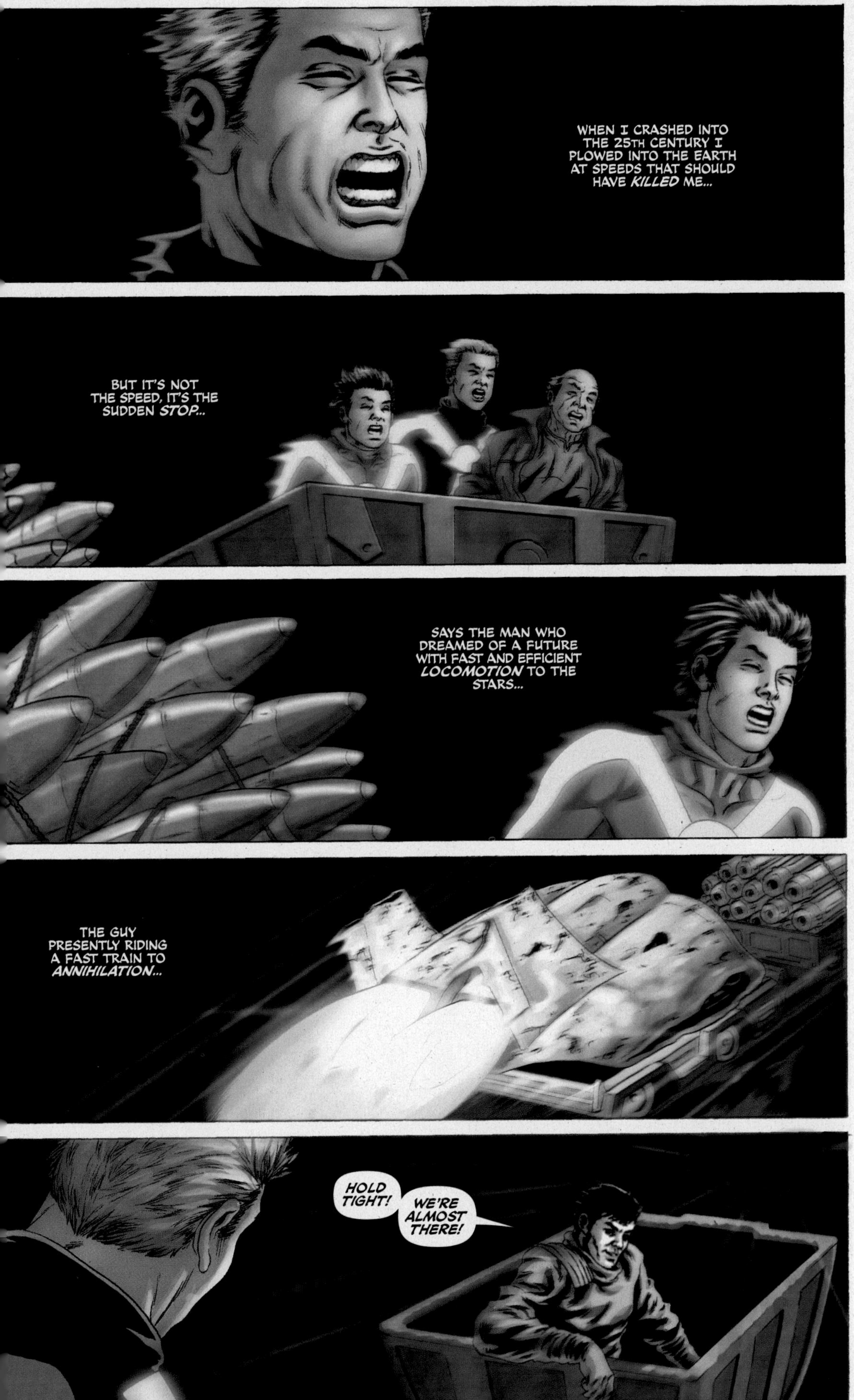
WHEN I CRASHED INTO THE 25TH CENTURY I PLOWED INTO THE EARTH AT SPEEDS THAT SHOULD HAVE *KILLED* ME...
BUT IT'S NOT THE SPEED, IT'S THE SUDDEN *STOP*...
SAYS THE MAN WHO DREAMED OF A FUTURE WITH FAST AND EFFICIENT *LOCOMOTION* TO THE STARS...
THE GUY PRESENTLY RIDING A FAST TRAIN TO *ANNIHILATION*...
HOLD TIGHT!
WE'RE ALMOST THERE!

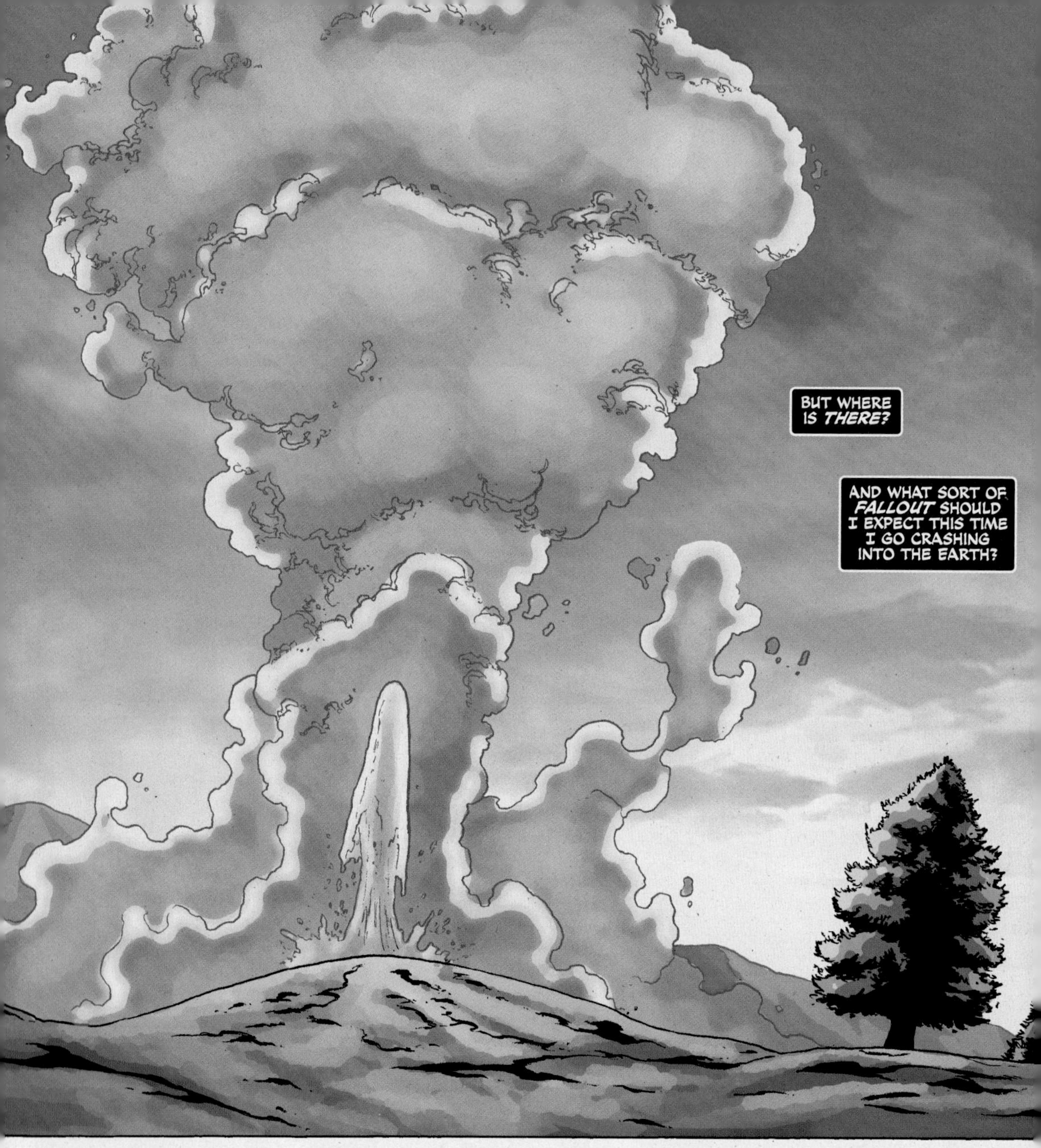
BUT WHERE IS *THERE?*
AND WHAT SORT OF *FALLOUT* SHOULD I EXPECT THIS TIME I GO CRASHING INTO THE EARTH?

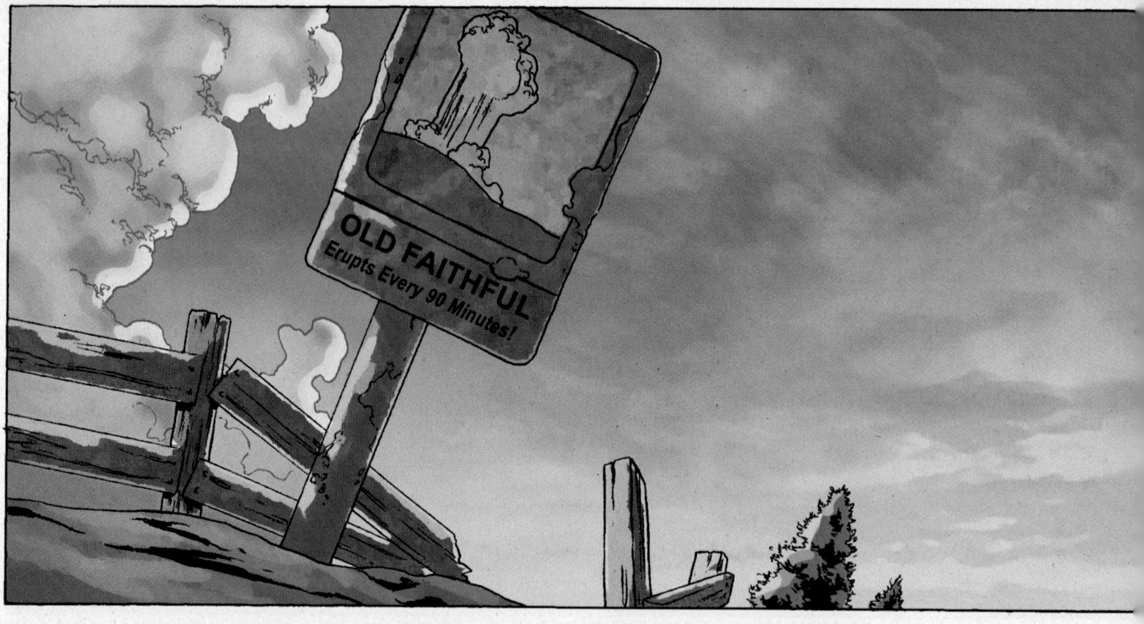
OLD FAITHFUL
Erupts Every 90 Minutes!

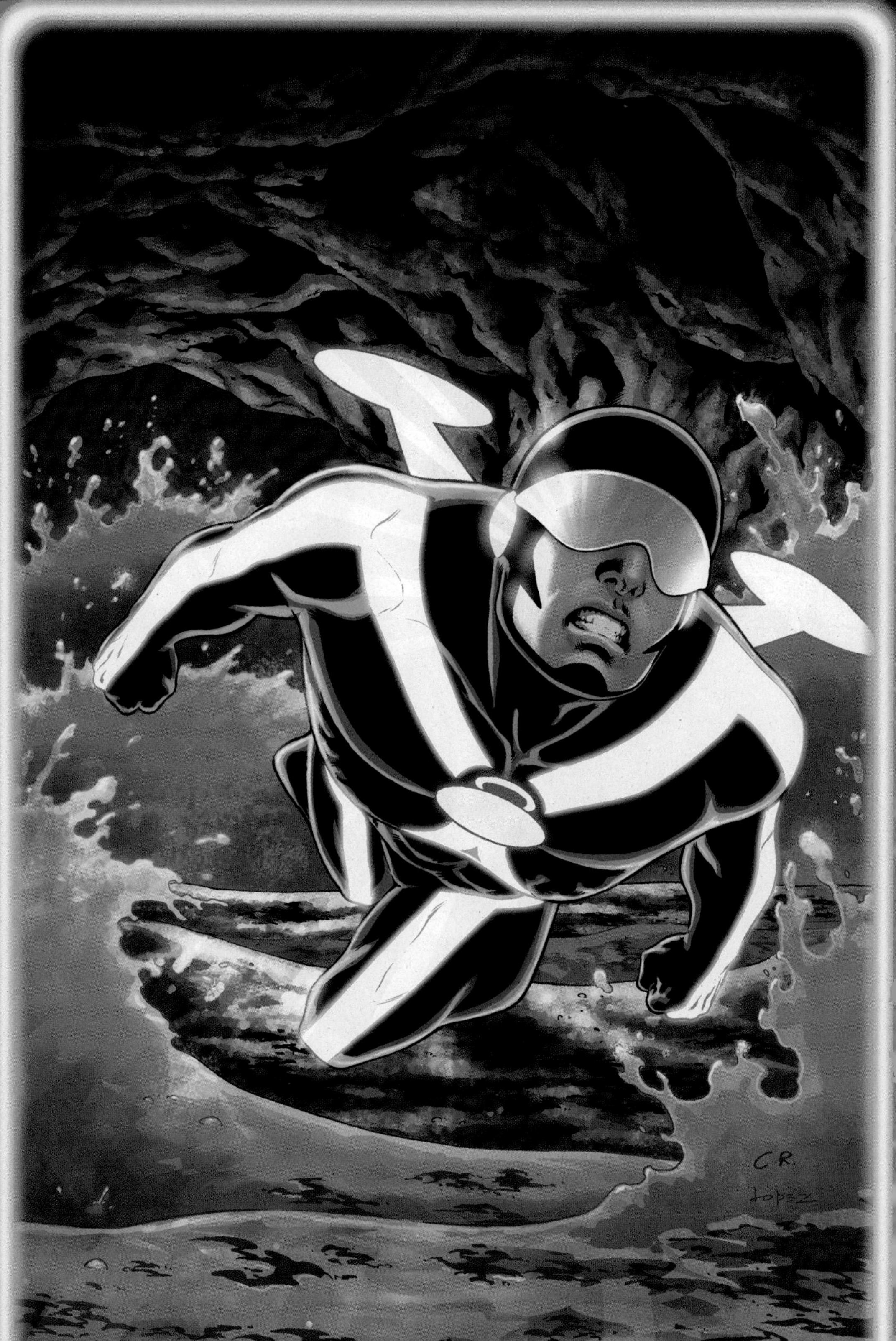
C.R.
Lopez

THE SPACE BENEATH PART TWO: The Fire Down Below

ISSUE EIGHT COVER BY CARLOS RAFAEL

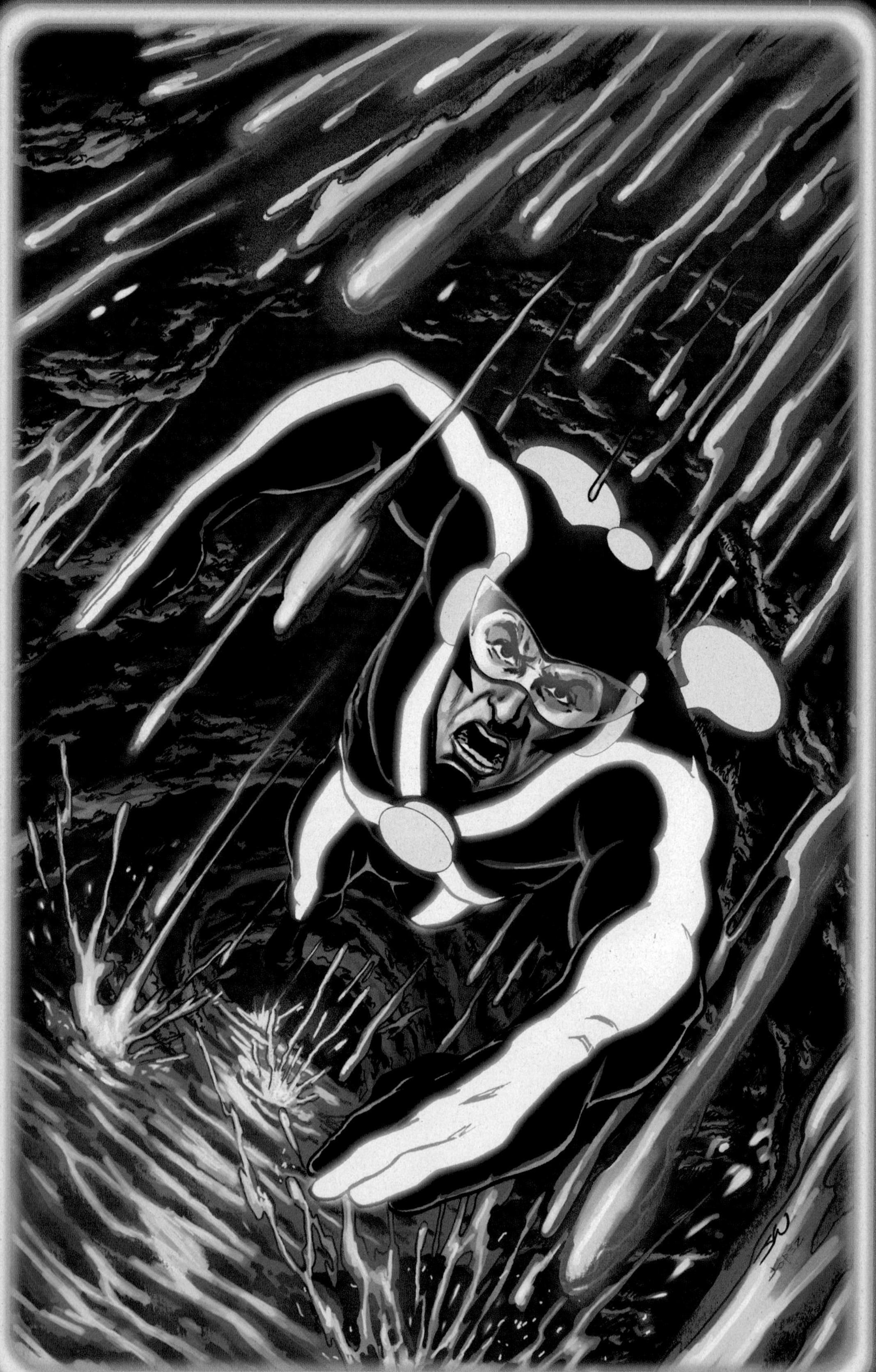

ALTERNATE COVER BY JOHN WATSON

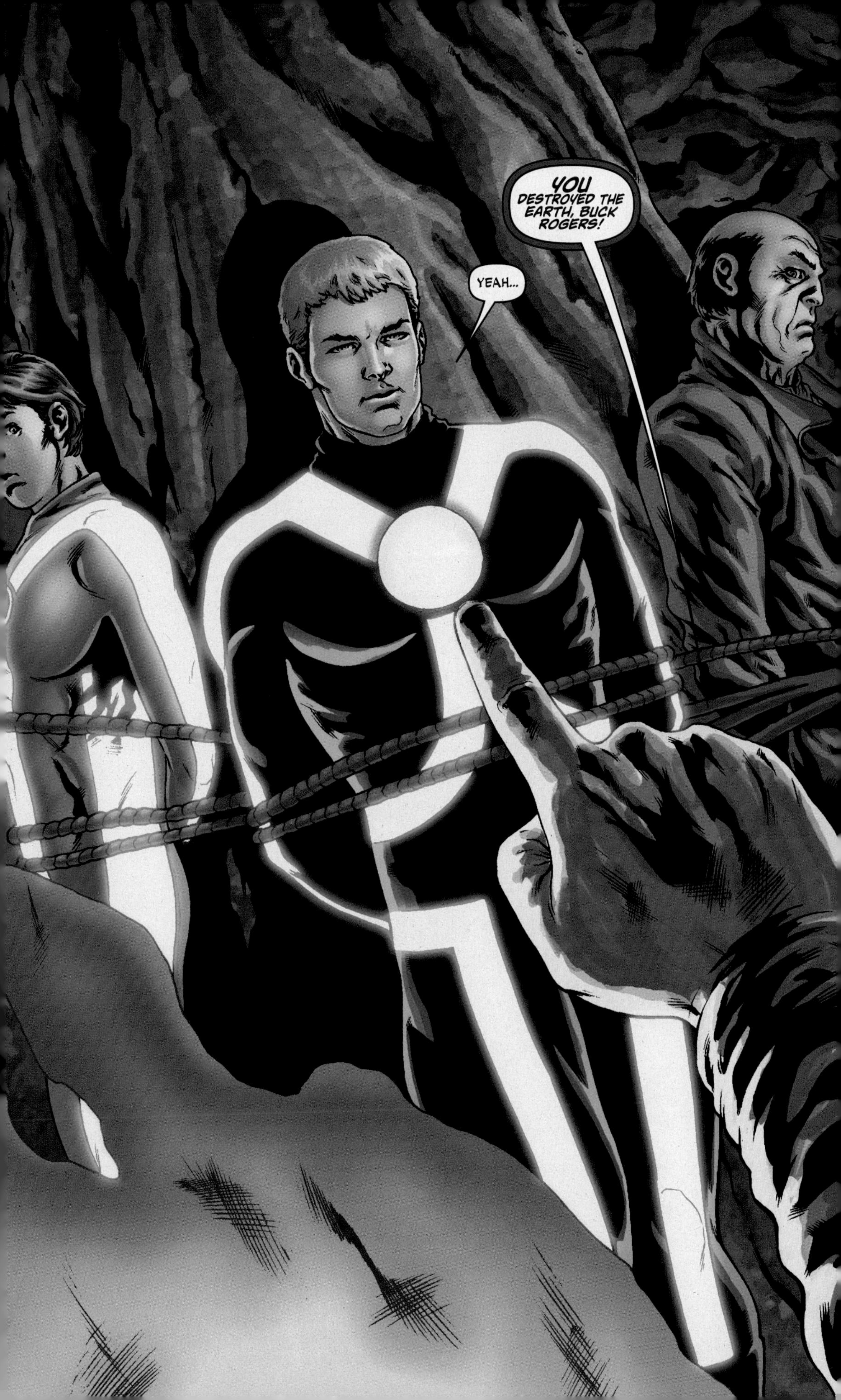
YOU DESTROYED THE EARTH, BUCK ROGERS!
YEAH...

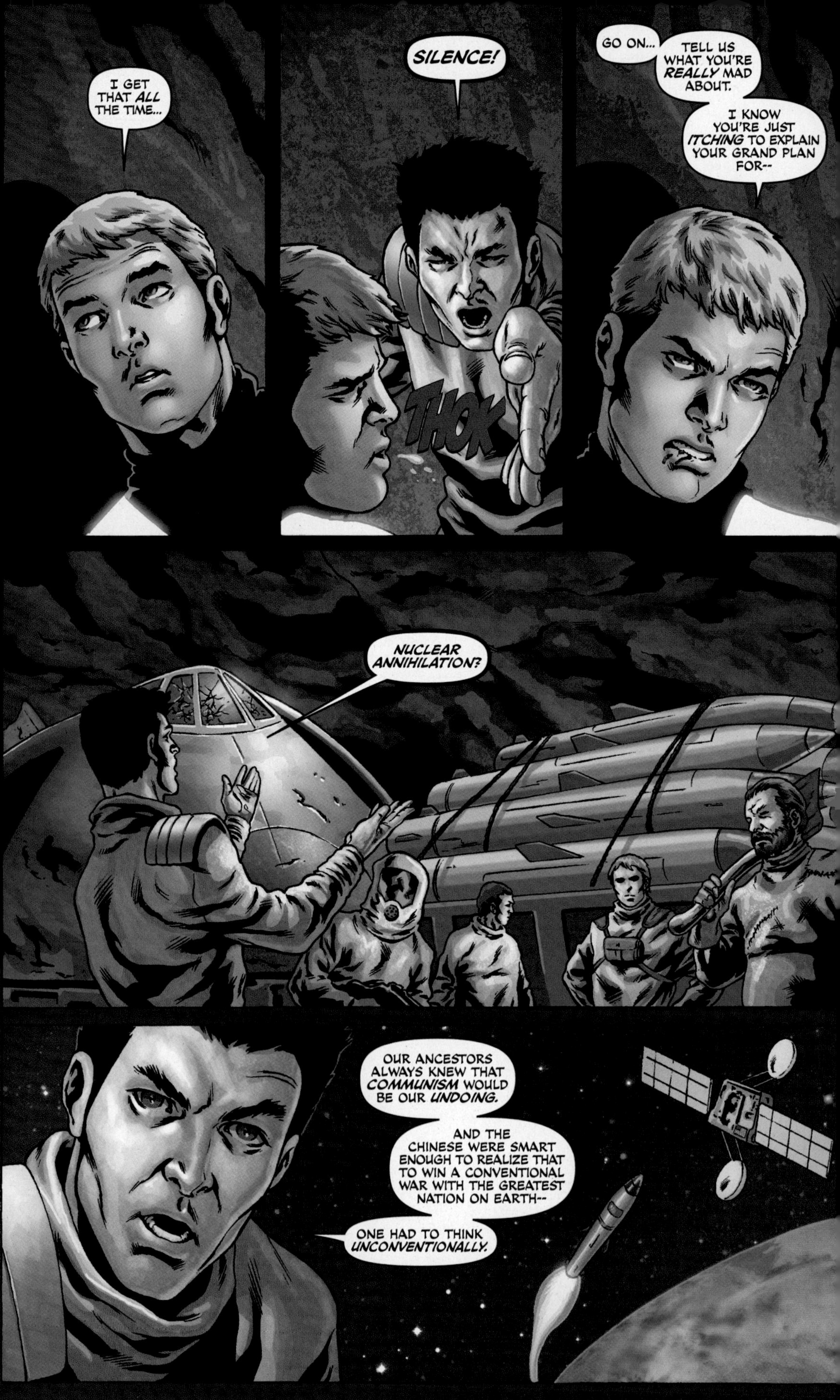
I GET THAT *ALL* THE TIME...
SILENCE!
THOK
GO ON...
TELL US WHAT YOU'RE *REALLY* MAD ABOUT.
I KNOW YOU'RE JUST *ITCHING* TO EXPLAIN YOUR GRAND PLAN FOR--
NUCLEAR ANNIHILATION?
OUR ANCESTORS ALWAYS KNEW THAT *COMMUNISM* WOULD BE OUR *UNDOING.*
AND THE CHINESE WERE SMART ENOUGH TO REALIZE THAT TO WIN A CONVENTIONAL WAR WITH THE GREATEST NATION ON EARTH--
ONE HAD TO THINK *UNCONVENTIONALLY.*

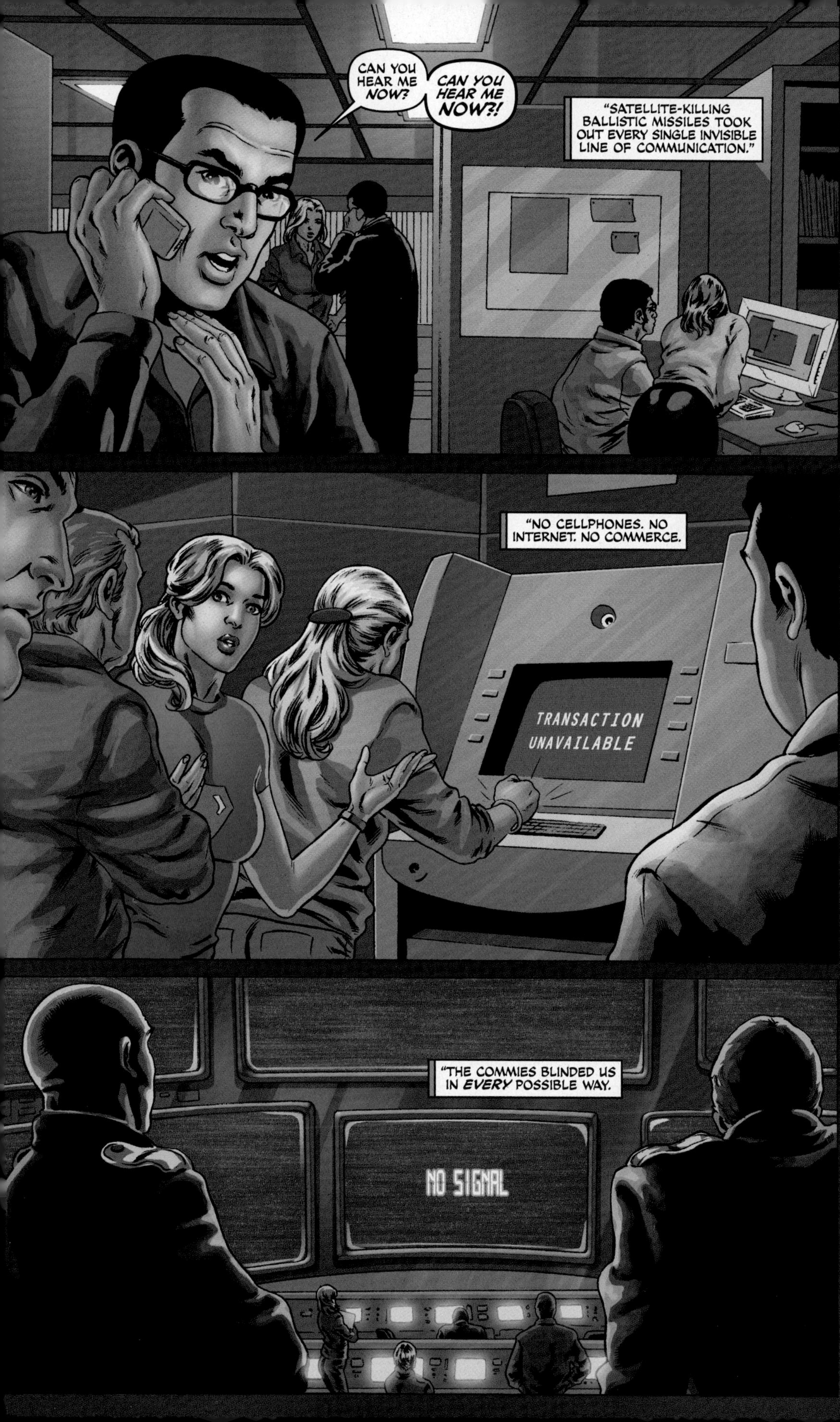
CAN YOU HEAR ME NOW?
CAN YOU HEAR ME NOW?!
"SATELLITE-KILLING BALLISTIC MISSILES TOOK OUT EVERY SINGLE INVISIBLE LINE OF COMMUNICATION."
"NO CELLPHONES. NO INTERNET. NO COMMERCE.
TRANSACTION UNAVAILABLE
"THE COMMIES BLINDED US IN *EVERY* POSSIBLE WAY.
NO SIGNAL

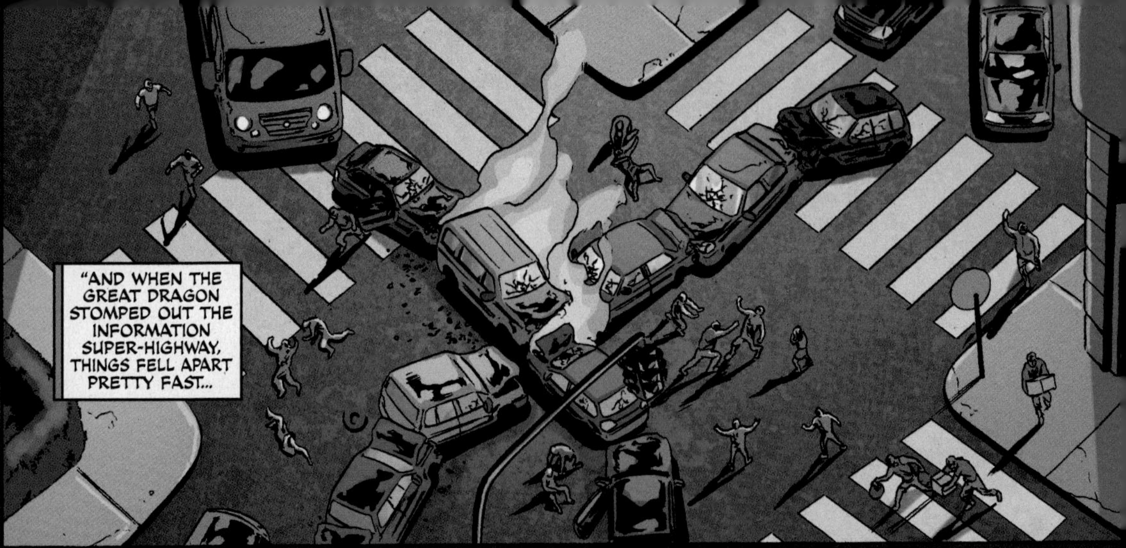
"AND WHEN THE GREAT DRAGON STOMPED OUT THE INFORMATION SUPER-HIGHWAY, THINGS FELL APART PRETTY FAST...

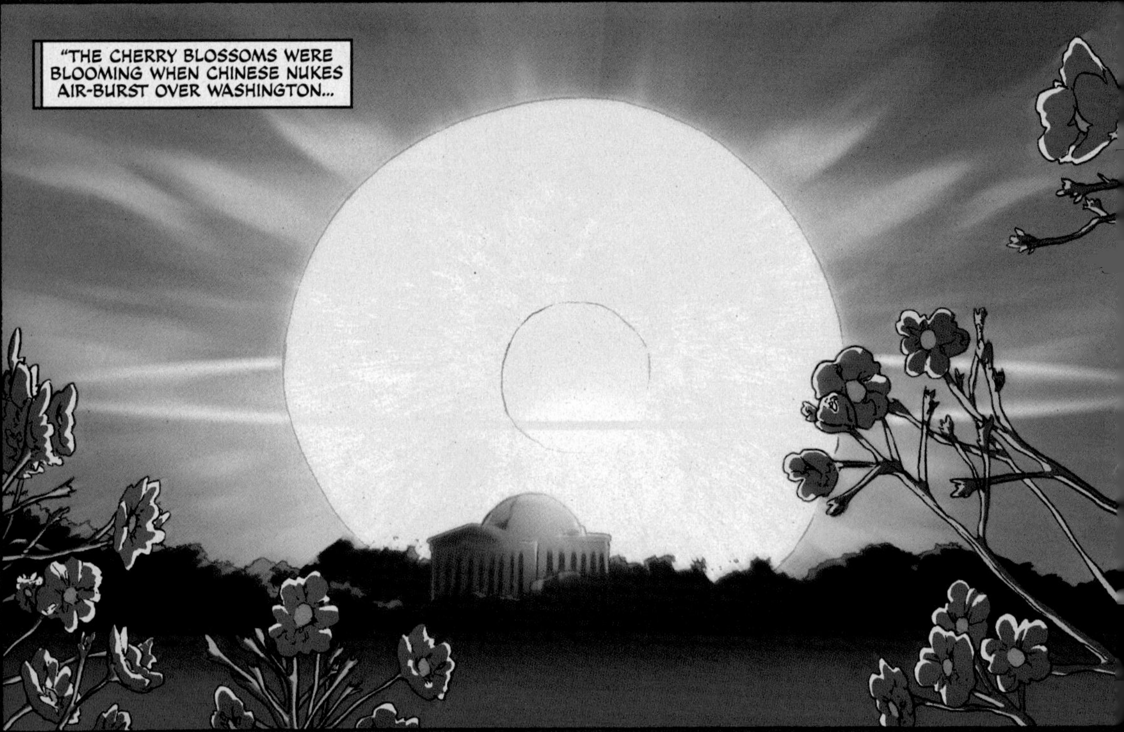
"THE CHERRY BLOSSOMS WERE BLOOMING WHEN CHINESE NUKES AIR-BURST OVER WASHINGTON...

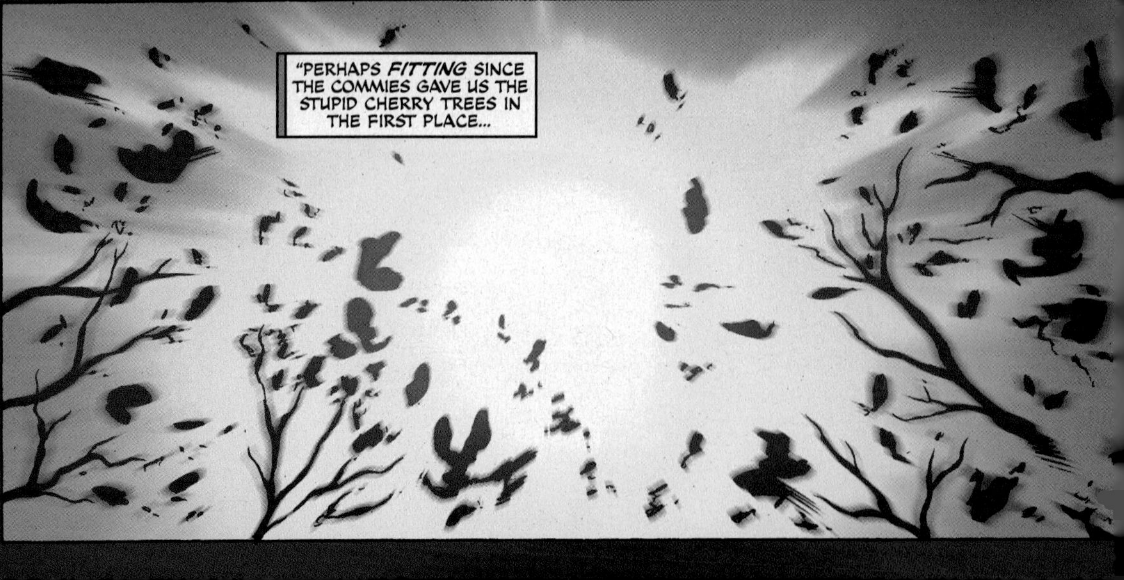
"PERHAPS *FITTING* SINCE THE COMMIES GAVE US THE STUPID CHERRY TREES IN THE FIRST PLACE...

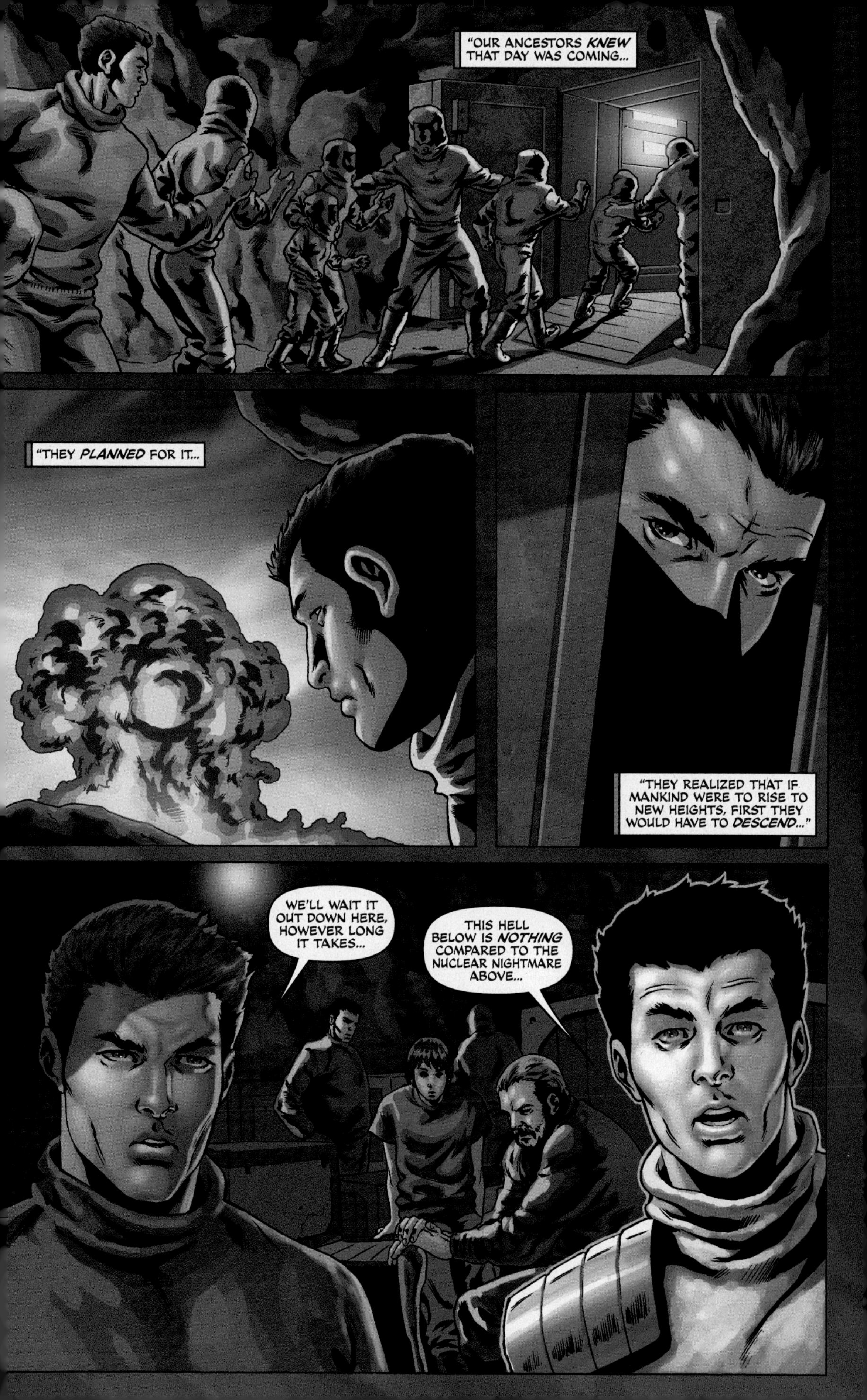
"OUR ANCESTORS KNEW THAT DAY WAS COMING...
"THEY PLANNED FOR IT...
"THEY REALIZED THAT IF MANKIND WERE TO RISE TO NEW HEIGHTS, FIRST THEY WOULD HAVE TO DESCEND..."
WE'LL WAIT IT OUT DOWN HERE, HOWEVER LONG IT TAKES...
THIS HELL BELOW IS NOTHING COMPARED TO THE NUCLEAR NIGHTMARE ABOVE...

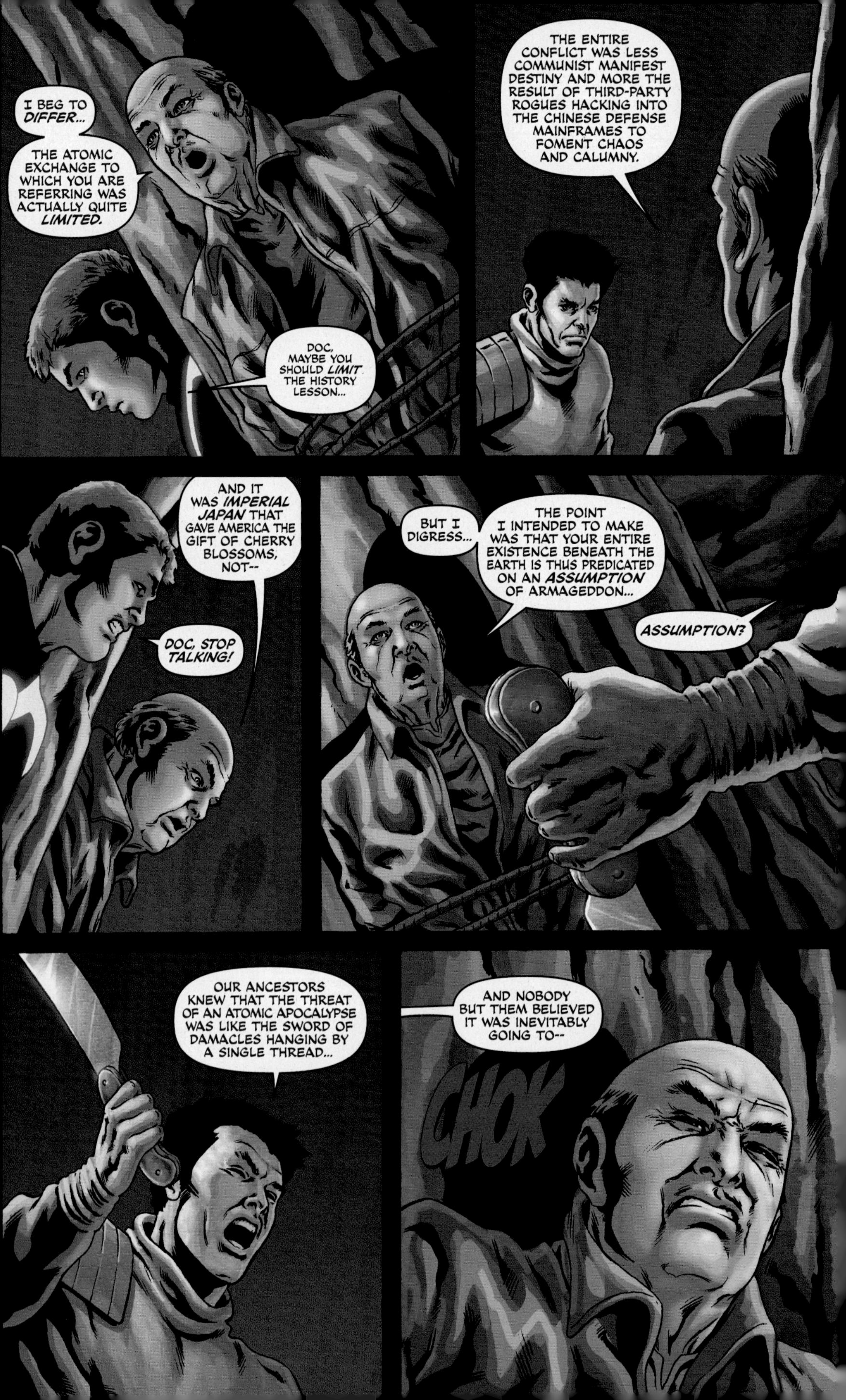
I BEG TO *DIFFER*...
THE ATOMIC EXCHANGE TO WHICH YOU ARE REFERRING WAS ACTUALLY QUITE *LIMITED.*
DOC, MAYBE YOU SHOULD *LIMIT* THE HISTORY LESSON...
THE ENTIRE CONFLICT WAS LESS COMMUNIST MANIFEST DESTINY AND MORE THE RESULT OF THIRD-PARTY ROGUES HACKING INTO THE CHINESE DEFENSE MAINFRAMES TO FOMENT CHAOS AND CALUMNY.
AND IT WAS *IMPERIAL JAPAN* THAT GAVE AMERICA THE GIFT OF CHERRY BLOSSOMS, NOT--
DOC, STOP TALKING!
BUT I DIGRESS...
THE POINT I INTENDED TO MAKE WAS THAT YOUR ENTIRE EXISTENCE BENEATH THE EARTH IS THUS PREDICATED ON AN *ASSUMPTION* OF ARMAGEDDON...
ASSUMPTION?
OUR ANCESTORS KNEW THAT THE THREAT OF AN ATOMIC APOCALYPSE WAS LIKE THE SWORD OF DAMACLES HANGING BY A SINGLE THREAD...
AND NOBODY BUT THEM BELIEVED IT WAS INEVITABLY GOING TO--
CHOK

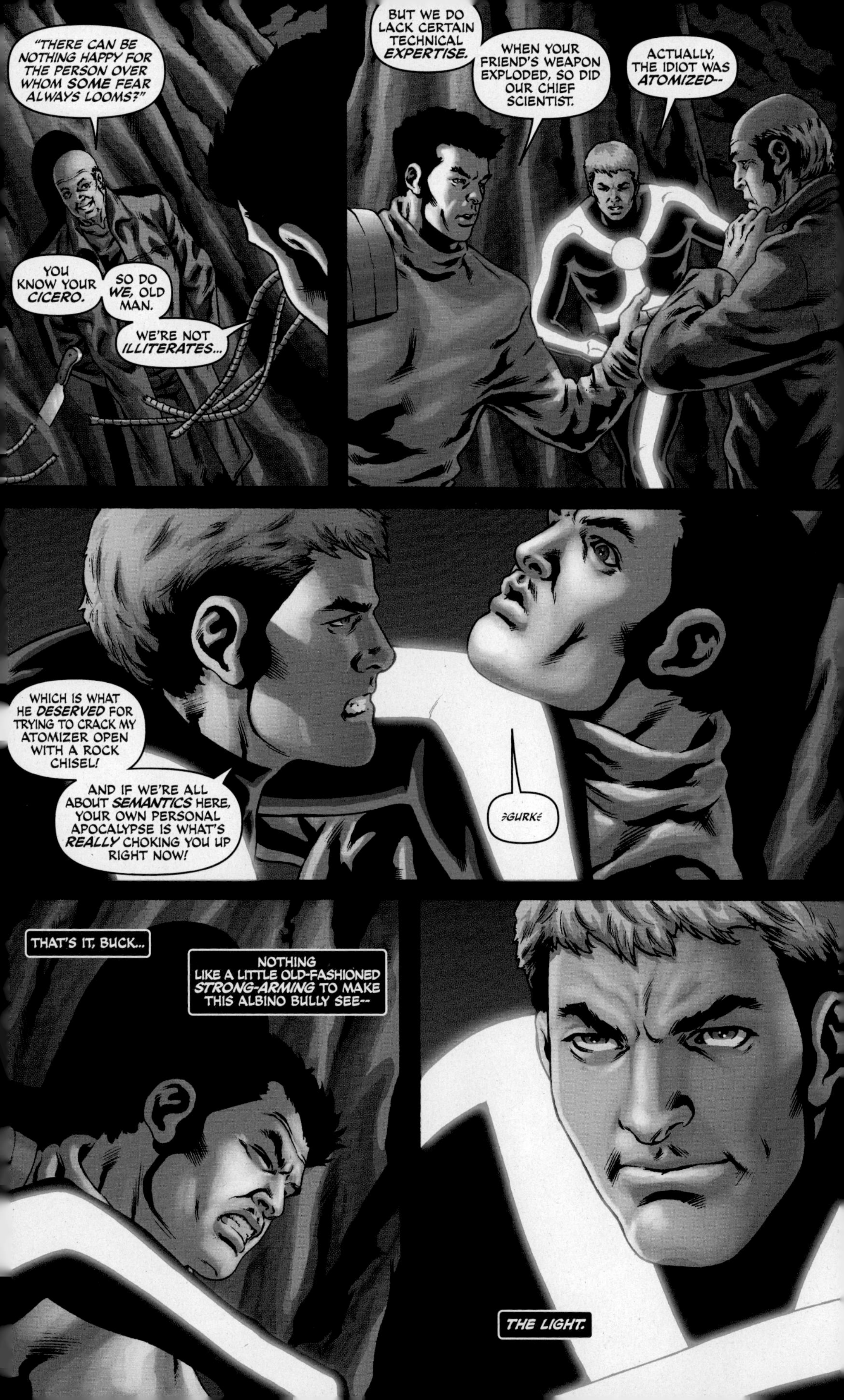
"THERE CAN BE NOTHING HAPPY FOR THE PERSON OVER WHOM SOME FEAR ALWAYS LOOMS?"
YOU KNOW YOUR CICERO.
SO DO WE, OLD MAN.
WE'RE NOT ILLITERATES...
BUT WE DO LACK CERTAIN TECHNICAL EXPERTISE.
WHEN YOUR FRIEND'S WEAPON EXPLODED, SO DID OUR CHIEF SCIENTIST.
ACTUALLY, THE IDIOT WAS ATOMIZED--
WHICH IS WHAT HE DESERVED FOR TRYING TO CRACK MY ATOMIZER OPEN WITH A ROCK CHISEL!
AND IF WE'RE ALL ABOUT SEMANTICS HERE, YOUR OWN PERSONAL APOCALYPSE IS WHAT'S REALLY CHOKING YOU UP RIGHT NOW!
GURK
THAT'S IT, BUCK...
NOTHING LIKE A LITTLE OLD-FASHIONED STRONG-ARMING TO MAKE THIS ALBINO BULLY SEE--
THE LIGHT.

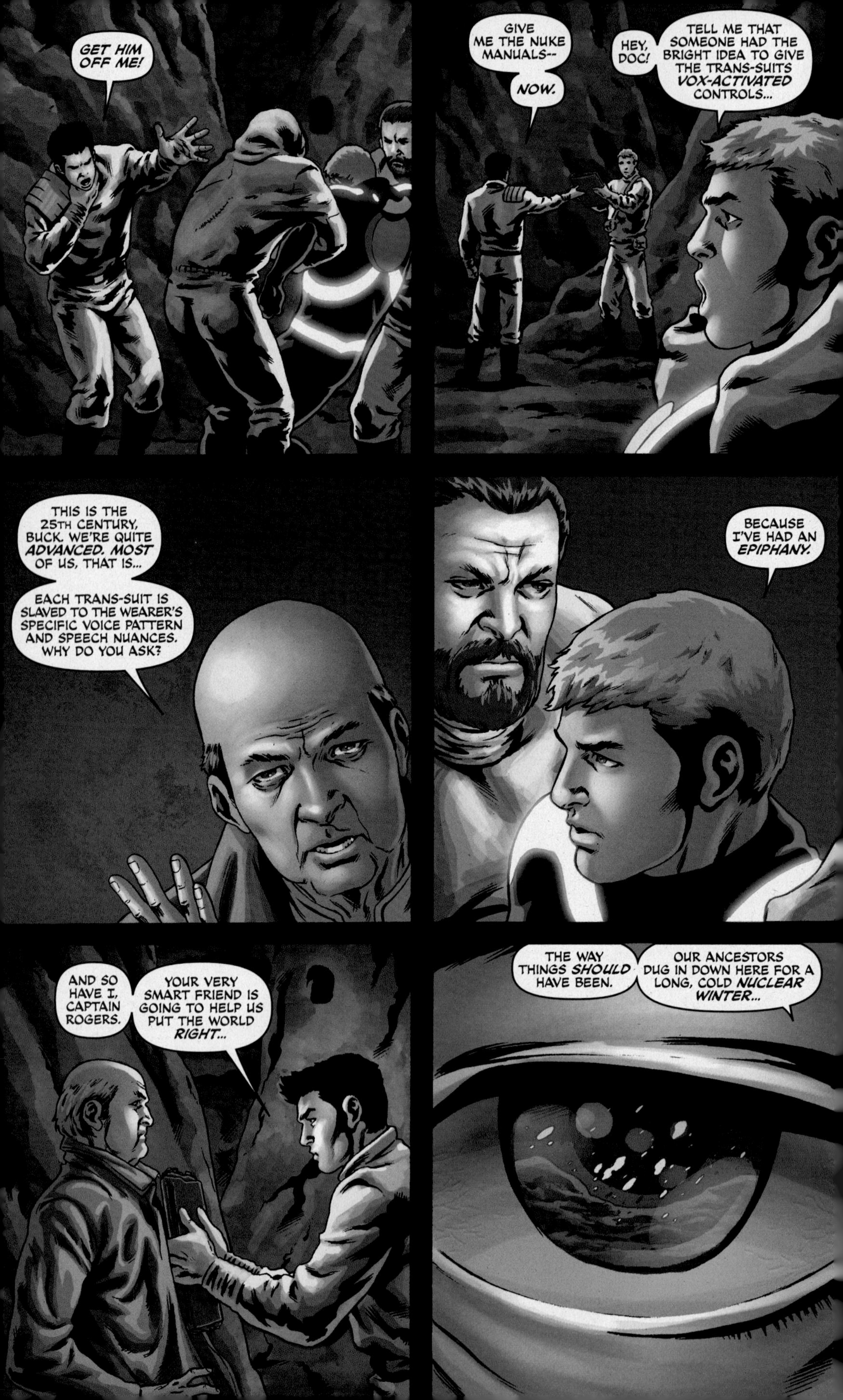
GET HIM OFF ME!
GIVE ME THE NUKE MANUALS--
NOW.
HEY, DOC!
TELL ME THAT SOMEONE HAD THE BRIGHT IDEA TO GIVE THE TRANS-SUITS VOX-ACTIVATED CONTROLS...
THIS IS THE 25TH CENTURY, BUCK. WE'RE QUITE ADVANCED. MOST OF US, THAT IS...
EACH TRANS-SUIT IS SLAVED TO THE WEARER'S SPECIFIC VOICE PATTERN AND SPEECH NUANCES. WHY DO YOU ASK?
BECAUSE I'VE HAD AN EPIPHANY.
AND SO HAVE I, CAPTAIN ROGERS.
YOUR VERY SMART FRIEND IS GOING TO HELP US PUT THE WORLD RIGHT...
THE WAY THINGS SHOULD HAVE BEEN.
OUR ANCESTORS DUG IN DOWN HERE FOR A LONG, COLD NUCLEAR WINTER...

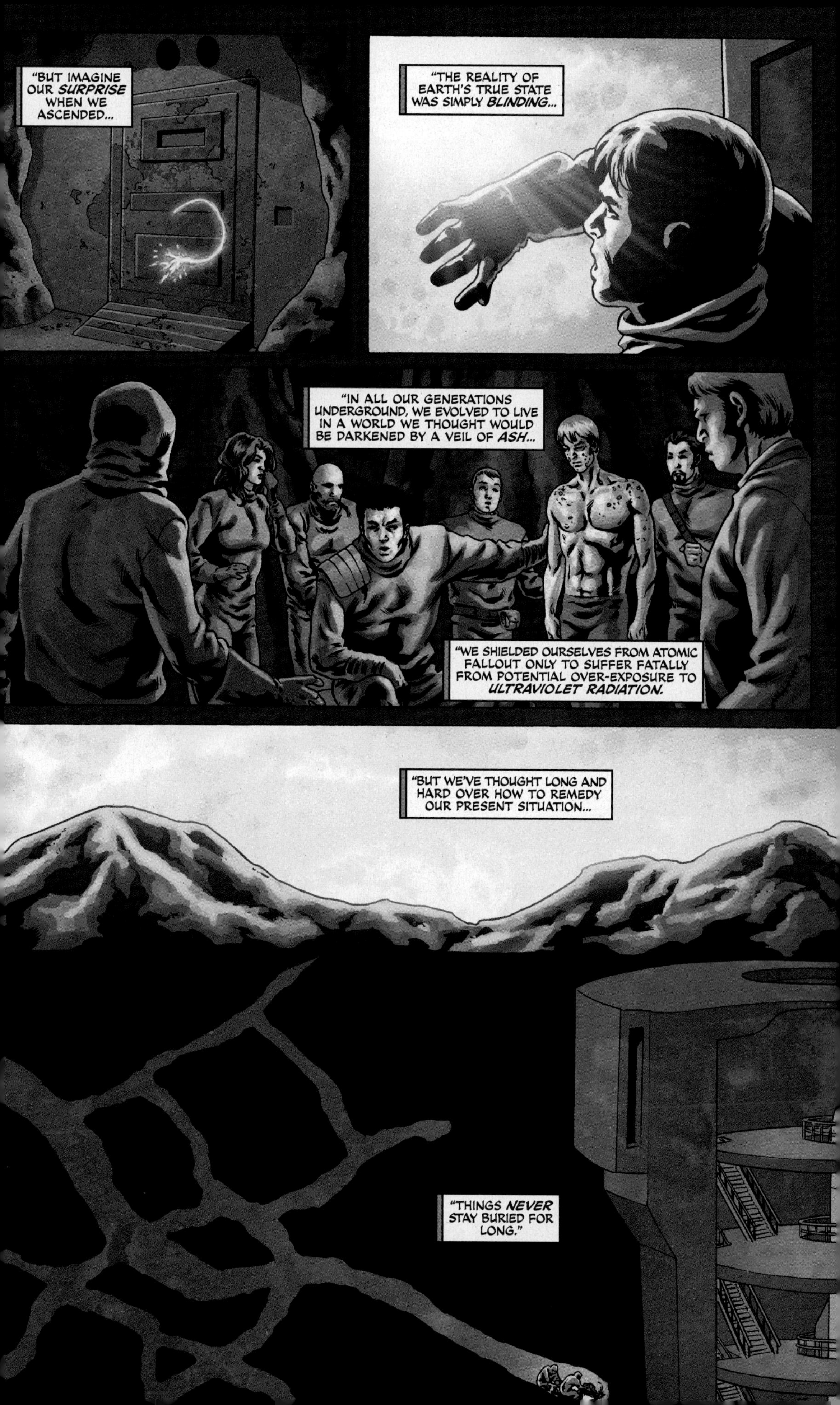
"BUT IMAGINE OUR SURPRISE WHEN WE ASCENDED...
"THE REALITY OF EARTH'S TRUE STATE WAS SIMPLY BLINDING...
"IN ALL OUR GENERATIONS UNDERGROUND, WE EVOLVED TO LIVE IN A WORLD WE THOUGHT WOULD BE DARKENED BY A VEIL OF ASH...
"WE SHIELDED OURSELVES FROM ATOMIC FALLOUT ONLY TO SUFFER FATALLY FROM POTENTIAL OVER-EXPOSURE TO ULTRAVIOLET RADIATION.
"BUT WE'VE THOUGHT LONG AND HARD OVER HOW TO REMEDY OUR PRESENT SITUATION...
"THINGS NEVER STAY BURIED FOR LONG."

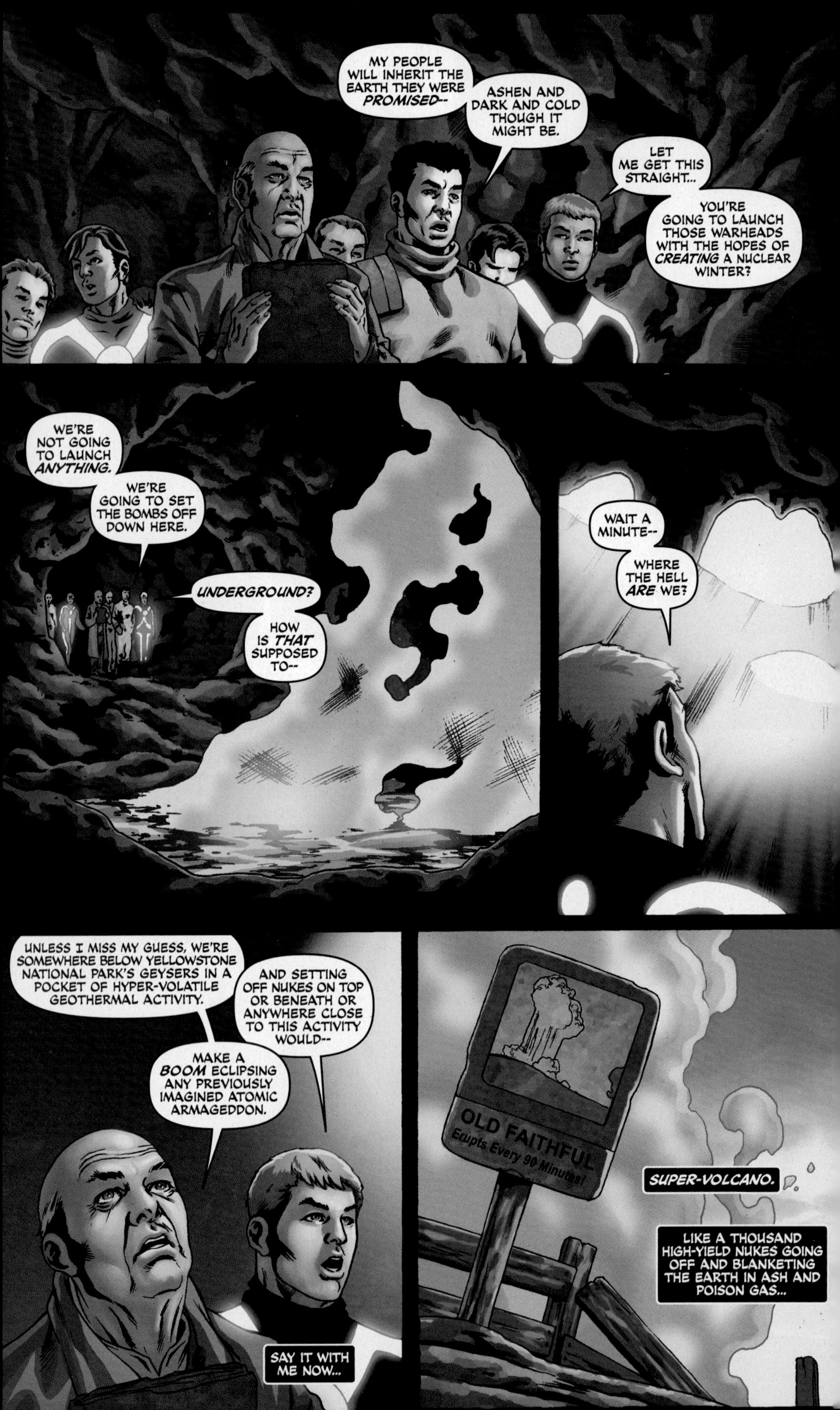

MY PEOPLE WILL INHERIT THE EARTH THEY WERE *PROMISED*--
ASHEN AND DARK AND COLD THOUGH IT MIGHT BE.
LET ME GET THIS STRAIGHT...
YOU'RE GOING TO LAUNCH THOSE WARHEADS WITH THE HOPES OF *CREATING* A NUCLEAR WINTER?
WE'RE NOT GOING TO LAUNCH *ANYTHING*.
WE'RE GOING TO SET THE BOMBS OFF DOWN HERE.
UNDERGROUND?
HOW IS *THAT* SUPPOSED TO--
WAIT A MINUTE--
WHERE THE HELL *ARE* WE?
UNLESS I MISS MY GUESS, WE'RE SOMEWHERE BELOW YELLOWSTONE NATIONAL PARK'S GEYSERS IN A POCKET OF HYPER-VOLATILE GEOTHERMAL ACTIVITY.
AND SETTING OFF NUKES ON TOP OR BENEATH OR ANYWHERE CLOSE TO THIS ACTIVITY WOULD--
MAKE A *BOOM* ECLIPSING ANY PREVIOUSLY IMAGINED ATOMIC ARMAGEDDON.
SAY IT WITH ME NOW...
OLD FAITHFUL
Erupts Every 90 Minutes!
SUPER-VOLCANO.
LIKE A THOUSAND HIGH-YIELD NUKES GOING OFF AND BLANKETING THE EARTH IN ASH AND POISON GAS...

AND EVENTUALLY BLOTTING OUT *THE SUN...*

AS YOU CAN SEE, *HAN* IS OFFERING TO LIGHT THE WAY TO A PROSPEROUS FUTURE FOR *ALL* OF EARTH--

NOT MERELY THE *UNIFIED ORGS,* COLONEL DEERING.

WE JUST BELIEVE OUR SHARE OF EARTH'S BOUNTY SHOULD BE SLIGHTLY *LARGER* GIVEN WHAT WE PROVIDE IN RETURN.

IT'S ALL THERE ON PARCHMENT IN THE TIME-HONORED CONVENTIONS OF DIPLOMACY BETWEEN NATIONS.

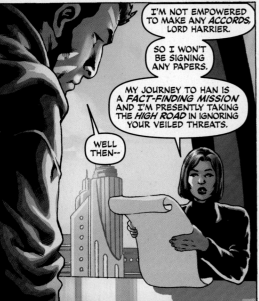

I'M NOT EMPOWERED TO MAKE ANY *ACCORDS,* LORD HARRIER.

SO I WON'T BE SIGNING ANY PAPERS.

MY JOURNEY TO HAN IS A *FACT-FINDING MISSION* AND I'M PRESENTLY TAKING THE *HIGH ROAD* IN IGNORING YOUR VEILED THREATS.

WELL THEN--

THESE ARE THE FACTS, WILMA.

HAN *IS* THE HIGH ROAD.

"IN FACT, HAN IS THE *HIGH GROUND* ABOVE *ALL* OF YOU EARTHBOUND PEASANTS."

EH?

FWASH

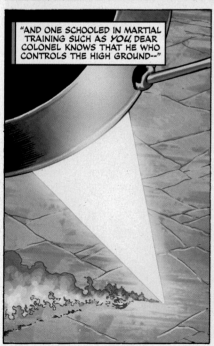

"AND ONE SCHOOLED IN MARTIAL TRAINING SUCH AS *YOU*, DEAR COLONEL KNOWS THAT HE WHO CONTROLS THE HIGH GROUND--"

CONTROLS *EVERYTHING.*

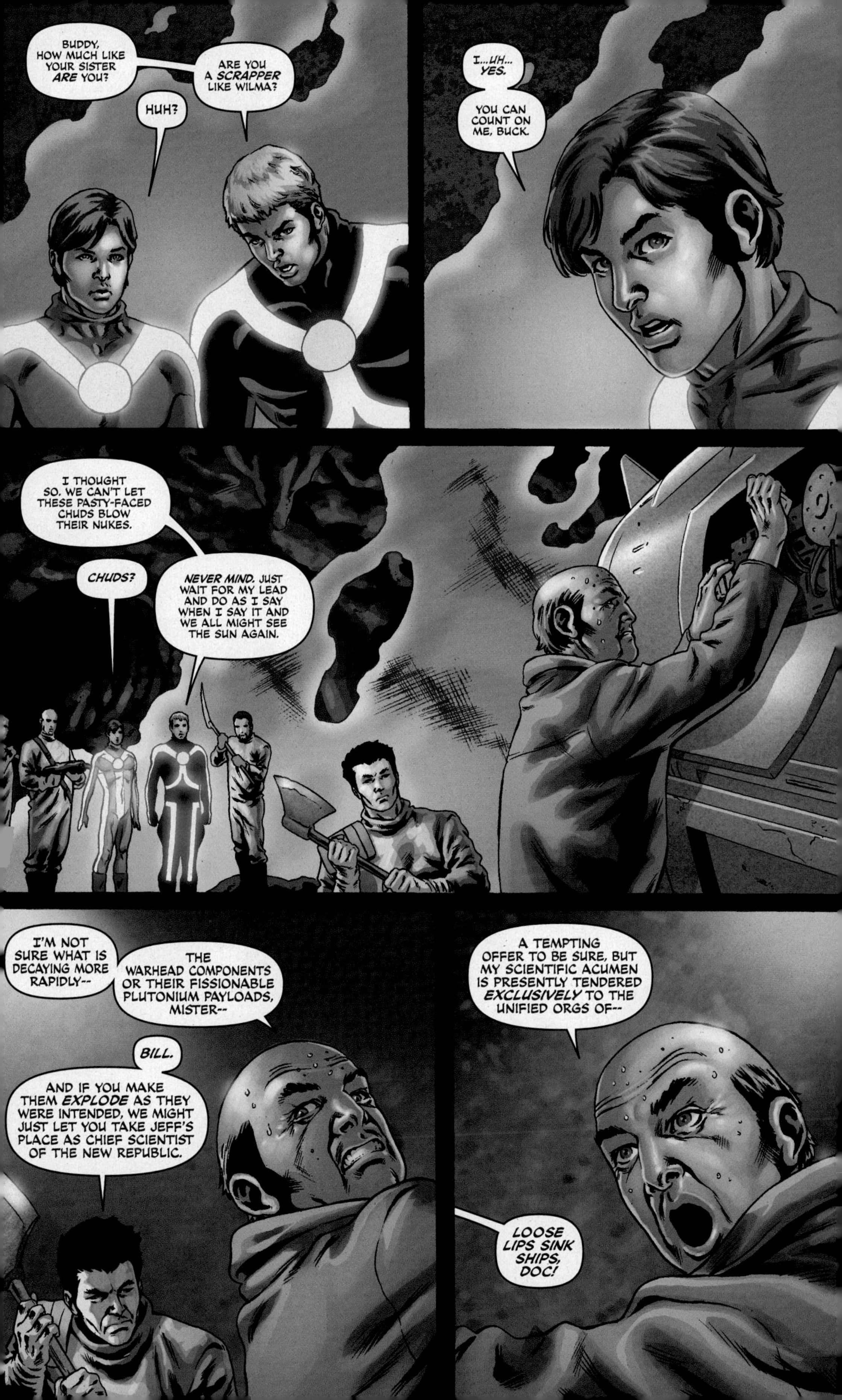
BUDDY, HOW MUCH LIKE YOUR SISTER *ARE* YOU?
HUH?
ARE YOU A *SCRAPPER* LIKE WILMA?
I...*UH*... *YES.*
YOU CAN COUNT ON ME, BUCK.
I THOUGHT SO. WE CAN'T LET THESE PASTY-FACED CHUDS BLOW THEIR NUKES.
CHUDS?
NEVER MIND. JUST WAIT FOR MY LEAD AND DO AS I SAY WHEN I SAY IT AND WE ALL MIGHT SEE THE SUN AGAIN.
I'M NOT SURE WHAT IS DECAYING MORE RAPIDLY--
THE WARHEAD COMPONENTS OR THEIR FISSIONABLE PLUTONIUM PAYLOADS, MISTER--
BILL.
AND IF YOU MAKE THEM *EXPLODE* AS THEY WERE INTENDED, WE MIGHT JUST LET YOU TAKE JEFF'S PLACE AS CHIEF SCIENTIST OF THE NEW REPUBLIC.
A TEMPTING OFFER TO BE SURE, BUT MY SCIENTIFIC ACUMEN IS PRESENTLY TENDERED *EXCLUSIVELY* TO THE UNIFIED ORGS OF--
LOOSE LIPS SINK SHIPS, DOC!

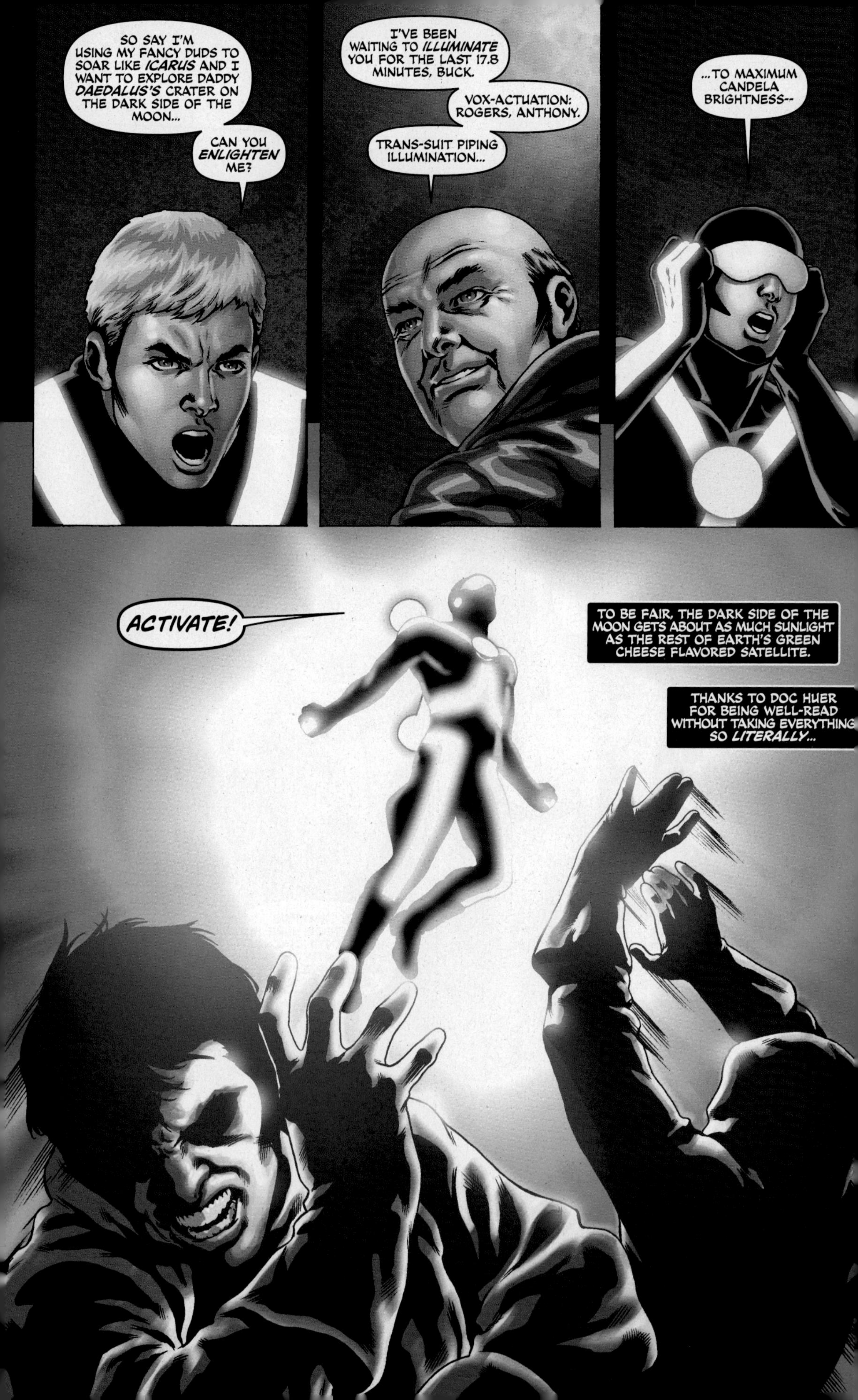
SO SAY I'M USING MY FANCY DUDS TO SOAR LIKE ICARUS AND I WANT TO EXPLORE DADDY DAEDALUS'S CRATER ON THE DARK SIDE OF THE MOON...
CAN YOU ENLIGHTEN ME?
I'VE BEEN WAITING TO ILLUMINATE YOU FOR THE LAST 17.8 MINUTES, BUCK.
VOX-ACTUATION: ROGERS, ANTHONY.
TRANS-SUIT PIPING ILLUMINATION...
...TO MAXIMUM CANDELA BRIGHTNESS--
ACTIVATE!
TO BE FAIR, THE DARK SIDE OF THE MOON GETS ABOUT AS MUCH SUNLIGHT AS THE REST OF EARTH'S GREEN CHEESE FLAVORED SATELLITE.
THANKS TO DOC HUER FOR BEING WELL-READ WITHOUT TAKING EVERYTHING SO LITERALLY...

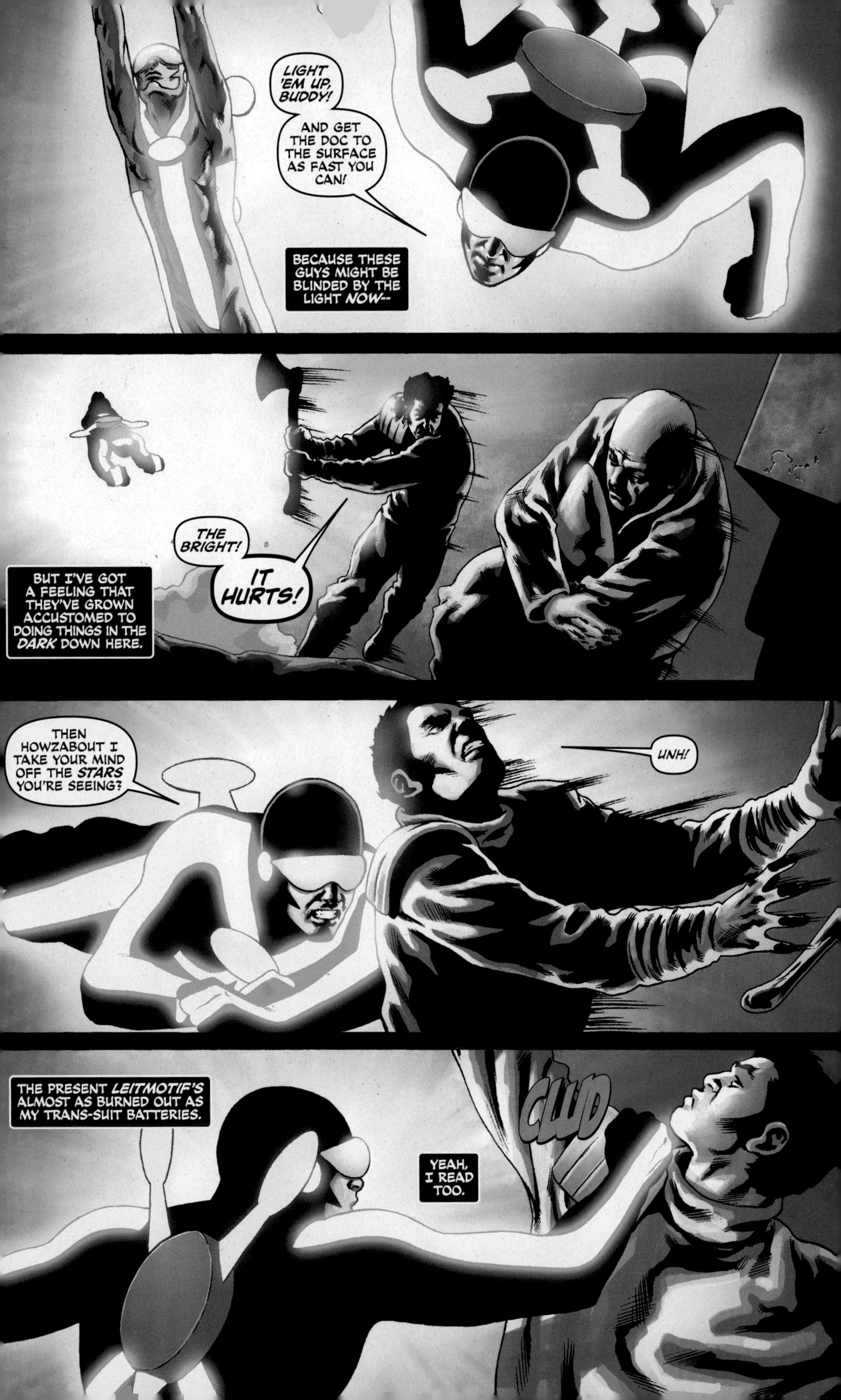
LIGHT 'EM UP, BUDDY!
AND GET THE DOC TO THE SURFACE AS FAST YOU CAN!
BECAUSE THESE GUYS MIGHT BE BLINDED BY THE LIGHT NOW--
THE BRIGHT!
IT HURTS!
BUT I'VE GOT A FEELING THAT THEY'VE GROWN ACCUSTOMED TO DOING THINGS IN THE DARK DOWN HERE.
THEN HOWZABOUT I TAKE YOUR MIND OFF THE STARS YOU'RE SEEING?
UNH!
THE PRESENT LEITMOTIF'S ALMOST AS BURNED OUT AS MY TRANS-SUIT BATTERIES.
CLUD
YEAH, I READ TOO.

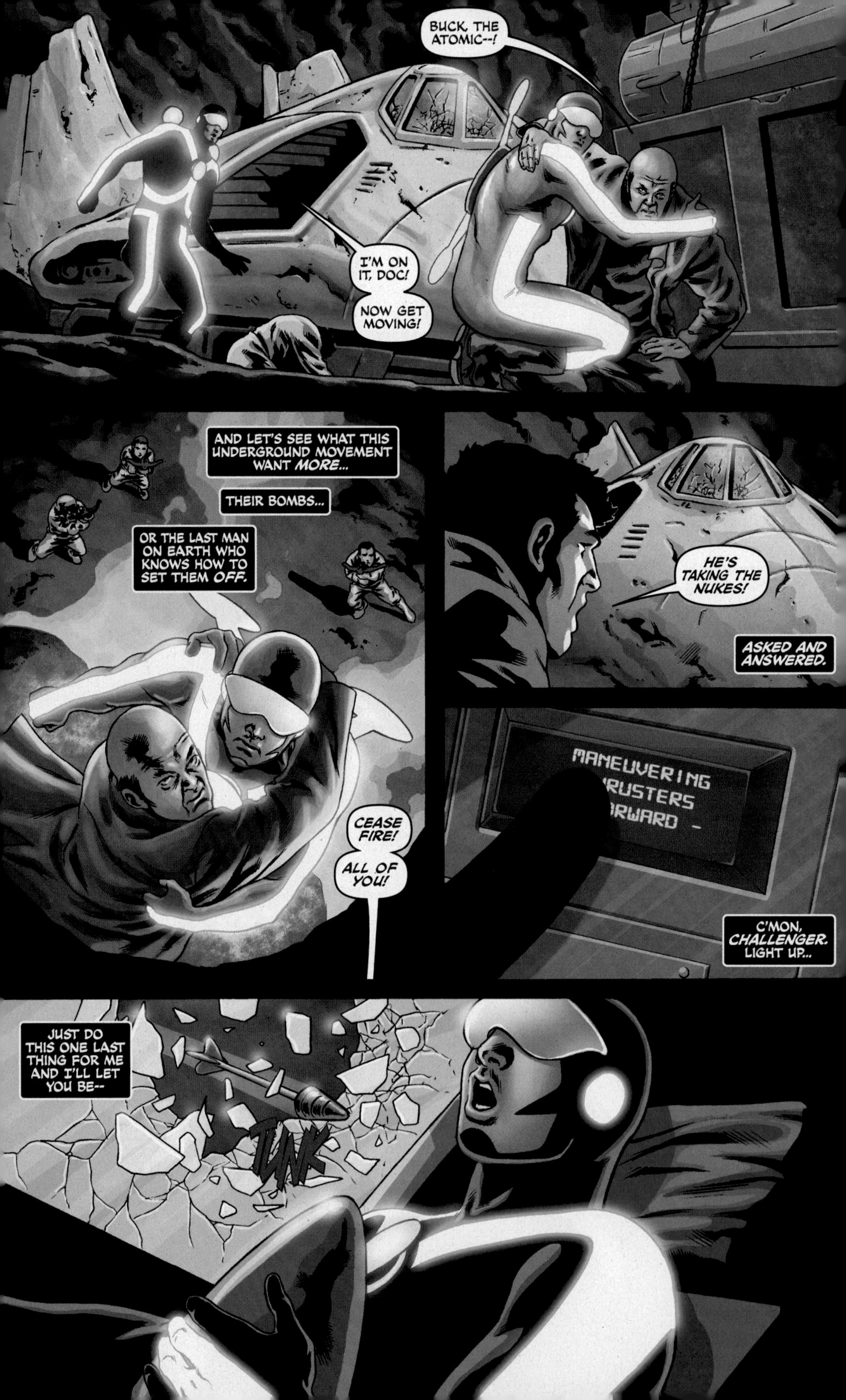
BUCK, THE ATOMIC--!
I'M ON IT, DOC!
NOW GET MOVING!
AND LET'S SEE WHAT THIS UNDERGROUND MOVEMENT WANT MORE...
THEIR BOMBS...
OR THE LAST MAN ON EARTH WHO KNOWS HOW TO SET THEM OFF.
HE'S TAKING THE NUKES!
ASKED AND ANSWERED.
CEASE FIRE!
ALL OF YOU!
MANEUVERING
RUSTERS
RWARD -
C'MON, CHALLENGER. LIGHT UP...
JUST DO THIS ONE LAST THING FOR ME AND I'LL LET YOU BE--
TUNK

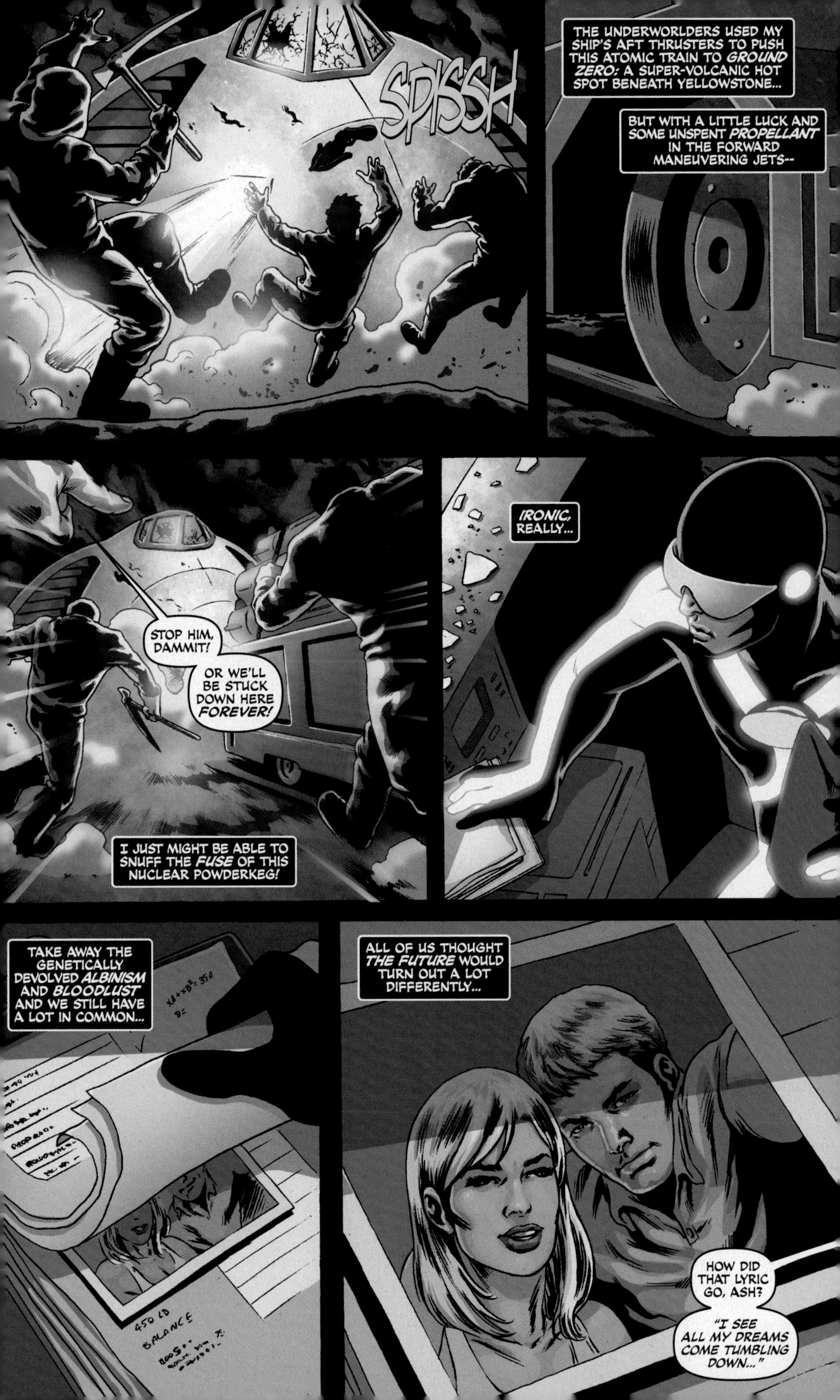
SPISSH
THE UNDERWORLDERS USED MY SHIP'S AFT THRUSTERS TO PUSH THIS ATOMIC TRAIN TO *GROUND ZERO:* A SUPER-VOLCANIC HOT SPOT BENEATH YELLOWSTONE...
BUT WITH A LITTLE LUCK AND SOME UNSPENT *PROPELLANT* IN THE FORWARD MANEUVERING JETS--
STOP HIM, DAMMIT!
OR WE'LL BE STUCK DOWN HERE *FOREVER!*
I JUST MIGHT BE ABLE TO SNUFF THE *FUSE* OF THIS NUCLEAR POWDERKEG!
IRONIC, REALLY...
TAKE AWAY THE GENETICALLY DEVOLVED *ALBINISM* AND *BLOODLUST* AND WE STILL HAVE A LOT IN COMMON...
ALL OF US THOUGHT *THE FUTURE* WOULD TURN OUT A LOT DIFFERENTLY...
HOW DID THAT LYRIC GO, ASH?
"I SEE ALL MY DREAMS COME TUMBLING DOWN..."

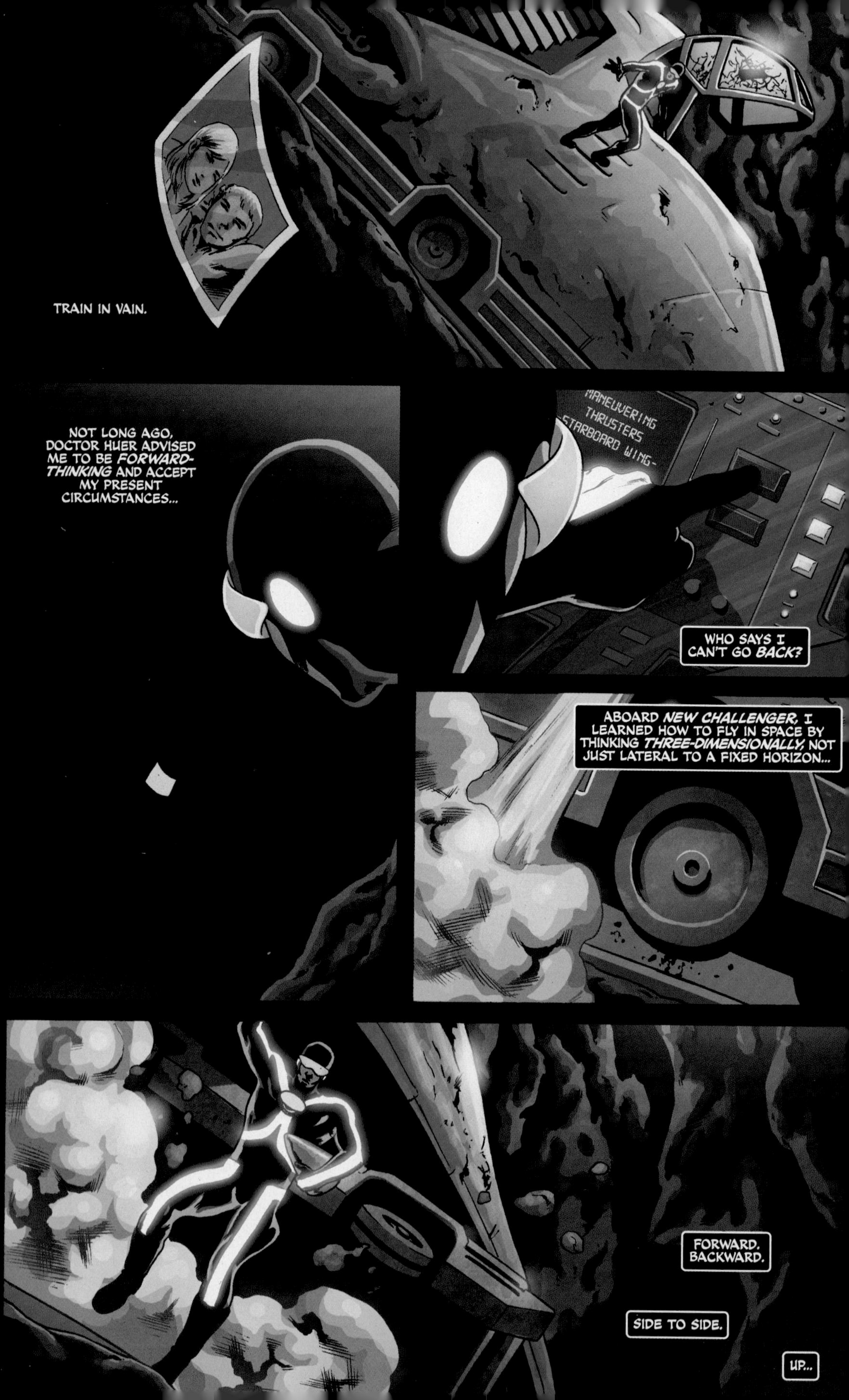

TRAIN IN VAIN.
NOT LONG AGO, DOCTOR HUER ADVISED ME TO BE *FORWARD-THINKING* AND ACCEPT MY PRESENT CIRCUMSTANCES...
MANEUVERING THRUSTERS STARBOARD WING-
WHO SAYS I CAN'T GO *BACK?*
ABOARD *NEW CHALLENGER,* I LEARNED HOW TO FLY IN SPACE BY THINKING *THREE-DIMENSIONALLY,* NOT JUST LATERAL TO A FIXED HORIZON...
FORWARD. BACKWARD.
SIDE TO SIDE.
UP...

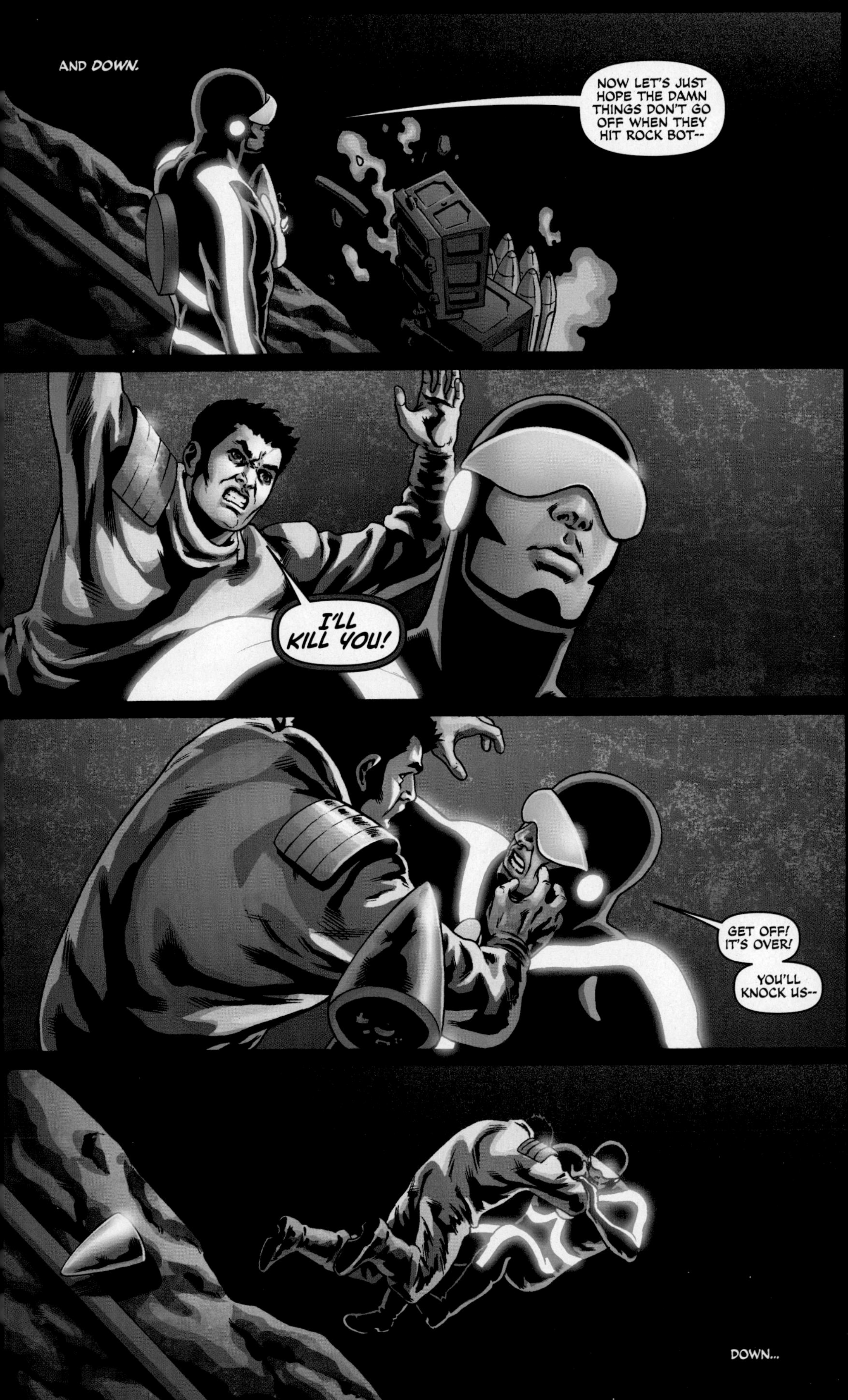
AND DOWN.
NOW LET'S JUST HOPE THE DAMN THINGS DON'T GO OFF WHEN THEY HIT ROCK BOT--
I'LL KILL YOU!
GET OFF! IT'S OVER!
YOU'LL KNOCK US--
DOWN...

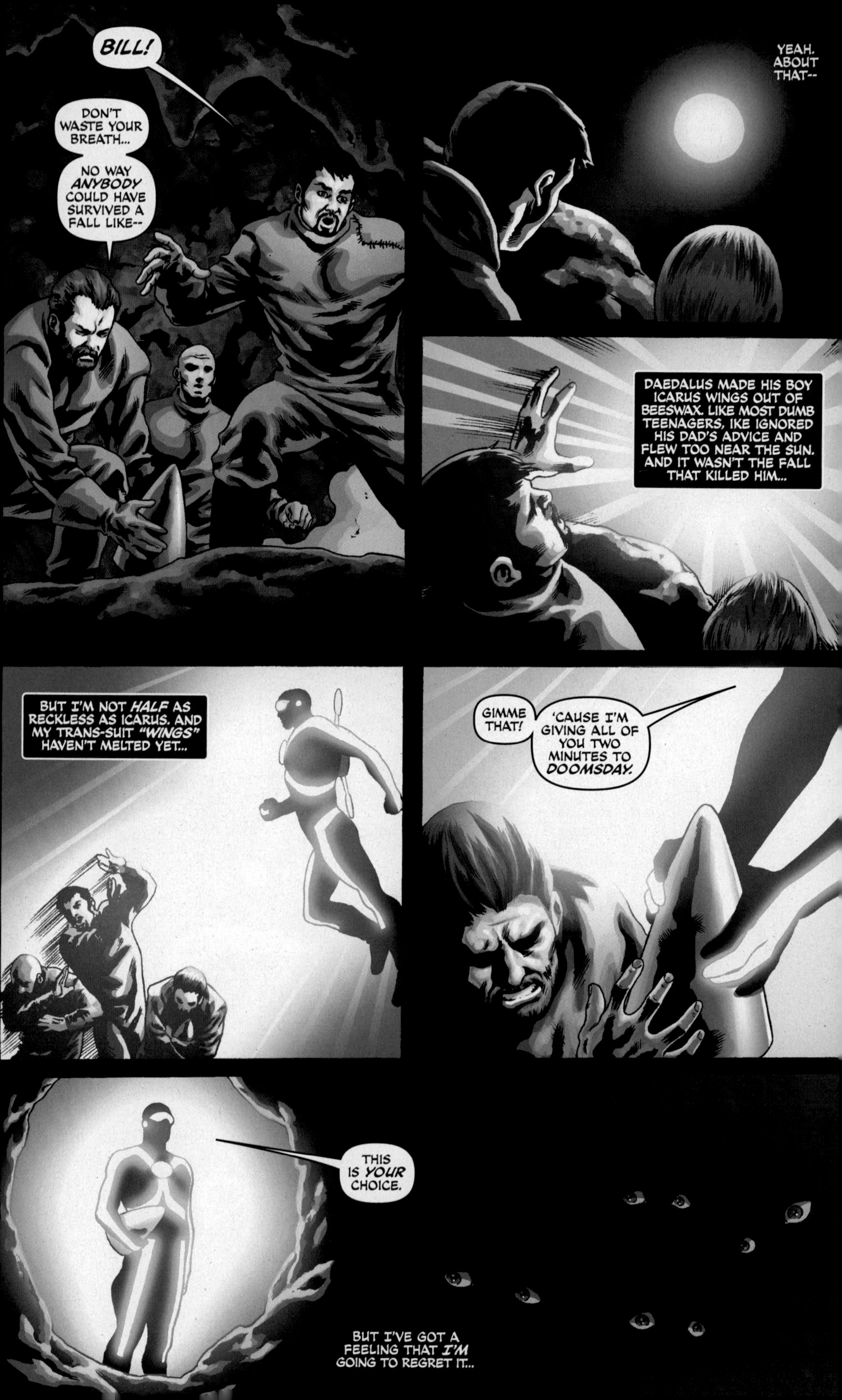
BILL!
DON'T WASTE YOUR BREATH...
NO WAY ANYBODY COULD HAVE SURVIVED A FALL LIKE--
YEAH. ABOUT THAT--
DAEDALUS MADE HIS BOY ICARUS WINGS OUT OF BEESWAX. LIKE MOST DUMB TEENAGERS, IKE IGNORED HIS DAD'S ADVICE AND FLEW TOO NEAR THE SUN. AND IT WASN'T THE FALL THAT KILLED HIM...
BUT I'M NOT HALF AS RECKLESS AS ICARUS. AND MY TRANS-SUIT "WINGS" HAVEN'T MELTED YET...
GIMME THAT!
'CAUSE I'M GIVING ALL OF YOU TWO MINUTES TO DOOMSDAY.
THIS IS YOUR CHOICE.
BUT I'VE GOT A FEELING THAT I'M GOING TO REGRET IT...

EVEN IF I'M ENDING THE *NUCLEAR THREAT* ONCE AND FOR ALL.

DOCTOR HUER, DO YOU THINK HE DID IT?

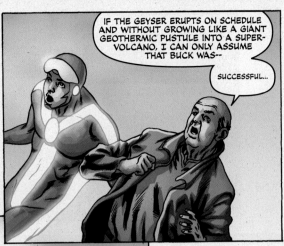

IF THE GEYSER ERUPTS ON SCHEDULE AND WITHOUT GROWING LIKE A GIANT GEOTHERMIC PUSTULE INTO A SUPER-VOLCANO, I CAN ONLY ASSUME THAT BUCK WAS--

SUCCESSFUL...

BUCK! YOU'RE ALIVE!

AND DESPITE THIS UNCONVENTIONAL *EXIT STRATEGY* FROM THIS CONFLICT, I FEEL LIKE I COULD USE A LONG, HOT SHOWER...

BUCK, THOSE PEOPLE...

WON'T BE BLANKETING THE EARTH IN ASH, DOC.

I OFFERED THEM A WAY BACK TO THE LIGHT...

BUT THE UNDERWORLDERS CHOSE TO DIG IN THEIR HEELS AND HUNKER *DOWN*...

EVERY LAST ONE OF THEM.

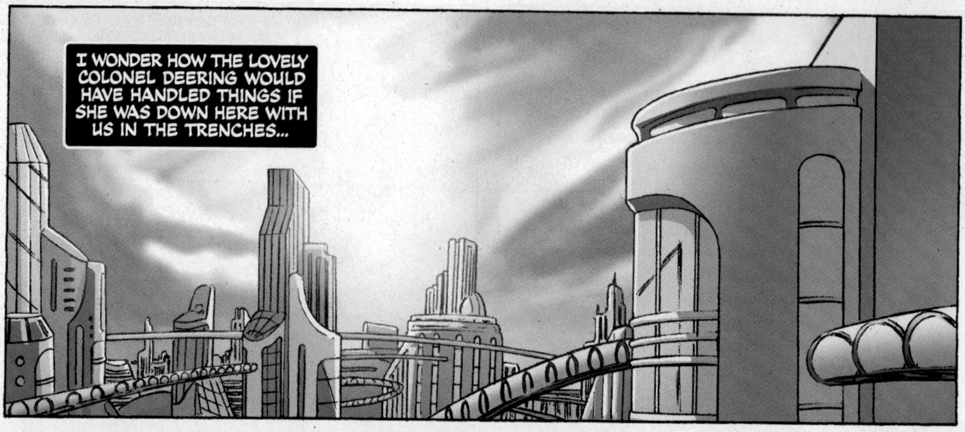
I WONDER HOW THE LOVELY COLONEL DEERING WOULD HAVE HANDLED THINGS IF SHE WAS DOWN HERE WITH US IN THE TRENCHES...

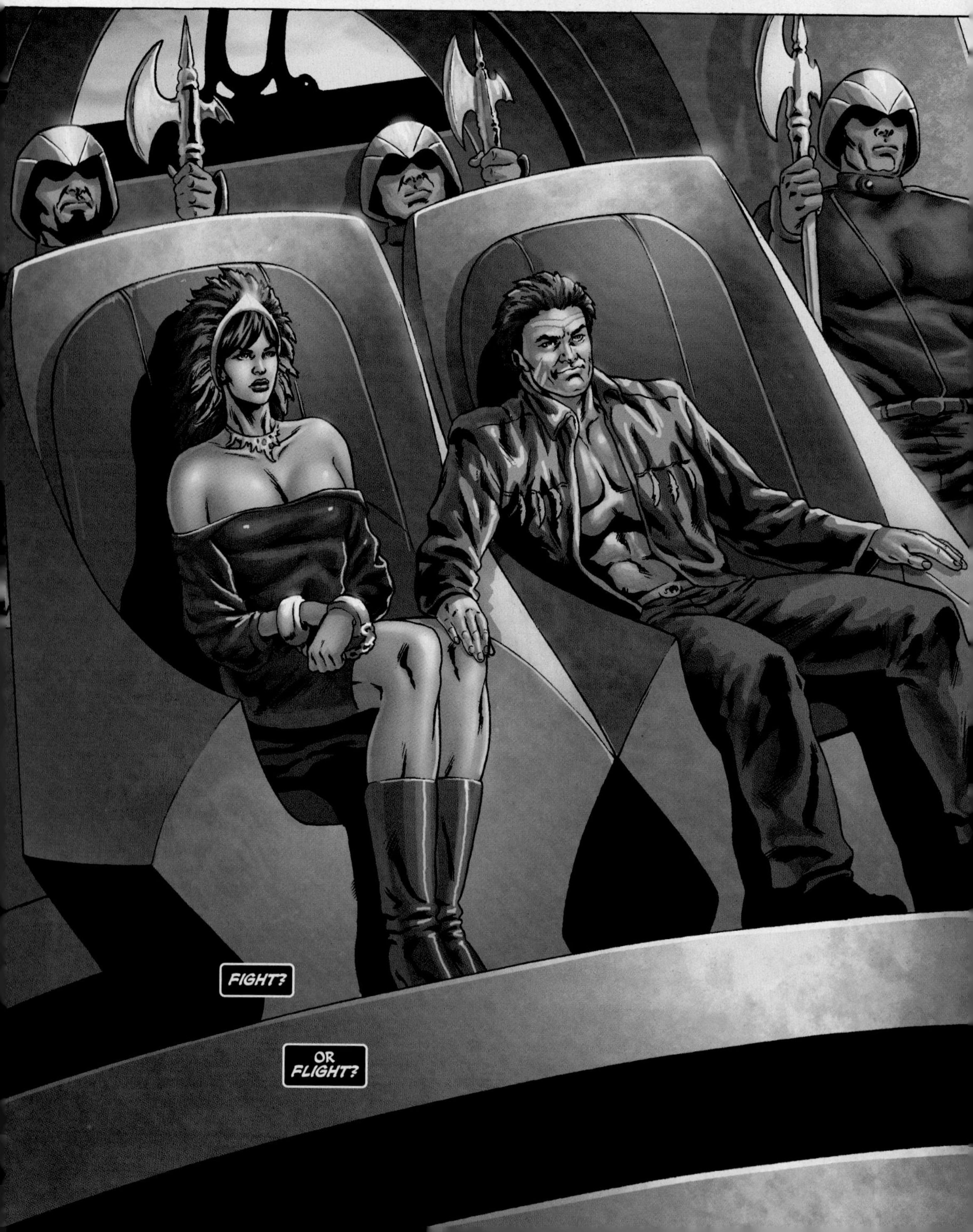
FIGHT?
OR FLIGHT?

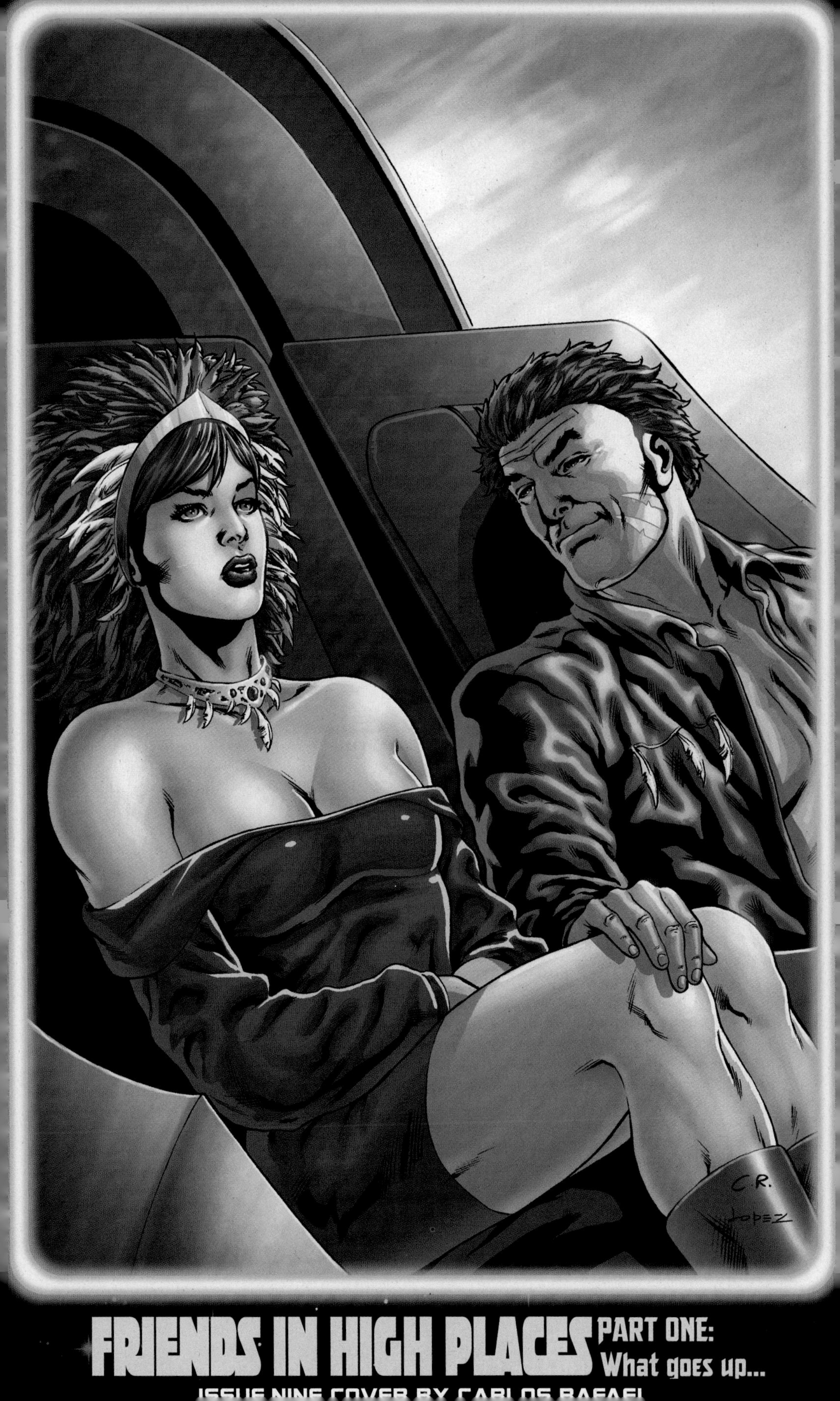
C.R.
LOPEZ

FRIENDS IN HIGH PLACES PART ONE: What goes up...

ISSUE NINE COVER BY CARLOS RAFAEL

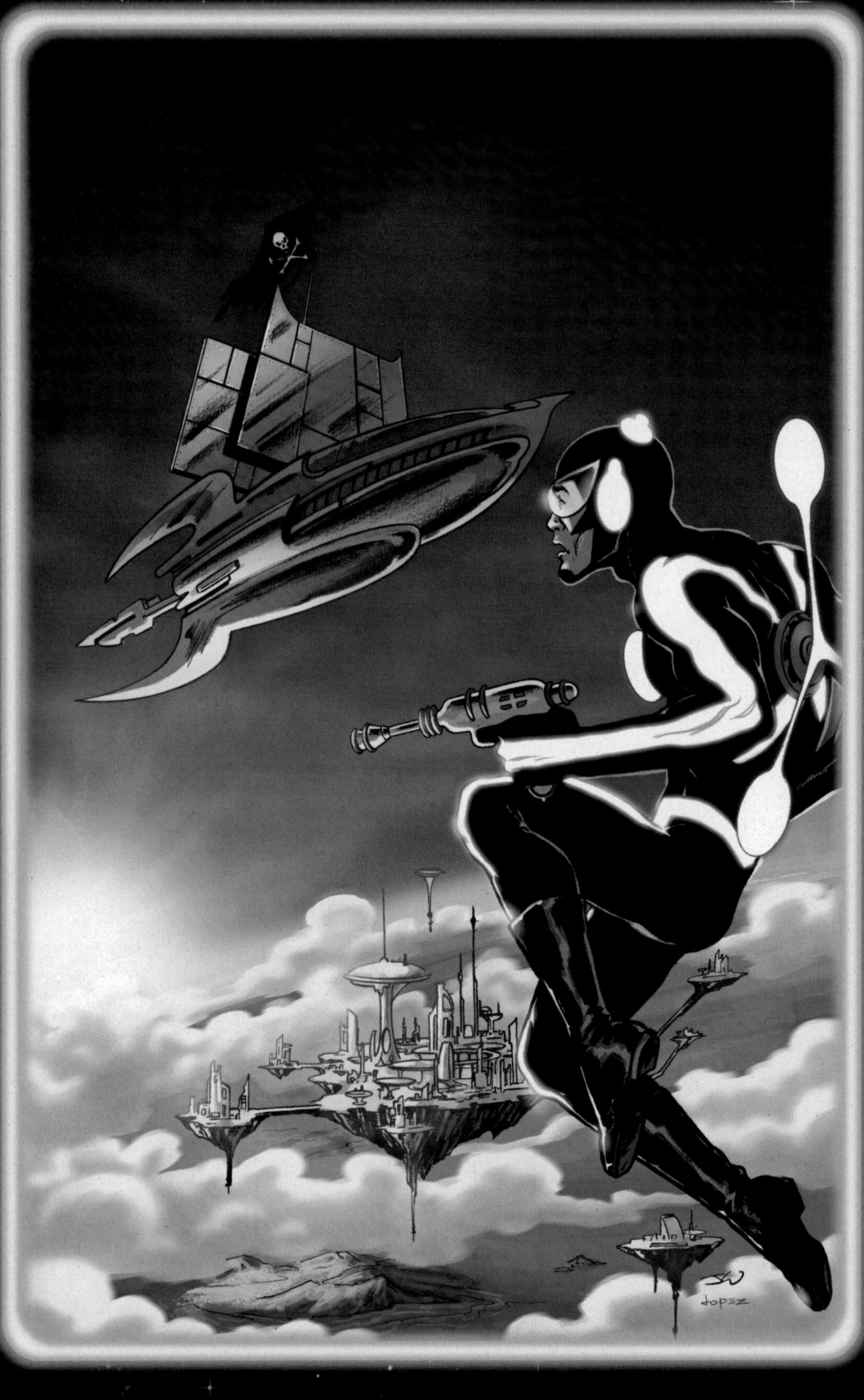
SW
Lopez

ALTERNATE COVER BY JOHN WATSON

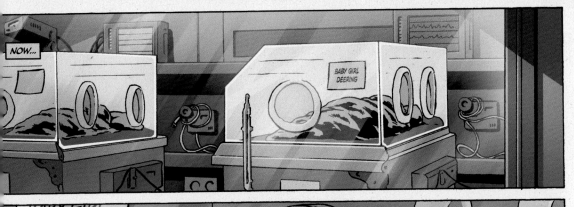

NOW...

BABY GIRL
DEERING

BABY GIRL
DEERING

TAP TAP TAP TAP

HEH. I THINK SHE *LIKES* ME...

SHE *SMILED*...

THAT'S NOT A *SMILE*, IT'S *GAS*.

TAPPING ON THE GLASS ONLY WAKES THE BABIES AND MAKES THEM *CRY*.

ARE YOU *DADDY*?

I...UH... WELL, YOU SEE--

IT'S *COMPLICATED*...

...ISN'T IT, ASHLEY?

GENTLEMEN, LET ME TELL YOU SOMETHING ABOUT US *DEERING* GIRLS...

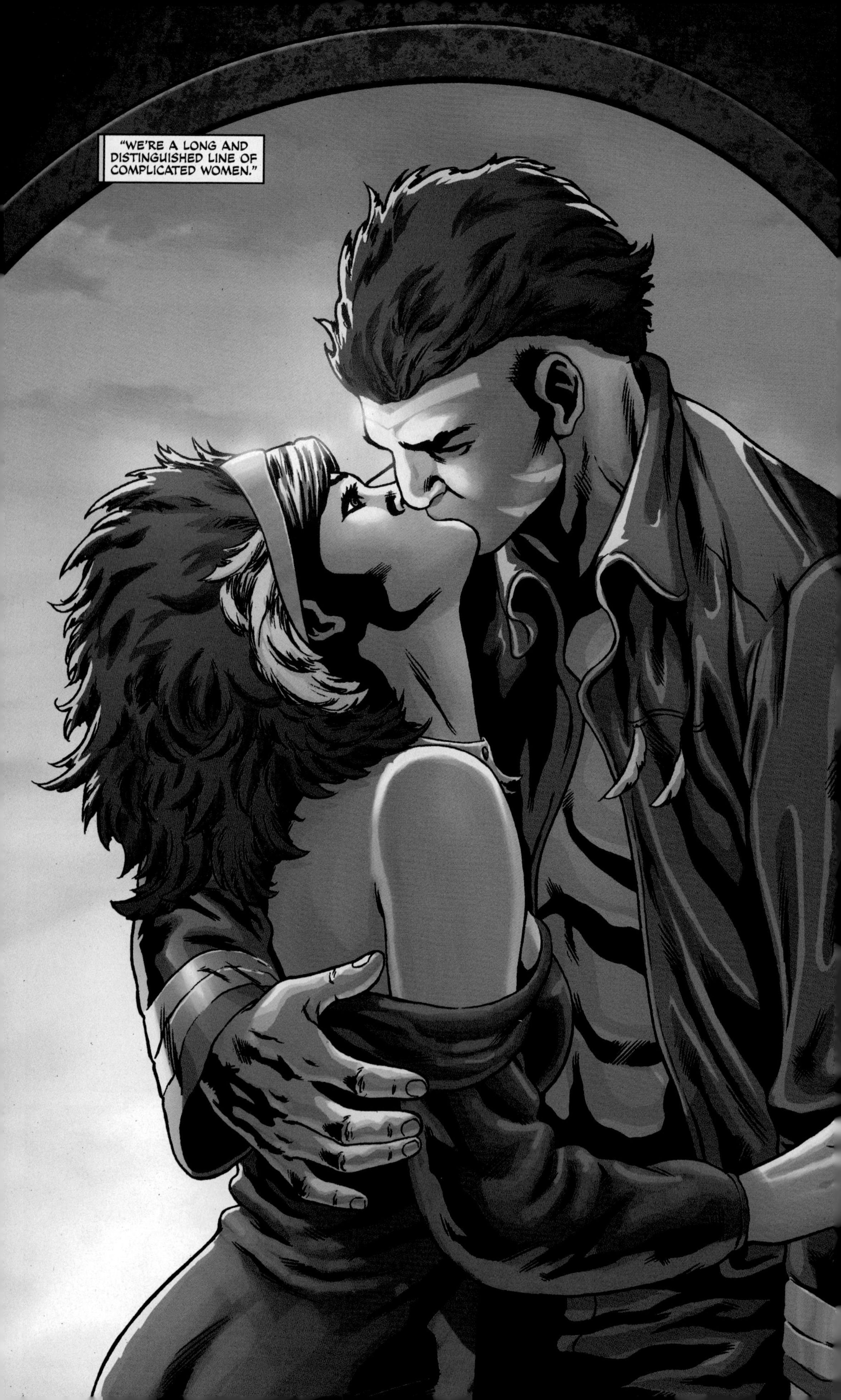
"WE'RE A LONG AND DISTINGUISHED LINE OF COMPLICATED WOMEN."

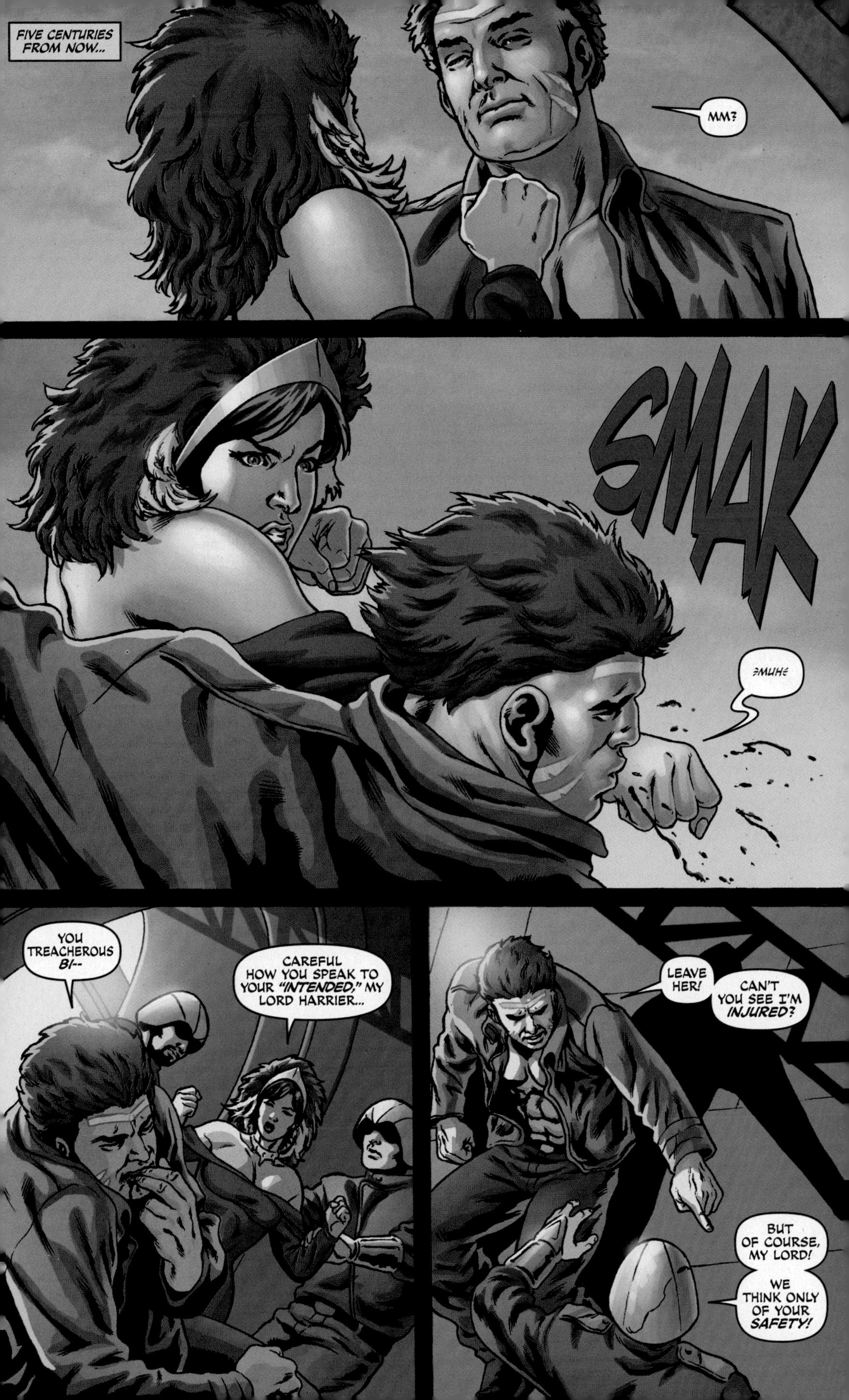
FIVE CENTURIES FROM NOW...
MM?
SMAK
MUH
YOU TREACHEROUS BI--
CAREFUL HOW YOU SPEAK TO YOUR "INTENDED," MY LORD HARRIER...
LEAVE HER!
CAN'T YOU SEE I'M INJURED?
BUT OF COURSE, MY LORD!
WE THINK ONLY OF YOUR SAFETY!

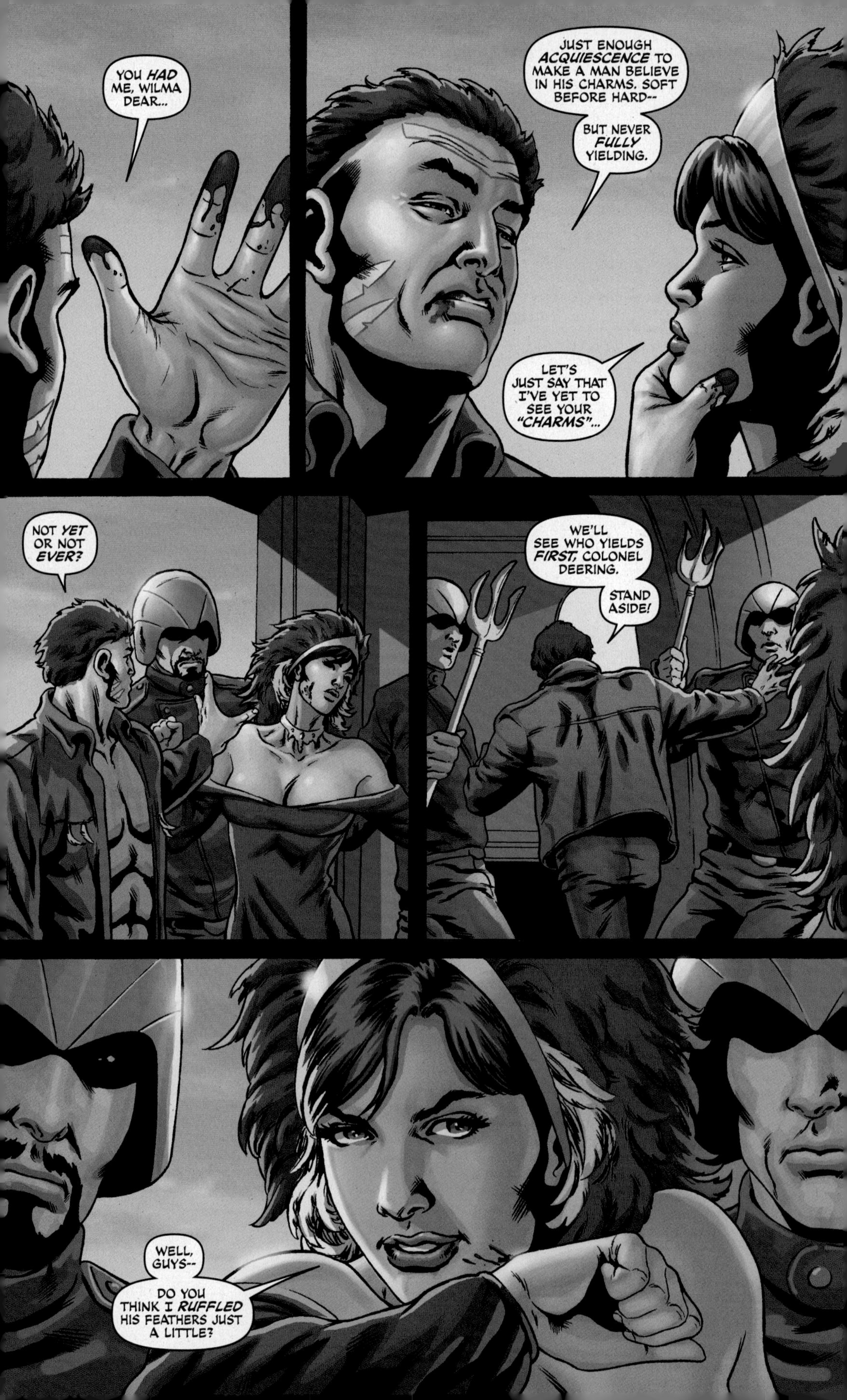
YOU *HAD* ME, WILMA DEAR...
JUST ENOUGH *ACQUIESCENCE* TO MAKE A MAN BELIEVE IN HIS CHARMS. SOFT BEFORE HARD--
BUT NEVER *FULLY* YIELDING.
LET'S JUST SAY THAT I'VE YET TO SEE YOUR *"CHARMS"*...
NOT *YET* OR NOT *EVER?*
WE'LL SEE WHO YIELDS *FIRST,* COLONEL DEERING.
STAND ASIDE!
WELL, GUYS--
DO YOU THINK I *RUFFLED* HIS FEATHERS JUST A LITTLE?

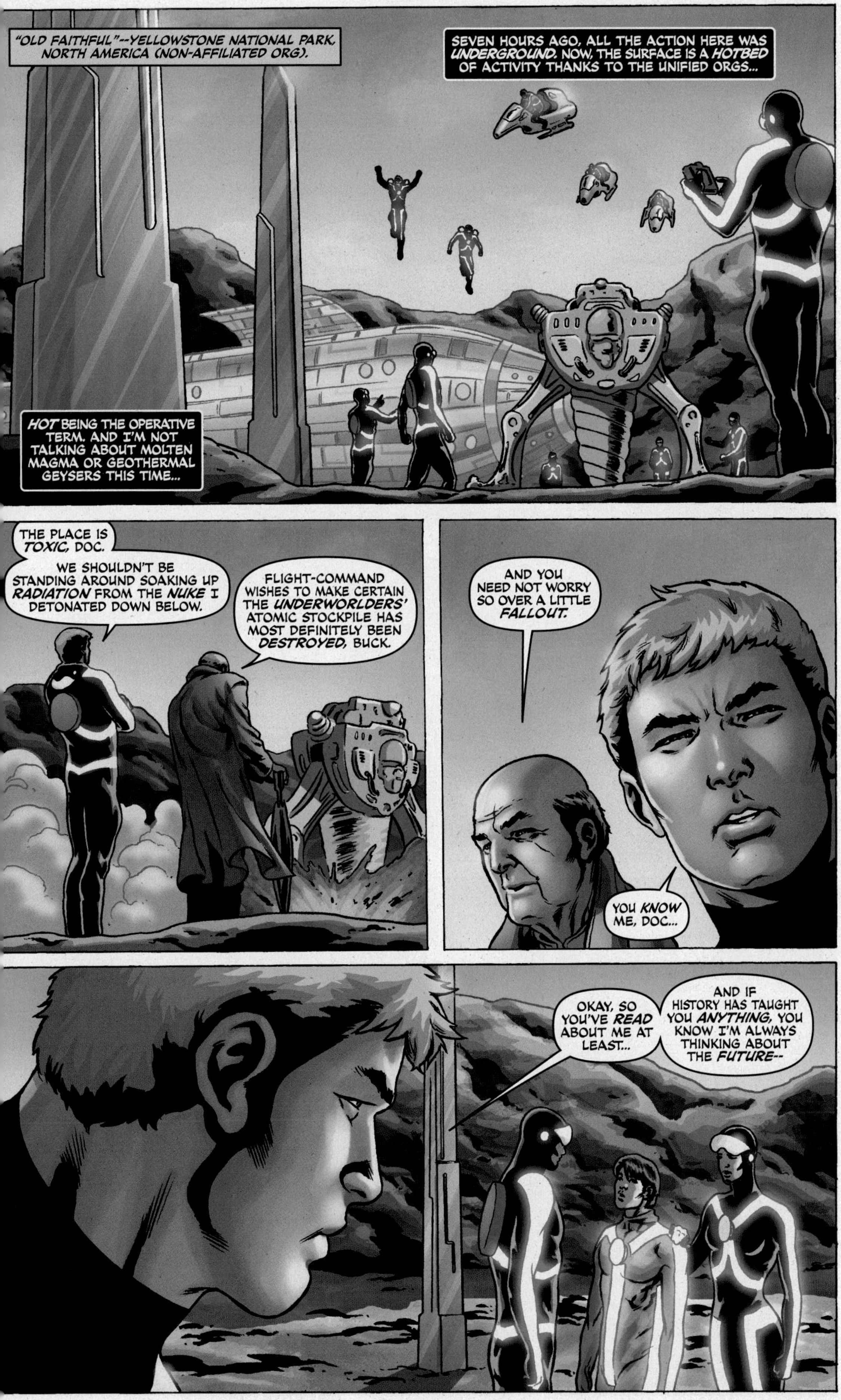
"OLD FAITHFUL"--YELLOWSTONE NATIONAL PARK, NORTH AMERICA (NON-AFFILIATED ORG).
SEVEN HOURS AGO, ALL THE ACTION HERE WAS UNDERGROUND. NOW, THE SURFACE IS A HOTBED OF ACTIVITY THANKS TO THE UNIFIED ORGS...
HOT BEING THE OPERATIVE TERM. AND I'M NOT TALKING ABOUT MOLTEN MAGMA OR GEOTHERMAL GEYSERS THIS TIME...
THE PLACE IS TOXIC, DOC.
WE SHOULDN'T BE STANDING AROUND SOAKING UP RADIATION FROM THE NUKE I DETONATED DOWN BELOW.
FLIGHT-COMMAND WISHES TO MAKE CERTAIN THE UNDERWORLDERS' ATOMIC STOCKPILE HAS MOST DEFINITELY BEEN DESTROYED, BUCK.
AND YOU NEED NOT WORRY SO OVER A LITTLE FALLOUT.
YOU KNOW ME, DOC...
OKAY, SO YOU'VE READ ABOUT ME AT LEAST...
AND IF HISTORY HAS TAUGHT YOU ANYTHING, YOU KNOW I'M ALWAYS THINKING ABOUT THE FUTURE--

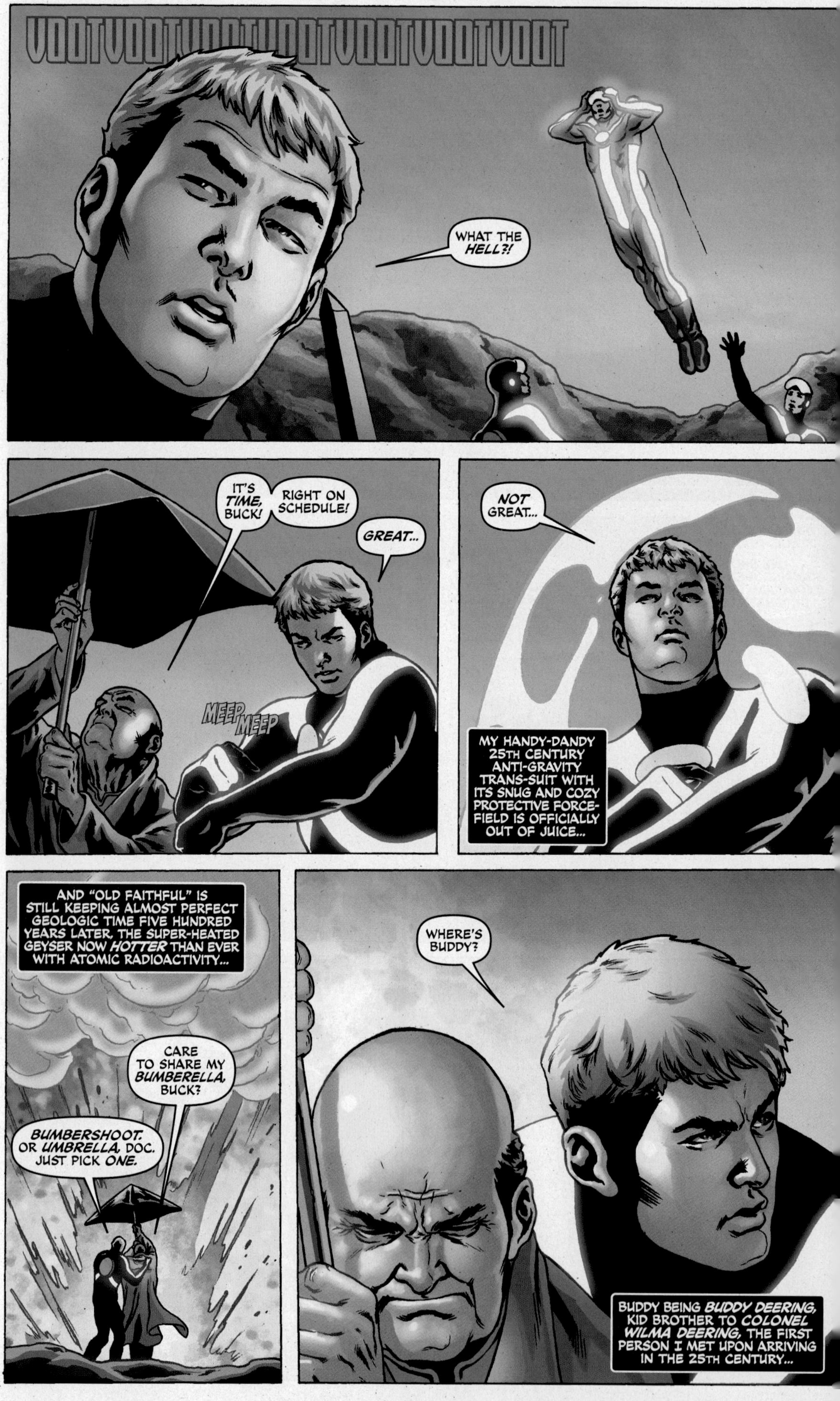
VOOTVOOTVOOTVOOTVOOTVOOTVOOT
WHAT THE HELL?!
IT'S TIME, BUCK!
RIGHT ON SCHEDULE!
GREAT...
MEEP MEEP
NOT GREAT...
MY HANDY-DANDY 25TH CENTURY ANTI-GRAVITY TRANS-SUIT WITH ITS SNUG AND COZY PROTECTIVE FORCE-FIELD IS OFFICIALLY OUT OF JUICE...
AND "OLD FAITHFUL" IS STILL KEEPING ALMOST PERFECT GEOLOGIC TIME FIVE HUNDRED YEARS LATER, THE SUPER-HEATED GEYSER NOW HOTTER THAN EVER WITH ATOMIC RADIOACTIVITY...
CARE TO SHARE MY BUMBERELLA, BUCK?
BUMBERSHOOT. OR UMBRELLA, DOC. JUST PICK ONE.
WHERE'S BUDDY?
BUDDY BEING BUDDY DEERING, KID BROTHER TO COLONEL WILMA DEERING, THE FIRST PERSON I MET UPON ARRIVING IN THE 25TH CENTURY...

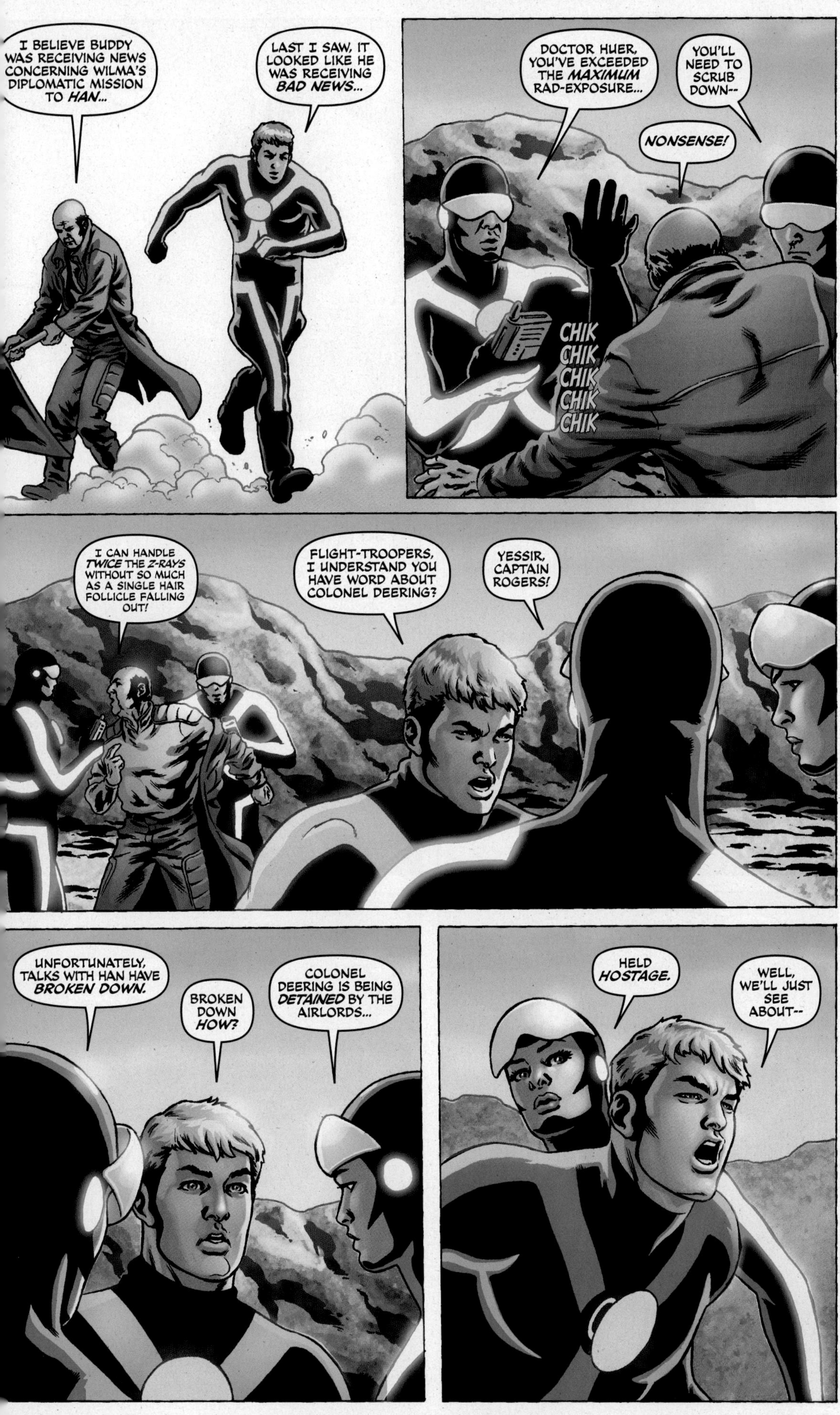

I BELIEVE BUDDY WAS RECEIVING NEWS CONCERNING WILMA'S DIPLOMATIC MISSION TO *HAN*...
LAST I SAW, IT LOOKED LIKE HE WAS RECEIVING *BAD NEWS*...
DOCTOR HUER, YOU'VE EXCEEDED THE *MAXIMUM* RAD-EXPOSURE...
YOU'LL NEED TO SCRUB DOWN--
NONSENSE!
CHIK CHIK CHIK CHIK CHIK
I CAN HANDLE *TWICE* THE *Z-RAYS* WITHOUT SO MUCH AS A SINGLE HAIR FOLLICLE FALLING OUT!
FLIGHT-TROOPERS, I UNDERSTAND YOU HAVE WORD ABOUT COLONEL DEERING?
YESSIR, CAPTAIN ROGERS!
UNFORTUNATELY, TALKS WITH HAN HAVE *BROKEN DOWN.*
BROKEN DOWN *HOW?*
COLONEL DEERING IS BEING *DETAINED* BY THE AIRLORDS...
HELD *HOSTAGE.*
WELL, WE'LL JUST SEE ABOUT--

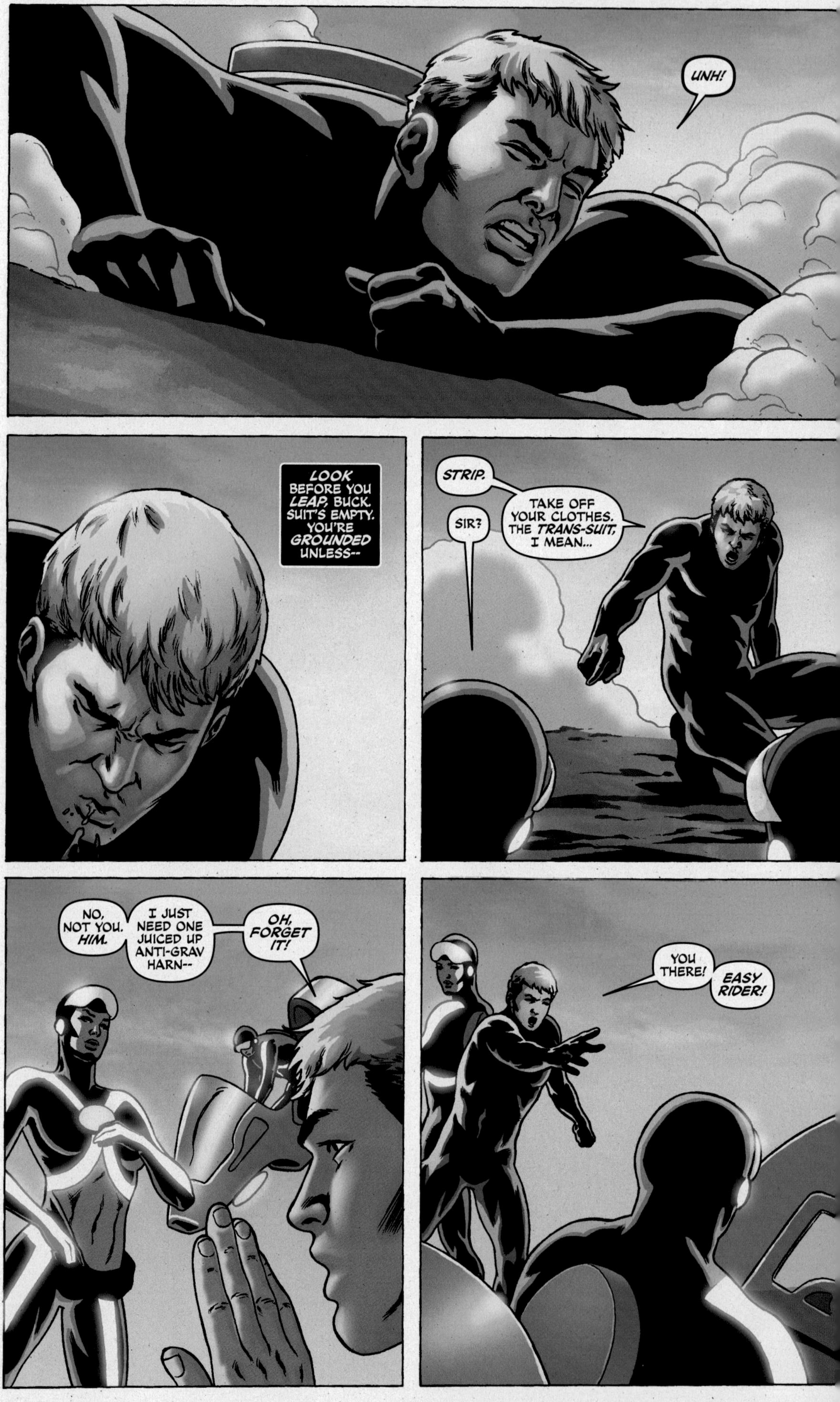
UNH!
LOOK BEFORE YOU LEAP, BUCK. SUIT'S EMPTY. YOU'RE GROUNDED UNLESS--
STRIP.
TAKE OFF YOUR CLOTHES. THE TRANS-SUIT, I MEAN...
SIR?
NO, NOT YOU. HIM.
I JUST NEED ONE JUICED UP ANTI-GRAV HARN--
OH, FORGET IT!
YOU THERE!
EASY RIDER!

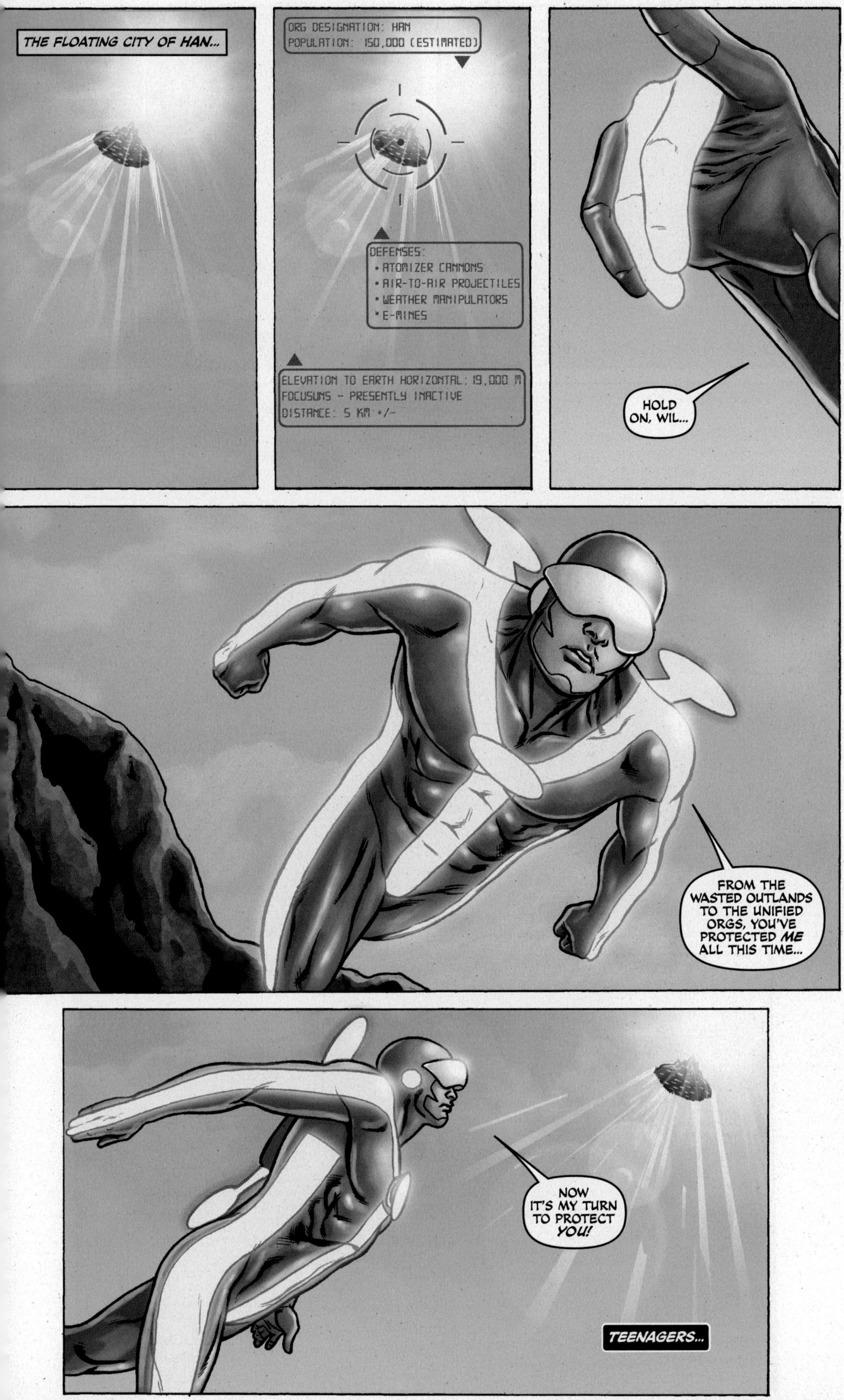
THE FLOATING CITY OF HAN...
ORG DESIGNATION: HAN
POPULATION: 150,000 (ESTIMATED)
DEFENSES:
• ATOMIZER CANNONS
• AIR-TO-AIR PROJECTILES
• WEATHER MANIPULATORS
• E-MINES
ELEVATION TO EARTH HORIZONTAL: 19,000 M
FOCUSUNS - PRESENTLY INACTIVE
DISTANCE: 5 KM +/-
HOLD ON, WIL...
FROM THE WASTED OUTLANDS TO THE UNIFIED ORGS, YOU'VE PROTECTED ME ALL THIS TIME...
NOW IT'S MY TURN TO PROTECT YOU!
TEENAGERS...

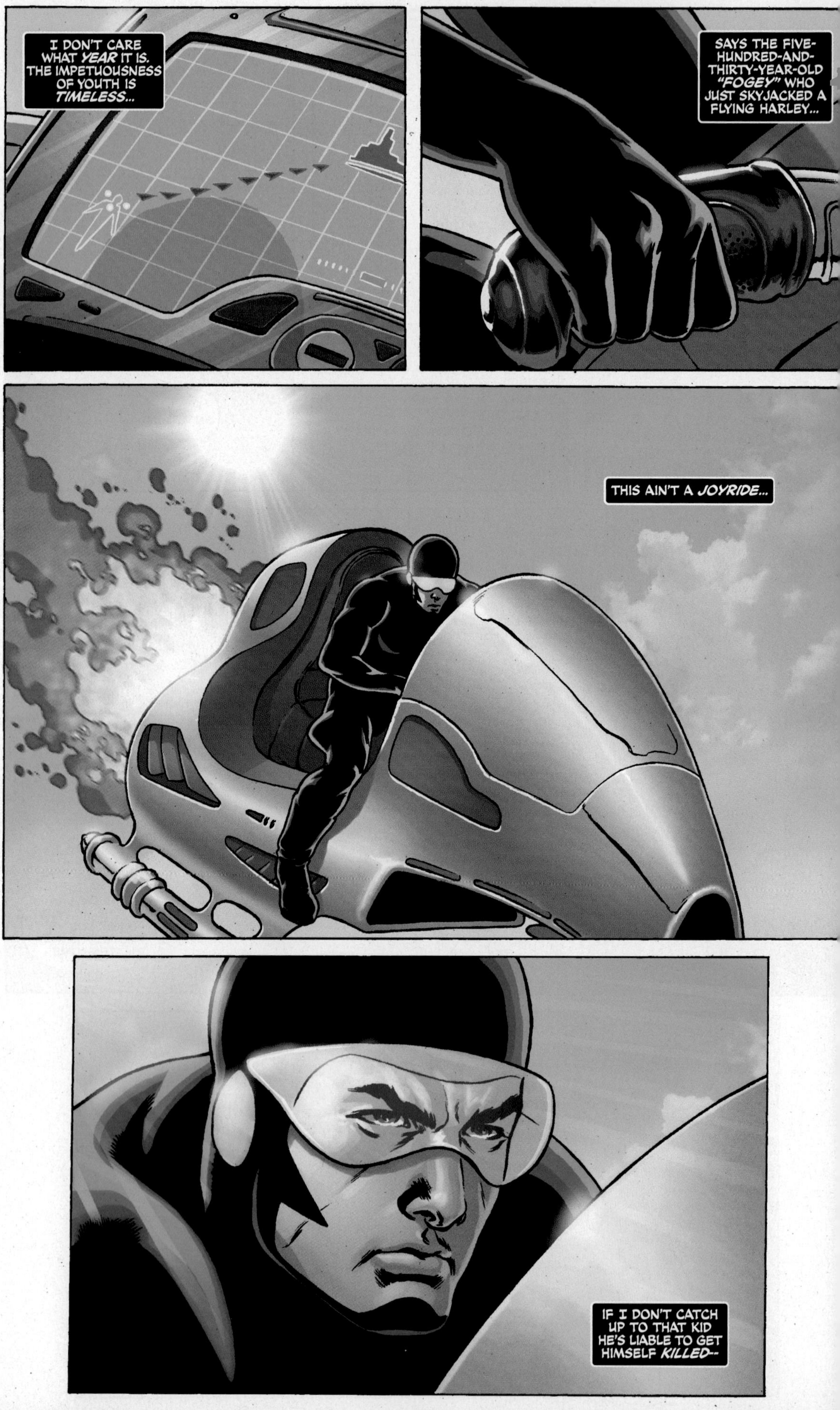
I DON'T CARE WHAT *YEAR* IT IS. THE IMPETUOUSNESS OF YOUTH IS *TIMELESS*...
SAYS THE FIVE-HUNDRED-AND-THIRTY-YEAR-OLD *"FOGEY"* WHO JUST SKYJACKED A FLYING HARLEY...
THIS AIN'T A *JOYRIDE*...
IF I DON'T CATCH UP TO THAT KID HE'S LIABLE TO GET HIMSELF *KILLED*--

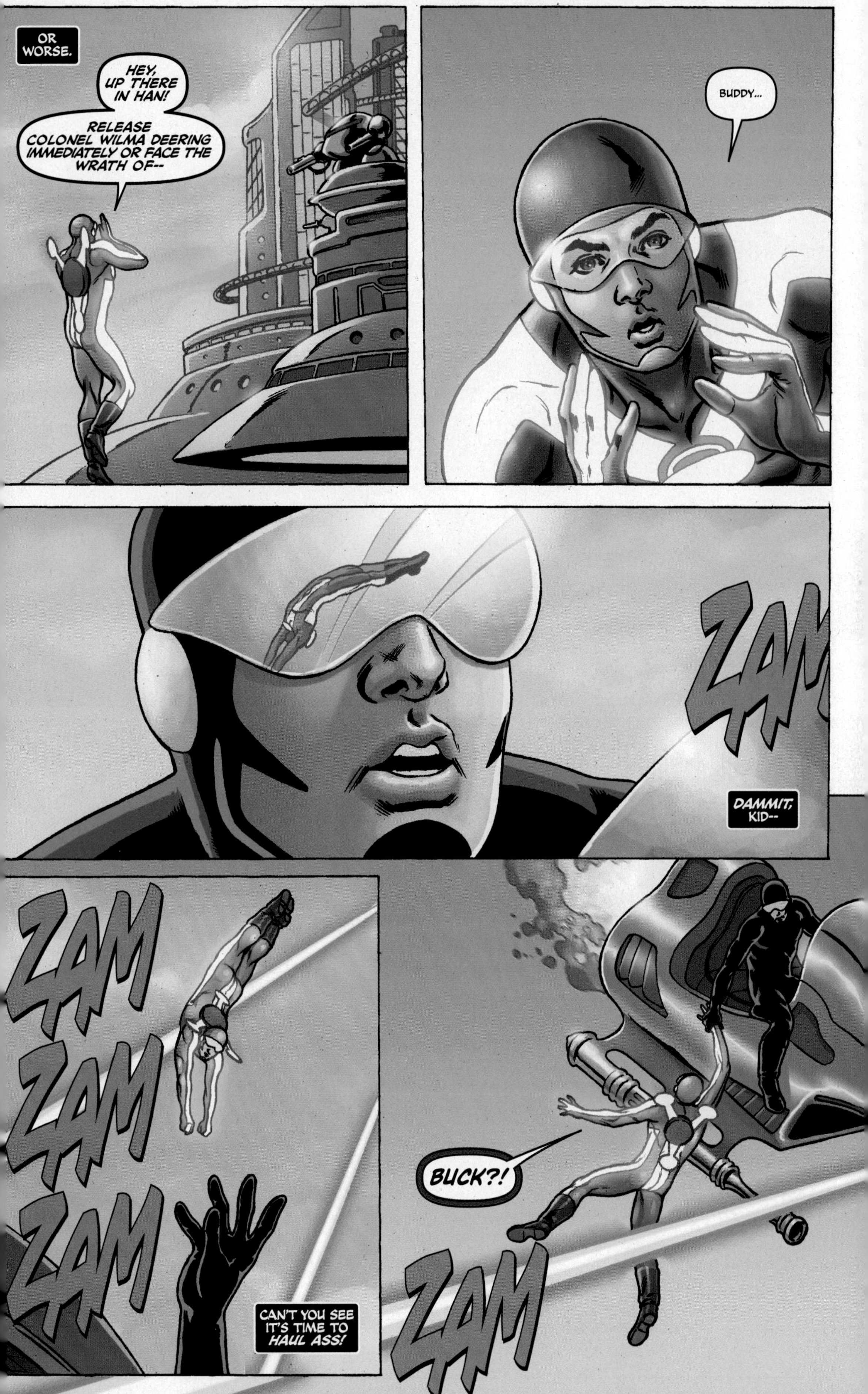
OR WORSE.
HEY, UP THERE IN HAN!
RELEASE COLONEL WILMA DEERING IMMEDIATELY OR FACE THE WRATH OF--
BUDDY...
ZAM
DAMMIT, KID--
ZAM
ZAM
ZAM
BUCK?!
ZAM
CAN'T YOU SEE IT'S TIME TO HAUL ASS!

CHOOM CHOOM CHOOM

E-MINES! THEY'RE LOCKED ON!

E-WHAT?!

STUDY UP ON FUTURISTIC WEAPONS WHEN THEY'RE *NOT* TRYING TO SEED THE CLOUDS WITH YOUR RED MISTY REMAINS, BUCK...

THESE AREN'T SMART BOMBS, THEY'RE *GENIUS* BOMBS...

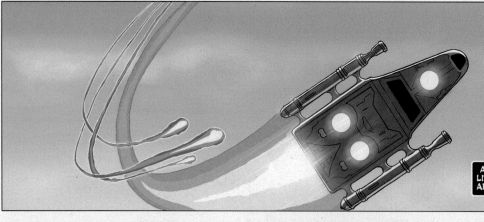

AND THE SPIKY LITTLE BUGGERS ARE *PERSISTENT.*

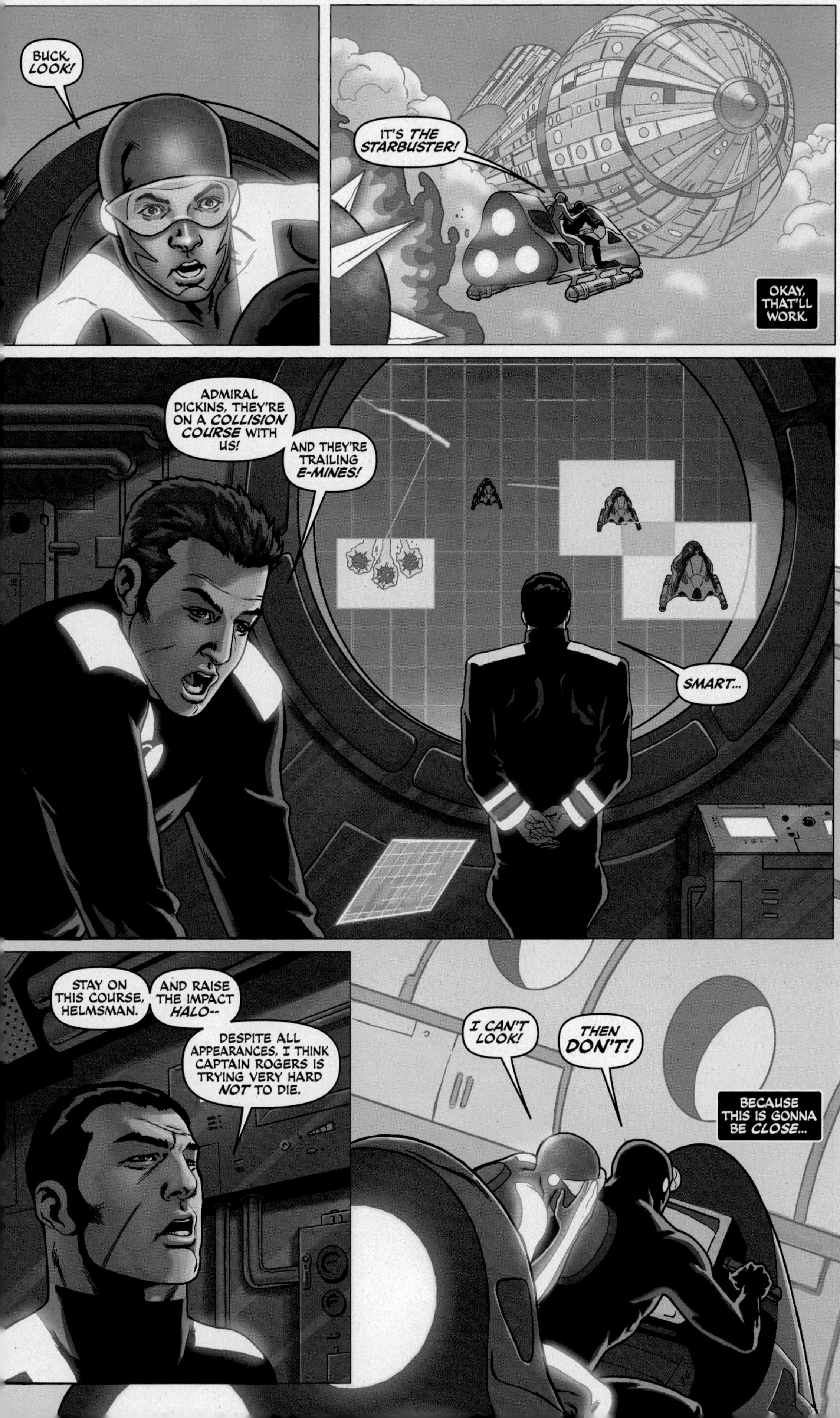
BUCK, LOOK!
IT'S THE STARBUSTER!
OKAY, THAT'LL WORK.
ADMIRAL DICKINS, THEY'RE ON A COLLISION COURSE WITH US!
AND THEY'RE TRAILING E-MINES!
SMART...
STAY ON THIS COURSE, HELMSMAN.
AND RAISE THE IMPACT HALO--
DESPITE ALL APPEARANCES, I THINK CAPTAIN ROGERS IS TRYING VERY HARD NOT TO DIE.
I CAN'T LOOK!
THEN DON'T!
BECAUSE THIS IS GONNA BE CLOSE...

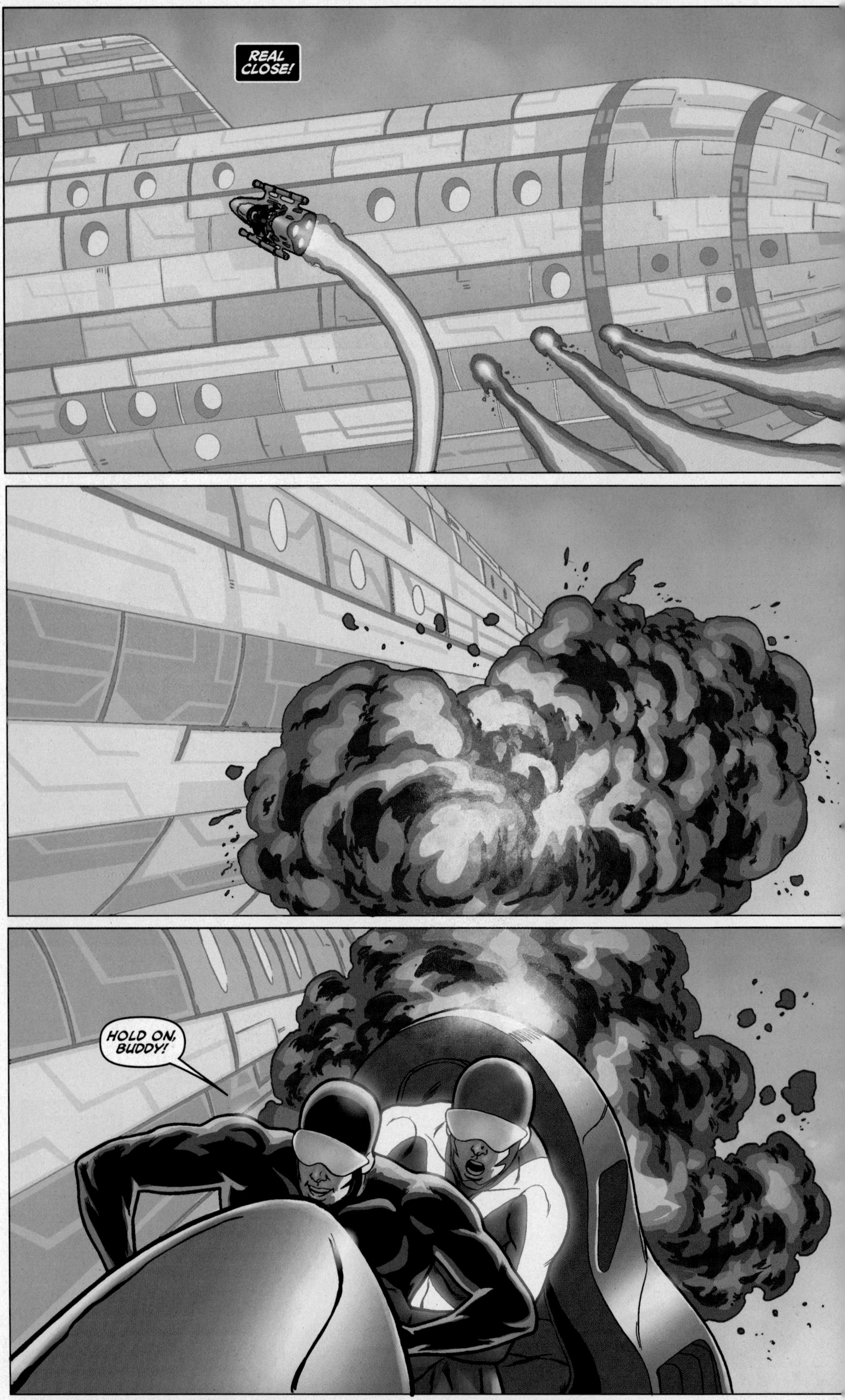
REAL CLOSE!
HOLD ON, BUDDY!

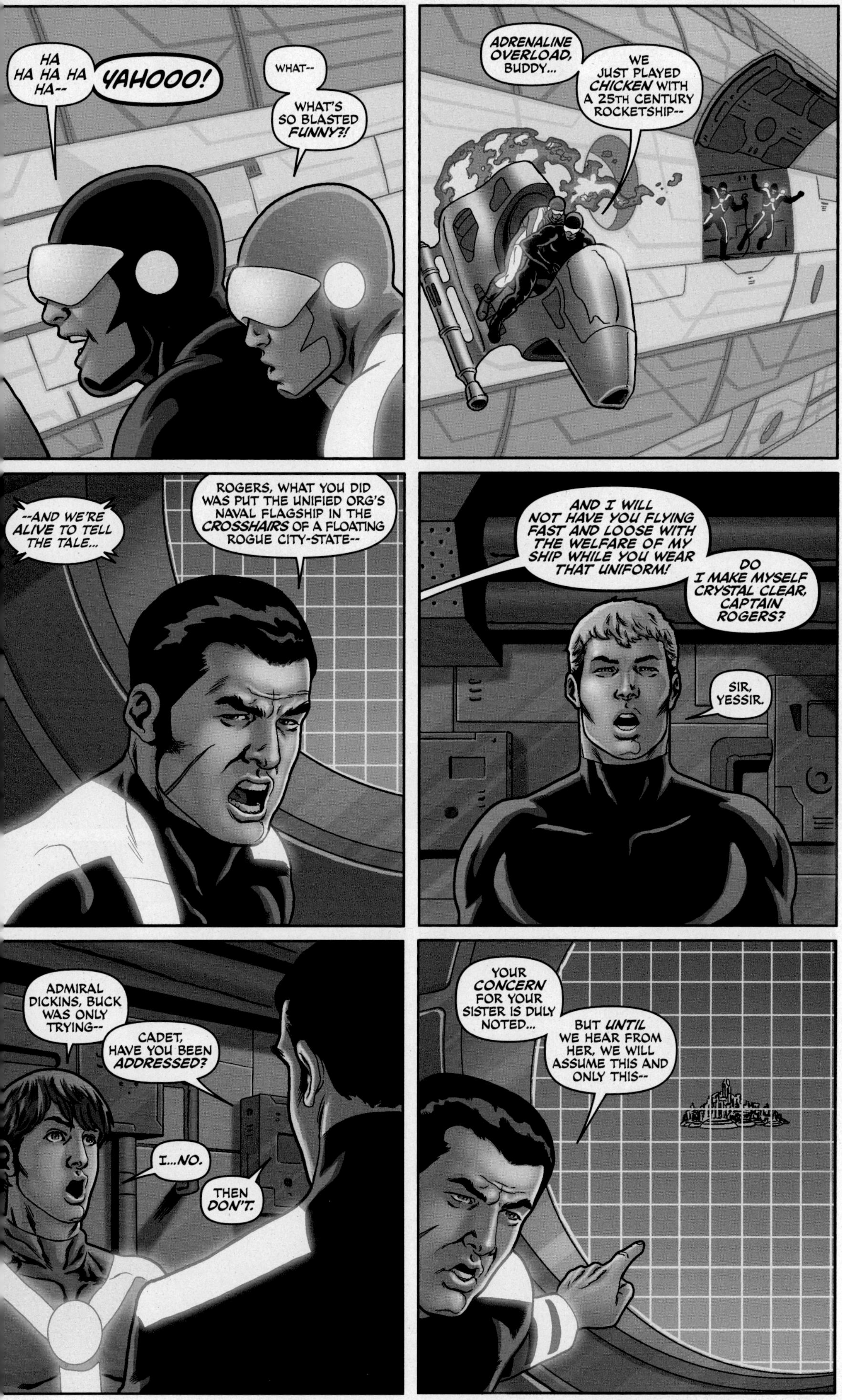

HA HA HA HA HA--
YAHOOO!
WHAT--
WHAT'S SO BLASTED FUNNY?!
ADRENALINE OVERLOAD, BUDDY...
WE JUST PLAYED CHICKEN WITH A 25TH CENTURY ROCKETSHIP--
--AND WE'RE ALIVE TO TELL THE TALE...
ROGERS, WHAT YOU DID WAS PUT THE UNIFIED ORG'S NAVAL FLAGSHIP IN THE CROSSHAIRS OF A FLOATING ROGUE CITY-STATE--
AND I WILL NOT HAVE YOU FLYING FAST AND LOOSE WITH THE WELFARE OF MY SHIP WHILE YOU WEAR THAT UNIFORM!
DO I MAKE MYSELF CRYSTAL CLEAR, CAPTAIN ROGERS?
SIR, YESSIR.
ADMIRAL DICKINS, BUCK WAS ONLY TRYING--
CADET, HAVE YOU BEEN ADDRESSED?
I...NO.
THEN DON'T.
YOUR CONCERN FOR YOUR SISTER IS DULY NOTED...
BUT UNTIL WE HEAR FROM HER, WE WILL ASSUME THIS AND ONLY THIS--

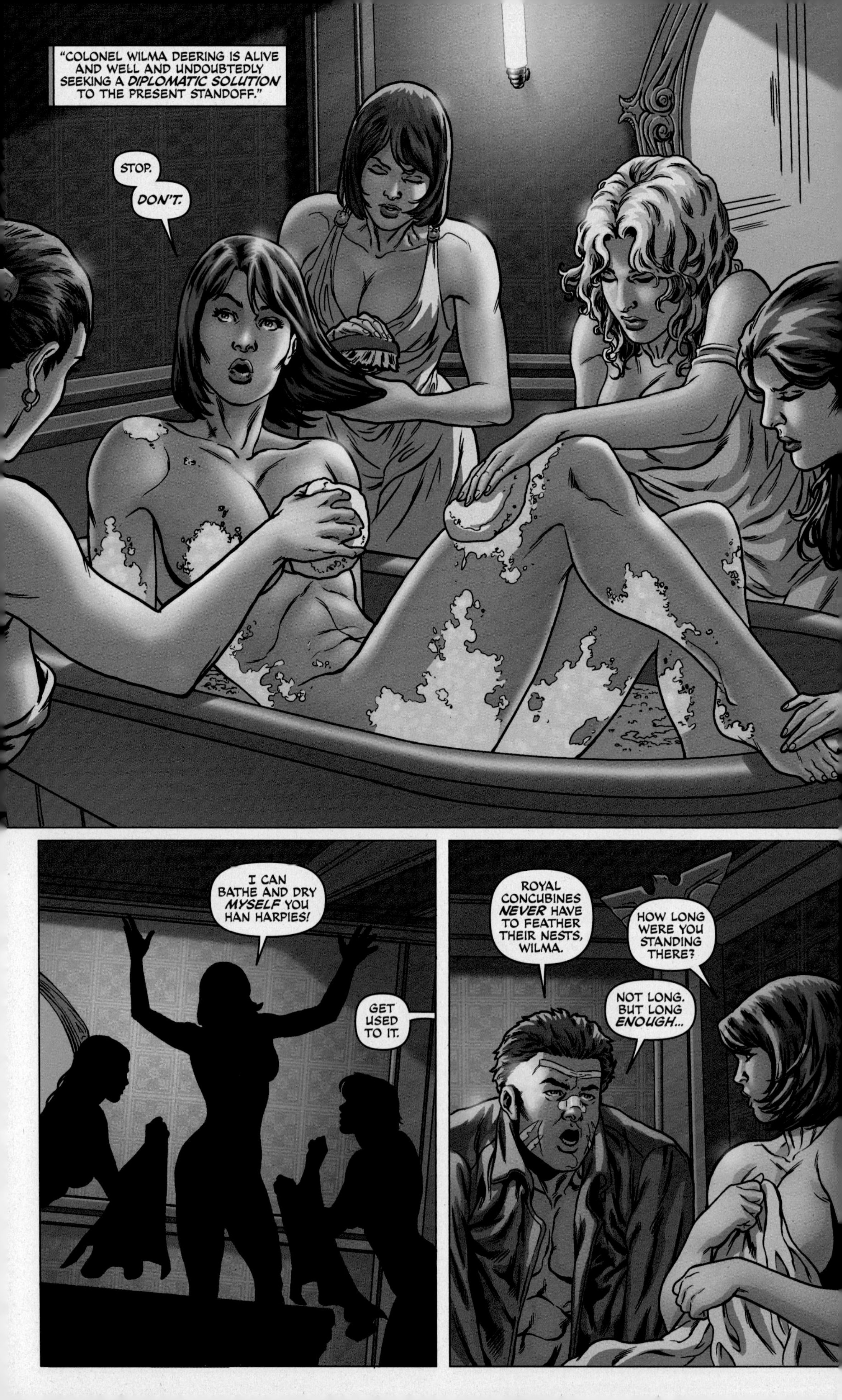
"COLONEL WILMA DEERING IS ALIVE AND WELL AND UNDOUBTEDLY SEEKING A DIPLOMATIC SOLUTION TO THE PRESENT STANDOFF."
STOP.
DON'T.
I CAN BATHE AND DRY MYSELF YOU HAN HARPIES!
GET USED TO IT.
ROYAL CONCUBINES NEVER HAVE TO FEATHER THEIR NESTS, WILMA.
HOW LONG WERE YOU STANDING THERE?
NOT LONG. BUT LONG ENOUGH...

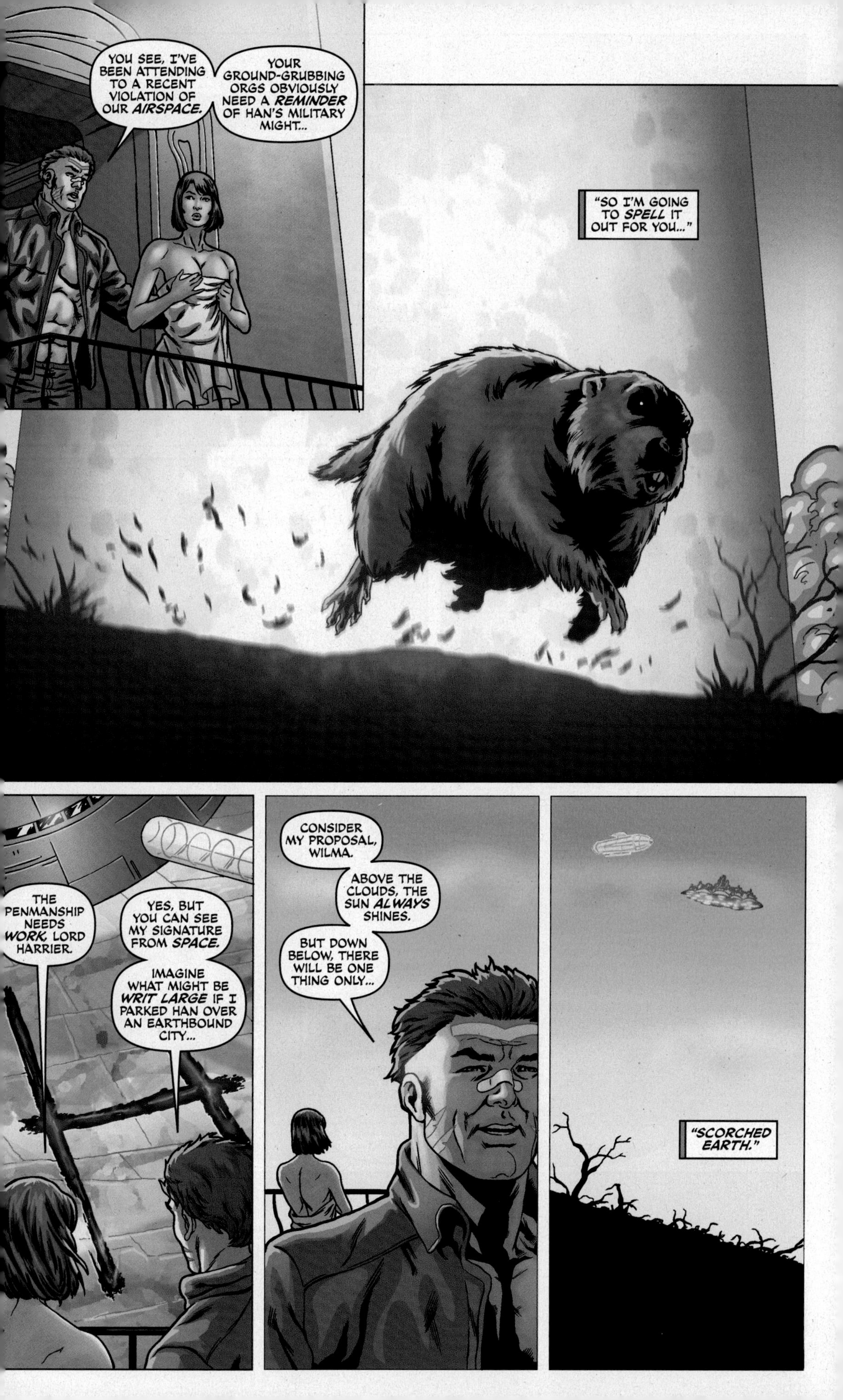
YOU SEE, I'VE BEEN ATTENDING TO A RECENT VIOLATION OF OUR AIRSPACE.
YOUR GROUND-GRUBBING ORGS OBVIOUSLY NEED A REMINDER OF HAN'S MILITARY MIGHT...
"SO I'M GOING TO SPELL IT OUT FOR YOU..."
THE PENMANSHIP NEEDS WORK, LORD HARRIER.
YES, BUT YOU CAN SEE MY SIGNATURE FROM SPACE.
IMAGINE WHAT MIGHT BE WRIT LARGE IF I PARKED HAN OVER AN EARTHBOUND CITY...
CONSIDER MY PROPOSAL, WILMA.
ABOVE THE CLOUDS, THE SUN ALWAYS SHINES.
BUT DOWN BELOW, THERE WILL BE ONE THING ONLY...
"SCORCHED EARTH."

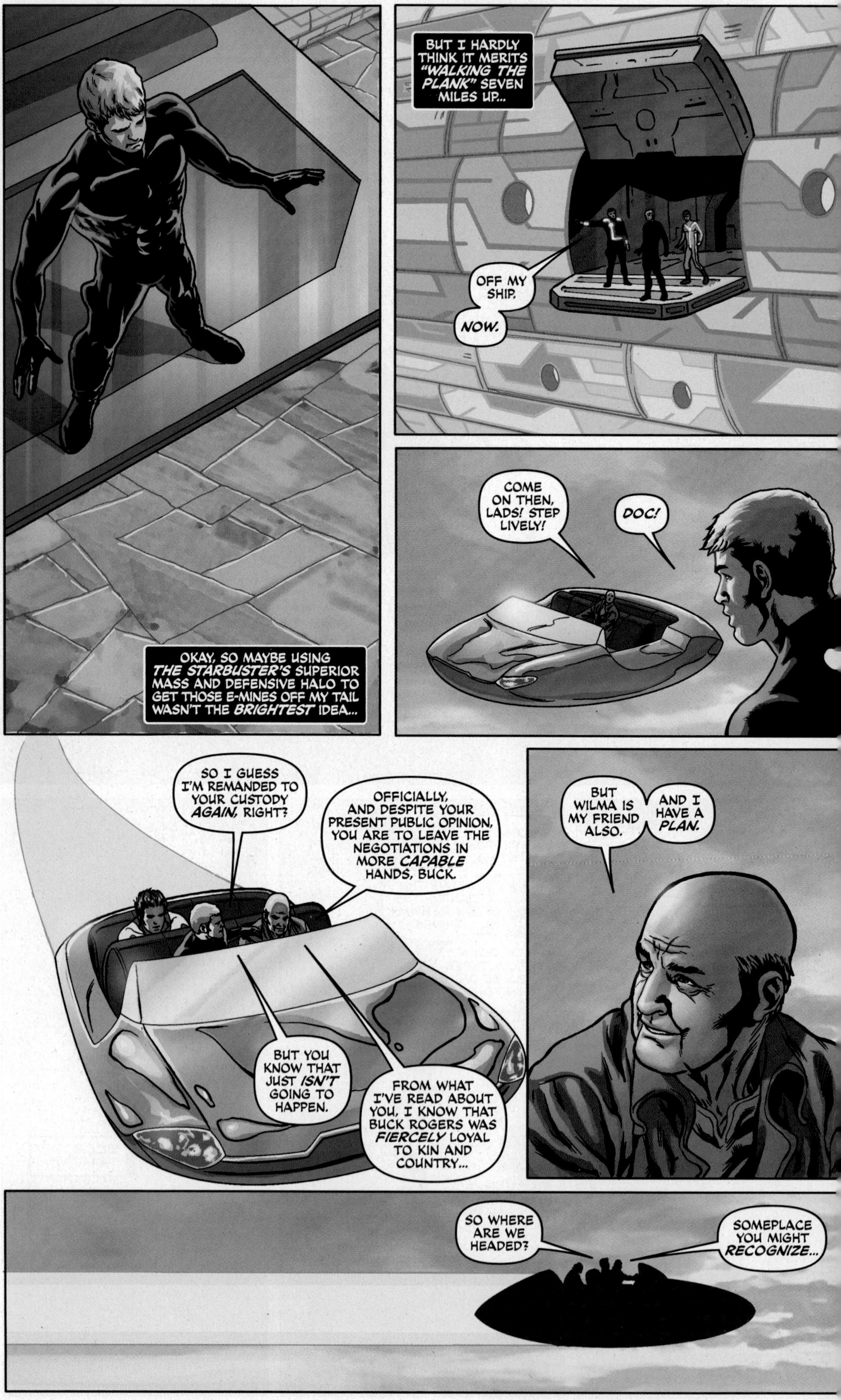
OKAY, SO MAYBE USING *THE STARBUSTER'S* SUPERIOR MASS AND DEFENSIVE HALO TO GET THOSE E-MINES OFF MY TAIL WASN'T THE *BRIGHTEST* IDEA...
BUT I HARDLY THINK IT MERITS *"WALKING THE PLANK"* SEVEN MILES UP...
OFF MY SHIP.
NOW.
COME ON THEN, LADS! STEP LIVELY!
DOC!
SO I GUESS I'M REMANDED TO YOUR CUSTODY *AGAIN*, RIGHT?
OFFICIALLY, AND DESPITE YOUR PRESENT PUBLIC OPINION, YOU ARE TO LEAVE THE NEGOTIATIONS IN MORE *CAPABLE* HANDS, BUCK.
BUT YOU KNOW THAT JUST *ISN'T* GOING TO HAPPEN.
FROM WHAT I'VE READ ABOUT YOU, I KNOW THAT BUCK ROGERS WAS *FIERCELY* LOYAL TO KIN AND COUNTRY...
BUT WILMA IS MY FRIEND ALSO.
AND I HAVE A *PLAN.*
SO WHERE ARE WE HEADED?
SOMEPLACE YOU MIGHT *RECOGNIZE...*

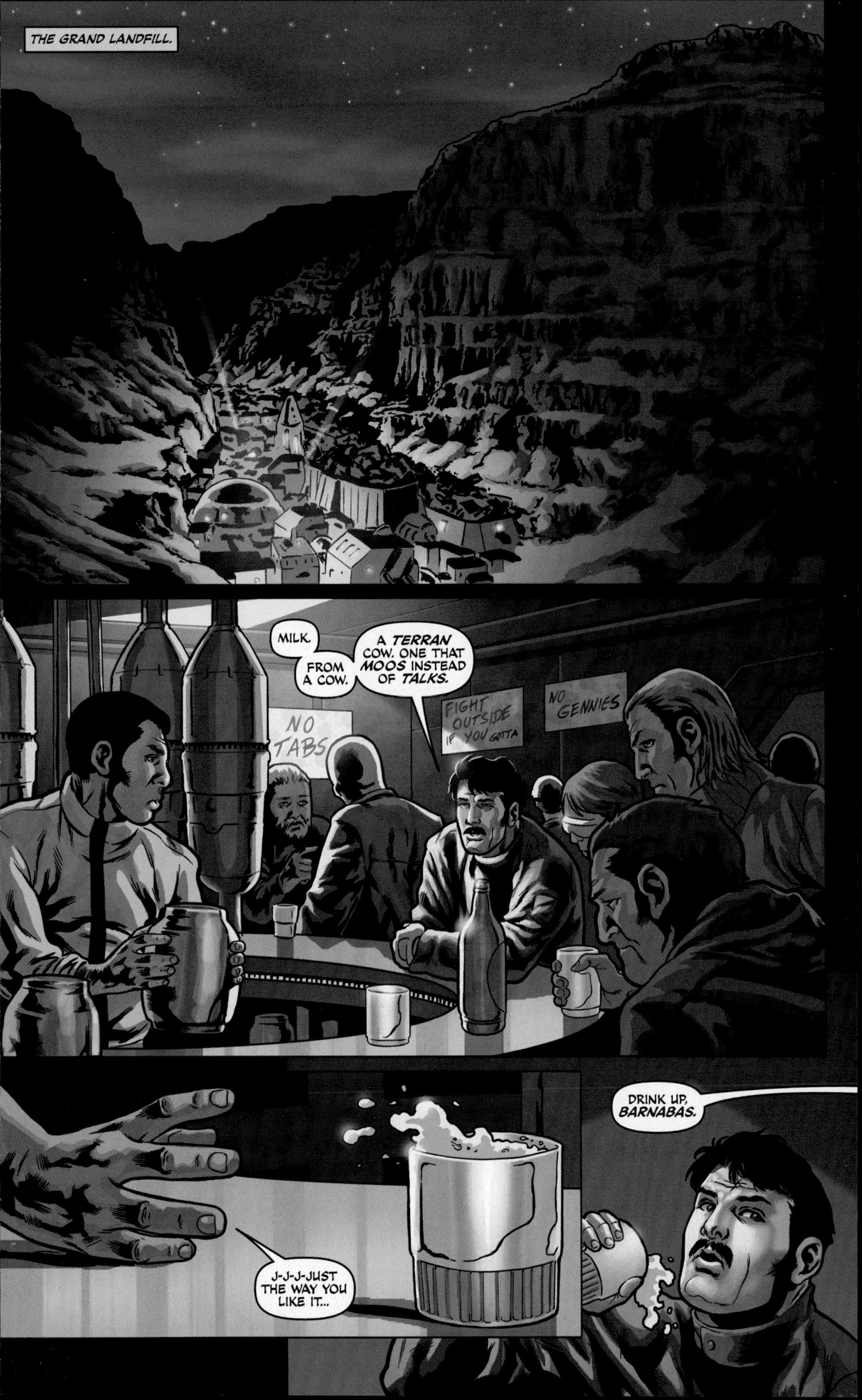
THE GRAND LANDFILL.
MILK.
FROM A COW.
A TERRAN COW. ONE THAT MOOS INSTEAD OF TALKS.
NO TABS
FIGHT OUTSIDE IF YOU GOTTA
NO GENNIES
DRINK UP, BARNABAS.
J-J-J-JUST THE WAY YOU LIKE IT...

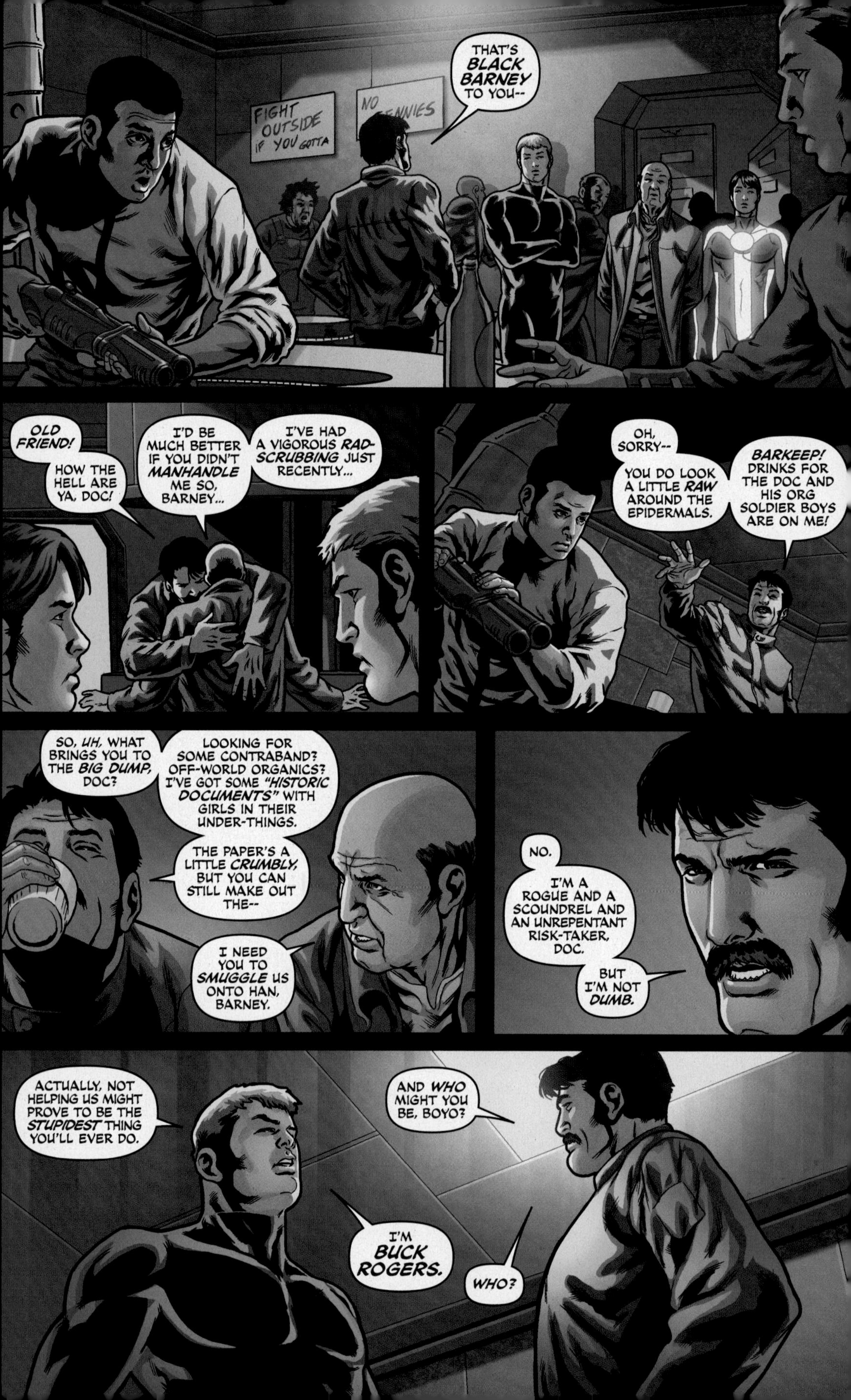
FIGHT OUTSIDE IF YOU GOTTA
NO [ ]ENNIES
THAT'S BLACK BARNEY TO YOU--
OLD FRIEND!
HOW THE HELL ARE YA, DOC!
I'D BE MUCH BETTER IF YOU DIDN'T MANHANDLE ME SO, BARNEY...
I'VE HAD A VIGOROUS RAD-SCRUBBING JUST RECENTLY...
OH, SORRY--
YOU DO LOOK A LITTLE RAW AROUND THE EPIDERMALS.
BARKEEP! DRINKS FOR THE DOC AND HIS ORG SOLDIER BOYS ARE ON ME!
SO, UH, WHAT BRINGS YOU TO THE BIG DUMP, DOC?
LOOKING FOR SOME CONTRABAND? OFF-WORLD ORGANICS? I'VE GOT SOME "HISTORIC DOCUMENTS" WITH GIRLS IN THEIR UNDER-THINGS.
THE PAPER'S A LITTLE CRUMBLY, BUT YOU CAN STILL MAKE OUT THE--
I NEED YOU TO SMUGGLE US ONTO HAN, BARNEY.
NO.
I'M A ROGUE AND A SCOUNDREL AND AN UNREPENTANT RISK-TAKER, DOC.
BUT I'M NOT DUMB.
ACTUALLY, NOT HELPING US MIGHT PROVE TO BE THE STUPIDEST THING YOU'LL EVER DO.
AND WHO MIGHT YOU BE, BOYO?
I'M BUCK ROGERS.
WHO?

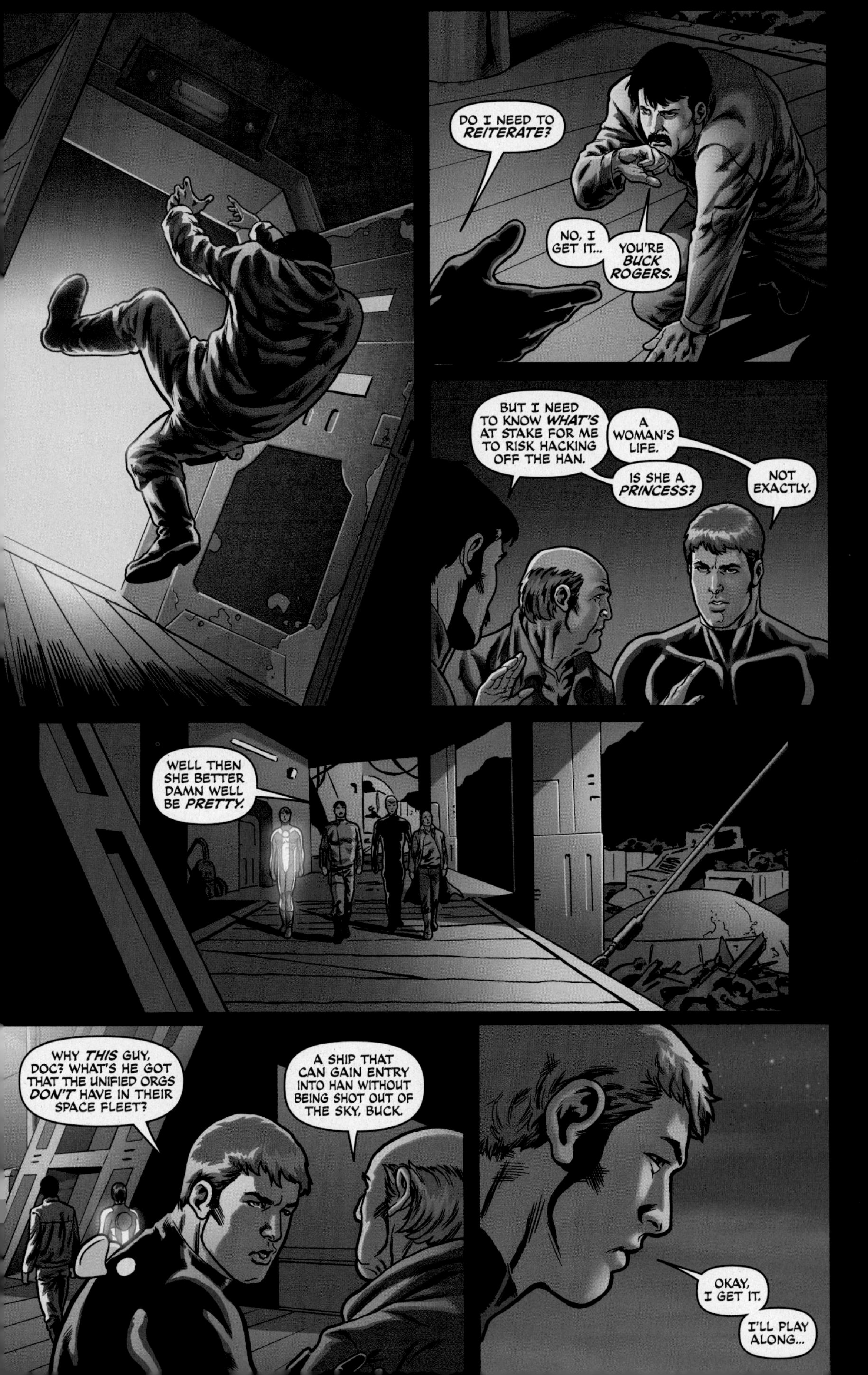
DO I NEED TO REITERATE?
NO, I GET IT...
YOU'RE BUCK ROGERS.
BUT I NEED TO KNOW WHAT'S AT STAKE FOR ME TO RISK HACKING OFF THE HAN.
A WOMAN'S LIFE.
IS SHE A PRINCESS?
NOT EXACTLY.
WELL THEN SHE BETTER DAMN WELL BE PRETTY.
WHY THIS GUY, DOC? WHAT'S HE GOT THAT THE UNIFIED ORGS DON'T HAVE IN THEIR SPACE FLEET?
A SHIP THAT CAN GAIN ENTRY INTO HAN WITHOUT BEING SHOT OUT OF THE SKY, BUCK.
OKAY, I GET IT.
I'LL PLAY ALONG...

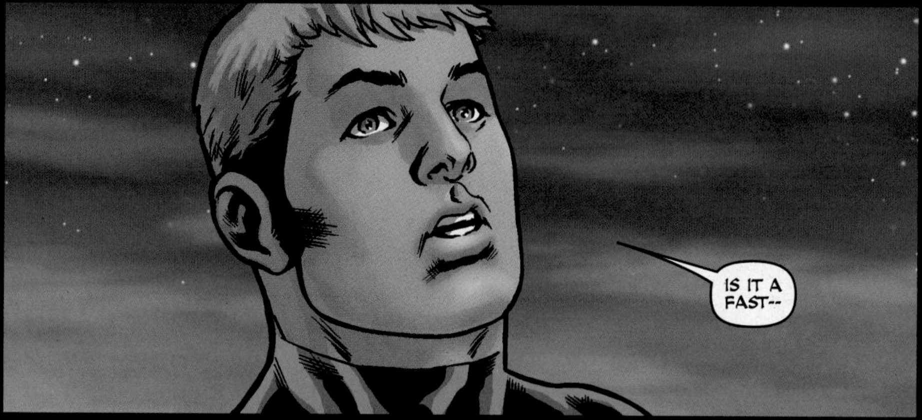
IS IT A FAST--

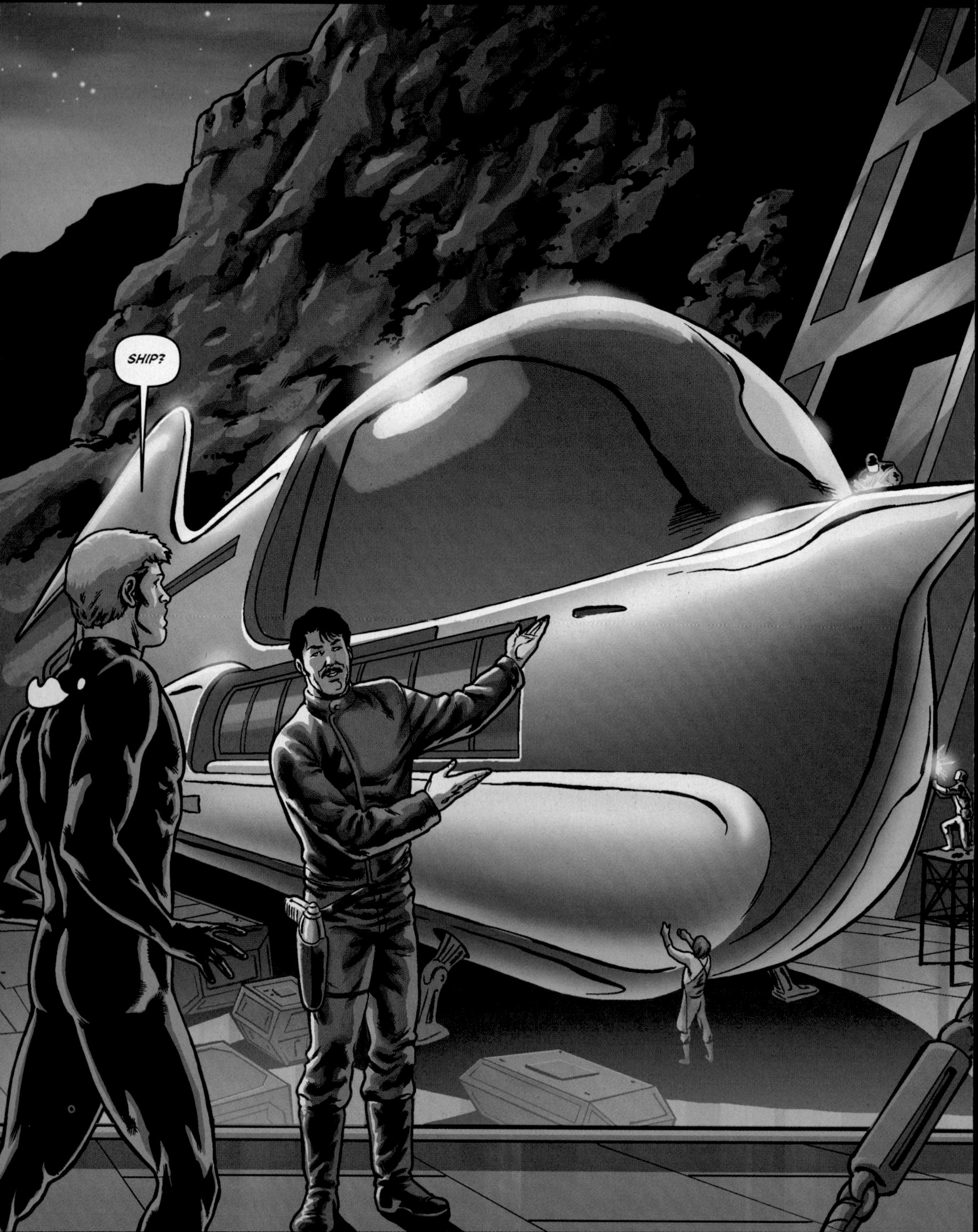
SHIP?

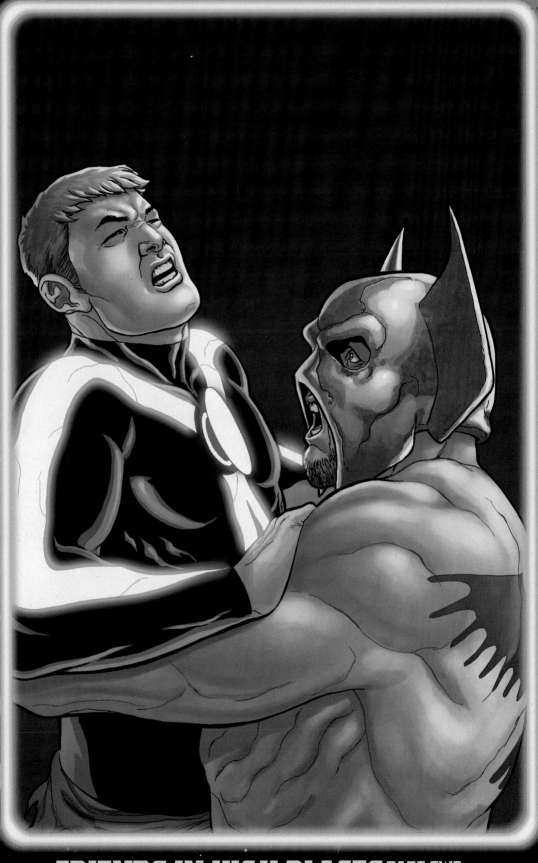

FRIENDS IN HIGH PLACES PART TWO: Fight or Flight

ISSUE TEN COVER BY CARLOS RAFAEL

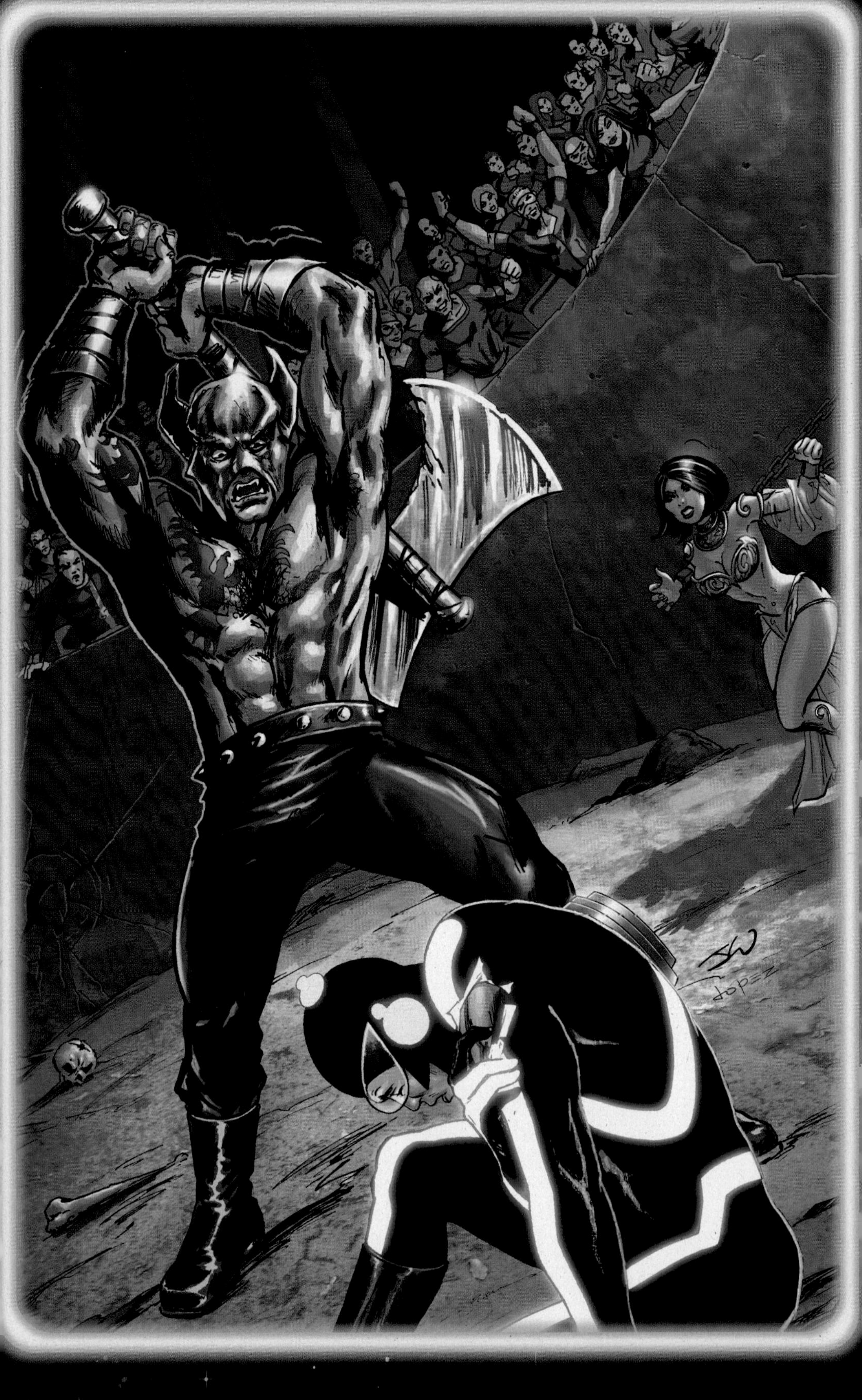

ALTERNATE COVER BY JOHN WATSON

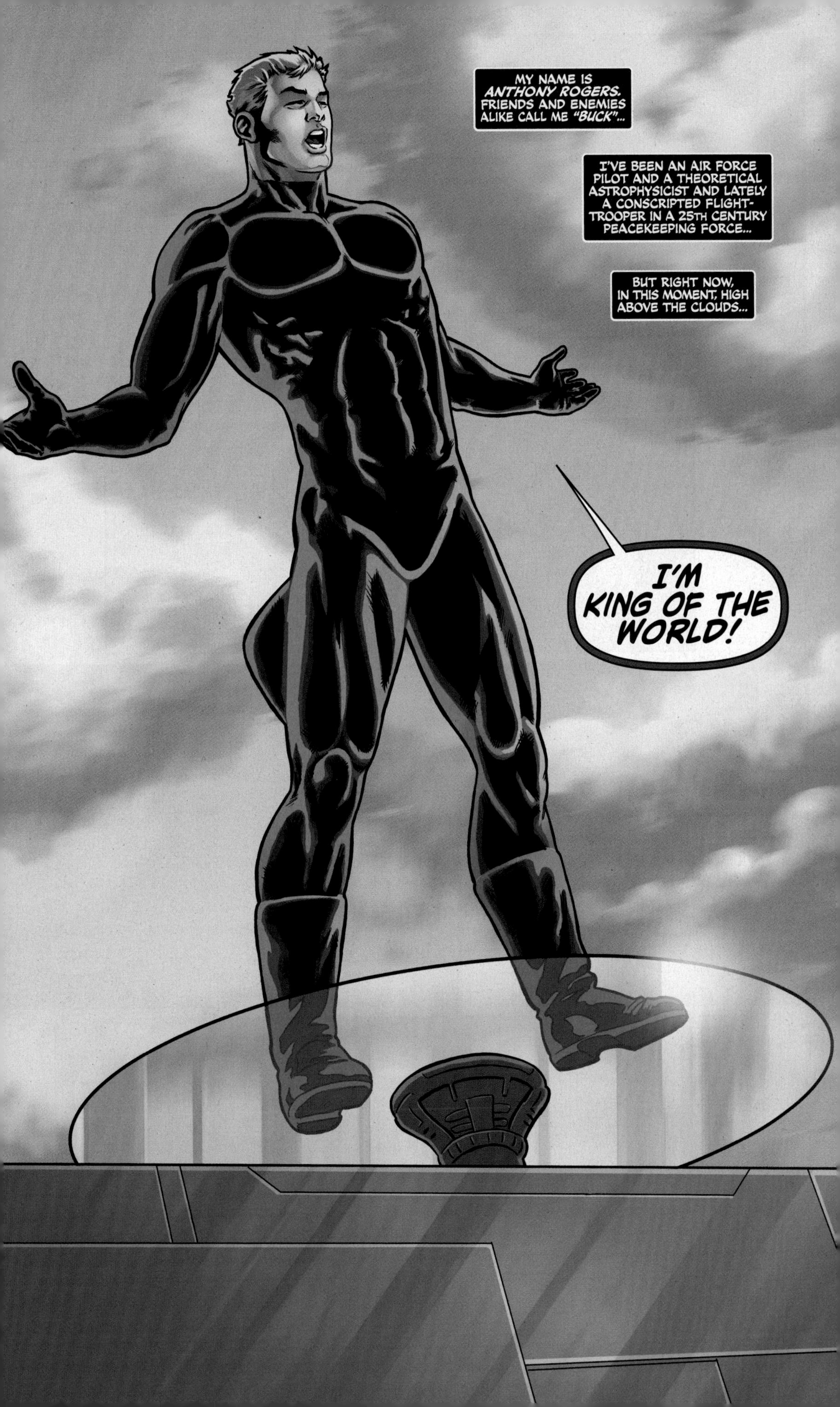
MY NAME IS *ANTHONY ROGERS.* FRIENDS AND ENEMIES ALIKE CALL ME *"BUCK"*...
I'VE BEEN AN AIR FORCE PILOT AND A THEORETICAL ASTROPHYSICIST AND LATELY A CONSCRIPTED FLIGHT-TROOPER IN A 25TH CENTURY PEACEKEEPING FORCE...
BUT RIGHT NOW, IN THIS MOMENT, HIGH ABOVE THE CLOUDS...
I'M KING OF THE WORLD!

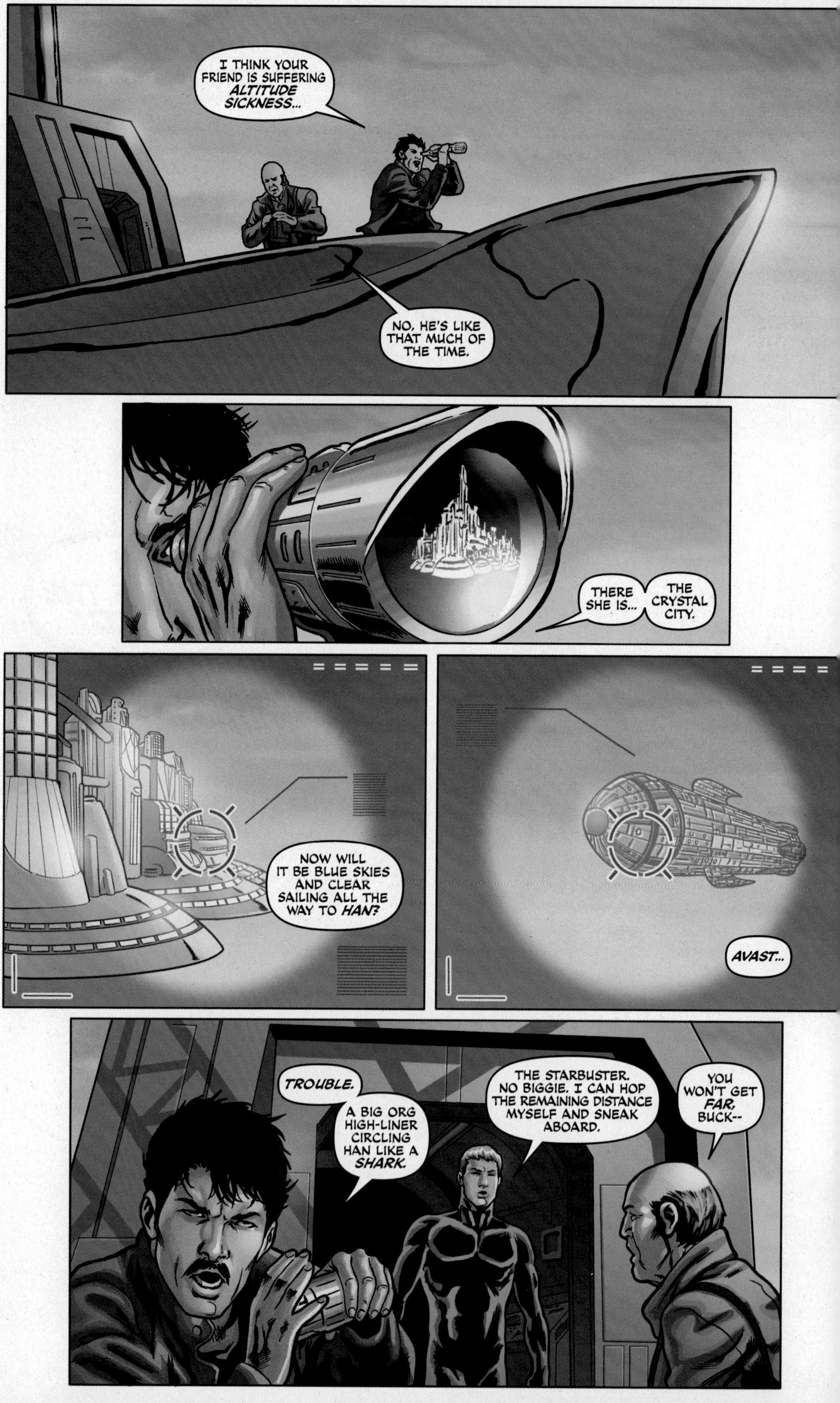
I THINK YOUR FRIEND IS SUFFERING *ALTITUDE SICKNESS...*
NO, HE'S LIKE THAT MUCH OF THE TIME.
THERE SHE IS...
THE CRYSTAL CITY.
NOW WILL IT BE BLUE SKIES AND CLEAR SAILING ALL THE WAY TO *HAN?*
AVAST...
TROUBLE.
A BIG ORG HIGH-LINER CIRCLING HAN LIKE A *SHARK.*
THE STARBUSTER. NO BIGGIE. I CAN HOP THE REMAINING DISTANCE MYSELF AND SNEAK ABOARD.
YOU WON'T GET *FAR,* BUCK--

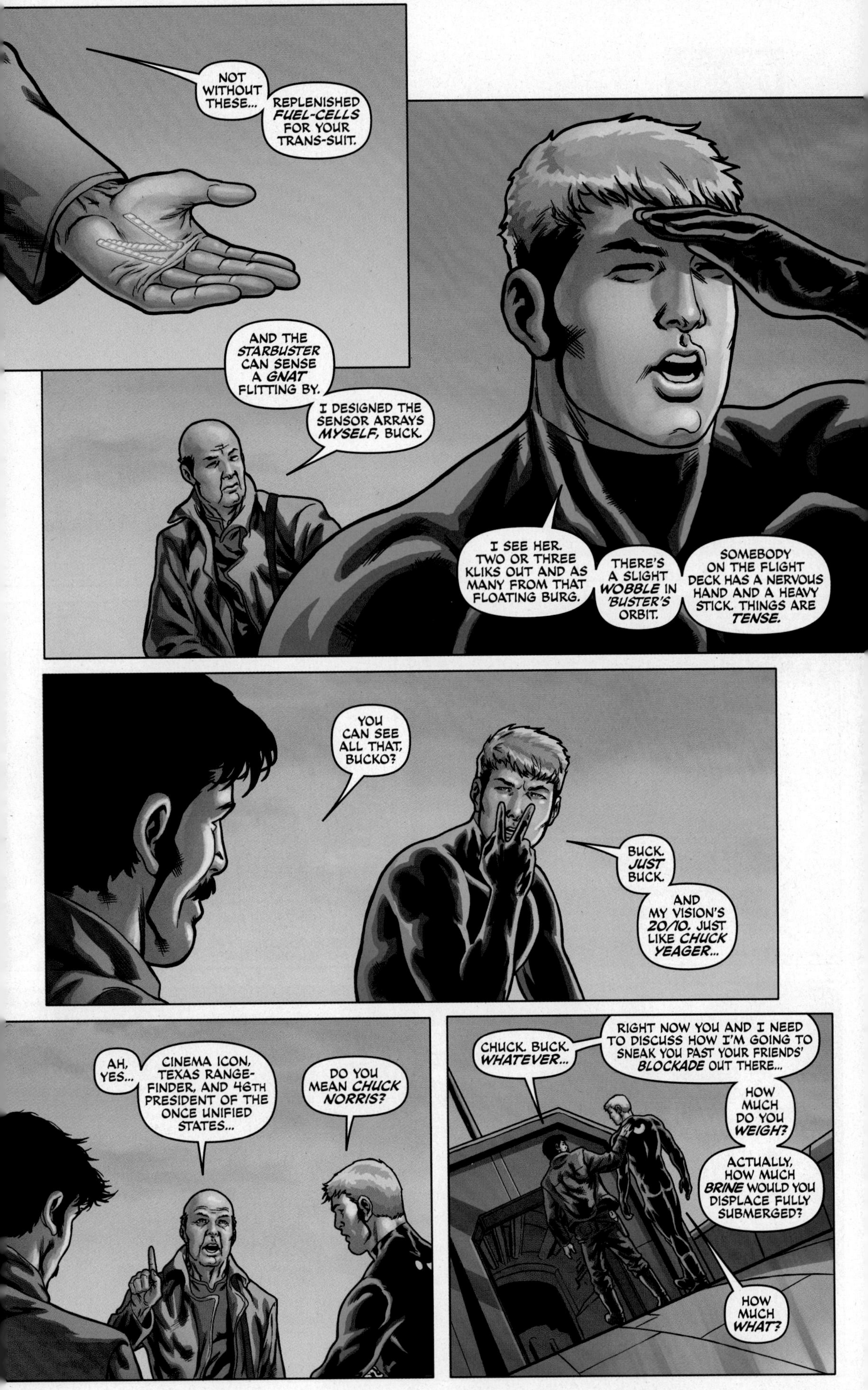

NOT WITHOUT THESE...
REPLENISHED FUEL-CELLS FOR YOUR TRANS-SUIT.
AND THE STARBUSTER CAN SENSE A GNAT FLITTING BY.
I DESIGNED THE SENSOR ARRAYS MYSELF, BUCK.
I SEE HER. TWO OR THREE KLIKS OUT AND AS MANY FROM THAT FLOATING BURG.
THERE'S A SLIGHT WOBBLE IN 'BUSTER'S ORBIT.
SOMEBODY ON THE FLIGHT DECK HAS A NERVOUS HAND AND A HEAVY STICK. THINGS ARE TENSE.
YOU CAN SEE ALL THAT, BUCKO?
BUCK. JUST BUCK.
AND MY VISION'S 20/10. JUST LIKE CHUCK YEAGER...
AH, YES...
CINEMA ICON, TEXAS RANGE-FINDER, AND 46TH PRESIDENT OF THE ONCE UNIFIED STATES...
DO YOU MEAN CHUCK NORRIS?
CHUCK. BUCK. WHATEVER...
RIGHT NOW YOU AND I NEED TO DISCUSS HOW I'M GOING TO SNEAK YOU PAST YOUR FRIENDS' BLOCKADE OUT THERE...
HOW MUCH DO YOU WEIGH?
ACTUALLY, HOW MUCH BRINE WOULD YOU DISPLACE FULLY SUBMERGED?
HOW MUCH WHAT?

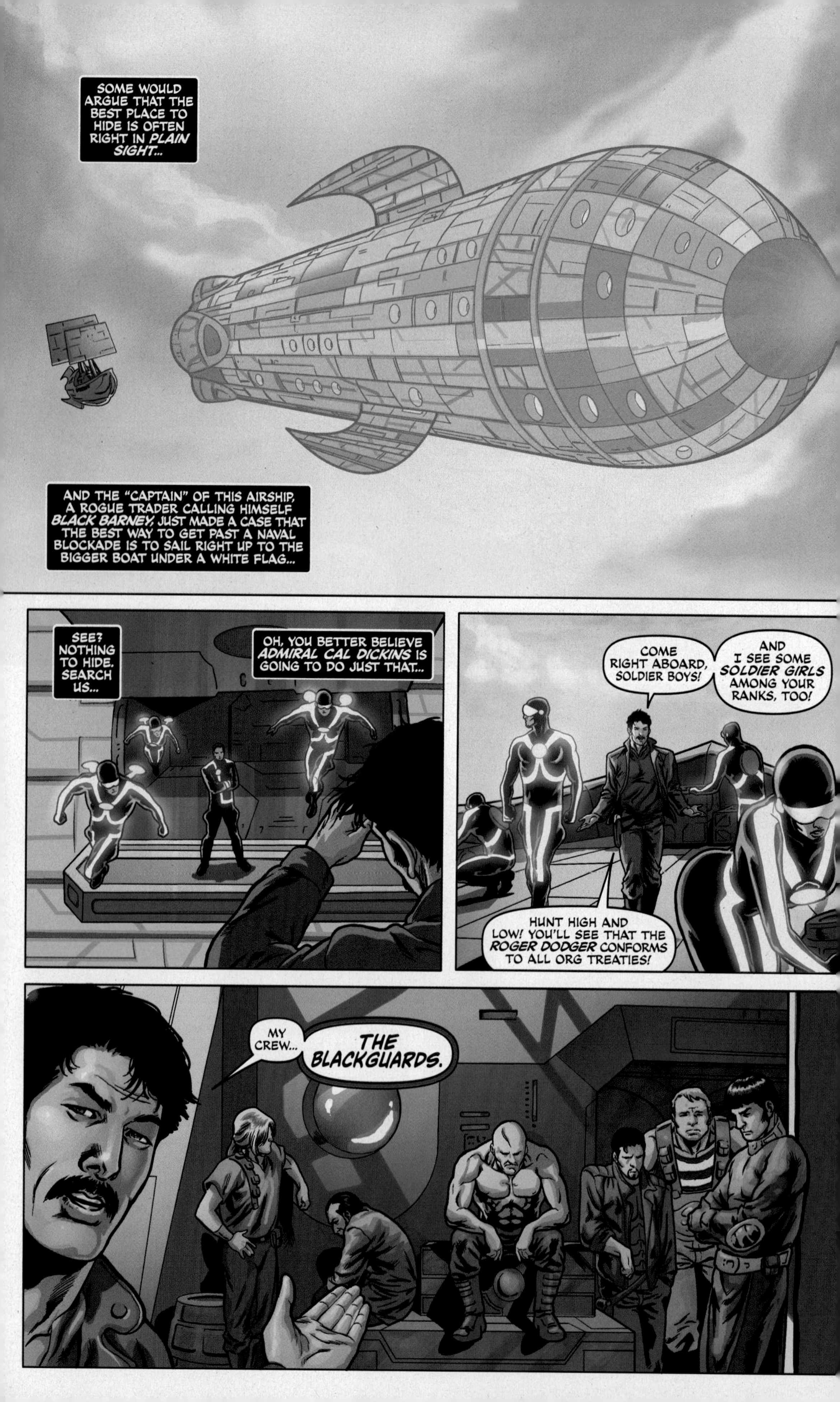
SOME WOULD ARGUE THAT THE BEST PLACE TO HIDE IS OFTEN RIGHT IN *PLAIN SIGHT*...
AND THE "CAPTAIN" OF THIS AIRSHIP, A ROGUE TRADER CALLING HIMSELF *BLACK BARNEY,* JUST MADE A CASE THAT THE BEST WAY TO GET PAST A NAVAL BLOCKADE IS TO SAIL RIGHT UP TO THE BIGGER BOAT UNDER A WHITE FLAG...
SEE? NOTHING TO HIDE. SEARCH US...
OH, YOU BETTER BELIEVE *ADMIRAL CAL DICKINS* IS GOING TO DO JUST THAT...
COME RIGHT ABOARD, SOLDIER BOYS!
AND I SEE SOME *SOLDIER GIRLS* AMONG YOUR RANKS, TOO!
HUNT HIGH AND LOW! YOU'LL SEE THAT THE *ROGER DODGER* CONFORMS TO ALL ORG TREATIES!
MY CREW...
THE BLACKGUARDS.

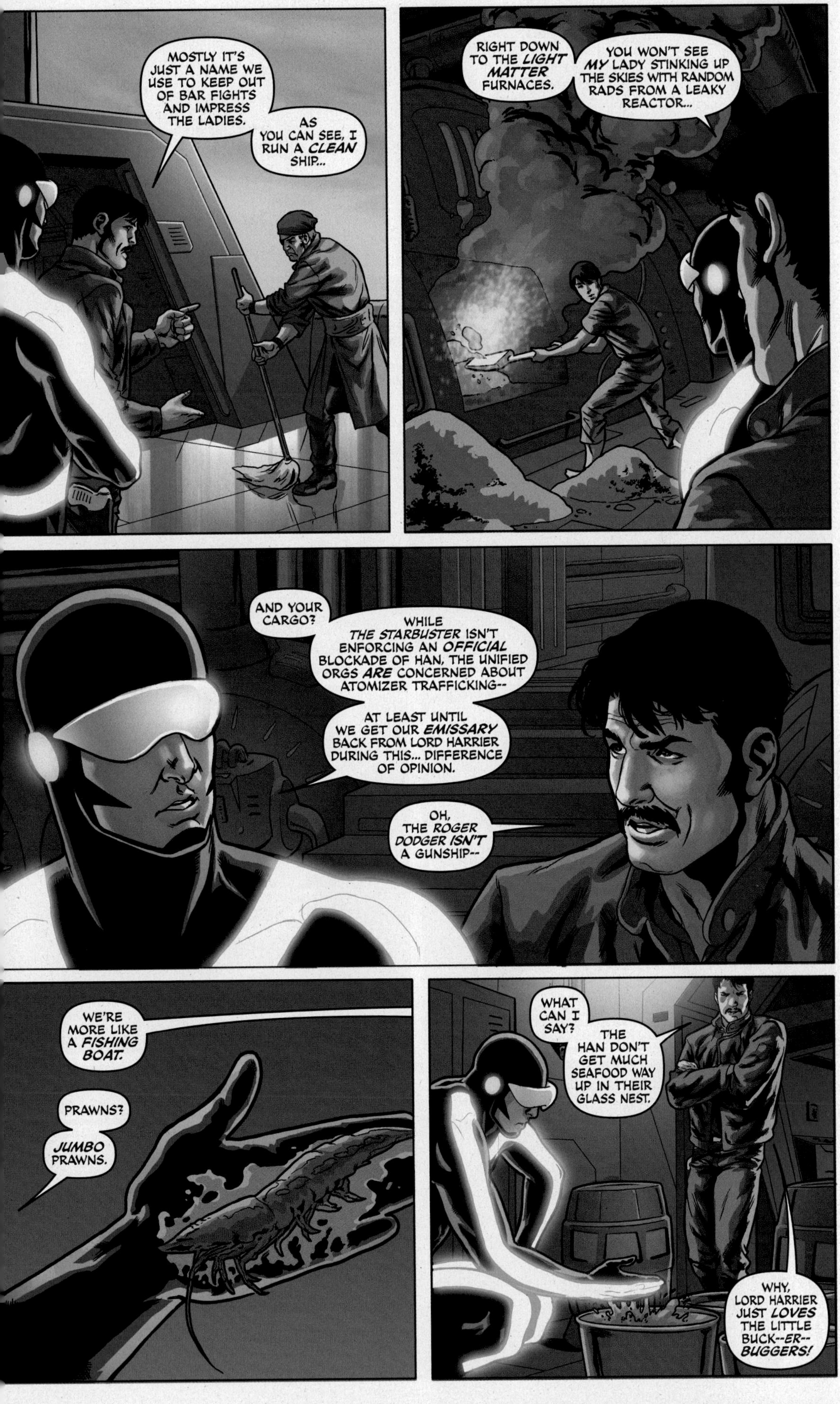
MOSTLY IT'S JUST A NAME WE USE TO KEEP OUT OF BAR FIGHTS AND IMPRESS THE LADIES.
AS YOU CAN SEE, I RUN A *CLEAN* SHIP...
RIGHT DOWN TO THE *LIGHT MATTER* FURNACES.
YOU WON'T SEE *MY* LADY STINKING UP THE SKIES WITH RANDOM RADS FROM A LEAKY REACTOR...
AND YOUR CARGO?
WHILE *THE STARBUSTER* ISN'T ENFORCING AN *OFFICIAL* BLOCKADE OF HAN, THE UNIFIED ORGS *ARE* CONCERNED ABOUT ATOMIZER TRAFFICKING--
AT LEAST UNTIL WE GET OUR *EMISSARY* BACK FROM LORD HARRIER DURING THIS... DIFFERENCE OF OPINION.
OH, THE *ROGER DODGER ISN'T* A GUNSHIP--
WE'RE MORE LIKE A *FISHING BOAT.*
PRAWNS?
JUMBO PRAWNS.
WHAT CAN I SAY?
THE HAN DON'T GET MUCH SEAFOOD WAY UP IN THEIR GLASS NEST.
WHY, LORD HARRIER JUST *LOVES* THE LITTLE BUCK--*ER*-- *BUGGERS!*

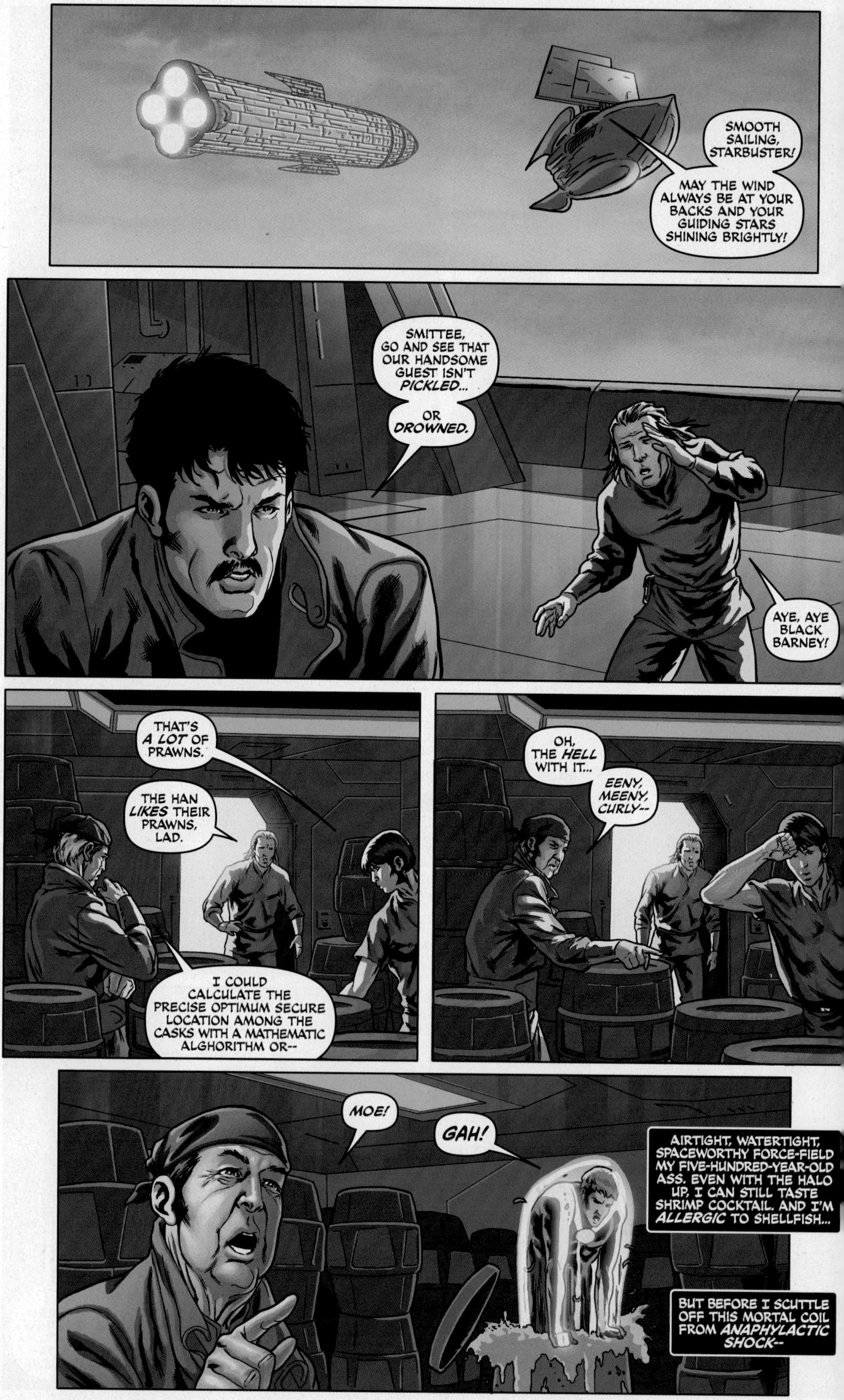
SMOOTH SAILING, STARBUSTER!
MAY THE WIND ALWAYS BE AT YOUR BACKS AND YOUR GUIDING STARS SHINING BRIGHTLY!
SMITTEE, GO AND SEE THAT OUR HANDSOME GUEST ISN'T PICKLED...
OR DROWNED.
AYE, AYE BLACK BARNEY!
THAT'S A LOT OF PRAWNS.
THE HAN LIKES THEIR PRAWNS, LAD.
I COULD CALCULATE THE PRECISE OPTIMUM SECURE LOCATION AMONG THE CASKS WITH A MATHEMATIC ALGHORITHM OR--
OH, THE HELL WITH IT...
EENY, MEENY, CURLY--
MOE!
GAH!
AIRTIGHT, WATERTIGHT, SPACEWORTHY FORCE-FIELD MY FIVE-HUNDRED-YEAR-OLD ASS. EVEN WITH THE HALO UP, I CAN STILL TASTE SHRIMP COCKTAIL. AND I'M ALLERGIC TO SHELLFISH...
BUT BEFORE I SCUTTLE OFF THIS MORTAL COIL FROM ANAPHYLACTIC SHOCK--

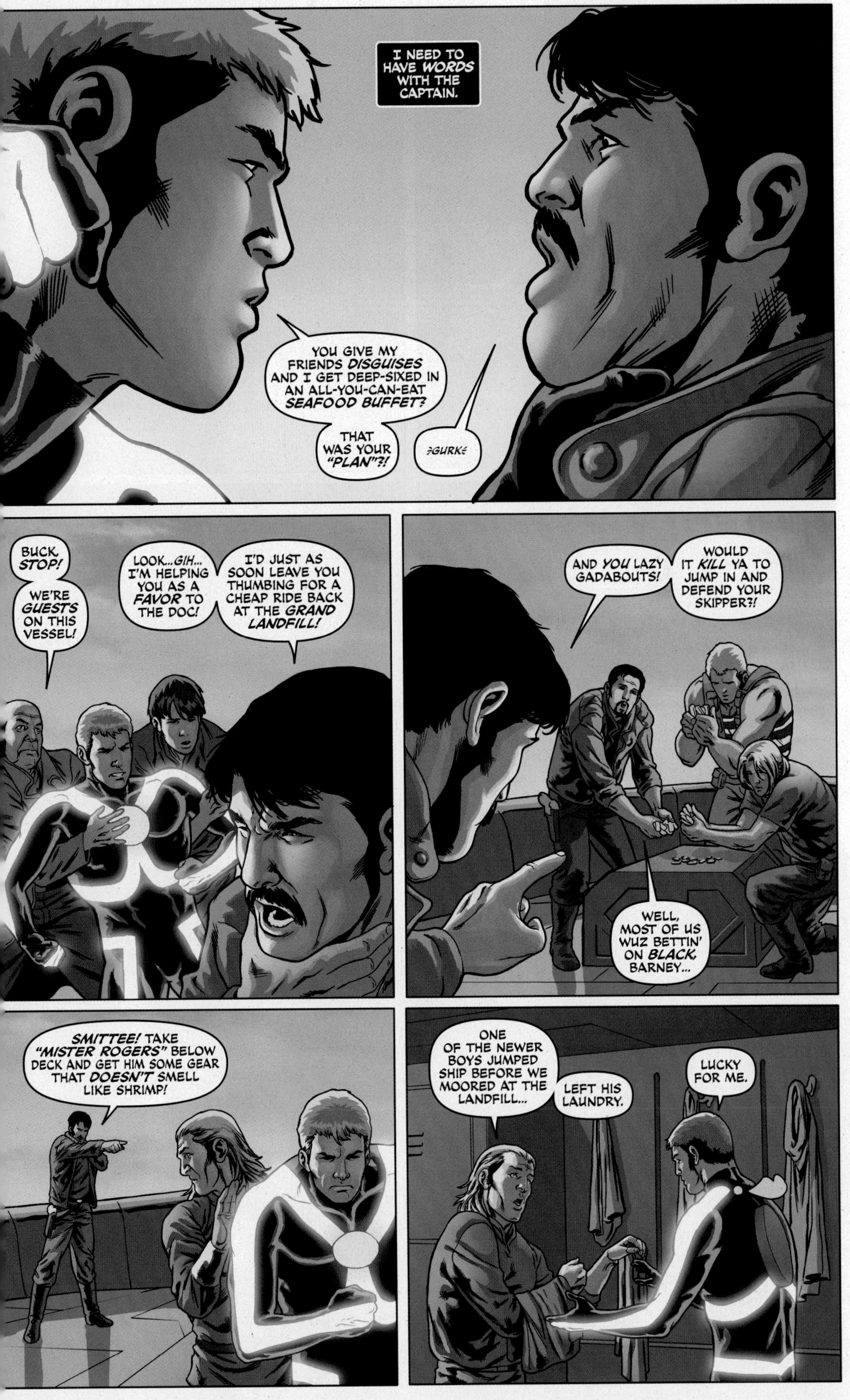
I NEED TO HAVE WORDS WITH THE CAPTAIN.
YOU GIVE MY FRIENDS DISGUISES AND I GET DEEP-SIXED IN AN ALL-YOU-CAN-EAT SEAFOOD BUFFET?
THAT WAS YOUR "PLAN"?!
GURK
BUCK, STOP!
WE'RE GUESTS ON THIS VESSEL!
LOOK...GIH... I'M HELPING YOU AS A FAVOR TO THE DOC!
I'D JUST AS SOON LEAVE YOU THUMBING FOR A CHEAP RIDE BACK AT THE GRAND LANDFILL!
AND YOU LAZY GADABOUTS!
WOULD IT KILL YA TO JUMP IN AND DEFEND YOUR SKIPPER?!
WELL, MOST OF US WUZ BETTIN' ON BLACK, BARNEY...
SMITTEE! TAKE "MISTER ROGERS" BELOW DECK AND GET HIM SOME GEAR THAT DOESN'T SMELL LIKE SHRIMP!
ONE OF THE NEWER BOYS JUMPED SHIP BEFORE WE MOORED AT THE LANDFILL...
LEFT HIS LAUNDRY.
LUCKY FOR ME.

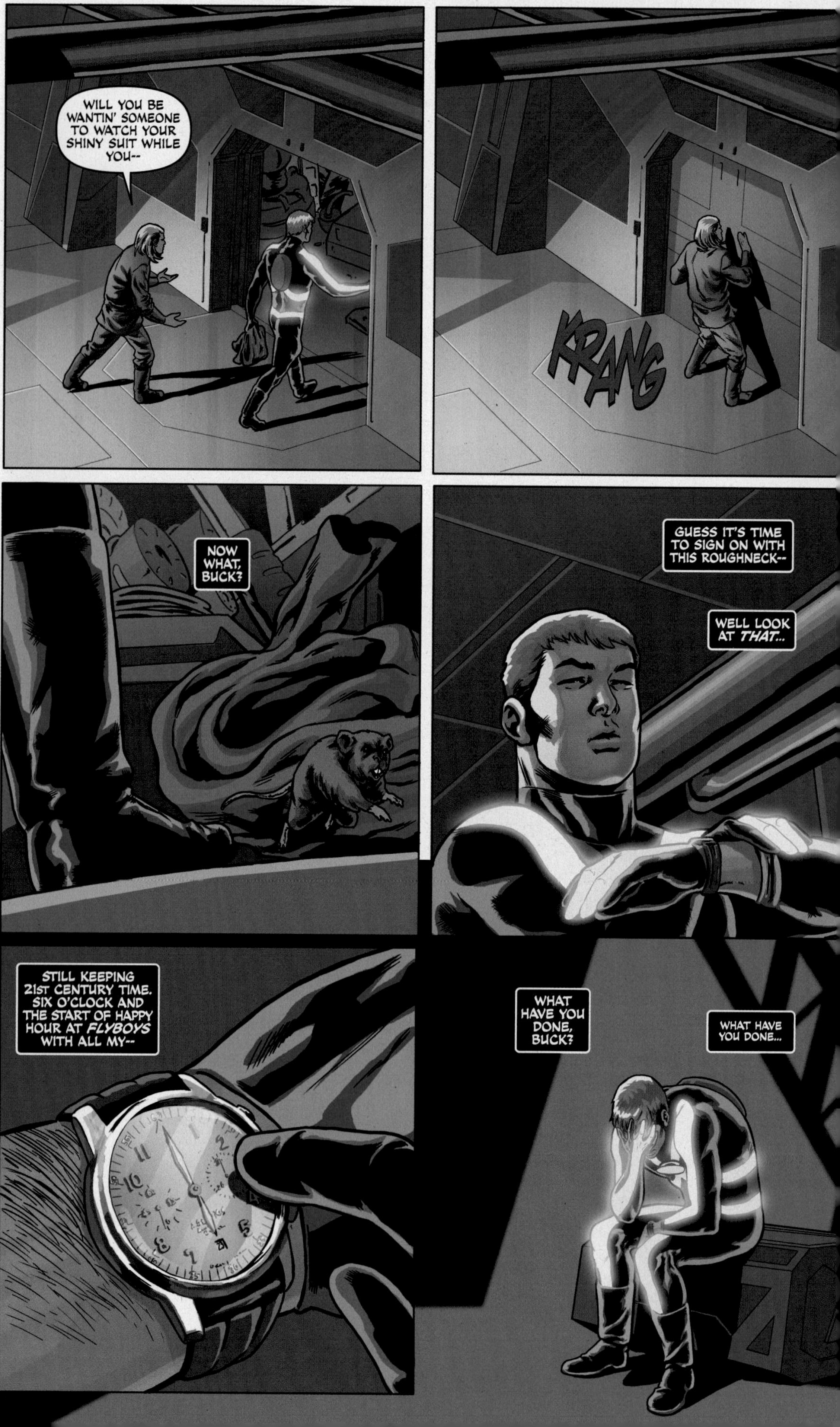
WILL YOU BE WANTIN' SOMEONE TO WATCH YOUR SHINY SUIT WHILE YOU--
KRANG
NOW WHAT, BUCK?
GUESS IT'S TIME TO SIGN ON WITH THIS ROUGHNECK--
WELL LOOK AT *THAT*...
STILL KEEPING 21ST CENTURY TIME. SIX O'CLOCK AND THE START OF HAPPY HOUR AT *FLYBOYS* WITH ALL MY--
WHAT HAVE YOU DONE, BUCK?
WHAT HAVE YOU DONE...

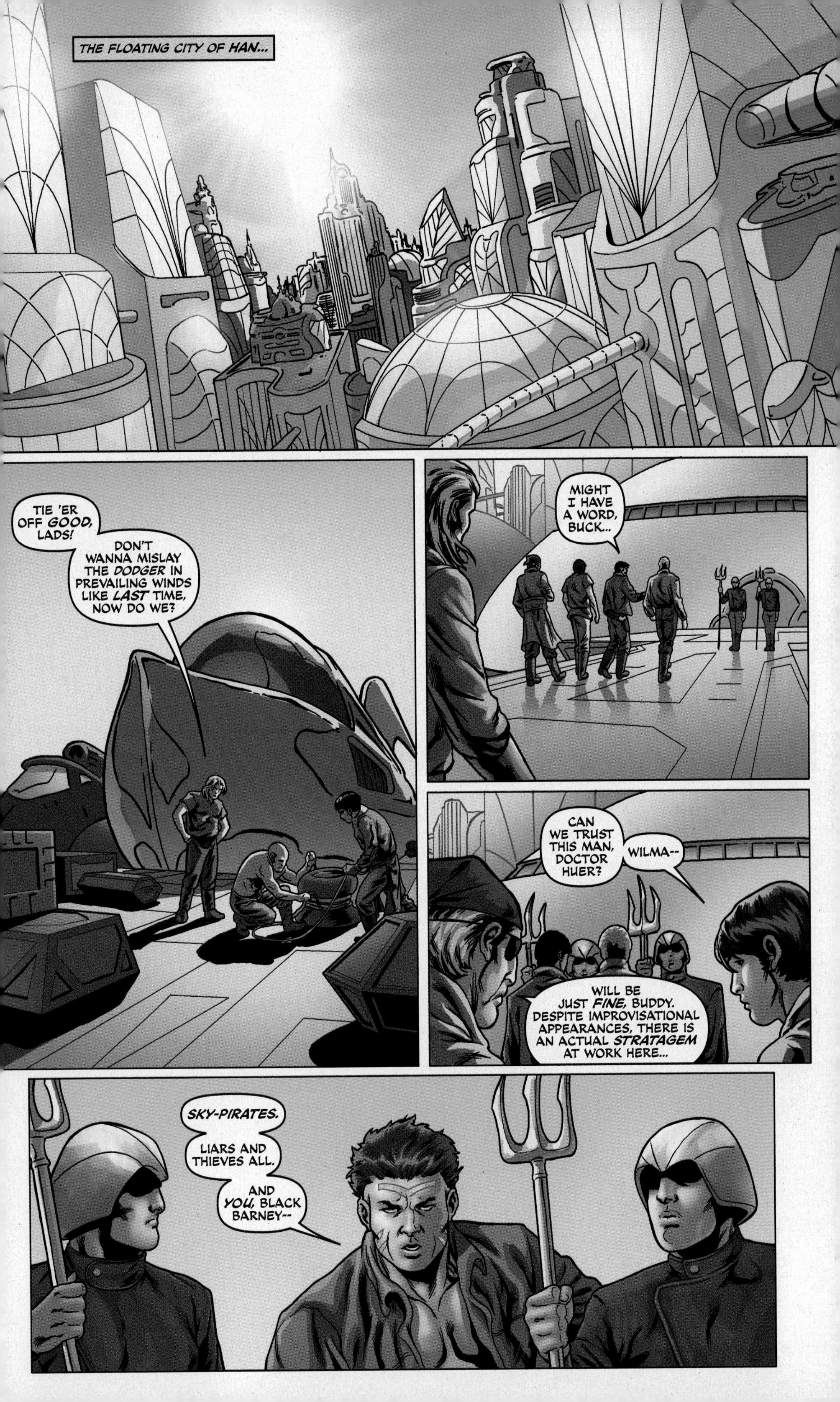
THE FLOATING CITY OF HAN...
TIE 'ER OFF GOOD, LADS!
DON'T WANNA MISLAY THE DODGER IN PREVAILING WINDS LIKE LAST TIME, NOW DO WE?
MIGHT I HAVE A WORD, BUCK...
CAN WE TRUST THIS MAN, DOCTOR HUER?
WILMA--
WILL BE JUST FINE, BUDDY. DESPITE IMPROVISATIONAL APPEARANCES, THERE IS AN ACTUAL STRATAGEM AT WORK HERE...
SKY-PIRATES.
LIARS AND THIEVES ALL.
AND YOU, BLACK BARNEY--

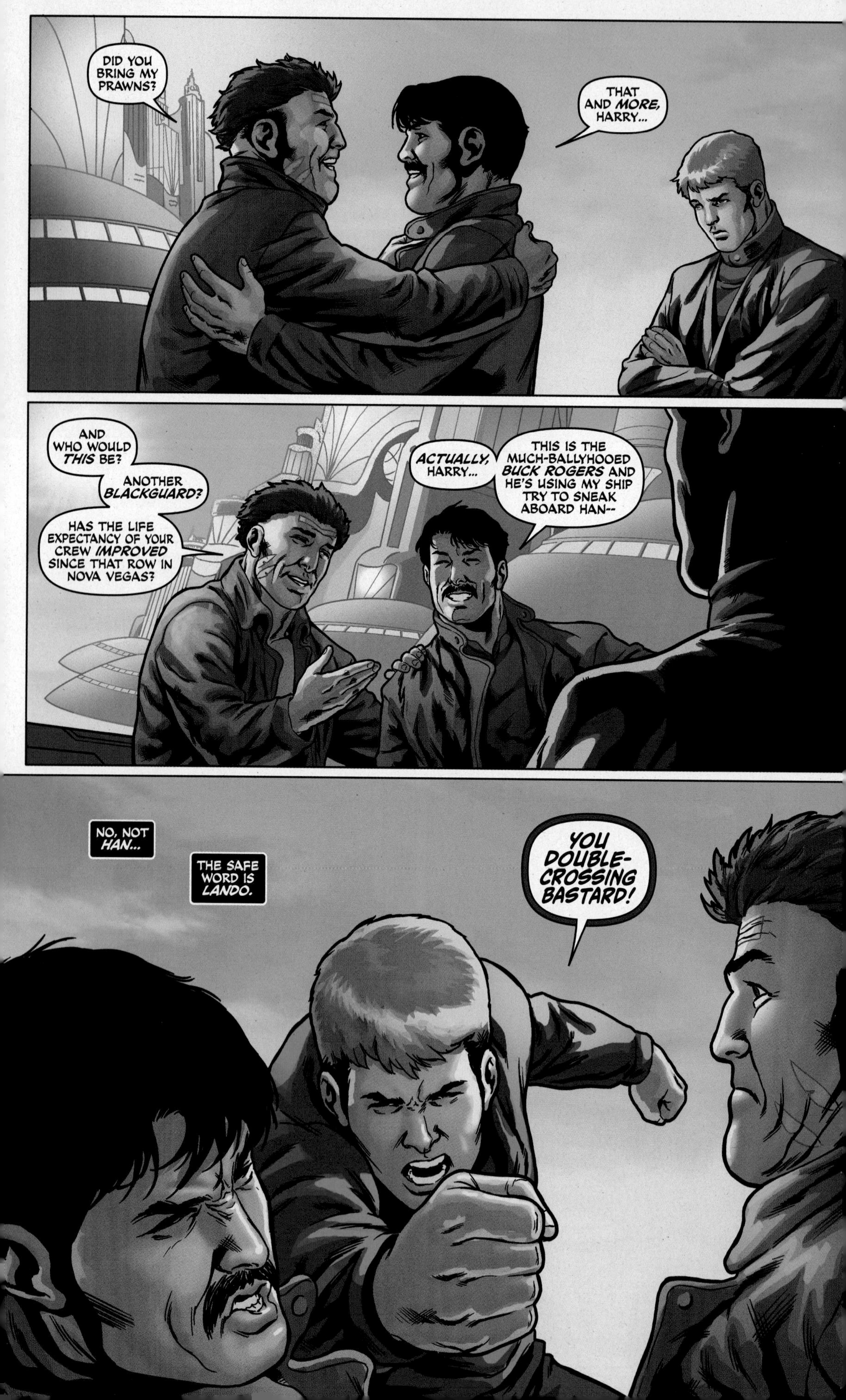
DID YOU BRING MY PRAWNS?
THAT AND *MORE,* HARRY...
AND WHO WOULD *THIS* BE?
ANOTHER *BLACKGUARD?*
HAS THE LIFE EXPECTANCY OF YOUR CREW *IMPROVED* SINCE THAT ROW IN NOVA VEGAS?
ACTUALLY, HARRY...
THIS IS THE MUCH-BALLYHOOED *BUCK ROGERS* AND HE'S USING MY SHIP TRY TO SNEAK ABOARD HAN--
NO, NOT *HAN...*
THE SAFE WORD IS *LANDO.*
YOU DOUBLE-CROSSING BASTARD!

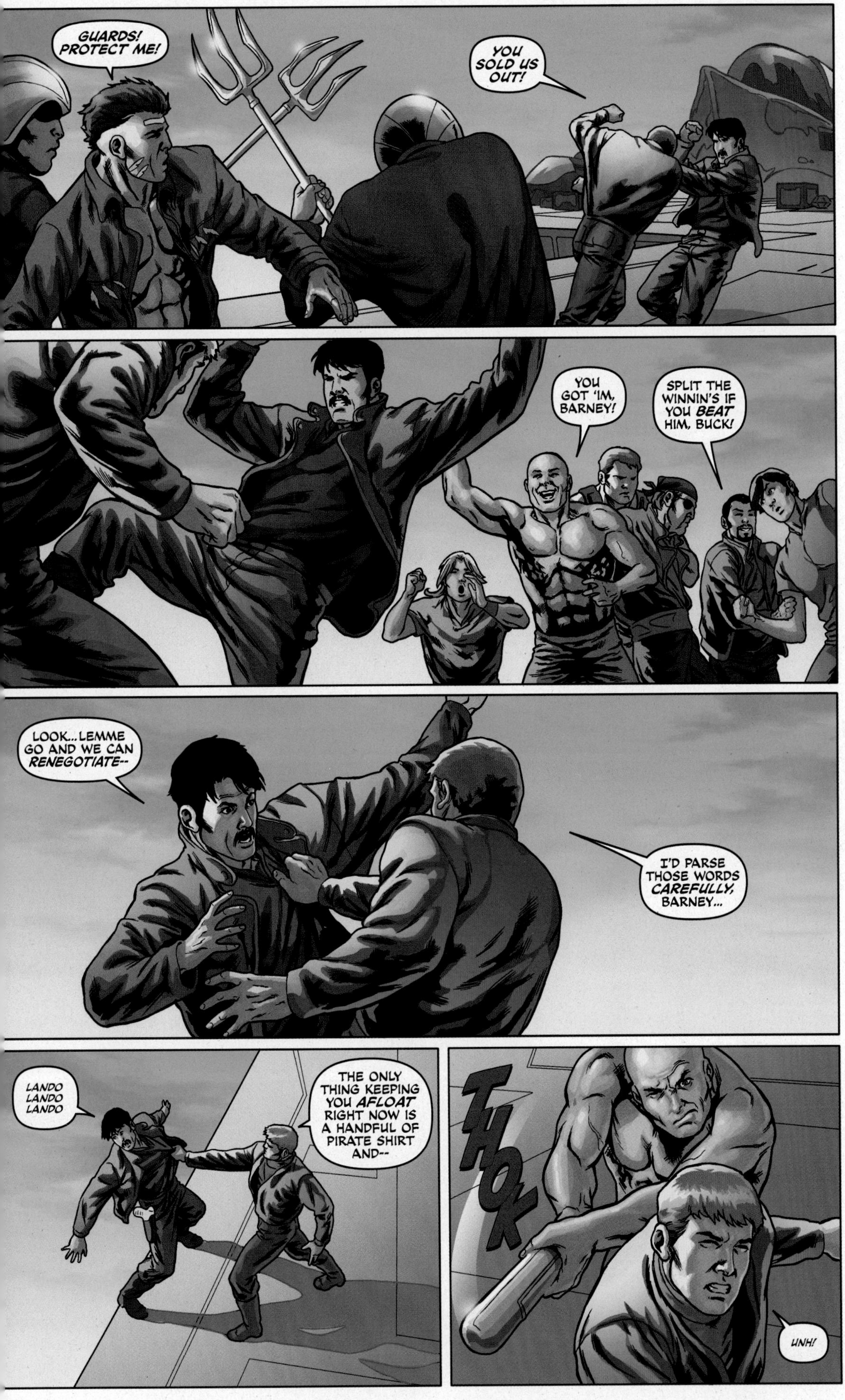
GUARDS! PROTECT ME!
YOU SOLD US OUT!
YOU GOT 'IM, BARNEY!
SPLIT THE WINNIN'S IF YOU BEAT HIM, BUCK!
LOOK... LEMME GO AND WE CAN RENEGOTIATE--
I'D PARSE THOSE WORDS CAREFULLY, BARNEY...
LANDO LANDO LANDO
THE ONLY THING KEEPING YOU AFLOAT RIGHT NOW IS A HANDFUL OF PIRATE SHIRT AND--
THOK
UNH!

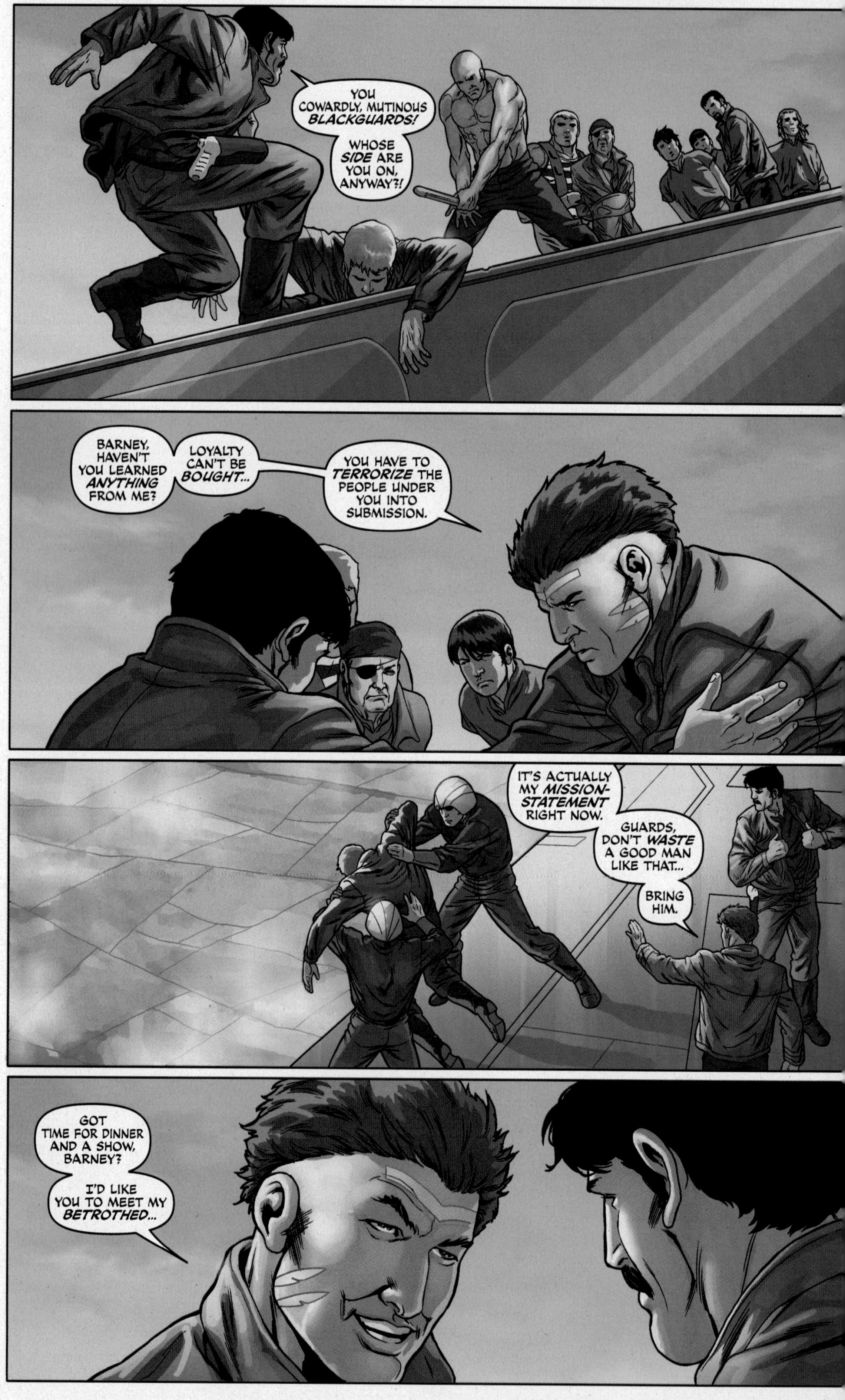
YOU COWARDLY, MUTINOUS *BLACKGUARDS!*
WHOSE *SIDE* ARE YOU ON, ANYWAY?!
BARNEY, HAVEN'T YOU LEARNED *ANYTHING* FROM ME?
LOYALTY CAN'T BE *BOUGHT*...
YOU HAVE TO *TERRORIZE* THE PEOPLE UNDER YOU INTO SUBMISSION.
IT'S ACTUALLY MY *MISSION-STATEMENT* RIGHT NOW.
GUARDS, DON'T *WASTE* A GOOD MAN LIKE THAT...
BRING HIM.
GOT TIME FOR DINNER AND A SHOW, BARNEY?
I'D LIKE YOU TO MEET MY *BETROTHED*...

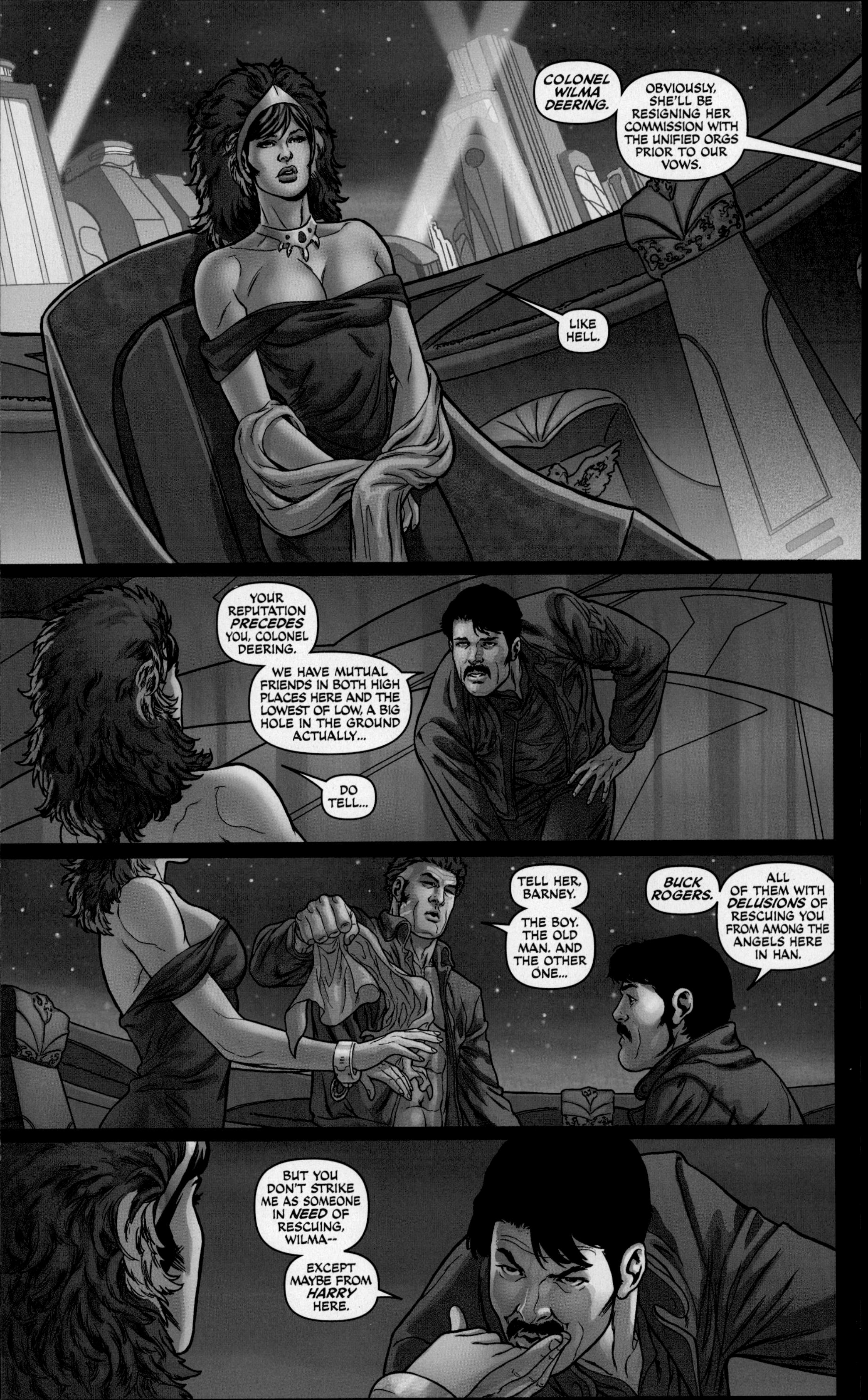
COLONEL WILMA DEERING.
OBVIOUSLY, SHE'LL BE RESIGNING HER COMMISSION WITH THE UNIFIED ORGS PRIOR TO OUR VOWS.
LIKE HELL.
YOUR REPUTATION PRECEDES YOU, COLONEL DEERING.
WE HAVE MUTUAL FRIENDS IN BOTH HIGH PLACES HERE AND THE LOWEST OF LOW, A BIG HOLE IN THE GROUND ACTUALLY...
DO TELL...
TELL HER, BARNEY.
THE BOY. THE OLD MAN. AND THE OTHER ONE...
BUCK ROGERS.
ALL OF THEM WITH DELUSIONS OF RESCUING YOU FROM AMONG THE ANGELS HERE IN HAN.
BUT YOU DON'T STRIKE ME AS SOMEONE IN NEED OF RESCUING, WILMA--
EXCEPT MAYBE FROM HARRY HERE.

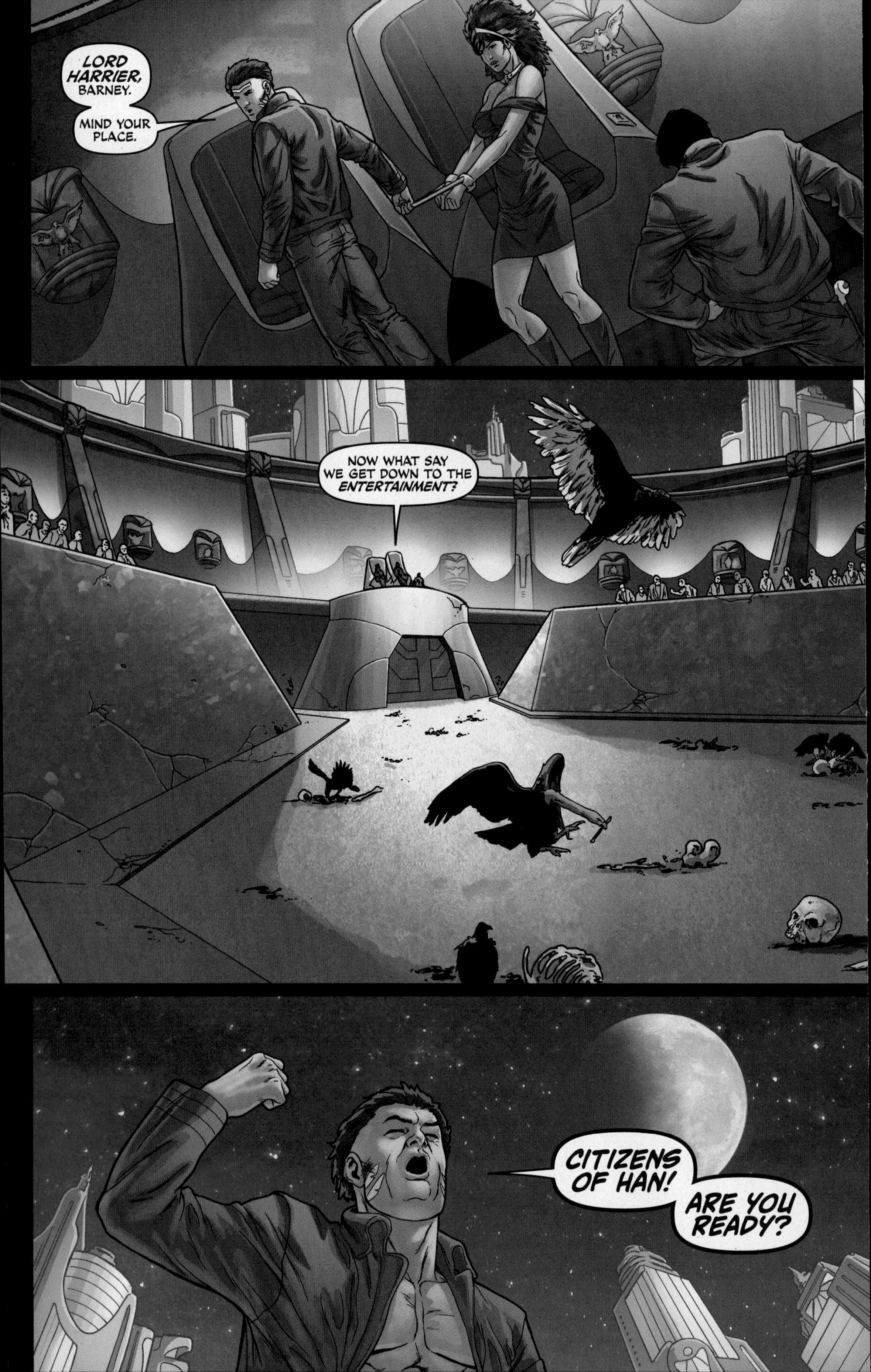
LORD HARRIER, BARNEY.
MIND YOUR PLACE.
NOW WHAT SAY WE GET DOWN TO THE ENTERTAINMENT?
CITIZENS OF HAN!
ARE YOU READY?

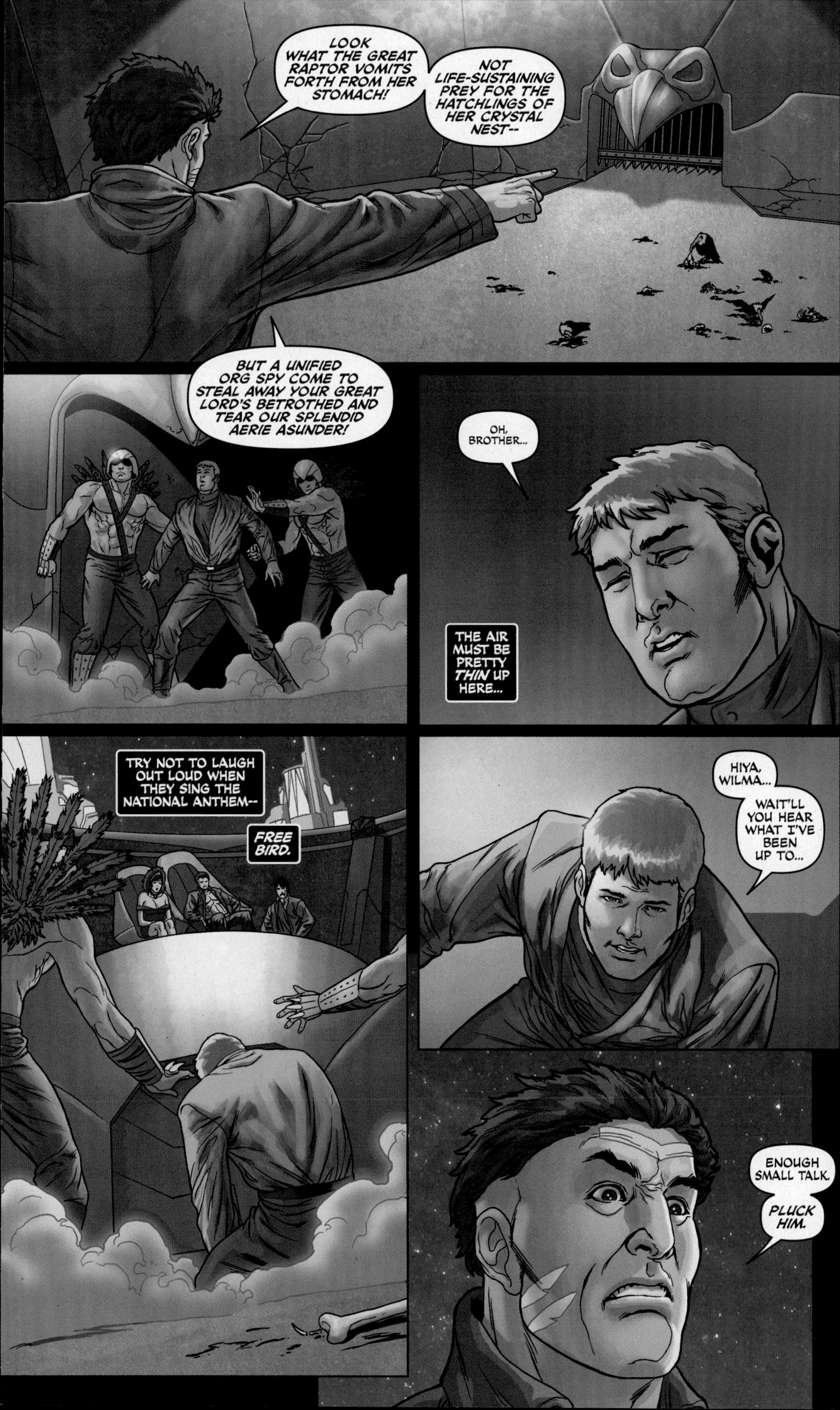
LOOK WHAT THE GREAT RAPTOR VOMITS FORTH FROM HER STOMACH!
NOT LIFE-SUSTAINING PREY FOR THE HATCHLINGS OF HER CRYSTAL NEST--
BUT A UNIFIED ORG SPY COME TO STEAL AWAY YOUR GREAT LORD'S BETROTHED AND TEAR OUR SPLENDID AERIE ASUNDER!
OH, BROTHER...
THE AIR MUST BE PRETTY THIN UP HERE...
TRY NOT TO LAUGH OUT LOUD WHEN THEY SING THE NATIONAL ANTHEM--
FREE BIRD.
HIYA, WILMA...
WAIT'LL YOU HEAR WHAT I'VE BEEN UP TO...
ENOUGH SMALL TALK.
PLUCK HIM.

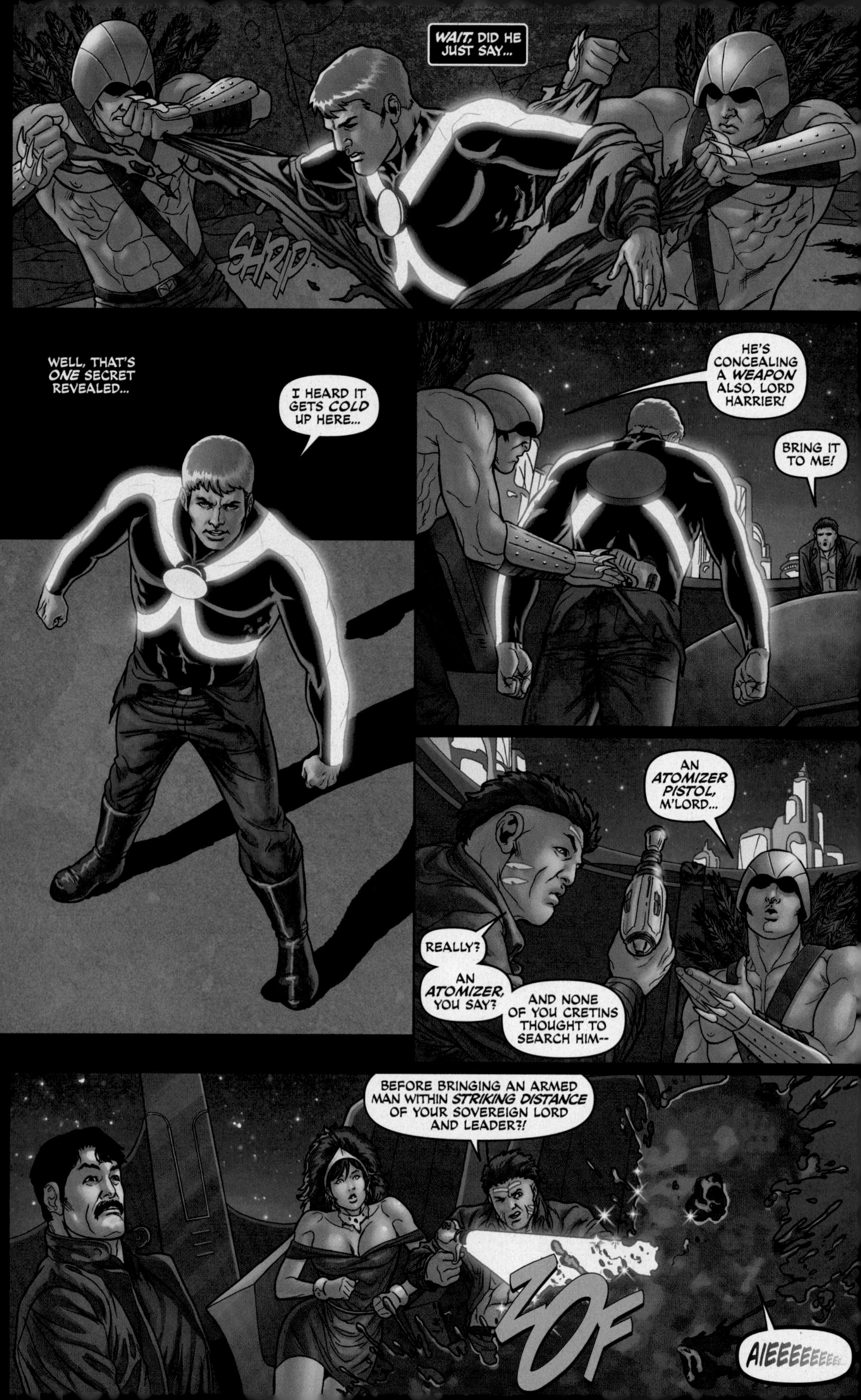
WAIT, DID HE JUST SAY...
SHRIP
WELL, THAT'S ONE SECRET REVEALED...
I HEARD IT GETS COLD UP HERE...
HE'S CONCEALING A WEAPON ALSO, LORD HARRIER!
BRING IT TO ME!
AN ATOMIZER PISTOL, M'LORD...
REALLY?
AN ATOMIZER, YOU SAY?
AND NONE OF YOU CRETINS THOUGHT TO SEARCH HIM--
BEFORE BRINGING AN ARMED MAN WITHIN STRIKING DISTANCE OF YOUR SOVEREIGN LORD AND LEADER?!
ZOOF
AIEEEEEEEEE...

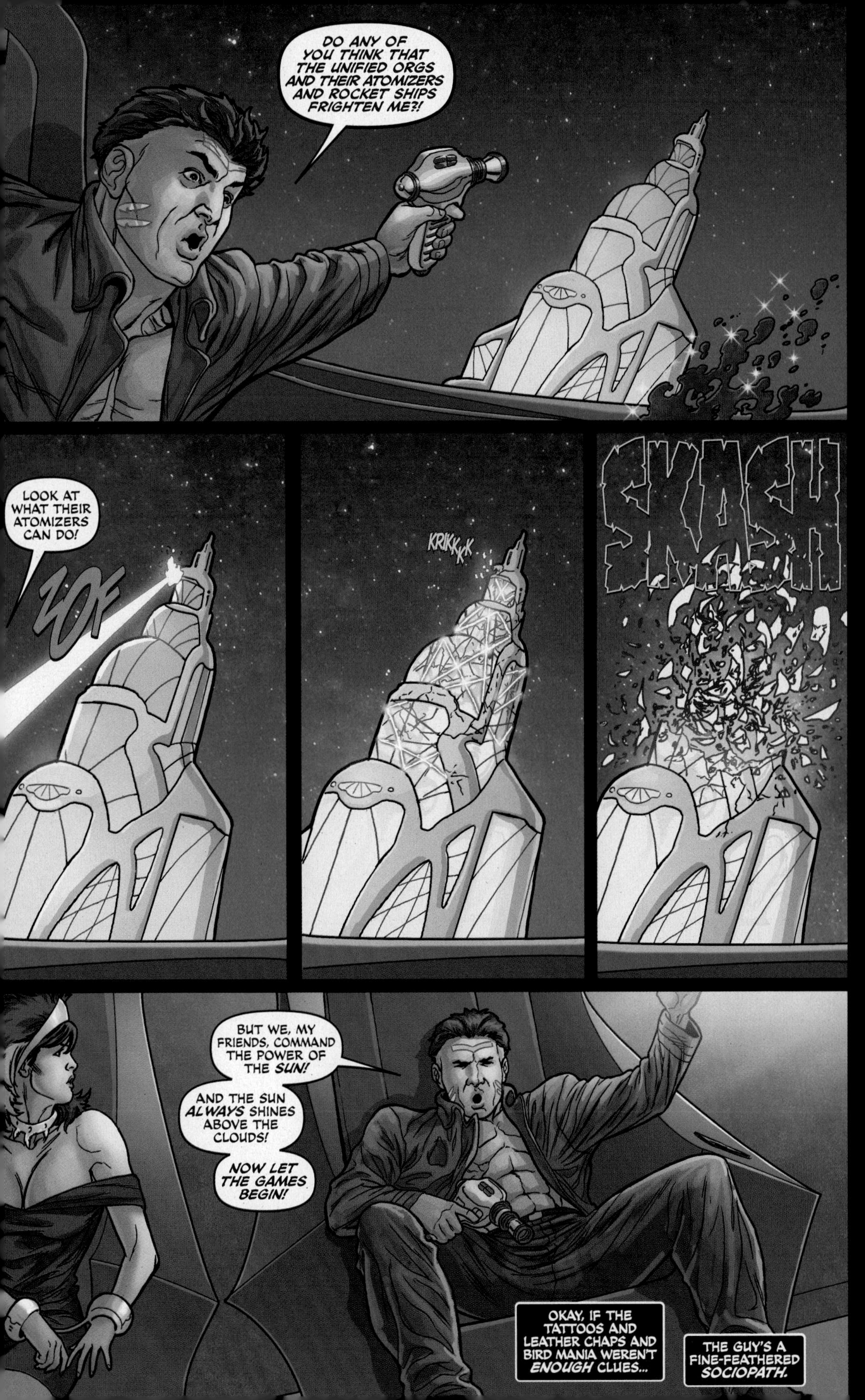

DO ANY OF YOU THINK THAT THE UNIFIED ORGS AND THEIR ATOMIZERS AND ROCKET SHIPS FRIGHTEN ME?!
LOOK AT WHAT THEIR ATOMIZERS CAN DO!
ZOF
KRIKKKK
SKASH
BUT WE, MY FRIENDS, COMMAND THE POWER OF THE *SUN!*
AND THE SUN *ALWAYS* SHINES ABOVE THE CLOUDS!
NOW LET THE GAMES BEGIN!
OKAY, IF THE TATTOOS AND LEATHER CHAPS AND BIRD MANIA WEREN'T *ENOUGH* CLUES...
THE GUY'S A FINE-FEATHERED *SOCIOPATH.*

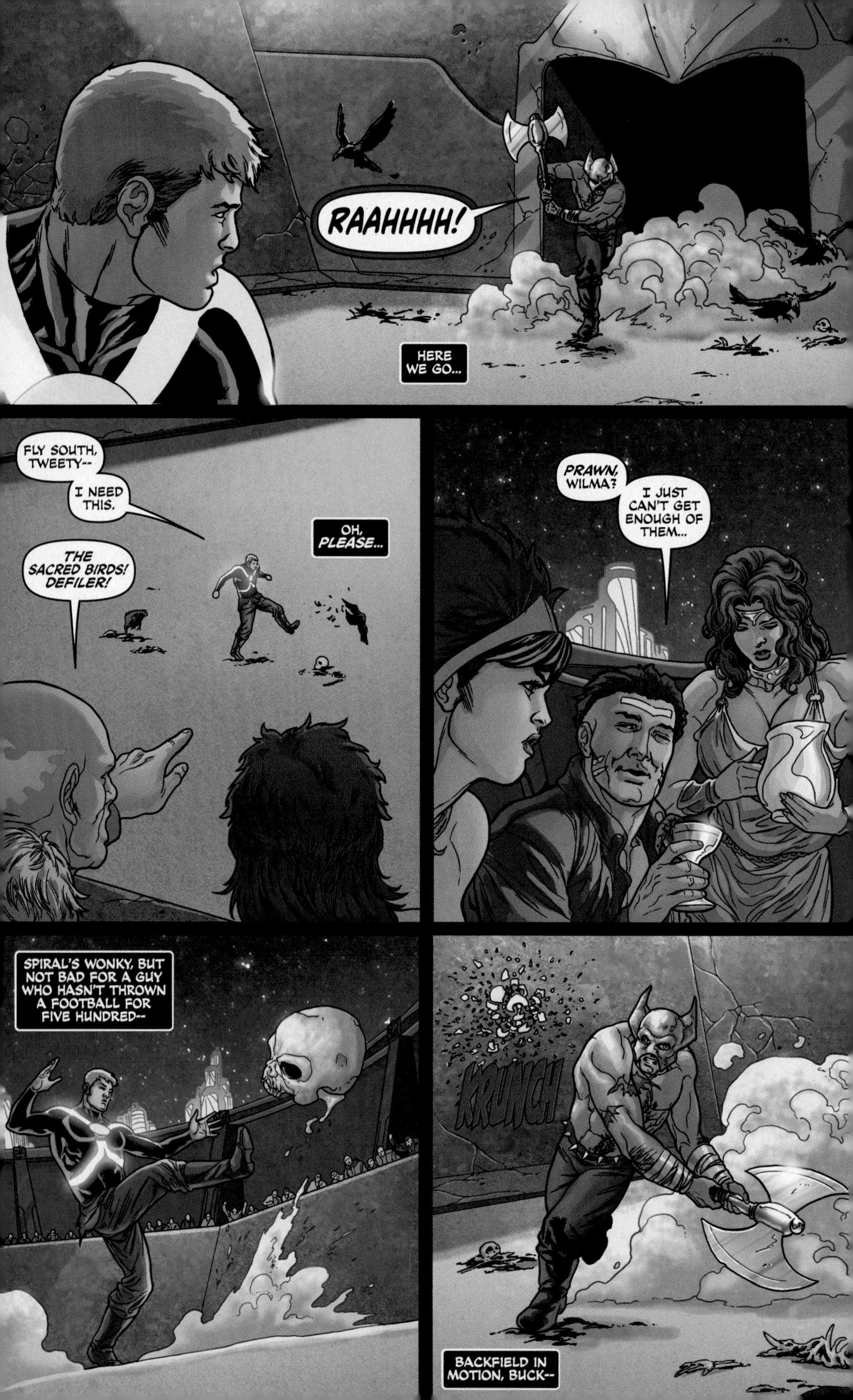
RAAHHHH!
HERE WE GO...
FLY SOUTH, TWEETY--
I NEED THIS.
OH, PLEASE...
THE SACRED BIRDS! DEFILER!
PRAWN, WILMA?
I JUST CAN'T GET ENOUGH OF THEM...
SPIRAL'S WONKY, BUT NOT BAD FOR A GUY WHO HASN'T THROWN A FOOTBALL FOR FIVE HUNDRED--
KRUNCH
BACKFIELD IN MOTION, BUCK--

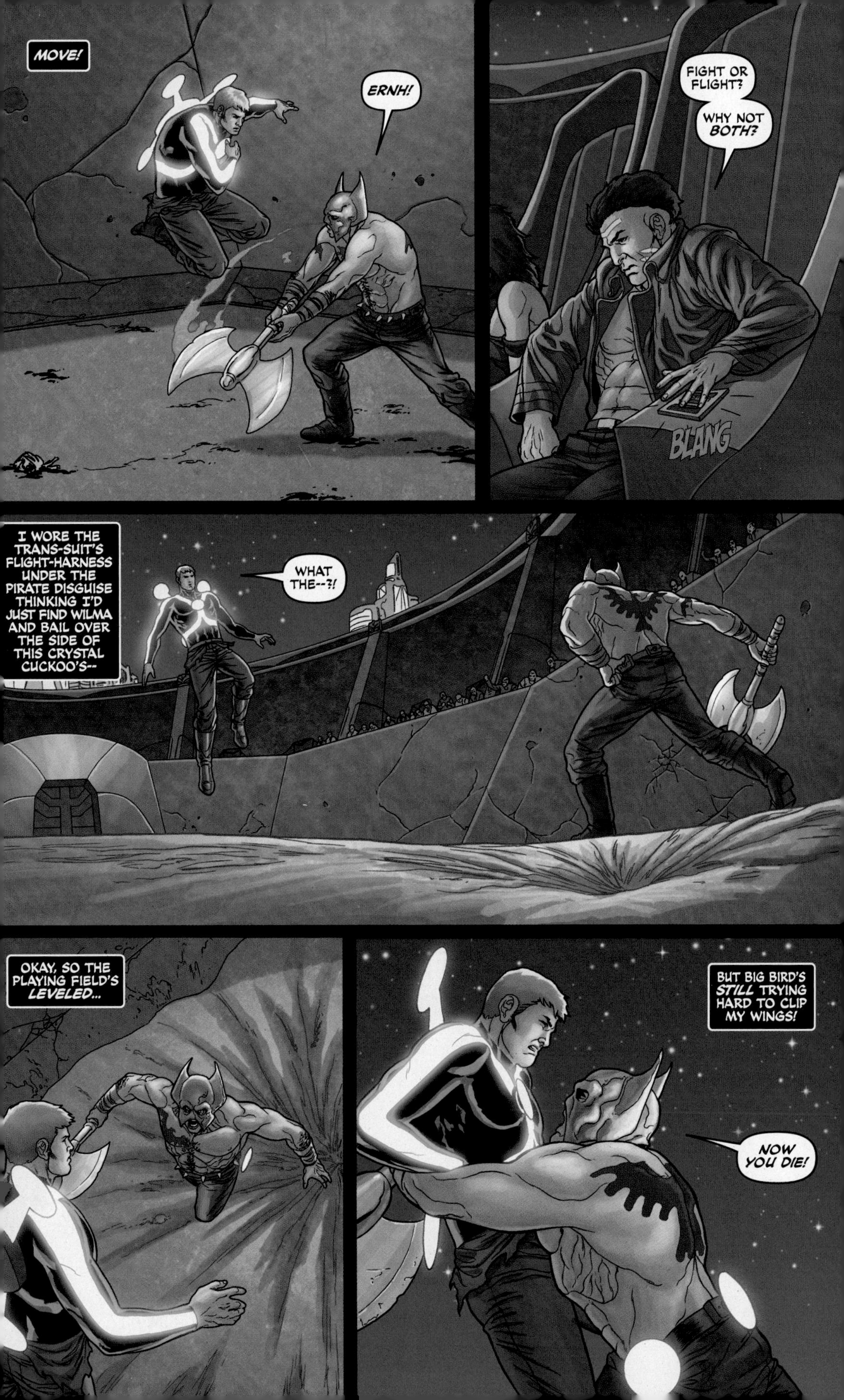

MOVE!
ERNH!
FIGHT OR FLIGHT?
WHY NOT BOTH?
BLANG
I WORE THE TRANS-SUIT'S FLIGHT-HARNESS UNDER THE PIRATE DISGUISE THINKING I'D JUST FIND WILMA AND BAIL OVER THE SIDE OF THIS CRYSTAL CUCKOO'S--
WHAT THE--?!
OKAY, SO THE PLAYING FIELD'S LEVELED...
BUT BIG BIRD'S STILL TRYING HARD TO CLIP MY WINGS!
NOW YOU DIE!

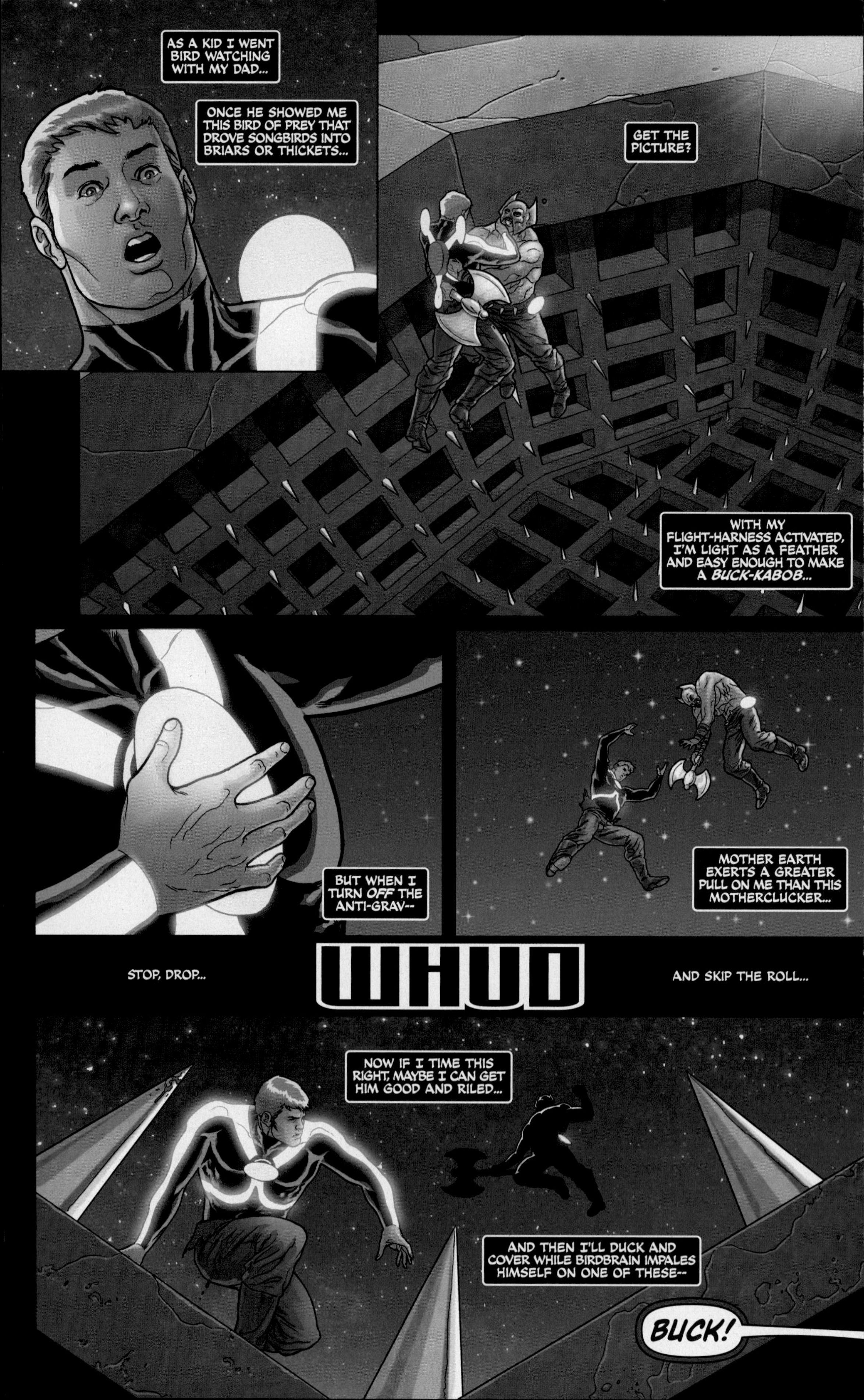
AS A KID I WENT BIRD WATCHING WITH MY DAD...
ONCE HE SHOWED ME THIS BIRD OF PREY THAT DROVE SONGBIRDS INTO BRIARS OR THICKETS...
GET THE PICTURE?
WITH MY FLIGHT-HARNESS ACTIVATED, I'M LIGHT AS A FEATHER AND EASY ENOUGH TO MAKE A *BUCK-KABOB*...
BUT WHEN I TURN *OFF* THE ANTI-GRAV--
MOTHER EARTH EXERTS A GREATER PULL ON ME THAN THIS MOTHERCLUCKER...
STOP, DROP...
WHUD
AND SKIP THE ROLL...
NOW IF I TIME THIS RIGHT, MAYBE I CAN GET HIM GOOD AND RILED...
AND THEN I'LL DUCK AND COVER WHILE BIRDBRAIN IMPALES HIMSELF ON ONE OF THESE--
BUCK!

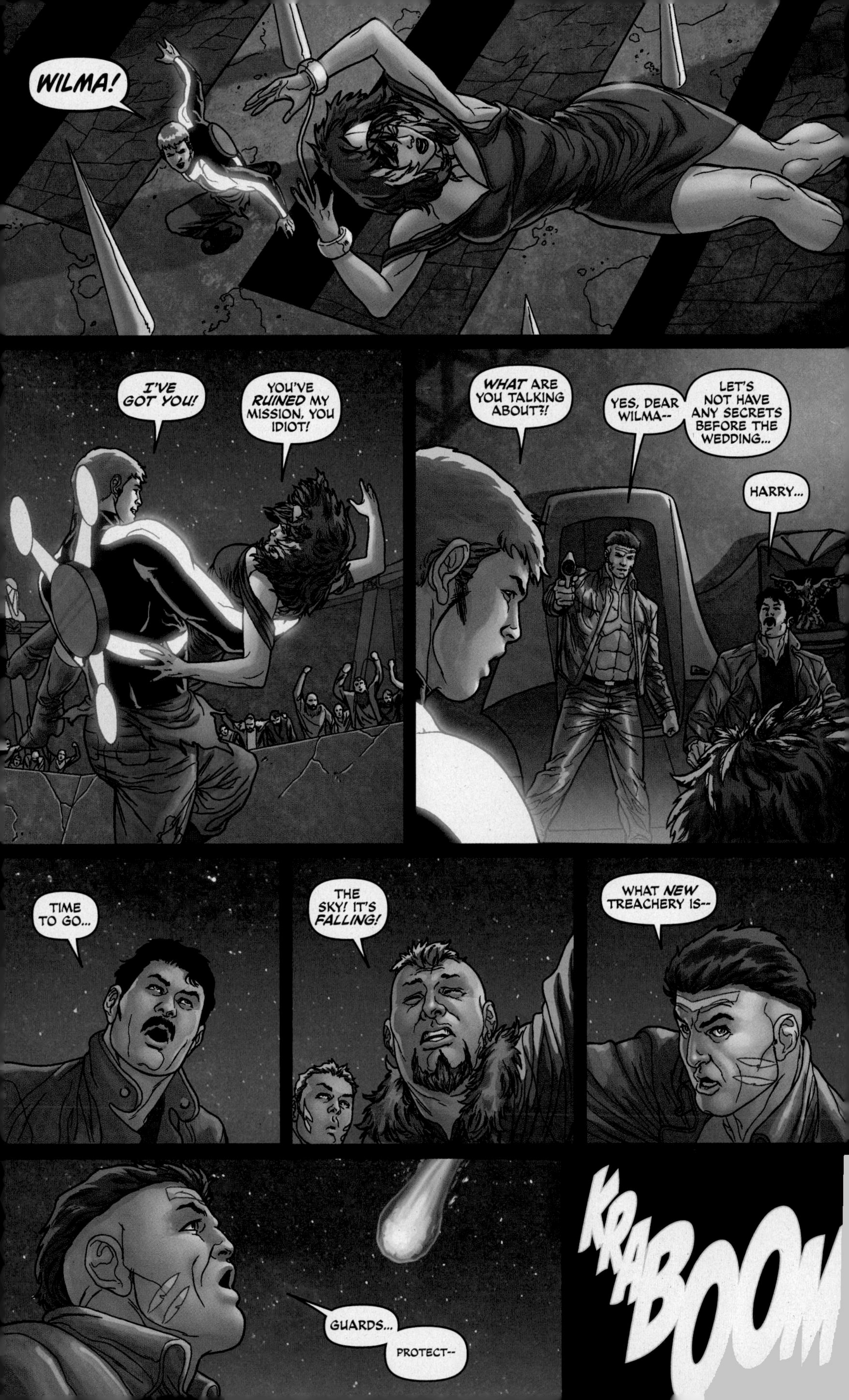
WILMA!
I'VE GOT YOU!
YOU'VE RUINED MY MISSION, YOU IDIOT!
WHAT ARE YOU TALKING ABOUT?!
YES, DEAR WILMA--
LET'S NOT HAVE ANY SECRETS BEFORE THE WEDDING...
HARRY...
TIME TO GO...
THE SKY! IT'S FALLING!
WHAT NEW TREACHERY IS--
GUARDS...
PROTECT--
KRABOOM

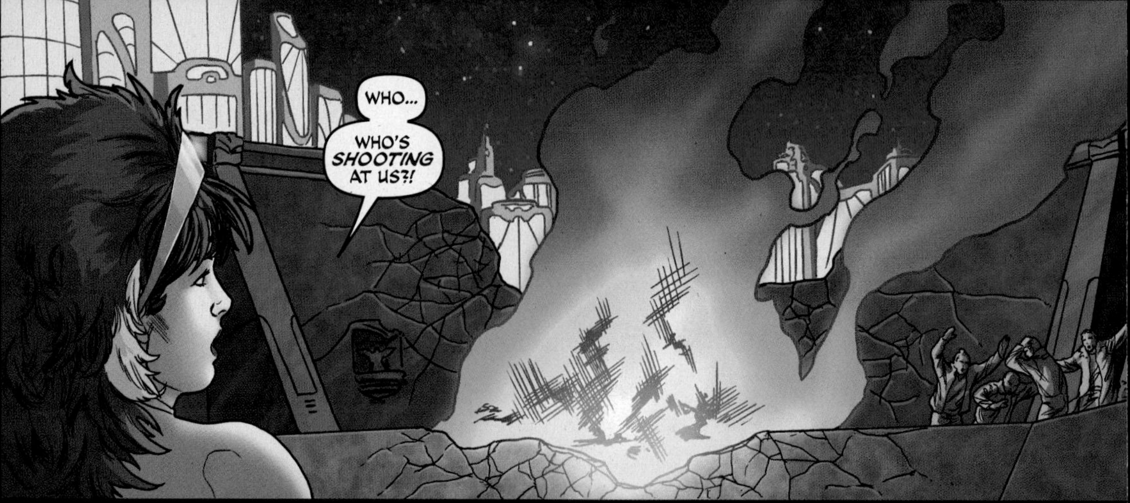
WHO...
WHO'S *SHOOTING* AT US?!

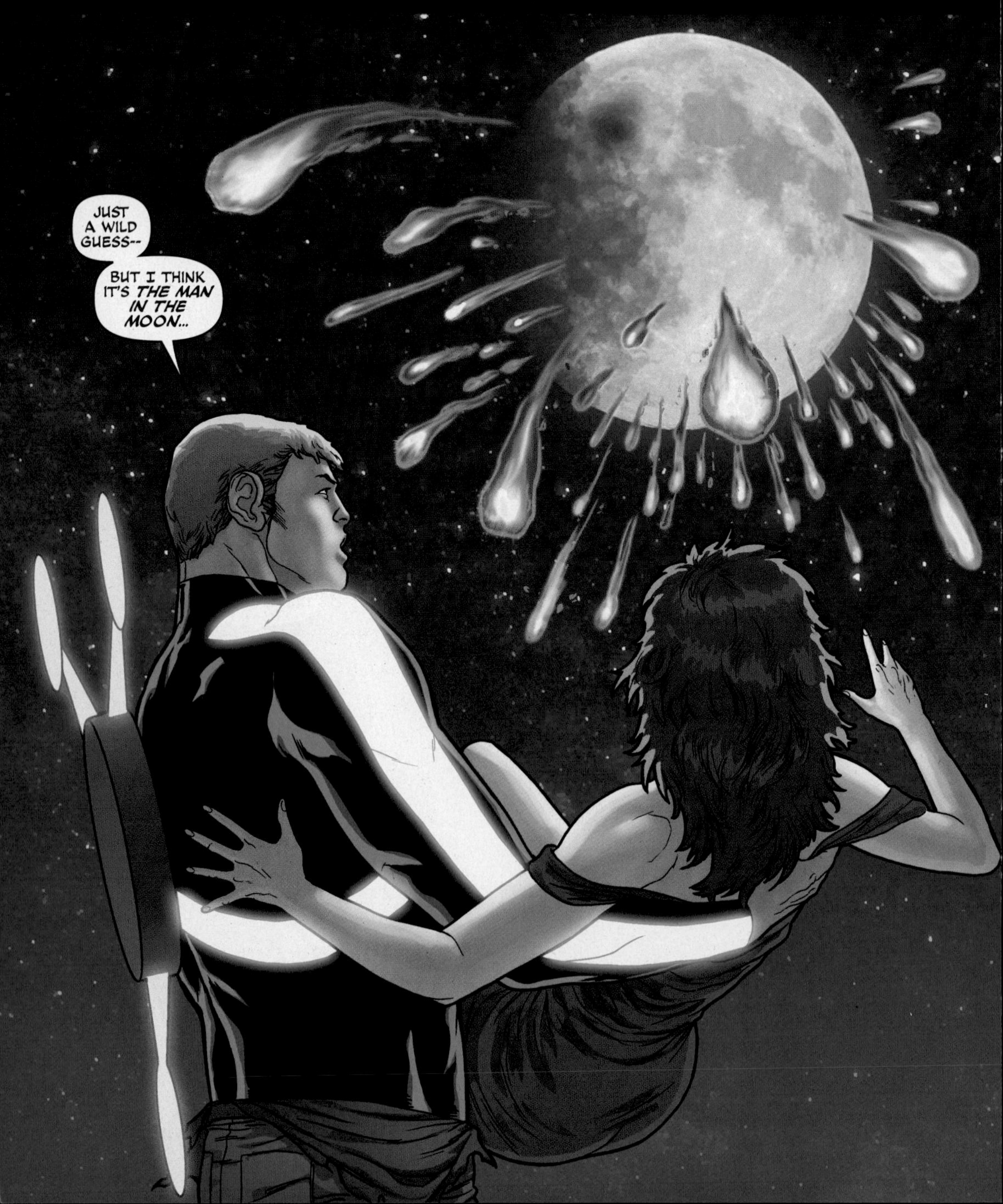
JUST A WILD GUESS--
BUT I THINK IT'S *THE MAN IN THE MOON*...

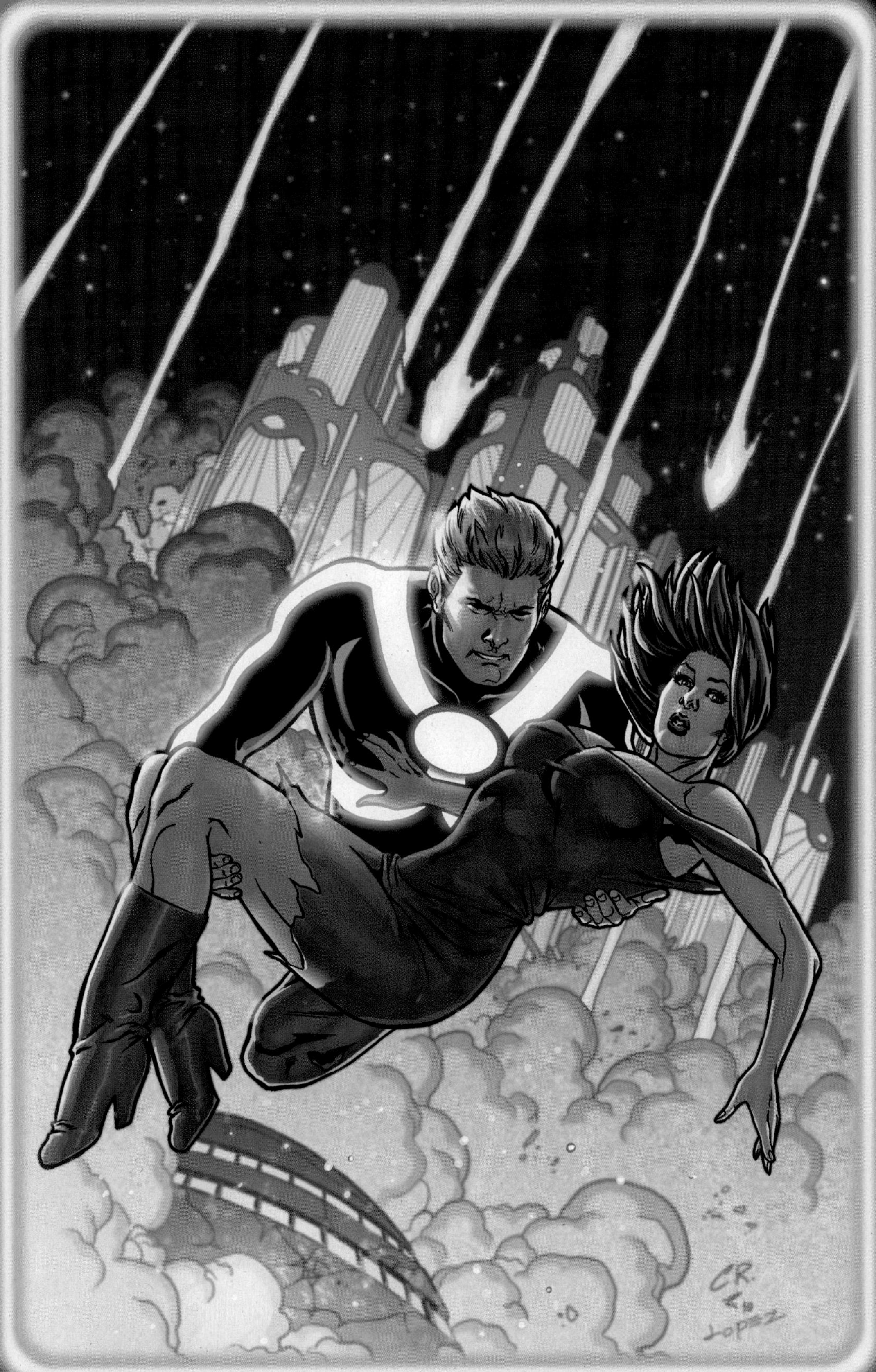

MOONSTRUCK PART ONE:
Tumbling Down

ISSUE ELEVEN COVER BY CARLOS RAFAEL

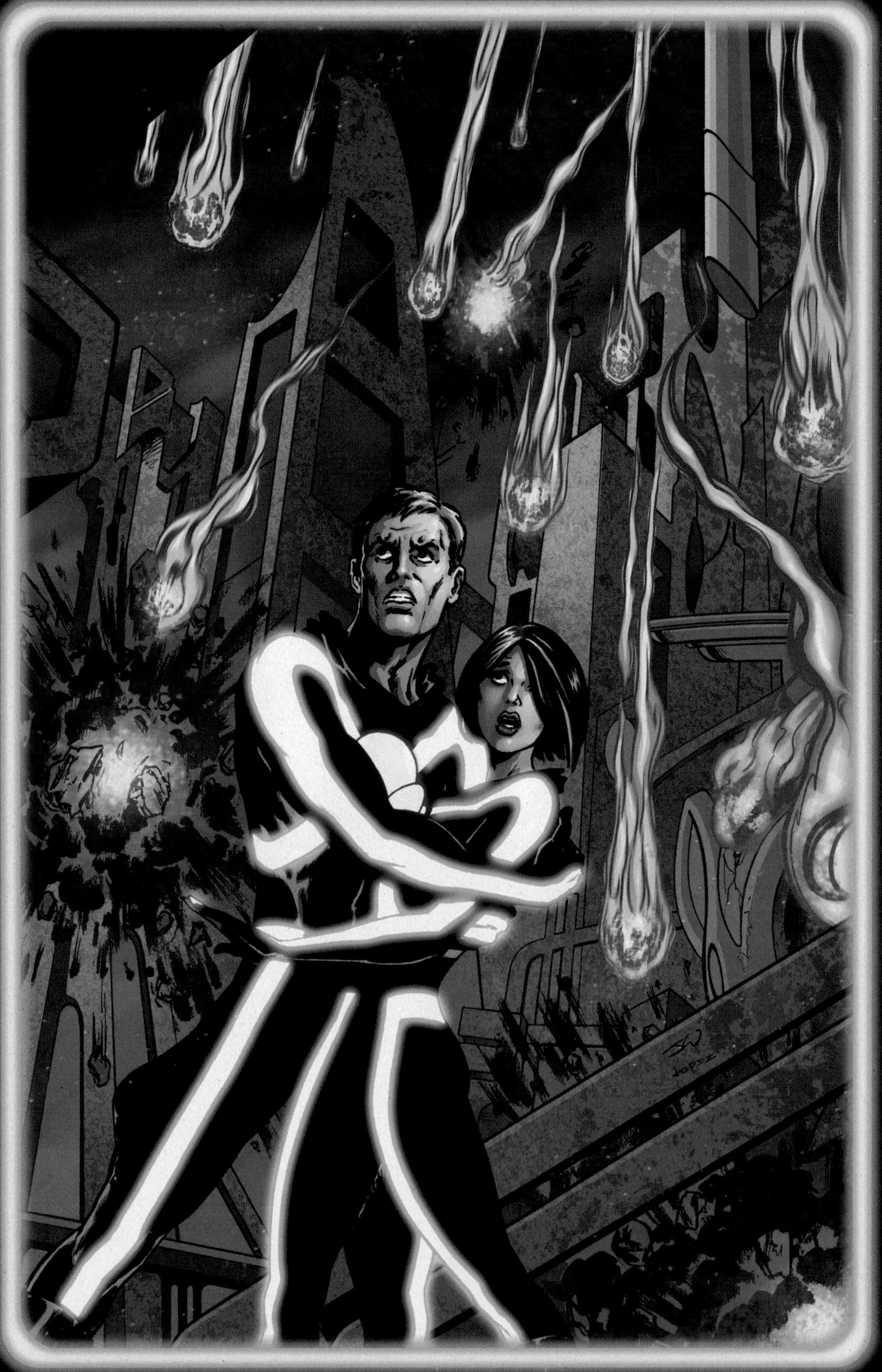

ALTERNATE COVER BY JOHN WATSON

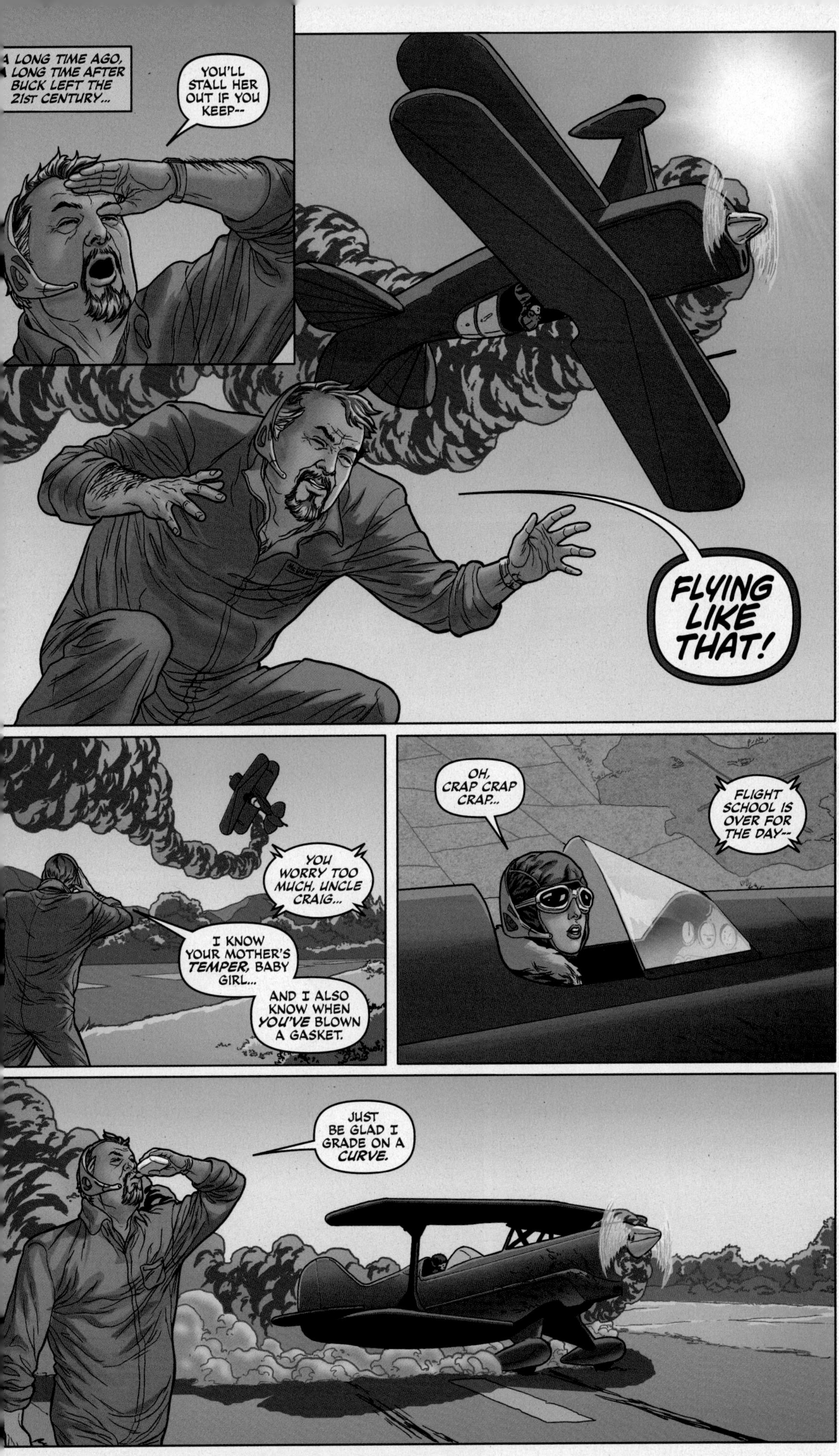
A LONG TIME AGO, A LONG TIME AFTER BUCK LEFT THE 21ST CENTURY...
YOU'LL STALL HER OUT IF YOU KEEP--
FLYING LIKE THAT!
YOU WORRY TOO MUCH, UNCLE CRAIG...
I KNOW YOUR MOTHER'S TEMPER, BABY GIRL...
AND I ALSO KNOW WHEN YOU'VE BLOWN A GASKET.
OH, CRAP CRAP CRAP...
FLIGHT SCHOOL IS OVER FOR THE DAY--
JUST BE GLAD I GRADE ON A CURVE.

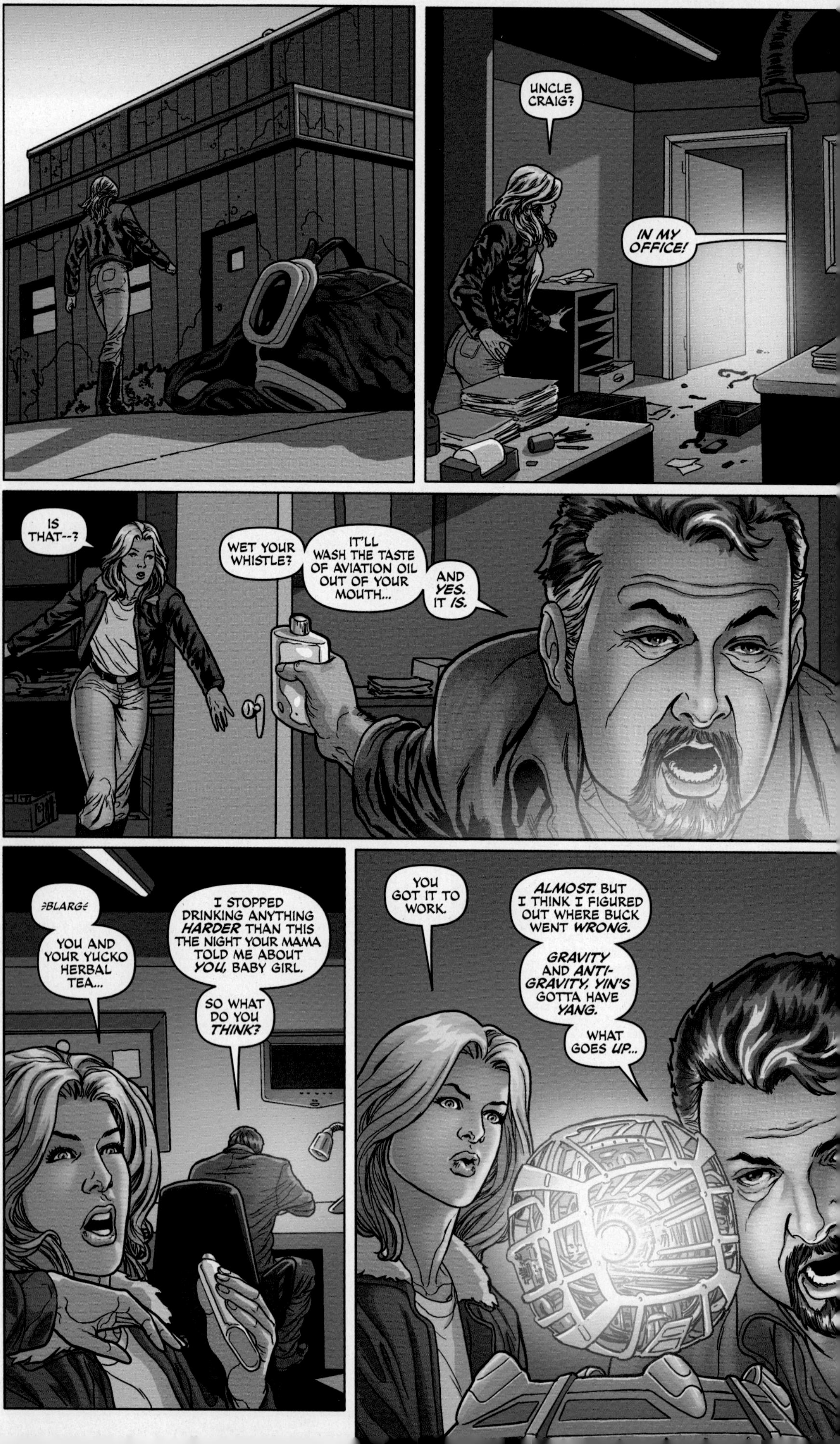
UNCLE CRAIG?
IN MY OFFICE!
IS THAT--?
WET YOUR WHISTLE?
IT'LL WASH THE TASTE OF AVIATION OIL OUT OF YOUR MOUTH...
AND YES. IT IS.
BLARG
YOU AND YOUR YUCKO HERBAL TEA...
I STOPPED DRINKING ANYTHING HARDER THAN THIS THE NIGHT YOUR MAMA TOLD ME ABOUT YOU, BABY GIRL.
SO WHAT DO YOU THINK?
YOU GOT IT TO WORK.
ALMOST. BUT I THINK I FIGURED OUT WHERE BUCK WENT WRONG.
GRAVITY AND ANTI-GRAVITY. YIN'S GOTTA HAVE YANG.
WHAT GOES UP...

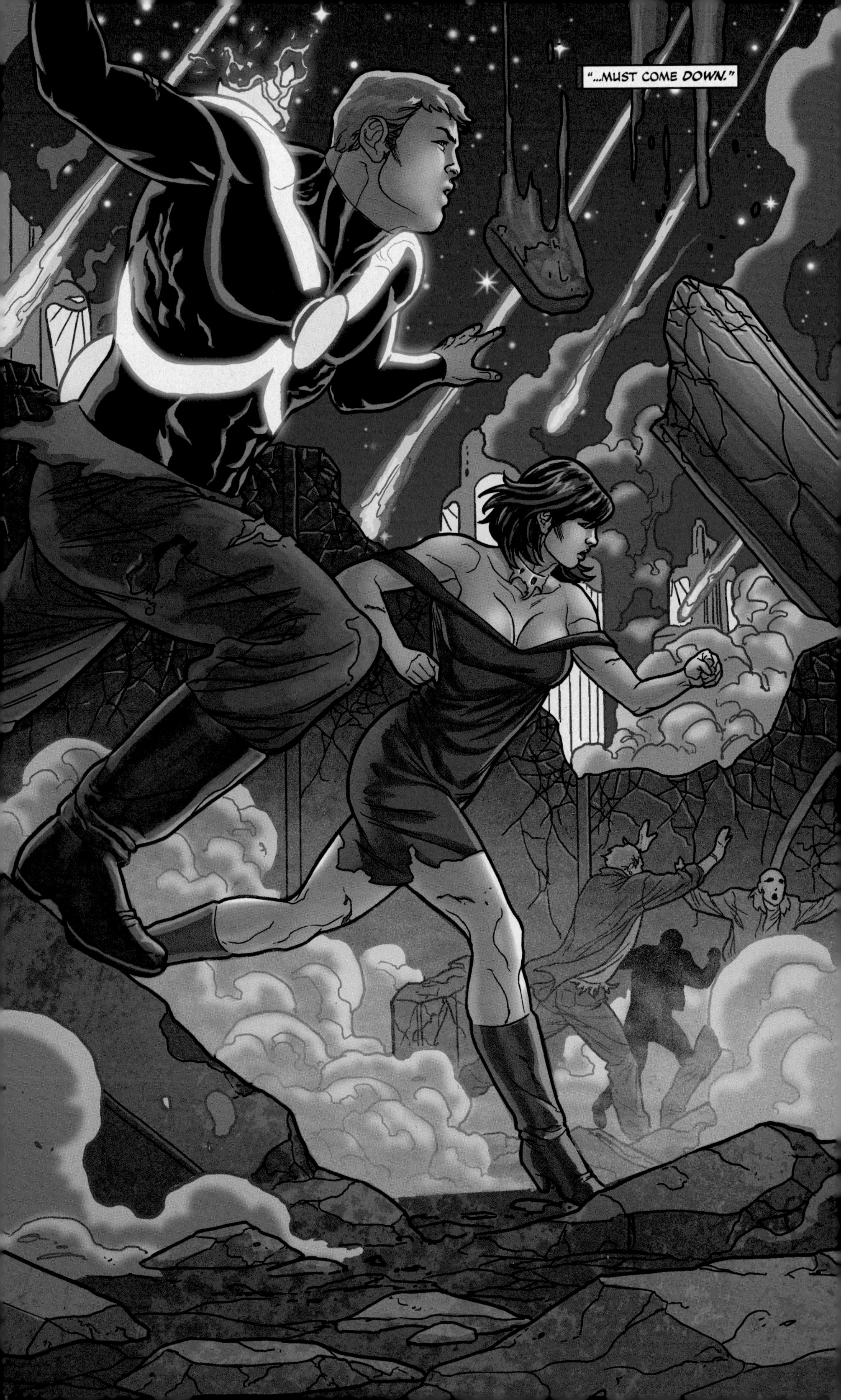
"...MUST COME DOWN."

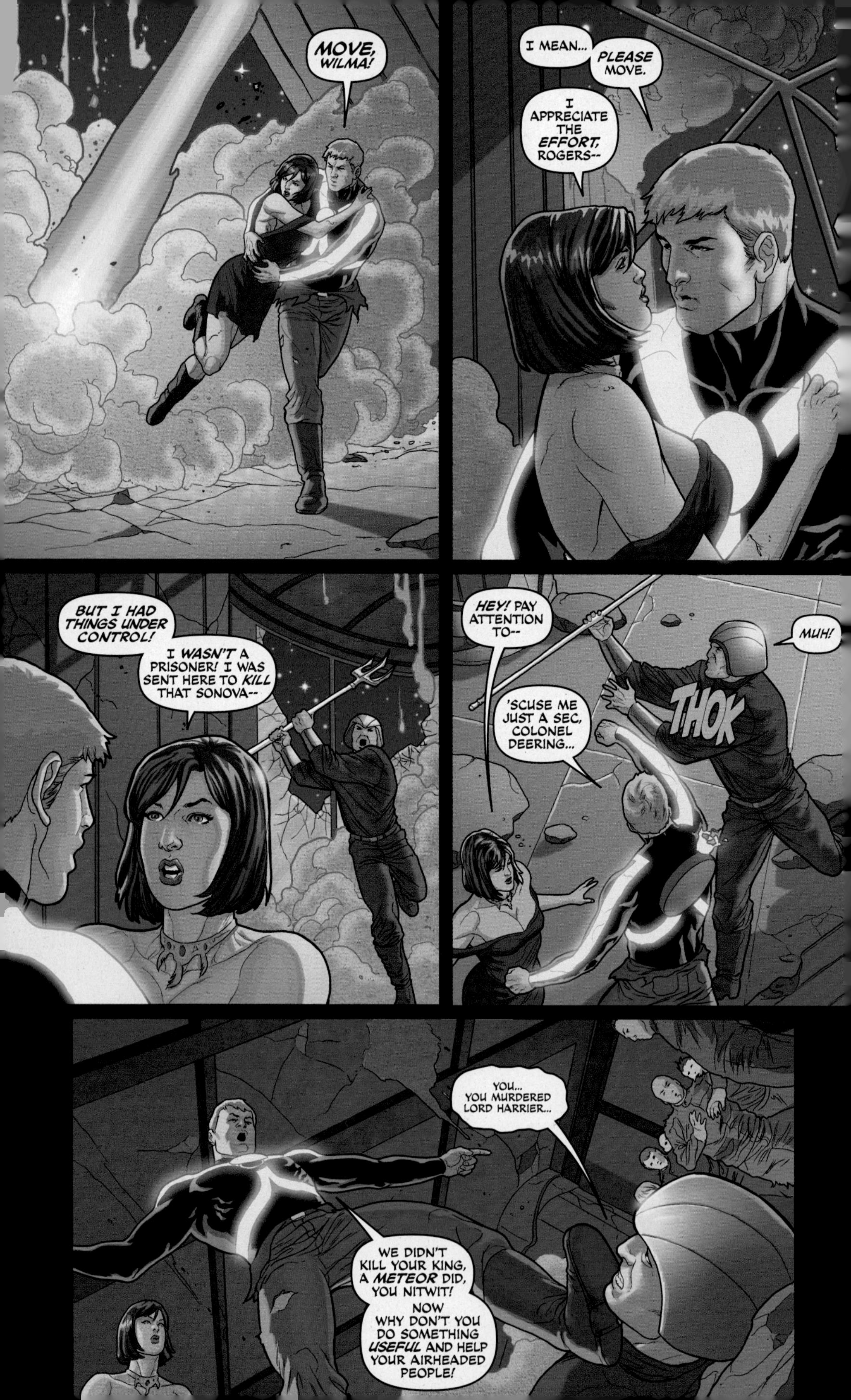
MOVE, WILMA!
I MEAN... PLEASE MOVE.
I APPRECIATE THE EFFORT, ROGERS--
BUT I HAD THINGS UNDER CONTROL!
I WASN'T A PRISONER! I WAS SENT HERE TO KILL THAT SONOVA--
HEY! PAY ATTENTION TO--
MUH!
'SCUSE ME JUST A SEC, COLONEL DEERING...
THOK
YOU... YOU MURDERED LORD HARRIER...
WE DIDN'T KILL YOUR KING, A METEOR DID, YOU NITWIT!
NOW WHY DON'T YOU DO SOMETHING USEFUL AND HELP YOUR AIRHEADED PEOPLE!

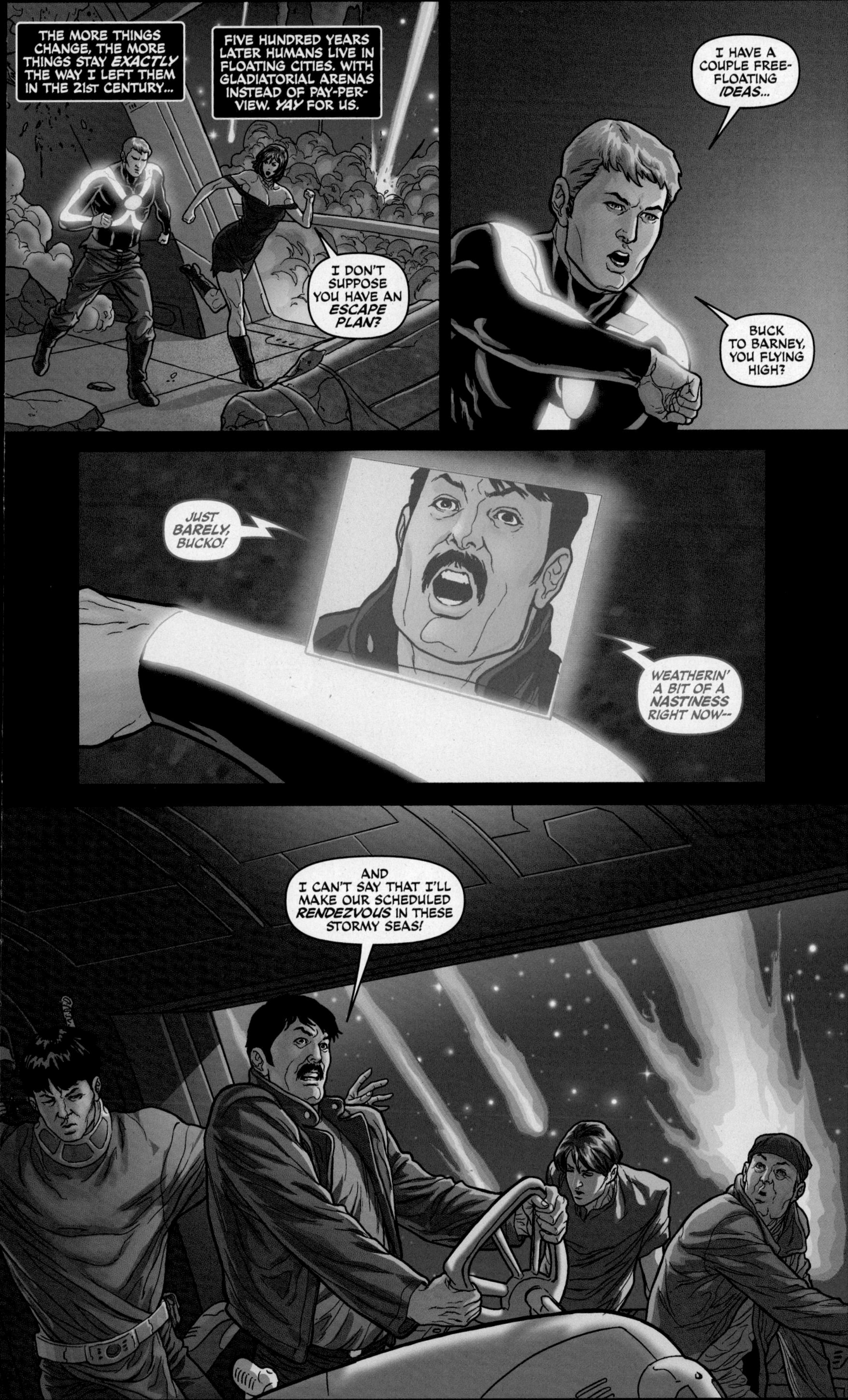
THE MORE THINGS CHANGE, THE MORE THINGS STAY EXACTLY THE WAY I LEFT THEM IN THE 21ST CENTURY...
FIVE HUNDRED YEARS LATER HUMANS LIVE IN FLOATING CITIES. WITH GLADIATORIAL ARENAS INSTEAD OF PAY-PER-VIEW. YAY FOR US.
I DON'T SUPPOSE YOU HAVE AN ESCAPE PLAN?
I HAVE A COUPLE FREE-FLOATING IDEAS...
BUCK TO BARNEY, YOU FLYING HIGH?
JUST BARELY, BUCKO!
WEATHERIN' A BIT OF A NASTINESS RIGHT NOW--
AND I CAN'T SAY THAT I'LL MAKE OUR SCHEDULED RENDEZVOUS IN THESE STORMY SEAS!

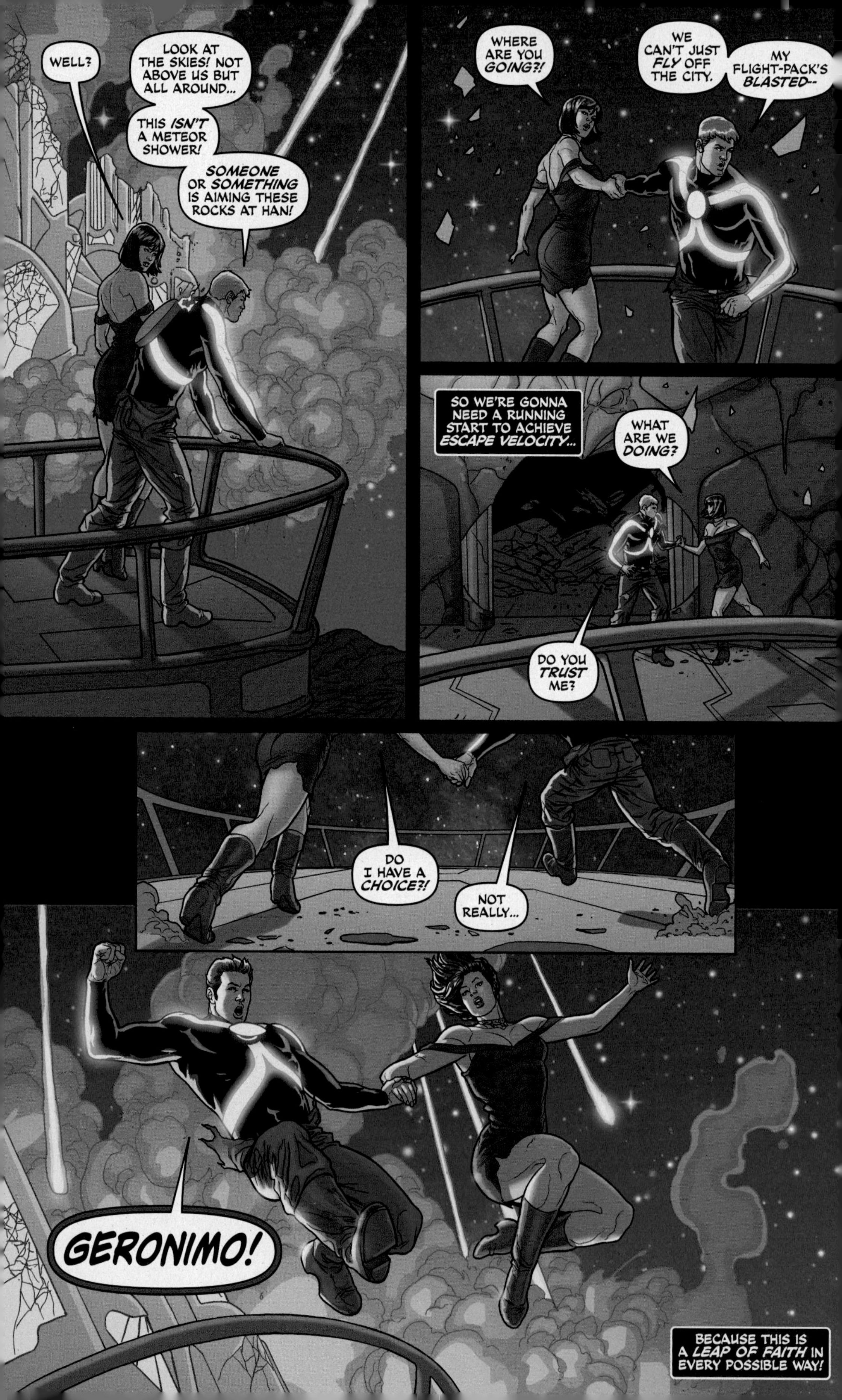
WELL?
LOOK AT THE SKIES! NOT ABOVE US BUT ALL AROUND...
THIS *ISN'T* A METEOR SHOWER!
SOMEONE OR *SOMETHING* IS AIMING THESE ROCKS AT HAN!
WHERE ARE YOU *GOING?!*
WE CAN'T JUST *FLY* OFF THE CITY.
MY FLIGHT-PACK'S *BLASTED*--
SO WE'RE GONNA NEED A RUNNING START TO ACHIEVE *ESCAPE VELOCITY*...
WHAT ARE WE *DOING?*
DO YOU *TRUST* ME?
DO I HAVE A *CHOICE?!*
NOT REALLY...
GERONIMO!
BECAUSE THIS IS A *LEAP OF FAITH* IN EVERY POSSIBLE WAY!

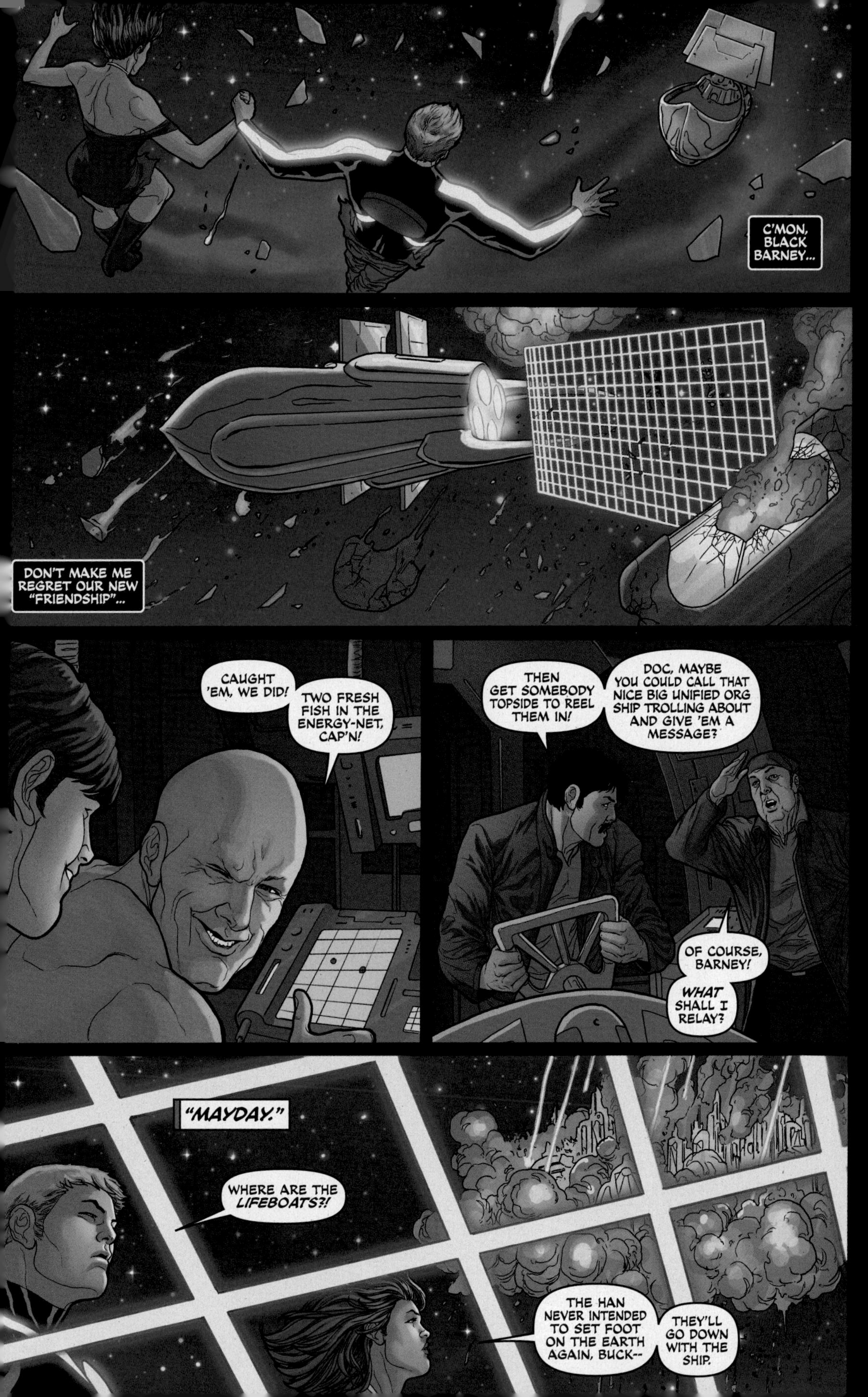
C'MON, BLACK BARNEY...
DON'T MAKE ME REGRET OUR NEW "FRIENDSHIP"...
CAUGHT 'EM, WE DID!
TWO FRESH FISH IN THE ENERGY-NET, CAP'N!
THEN GET SOMEBODY TOPSIDE TO REEL THEM IN!
DOC, MAYBE YOU COULD CALL THAT NICE BIG UNIFIED ORG SHIP TROLLING ABOUT AND GIVE 'EM A MESSAGE?
OF COURSE, BARNEY!
WHAT SHALL I RELAY?
"MAYDAY."
WHERE ARE THE *LIFEBOATS?!*
THE HAN NEVER INTENDED TO SET FOOT ON THE EARTH AGAIN, BUCK--
THEY'LL GO DOWN WITH THE SHIP.

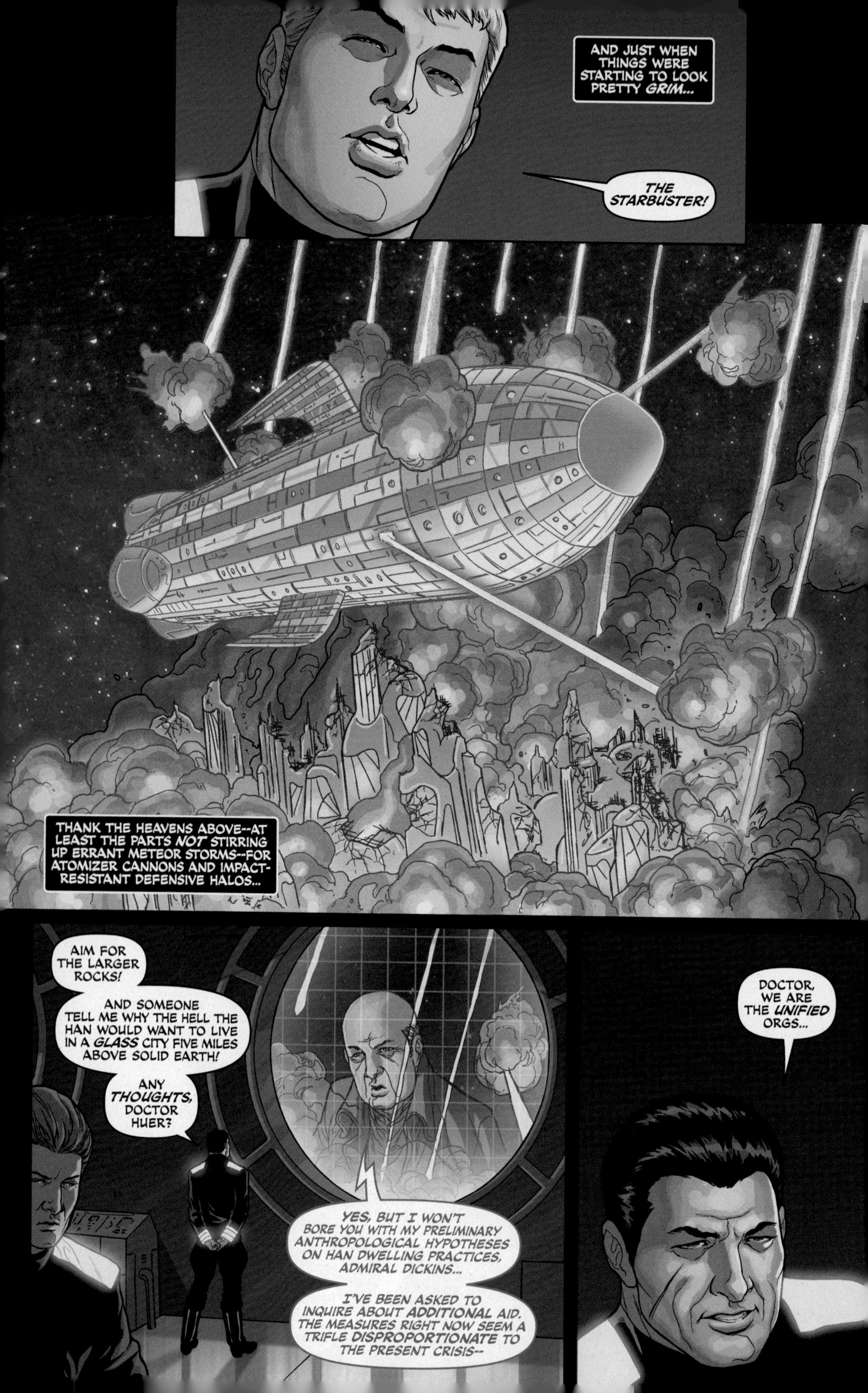
AND JUST WHEN THINGS WERE STARTING TO LOOK PRETTY *GRIM*...
THE STARBUSTER!
THANK THE HEAVENS ABOVE--AT LEAST THE PARTS *NOT* STIRRING UP ERRANT METEOR STORMS--FOR ATOMIZER CANNONS AND IMPACT-RESISTANT DEFENSIVE HALOS...
AIM FOR THE LARGER ROCKS!
AND SOMEONE TELL ME WHY THE HELL THE HAN WOULD WANT TO LIVE IN A *GLASS* CITY FIVE MILES ABOVE SOLID EARTH!
ANY *THOUGHTS,* DOCTOR HUER?
YES, BUT I WON'T BORE YOU WITH MY PRELIMINARY ANTHROPOLOGICAL HYPOTHESES ON HAN DWELLING PRACTICES, ADMIRAL DICKINS...
I'VE BEEN ASKED TO INQUIRE ABOUT ***ADDITIONAL*** *AID. THE MEASURES RIGHT NOW SEEM A TRIFLE* ***DISPROPORTIONATE*** *TO THE PRESENT CRISIS--*
DOCTOR, WE ARE THE *UNIFIED* ORGS...

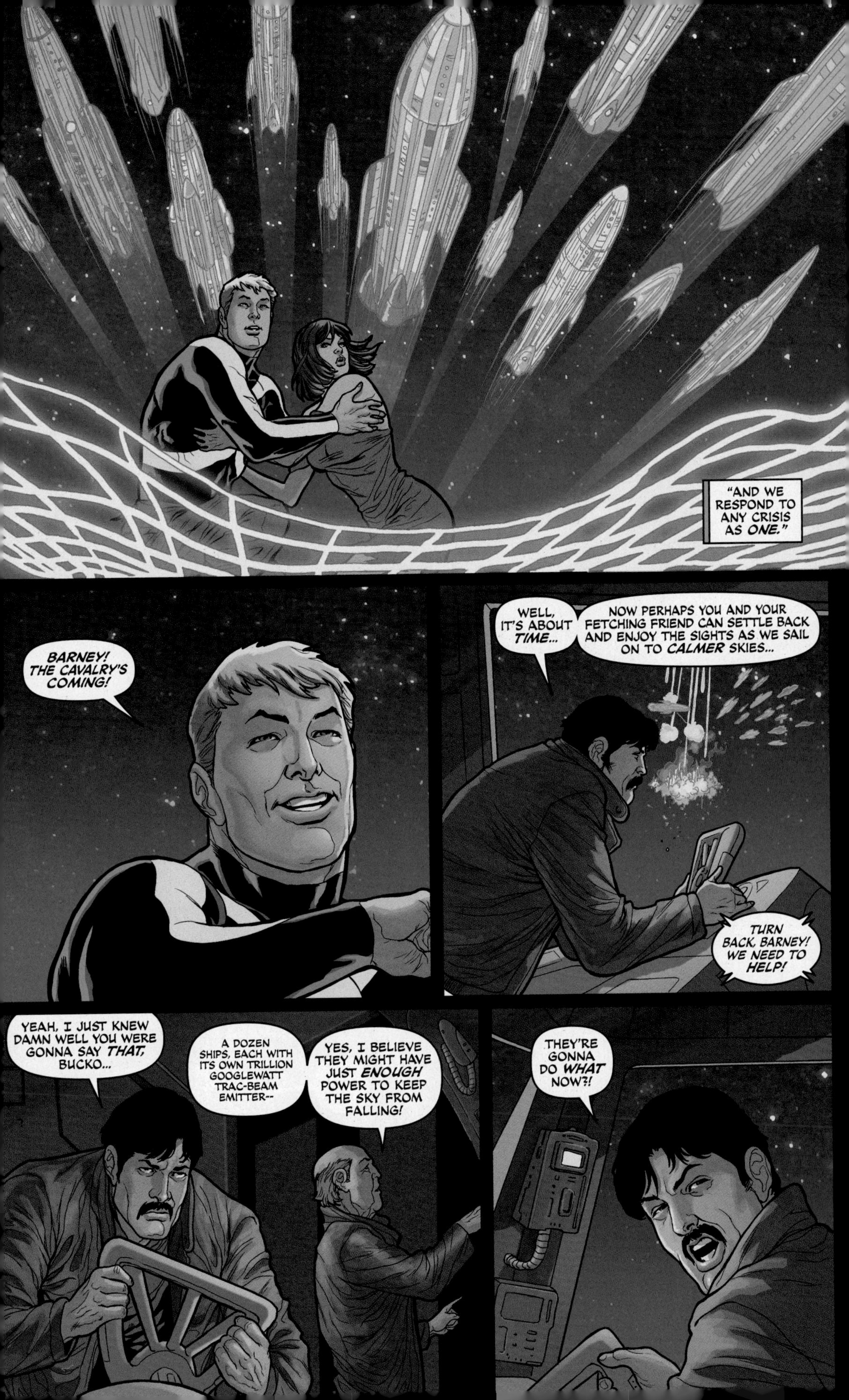
"AND WE RESPOND TO ANY CRISIS AS ONE."
BARNEY! THE CAVALRY'S COMING!
WELL, IT'S ABOUT TIME...
NOW PERHAPS YOU AND YOUR FETCHING FRIEND CAN SETTLE BACK AND ENJOY THE SIGHTS AS WE SAIL ON TO CALMER SKIES...
TURN BACK, BARNEY! WE NEED TO HELP!
YEAH, I JUST KNEW DAMN WELL YOU WERE GONNA SAY THAT, BUCKO...
A DOZEN SHIPS, EACH WITH ITS OWN TRILLION GOOGLEWATT TRAC-BEAM EMITTER--
YES, I BELIEVE THEY MIGHT HAVE JUST ENOUGH POWER TO KEEP THE SKY FROM FALLING!
THEY'RE GONNA DO WHAT NOW?!

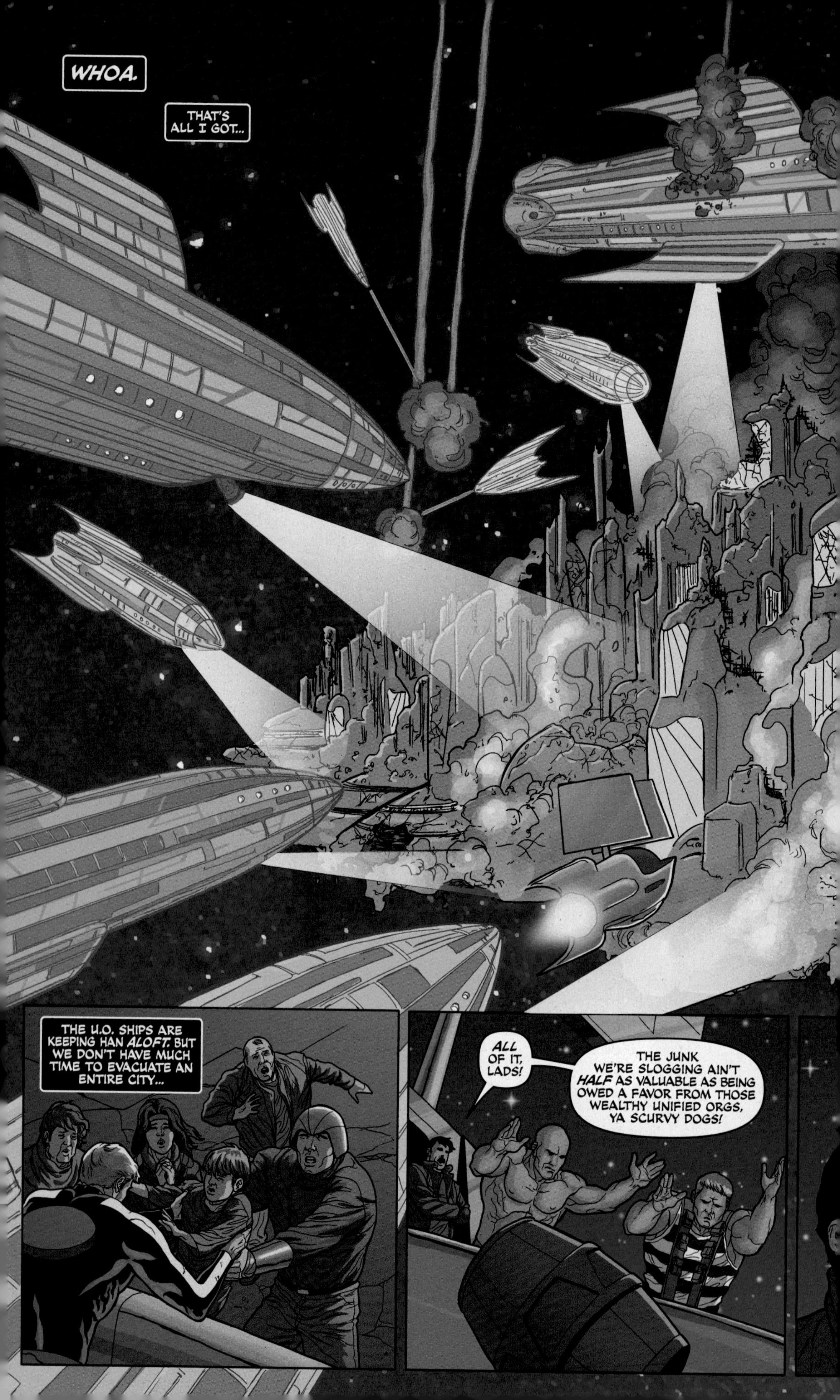
WHOA.
THAT'S ALL I GOT...
THE U.O. SHIPS ARE KEEPING HAN ALOFT, BUT WE DON'T HAVE MUCH TIME TO EVACUATE AN ENTIRE CITY...
ALL OF IT, LADS!
THE JUNK WE'RE SLOGGING AIN'T HALF AS VALUABLE AS BEING OWED A FAVOR FROM THOSE WEALTHY UNIFIED ORGS, YA SCURVY DOGS!

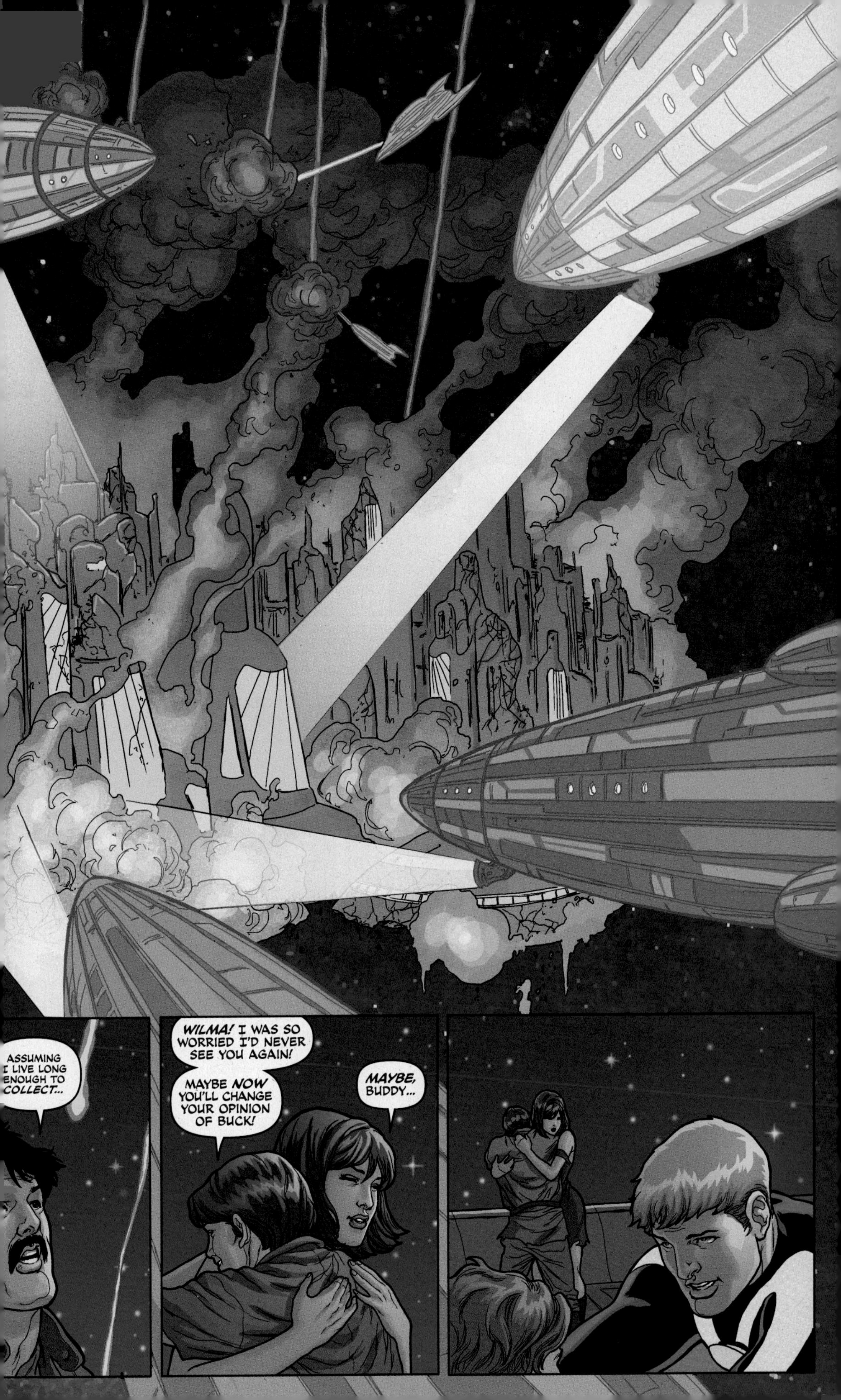
ASSUMING I LIVE LONG ENOUGH TO COLLECT...
WILMA! I WAS SO WORRIED I'D NEVER SEE YOU AGAIN!
MAYBE NOW YOU'LL CHANGE YOUR OPINION OF BUCK!
MAYBE, BUDDY...

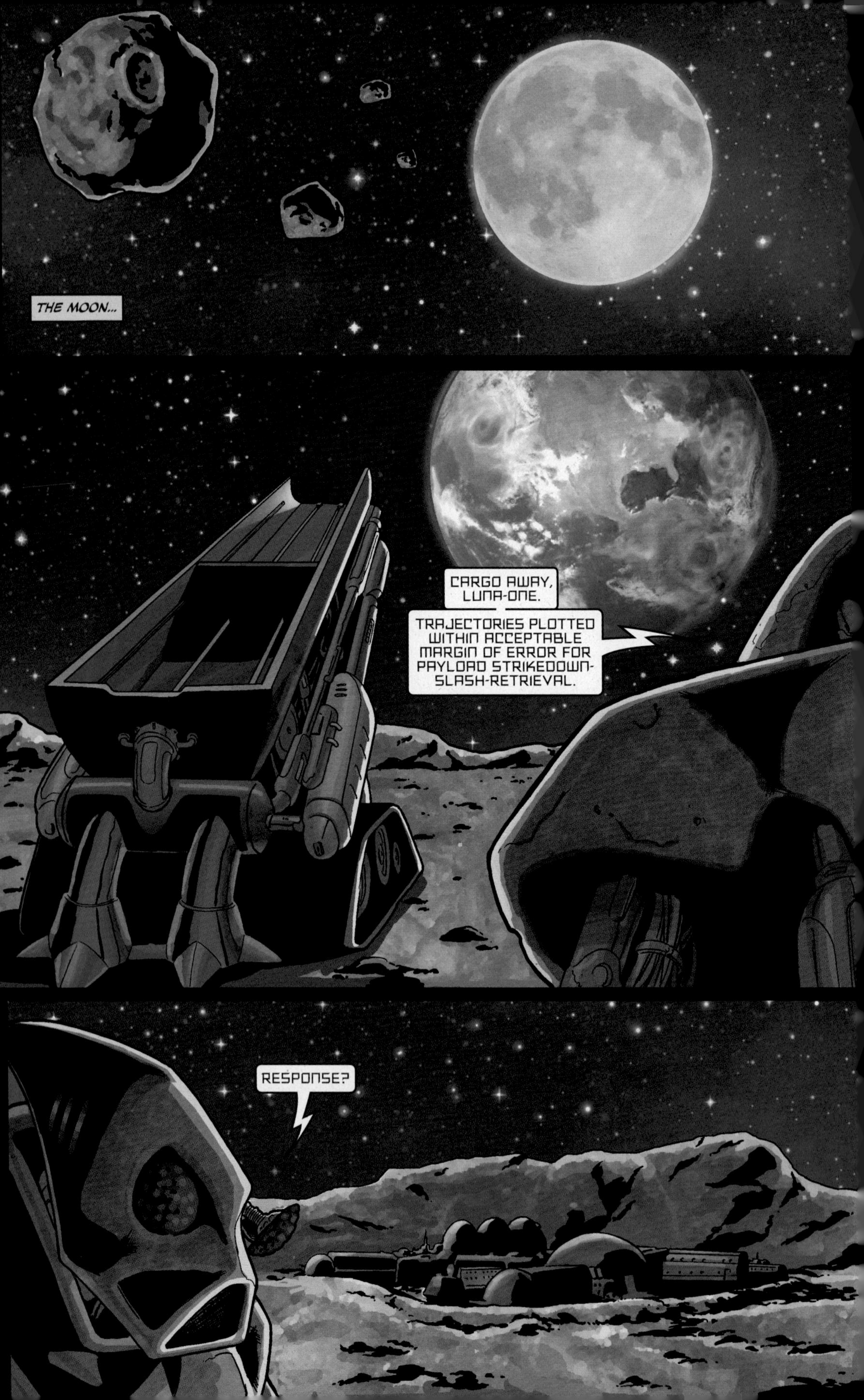
THE MOON...
CARGO AWAY, LUNA-ONE.
TRAJECTORIES PLOTTED WITHIN ACCEPTABLE MARGIN OF ERROR FOR PAYLOAD STRIKEDOWN-SLASH-RETRIEVAL.
RESPONSE?

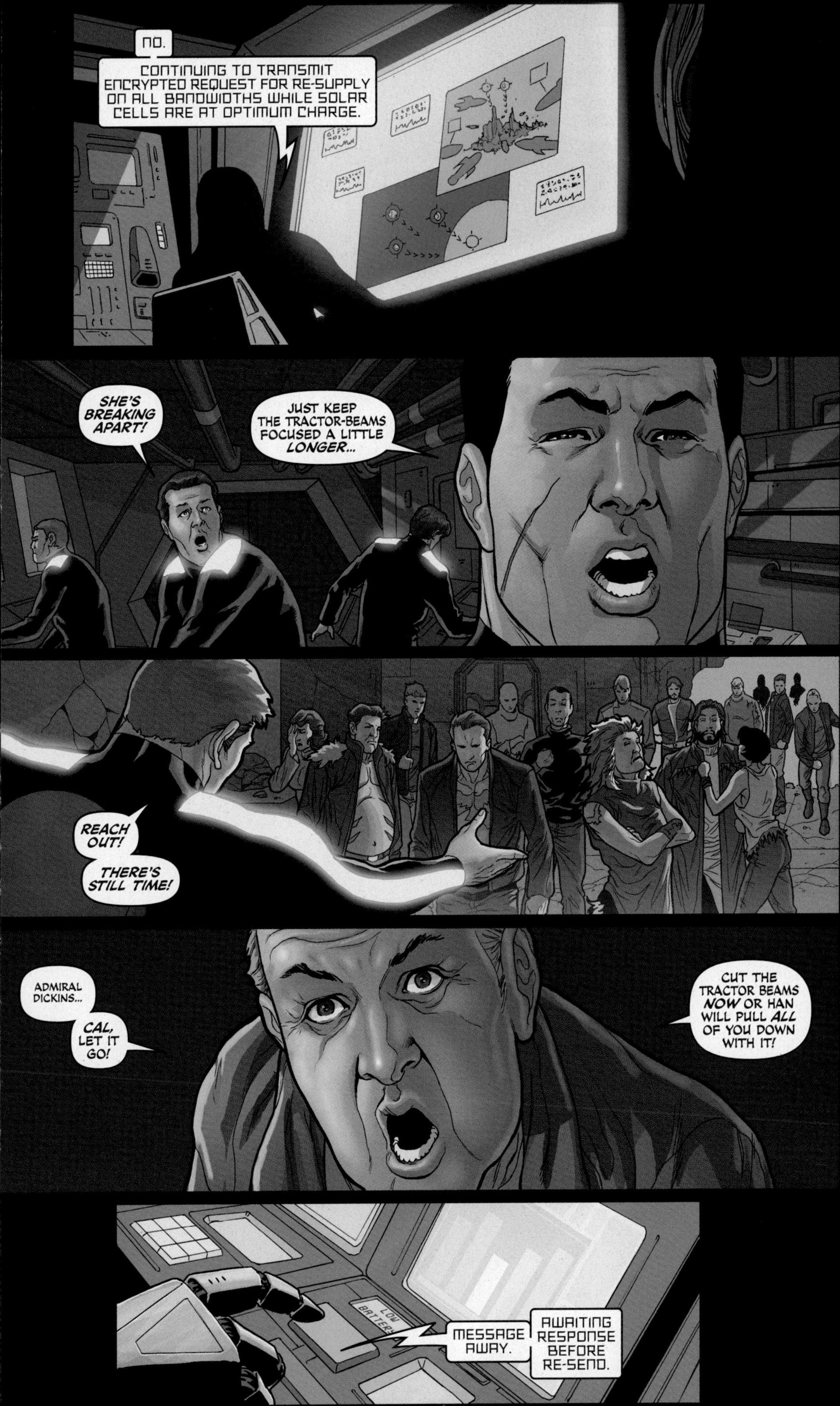
NO.
CONTINUING TO TRANSMIT ENCRYPTED REQUEST FOR RE-SUPPLY ON ALL BANDWIDTHS WHILE SOLAR CELLS ARE AT OPTIMUM CHARGE.
SHE'S BREAKING APART!
JUST KEEP THE TRACTOR-BEAMS FOCUSED A LITTLE LONGER...
REACH OUT!
THERE'S STILL TIME!
ADMIRAL DICKINS...
CAL, LET IT GO!
CUT THE TRACTOR BEAMS NOW OR HAN WILL PULL ALL OF YOU DOWN WITH IT!
LOW BATTERY
MESSAGE AWAY.
AWAITING RESPONSE BEFORE RE-SEND.

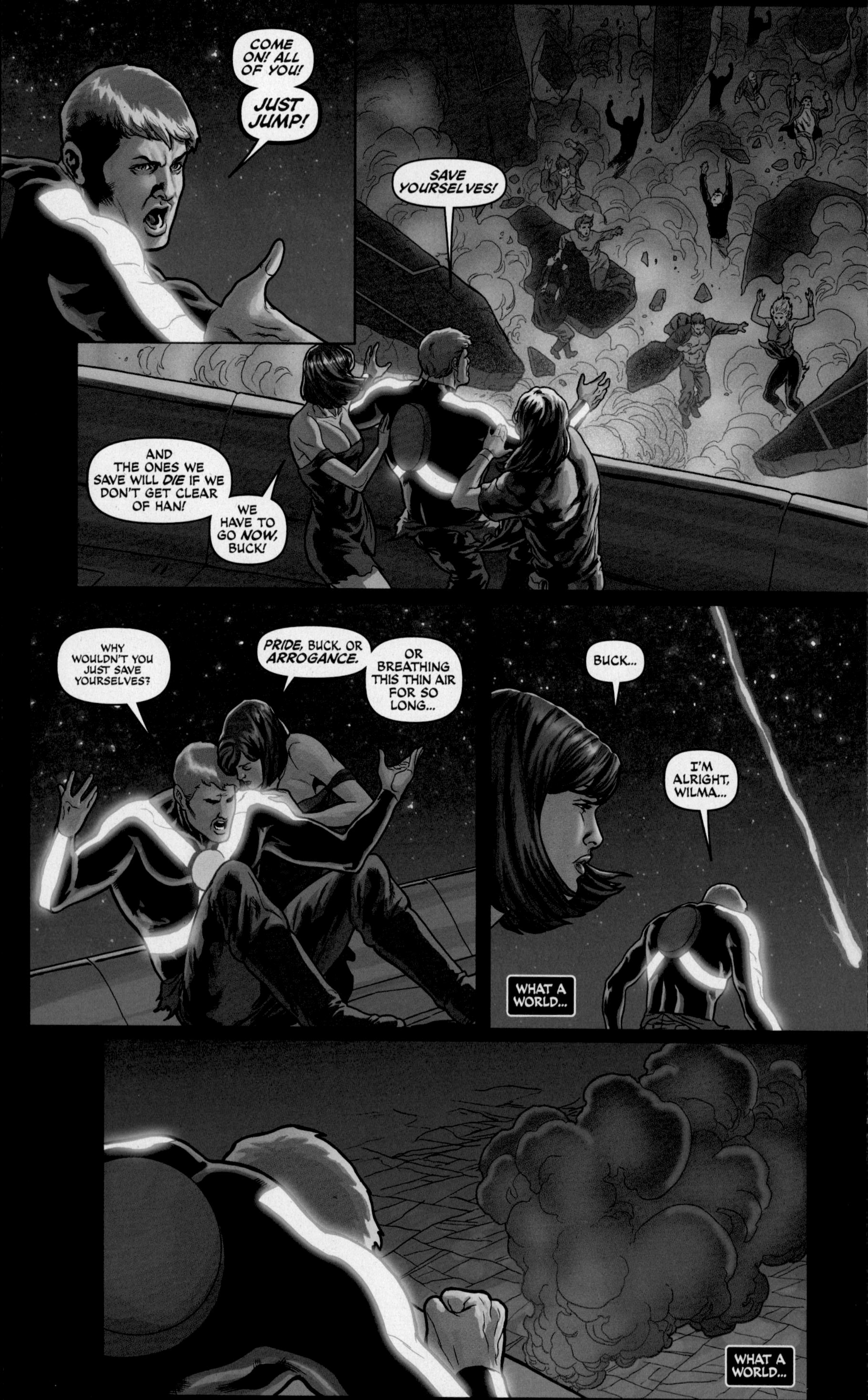
COME ON! ALL OF YOU!
JUST JUMP!
SAVE YOURSELVES!
AND THE ONES WE SAVE WILL DIE IF WE DON'T GET CLEAR OF HAN!
WE HAVE TO GO NOW, BUCK!
WHY WOULDN'T YOU JUST SAVE YOURSELVES?
PRIDE, BUCK. OR ARROGANCE.
OR BREATHING THIS THIN AIR FOR SO LONG...
BUCK...
I'M ALRIGHT, WILMA...
WHAT A WORLD...
WHAT A WORLD...

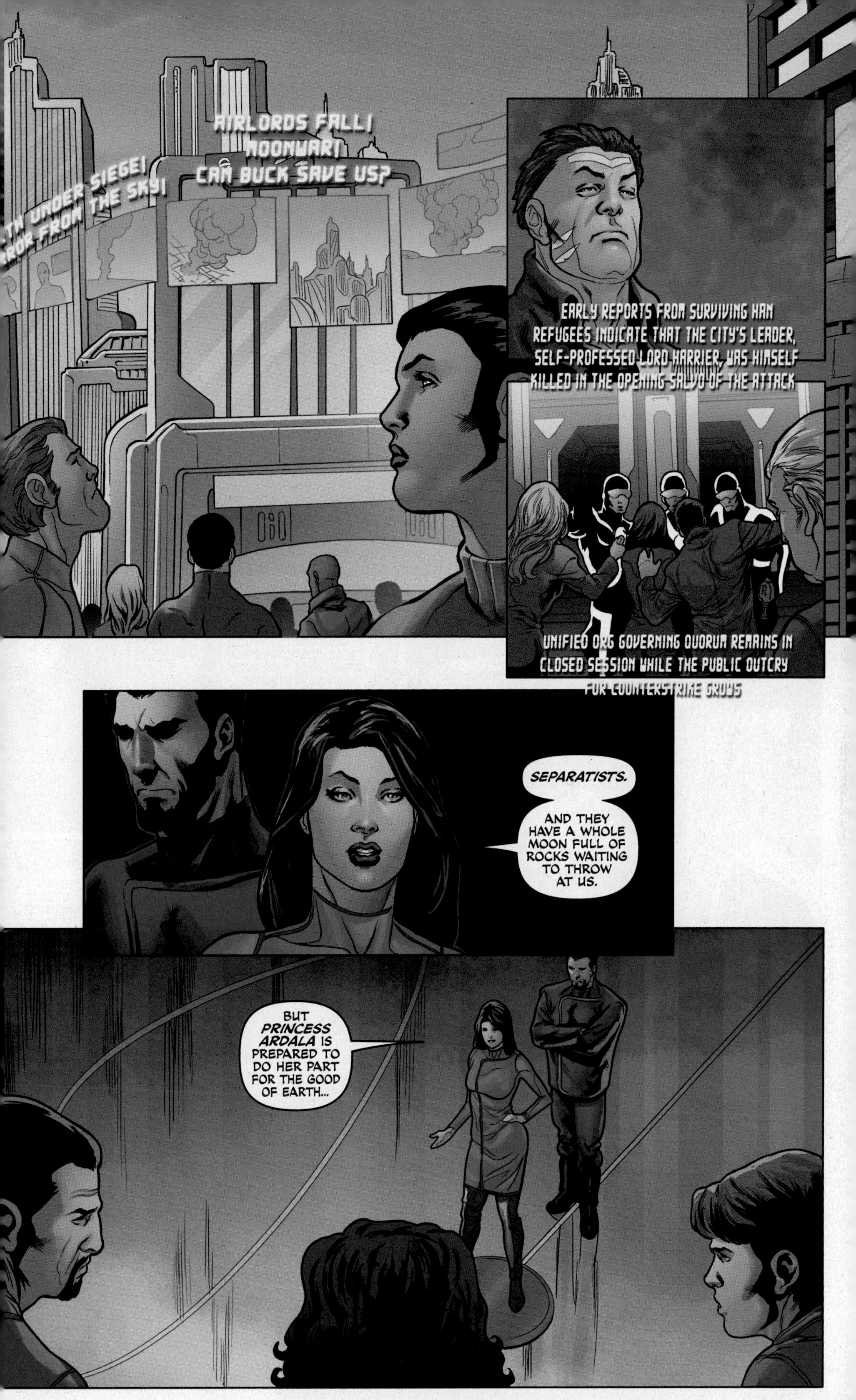
AIRLORDS FALL!
MOONWAR!
CAN BUCK SAVE US?
UNDER SIEGE!
FROM THE SKY!
EARLY REPORTS FROM SURVIVING HAN REFUGEES INDICATE THAT THE CITY'S LEADER, SELF-PROFESSED LORD HARRIER, WAS HIMSELF KILLED IN THE OPENING SALVO OF THE ATTACK
UNIFIED ORG GOVERNING QUORUM REMAINS IN CLOSED SESSION WHILE THE PUBLIC OUTCRY FOR COUNTERSTRIKE GROWS
SEPARATISTS.
AND THEY HAVE A WHOLE MOON FULL OF ROCKS WAITING TO THROW AT US.
BUT *PRINCESS ARDALA* IS PREPARED TO DO HER PART FOR THE GOOD OF EARTH...

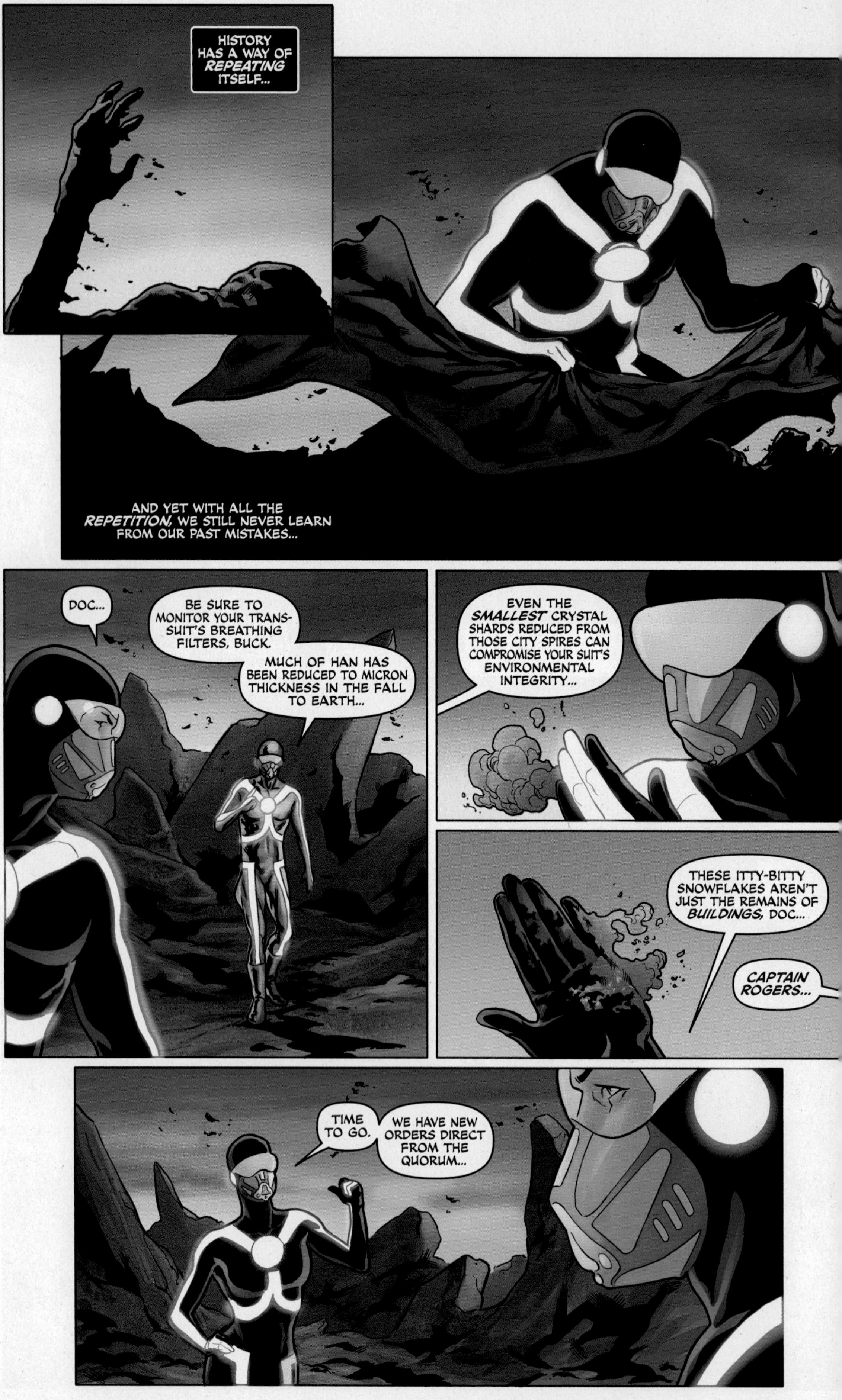
HISTORY HAS A WAY OF *REPEATING* ITSELF...
AND YET WITH ALL THE *REPETITION,* WE STILL NEVER LEARN FROM OUR PAST MISTAKES...
DOC...
BE SURE TO MONITOR YOUR TRANS-SUIT'S BREATHING FILTERS, BUCK.
MUCH OF HAN HAS BEEN REDUCED TO MICRON THICKNESS IN THE FALL TO EARTH...
EVEN THE *SMALLEST* CRYSTAL SHARDS REDUCED FROM THOSE CITY SPIRES CAN COMPROMISE YOUR SUIT'S ENVIRONMENTAL INTEGRITY...
THESE ITTY-BITTY SNOWFLAKES AREN'T JUST THE REMAINS OF *BUILDINGS,* DOC...
CAPTAIN ROGERS...
TIME TO GO.
WE HAVE NEW ORDERS DIRECT FROM THE QUORUM...

SO WE'RE BACK TO "CAPTAIN ROGERS"...

ONE STEP FORWARD, TWO STEPS BACK...

I CAN'T BELIEVE WE'RE GOING TO THE MOON!

CAPTAIN ROGERS IS GOING TO THE MOON. I AM GOING TO THE MOON.

YOU'RE NOT GOING ANYWHERE EXCEPT HOME.

JUST AS SOON AS I SECURE AN ARMED ESCORT FOR YOU AND THE GOOD DOCTOR, LITTLE BROTHER...

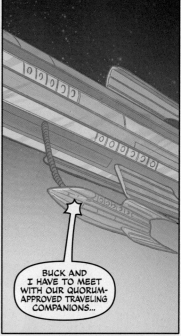

BUCK AND I HAVE TO MEET WITH OUR QUORUM-APPROVED TRAVELING COMPANIONS...

YOU!

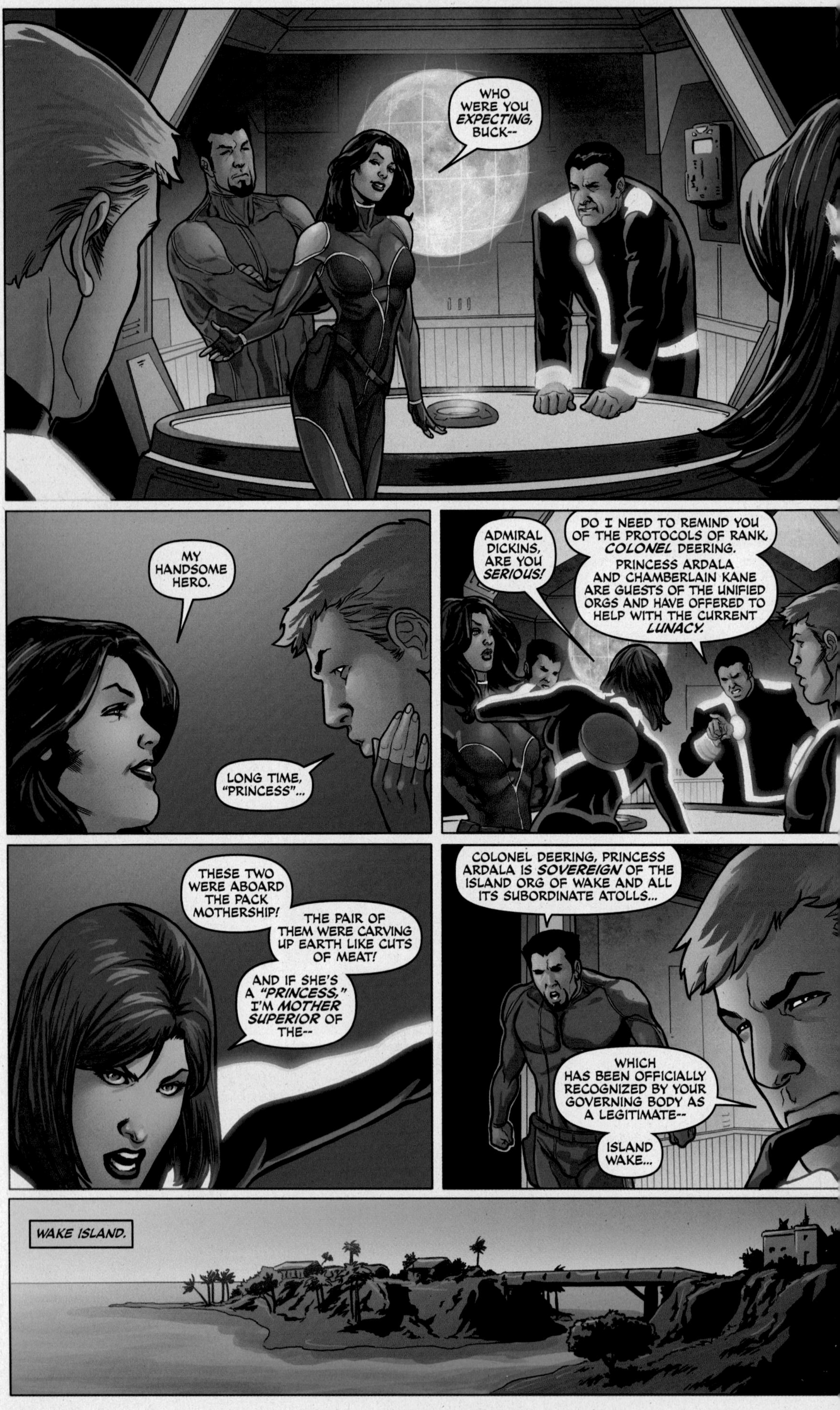
WHO WERE YOU EXPECTING, BUCK--
MY HANDSOME HERO.
LONG TIME, "PRINCESS"...
ADMIRAL DICKINS, ARE YOU SERIOUS!
DO I NEED TO REMIND YOU OF THE PROTOCOLS OF RANK, COLONEL DEERING.
PRINCESS ARDALA AND CHAMBERLAIN KANE ARE GUESTS OF THE UNIFIED ORGS AND HAVE OFFERED TO HELP WITH THE CURRENT LUNACY.
THESE TWO WERE ABOARD THE PACK MOTHERSHIP!
THE PAIR OF THEM WERE CARVING UP EARTH LIKE CUTS OF MEAT!
AND IF SHE'S A "PRINCESS," I'M MOTHER SUPERIOR OF THE--
COLONEL DEERING, PRINCESS ARDALA IS SOVEREIGN OF THE ISLAND ORG OF WAKE AND ALL ITS SUBORDINATE ATOLLS...
WHICH HAS BEEN OFFICIALLY RECOGNIZED BY YOUR GOVERNING BODY AS A LEGITIMATE--
ISLAND WAKE...
WAKE ISLAND.

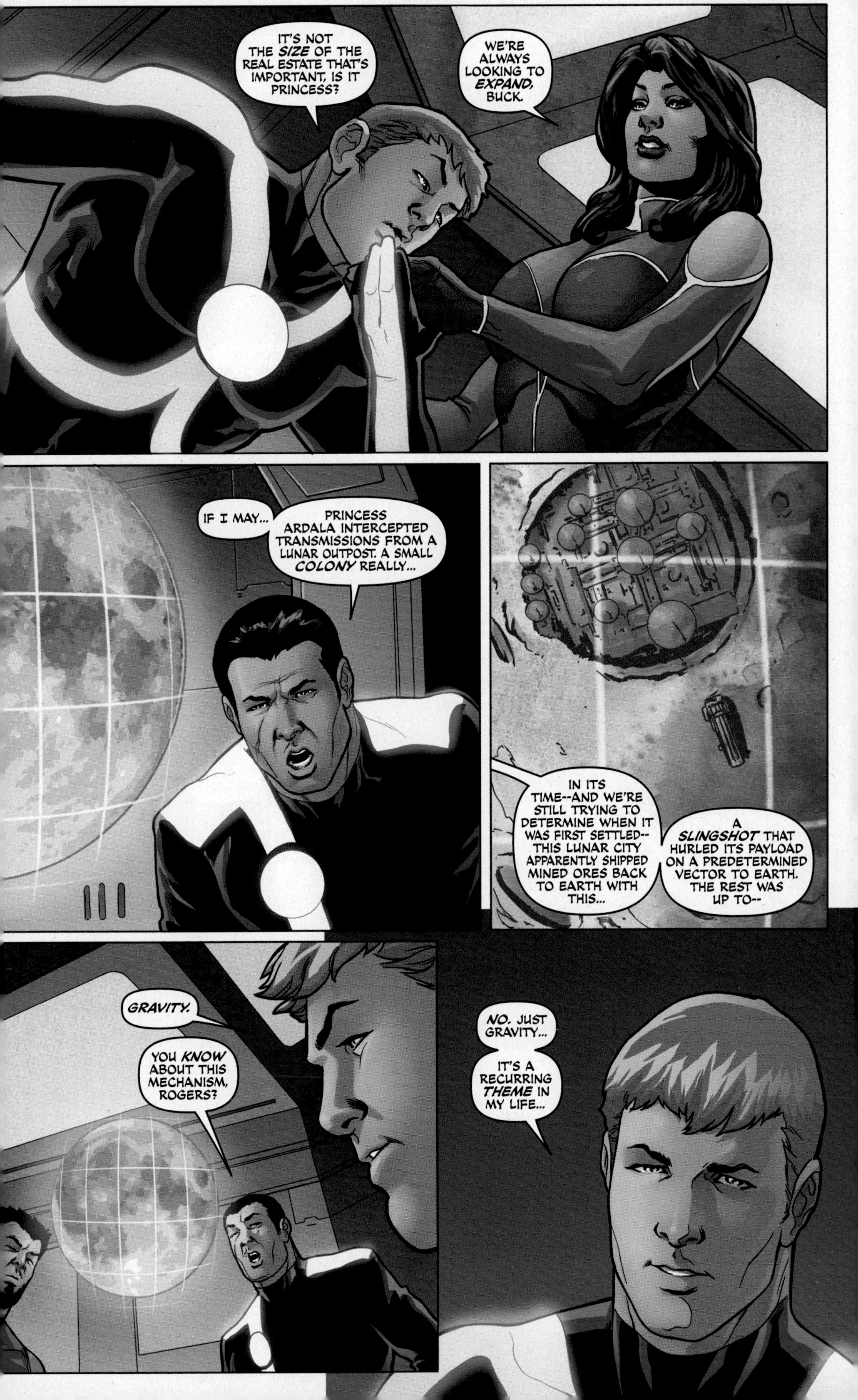
IT'S NOT THE SIZE OF THE REAL ESTATE THAT'S IMPORTANT, IS IT PRINCESS?
WE'RE ALWAYS LOOKING TO EXPAND, BUCK.
IF I MAY...
PRINCESS ARDALA INTERCEPTED TRANSMISSIONS FROM A LUNAR OUTPOST. A SMALL COLONY REALLY...
IN ITS TIME--AND WE'RE STILL TRYING TO DETERMINE WHEN IT WAS FIRST SETTLED--THIS LUNAR CITY APPARENTLY SHIPPED MINED ORES BACK TO EARTH WITH THIS...
A SLINGSHOT THAT HURLED ITS PAYLOAD ON A PREDETERMINED VECTOR TO EARTH. THE REST WAS UP TO--
GRAVITY.
YOU KNOW ABOUT THIS MECHANISM, ROGERS?
NO. JUST GRAVITY...
IT'S A RECURRING THEME IN MY LIFE...

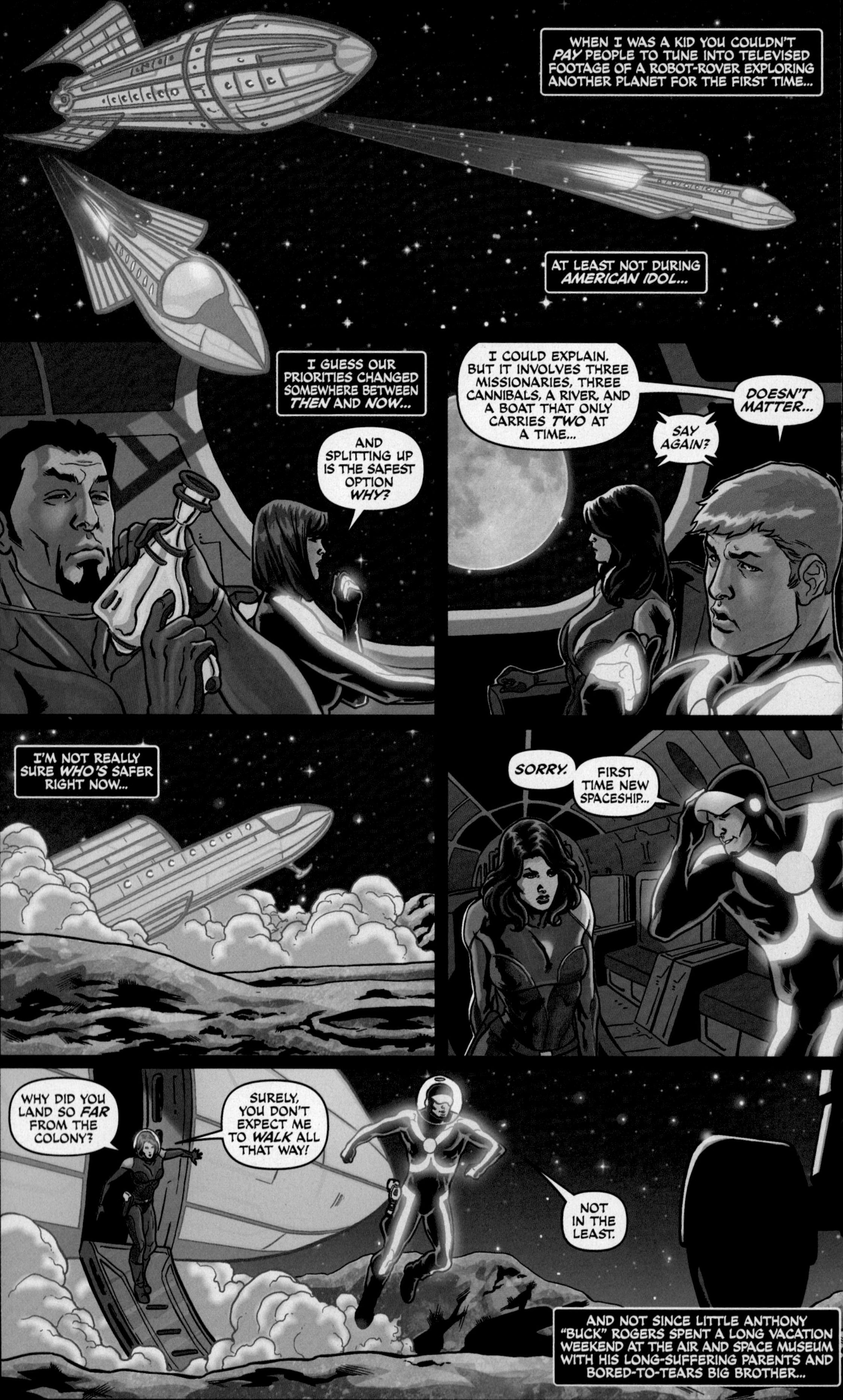
WHEN I WAS A KID YOU COULDN'T PAY PEOPLE TO TUNE INTO TELEVISED FOOTAGE OF A ROBOT-ROVER EXPLORING ANOTHER PLANET FOR THE FIRST TIME...
AT LEAST NOT DURING AMERICAN IDOL...
I GUESS OUR PRIORITIES CHANGED SOMEWHERE BETWEEN THEN AND NOW...
AND SPLITTING UP IS THE SAFEST OPTION WHY?
I COULD EXPLAIN. BUT IT INVOLVES THREE MISSIONARIES, THREE CANNIBALS, A RIVER, AND A BOAT THAT ONLY CARRIES TWO AT A TIME...
SAY AGAIN?
DOESN'T MATTER...
I'M NOT REALLY SURE WHO'S SAFER RIGHT NOW...
SORRY.
FIRST TIME NEW SPACESHIP...
WHY DID YOU LAND SO FAR FROM THE COLONY?
SURELY, YOU DON'T EXPECT ME TO WALK ALL THAT WAY!
NOT IN THE LEAST.
AND NOT SINCE LITTLE ANTHONY "BUCK" ROGERS SPENT A LONG VACATION WEEKEND AT THE AIR AND SPACE MUSEUM WITH HIS LONG-SUFFERING PARENTS AND BORED-TO-TEARS BIG BROTHER...

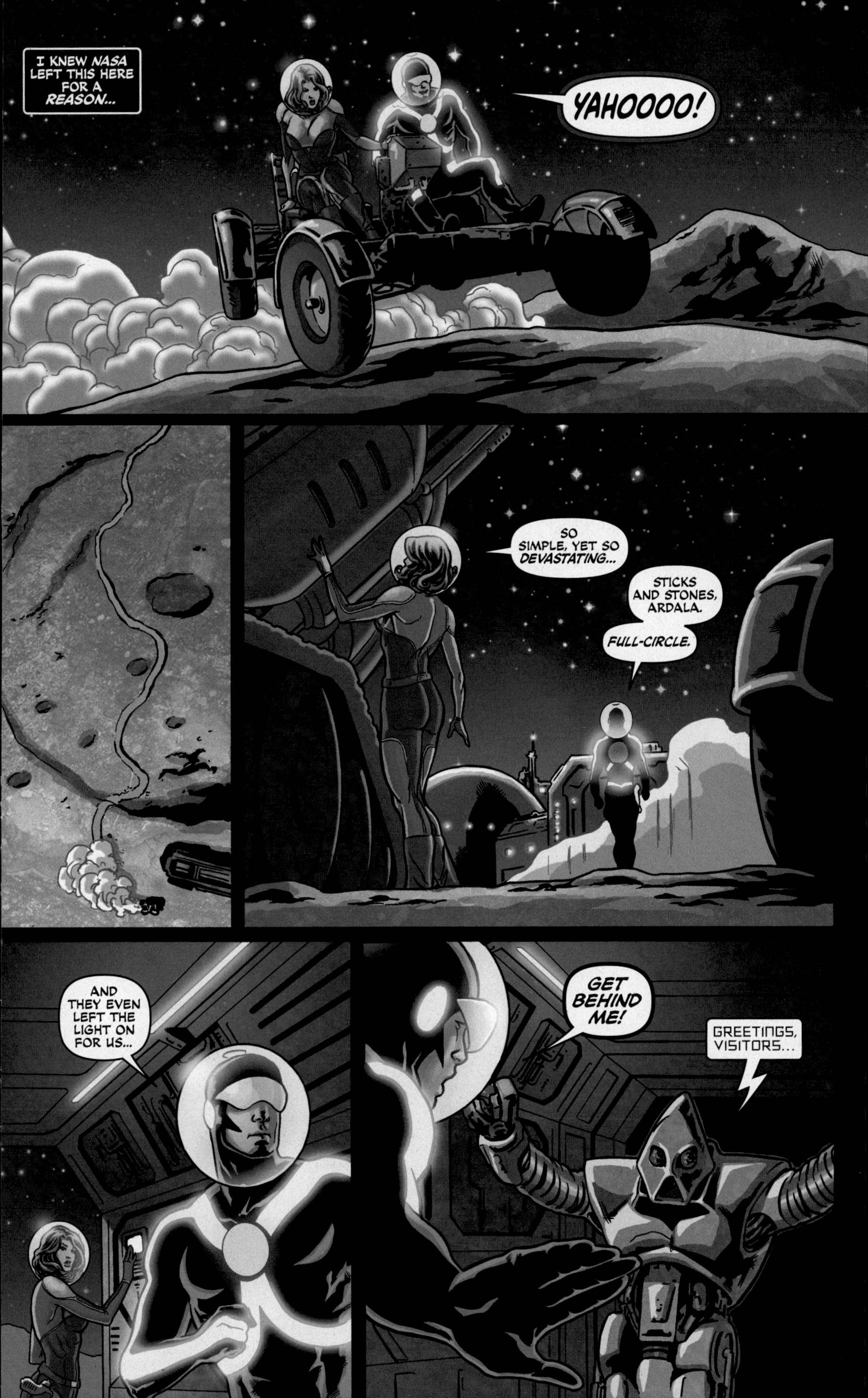
I KNEW NASA LEFT THIS HERE FOR A REASON...
YAHOOOO!
SO SIMPLE, YET SO DEVASTATING...
STICKS AND STONES, ARDALA.
FULL-CIRCLE.
AND THEY EVEN LEFT THE LIGHT ON FOR US...
GET BEHIND ME!
GREETINGS, VISITORS...

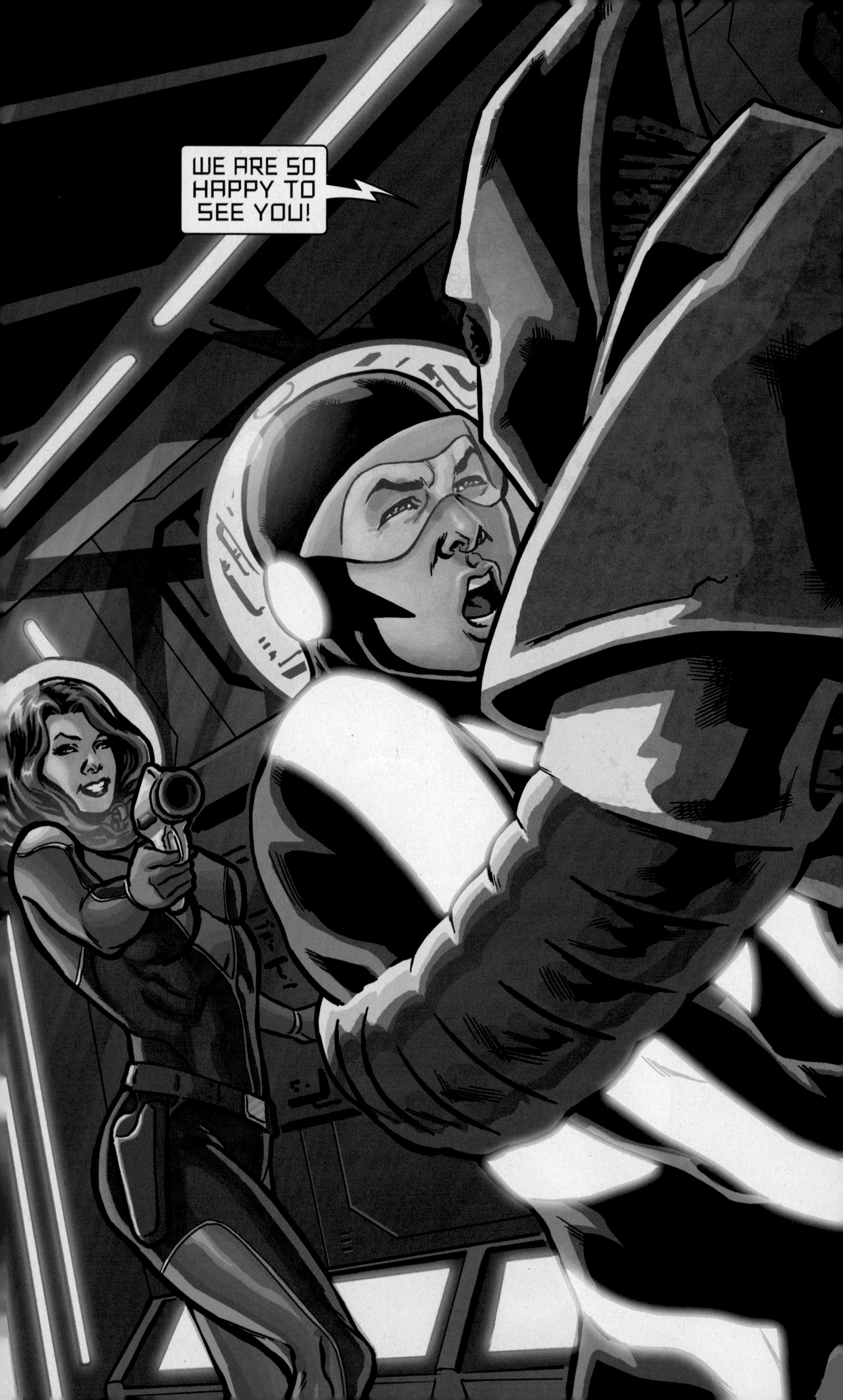
WE ARE SO HAPPY TO SEE YOU!

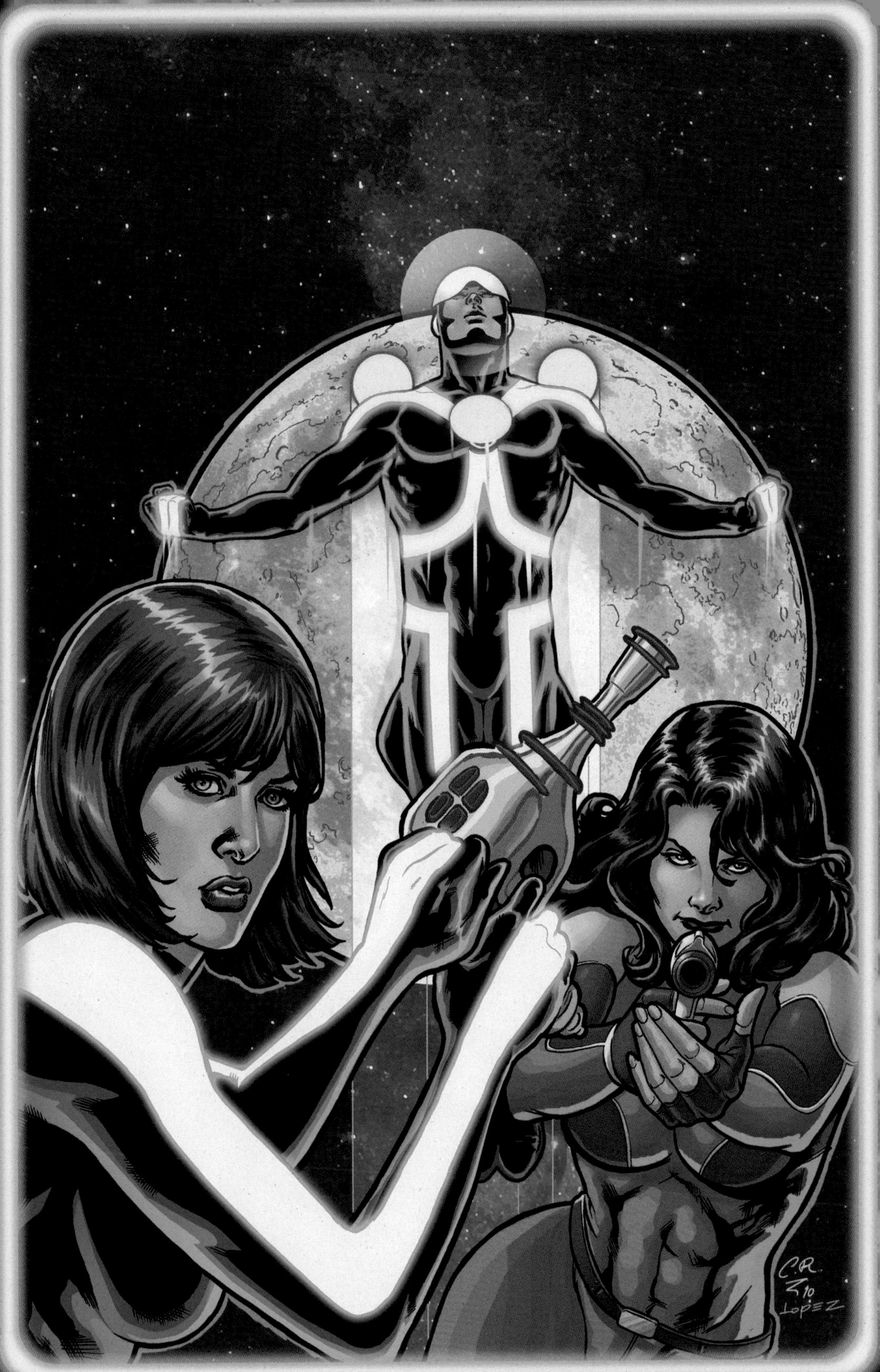

MOONSTRUCK PART TWO:
Shoot the Moon!

ISSUE TWELVE COVER BY CARLOS RAFAEL

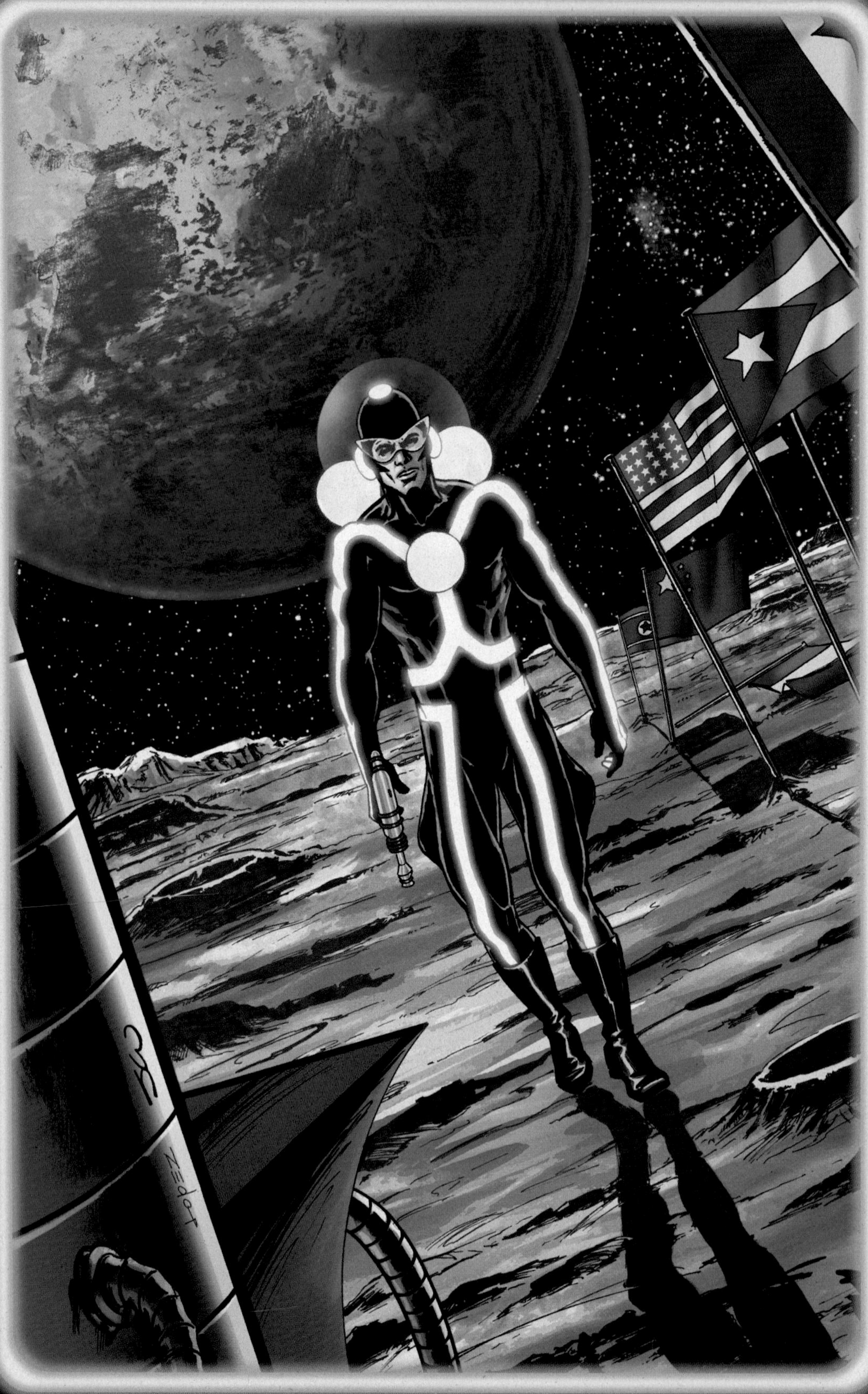

ALTERNATE COVER BY JOHN WATSON

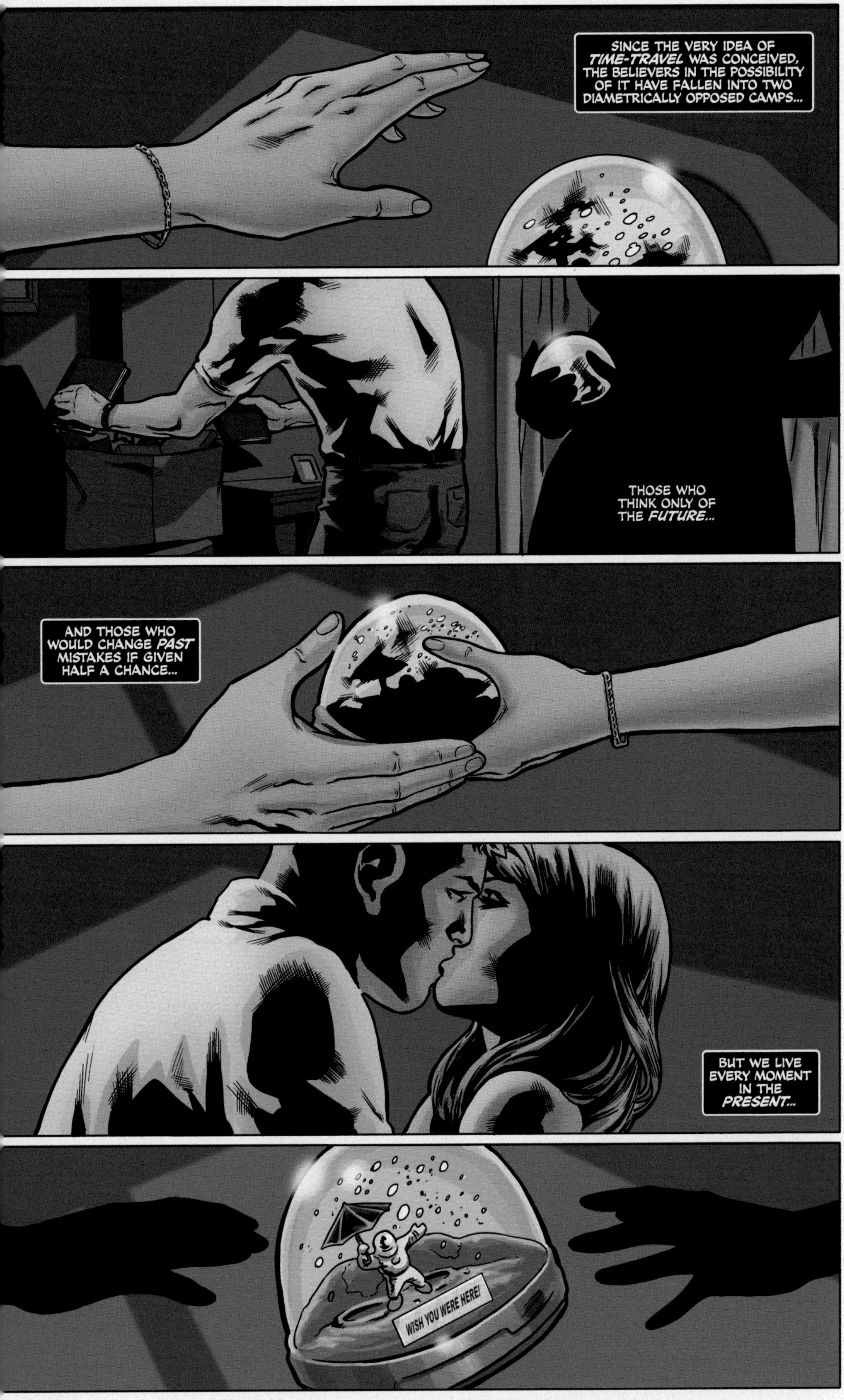
SINCE THE VERY IDEA OF TIME-TRAVEL WAS CONCEIVED, THE BELIEVERS IN THE POSSIBILITY OF IT HAVE FALLEN INTO TWO DIAMETRICALLY OPPOSED CAMPS...
THOSE WHO THINK ONLY OF THE FUTURE...
AND THOSE WHO WOULD CHANGE PAST MISTAKES IF GIVEN HALF A CHANCE...
BUT WE LIVE EVERY MOMENT IN THE PRESENT...
WISH YOU WERE HERE!

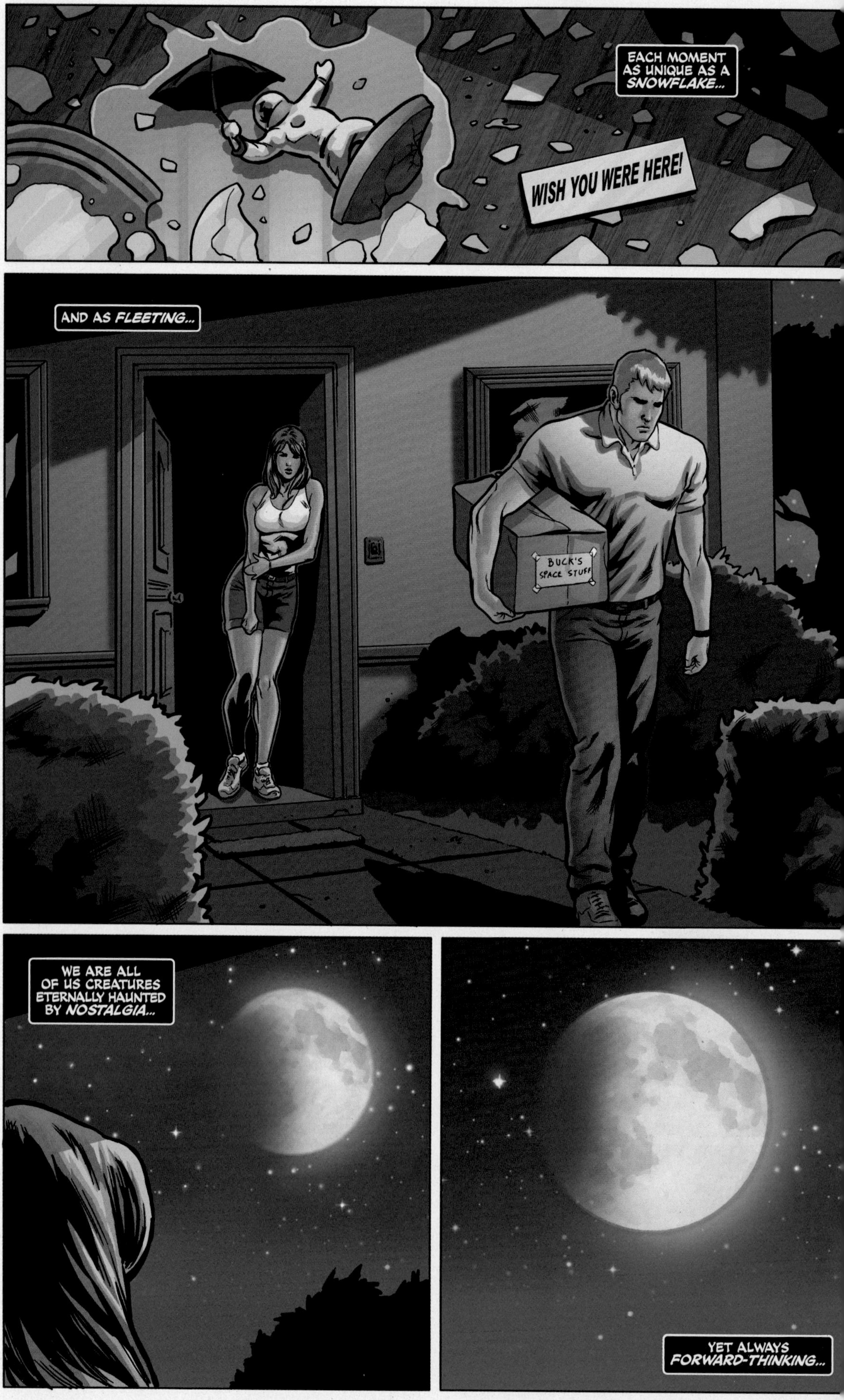
EACH MOMENT AS UNIQUE AS A SNOWFLAKE...
WISH YOU WERE HERE!
AND AS FLEETING...
BUCK'S SPACE STUFF
WE ARE ALL OF US CREATURES ETERNALLY HAUNTED BY NOSTALGIA...
YET ALWAYS FORWARD-THINKING...

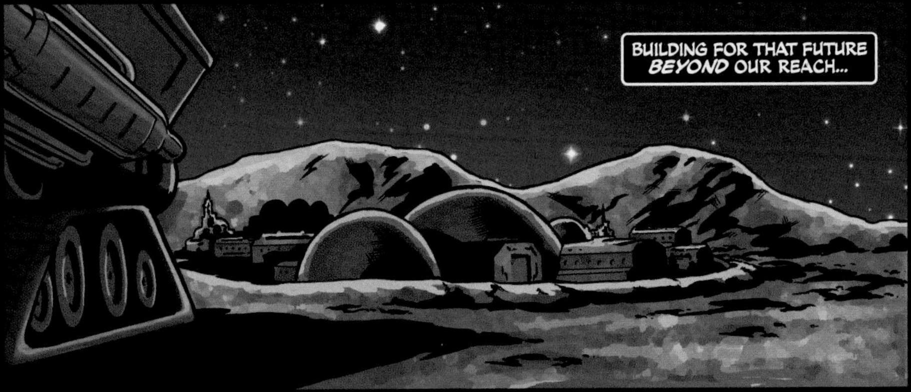
BUILDING FOR THAT FUTURE *BEYOND* OUR REACH...

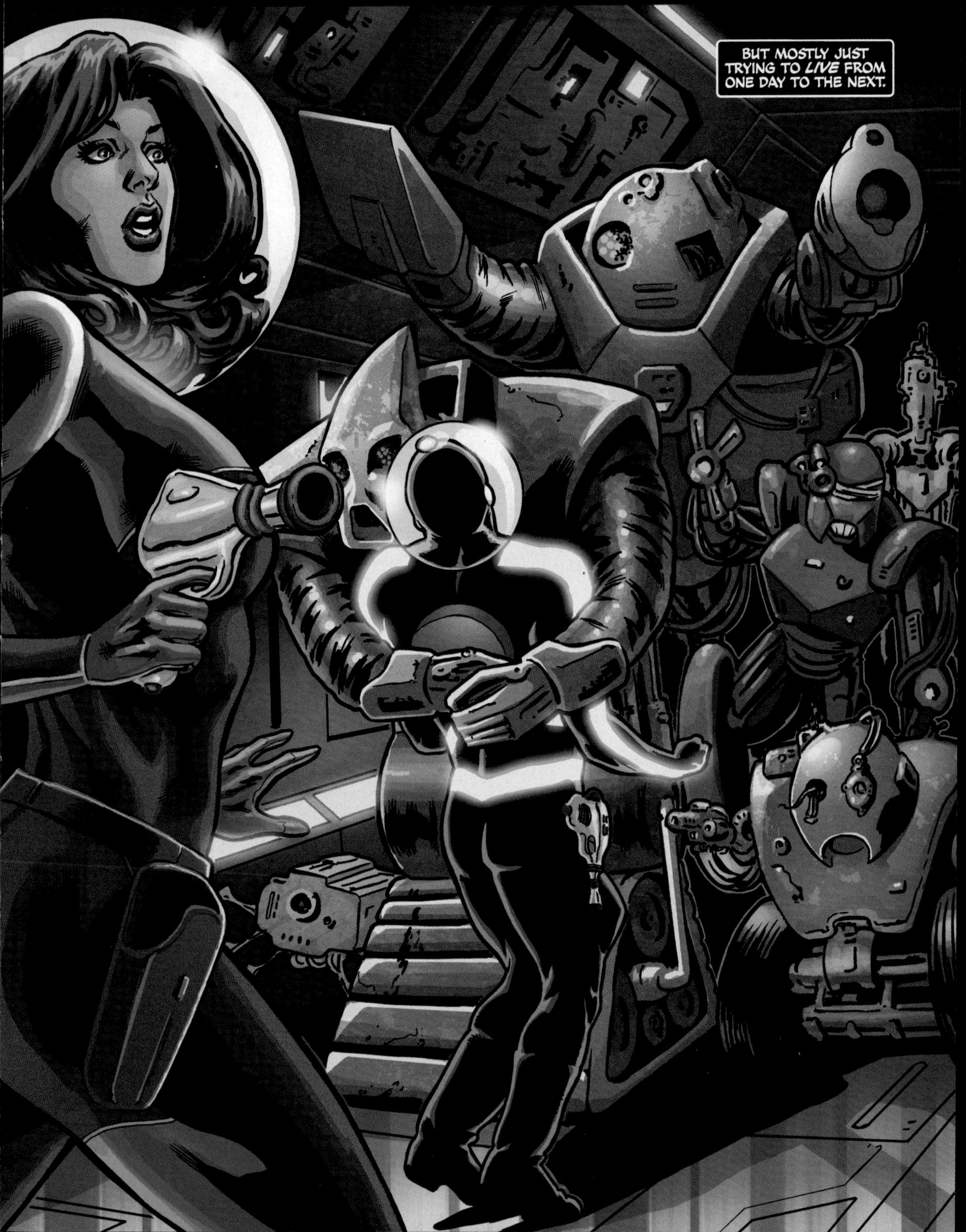
BUT MOSTLY JUST TRYING TO *LIVE* FROM ONE DAY TO THE NEXT.

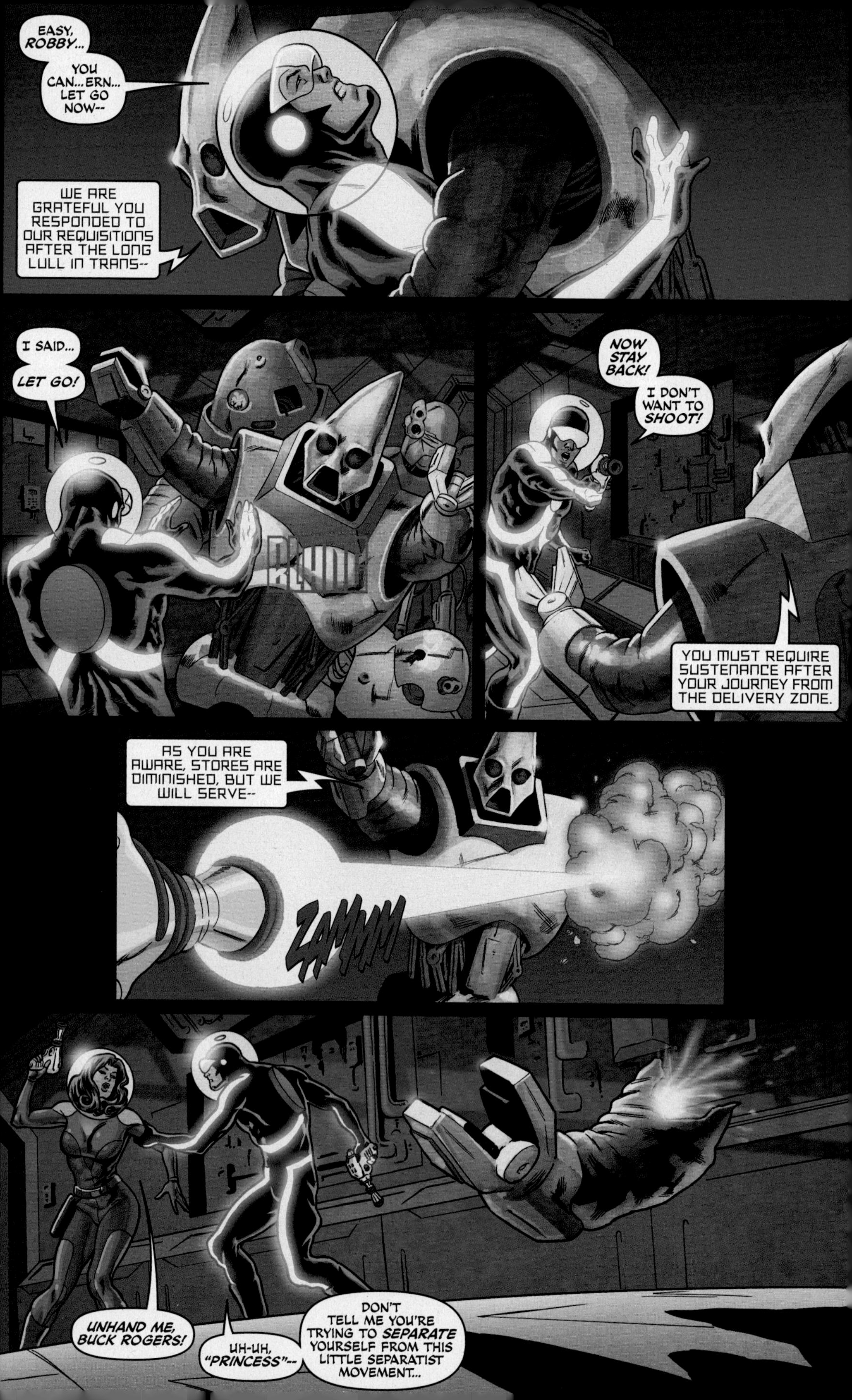
EASY, ROBBY...
YOU CAN...ERN... LET GO NOW--
WE ARE GRATEFUL YOU RESPONDED TO OUR REQUISITIONS AFTER THE LONG LULL IN TRANS--
I SAID...
LET GO!
BLHUK
NOW STAY BACK!
I DON'T WANT TO SHOOT!
YOU MUST REQUIRE SUSTENANCE AFTER YOUR JOURNEY FROM THE DELIVERY ZONE.
AS YOU ARE AWARE, STORES ARE DIMINISHED, BUT WE WILL SERVE--
ZAMMM
UNHAND ME, BUCK ROGERS!
UH-UH, "PRINCESS"--
DON'T TELL ME YOU'RE TRYING TO SEPARATE YOURSELF FROM THIS LITTLE SEPARATIST MOVEMENT...

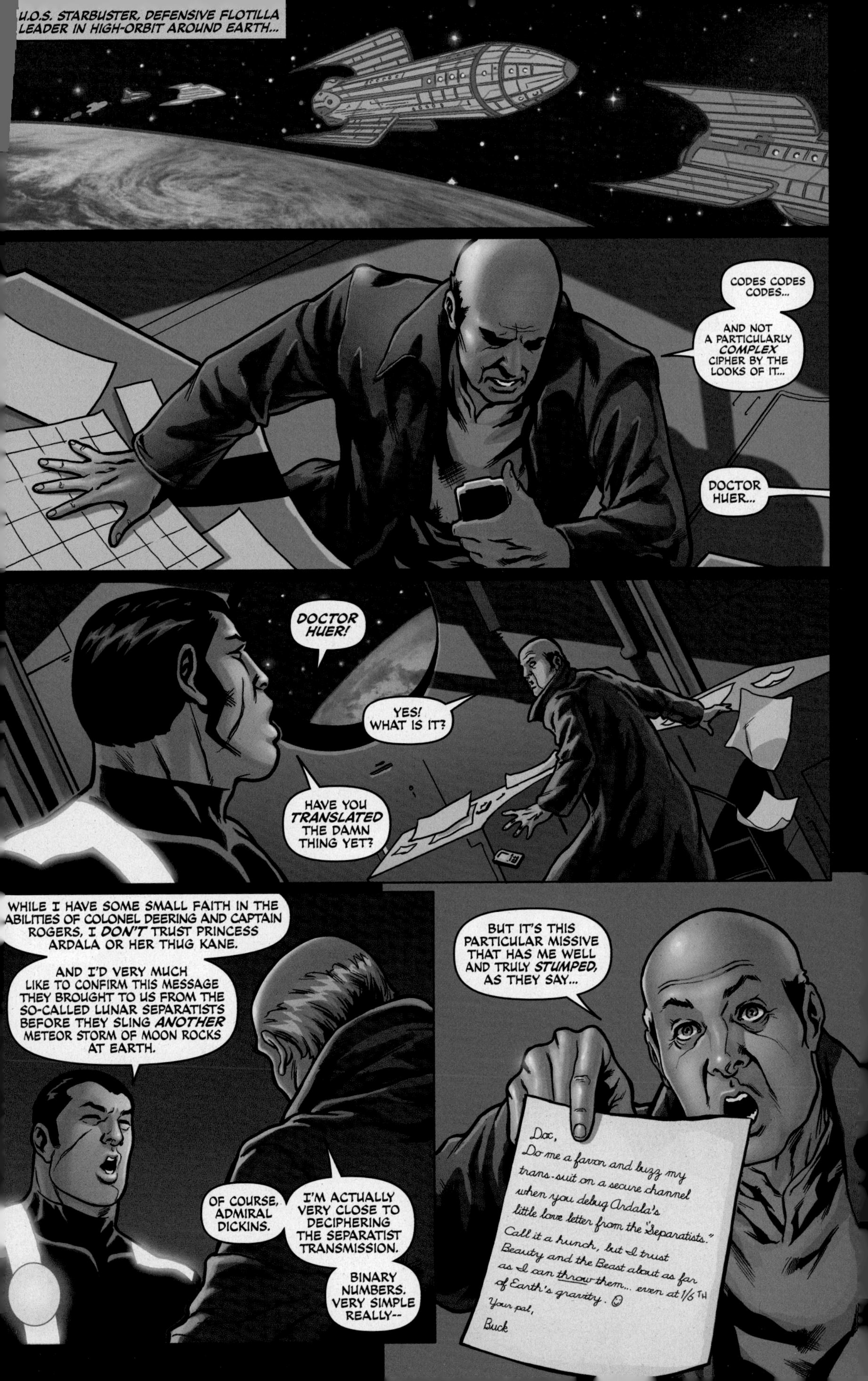
U.O.S. STARBUSTER, DEFENSIVE FLOTILLA LEADER IN HIGH-ORBIT AROUND EARTH...
CODES CODES CODES...
AND NOT A PARTICULARLY COMPLEX CIPHER BY THE LOOKS OF IT...
DOCTOR HUER...
DOCTOR HUER!
YES! WHAT IS IT?
HAVE YOU TRANSLATED THE DAMN THING YET?
WHILE I HAVE SOME SMALL FAITH IN THE ABILITIES OF COLONEL DEERING AND CAPTAIN ROGERS, I DON'T TRUST PRINCESS ARDALA OR HER THUG KANE.
AND I'D VERY MUCH LIKE TO CONFIRM THIS MESSAGE THEY BROUGHT TO US FROM THE SO-CALLED LUNAR SEPARATISTS BEFORE THEY SLING ANOTHER METEOR STORM OF MOON ROCKS AT EARTH.
OF COURSE, ADMIRAL DICKINS.
I'M ACTUALLY VERY CLOSE TO DECIPHERING THE SEPARATIST TRANSMISSION.
BINARY NUMBERS. VERY SIMPLE REALLY--
BUT IT'S THIS PARTICULAR MISSIVE THAT HAS ME WELL AND TRULY STUMPED, AS THEY SAY...
Doc,
Do me a favor and buzz my trans-suit on a secure channel when you debug Ardala's little love letter from the "Separatists."
Call it a hunch, but I trust Beauty and the Beast about as far as I can throw them... even at 1/6TH of Earth's gravity. ☺
Your pal,
Buck

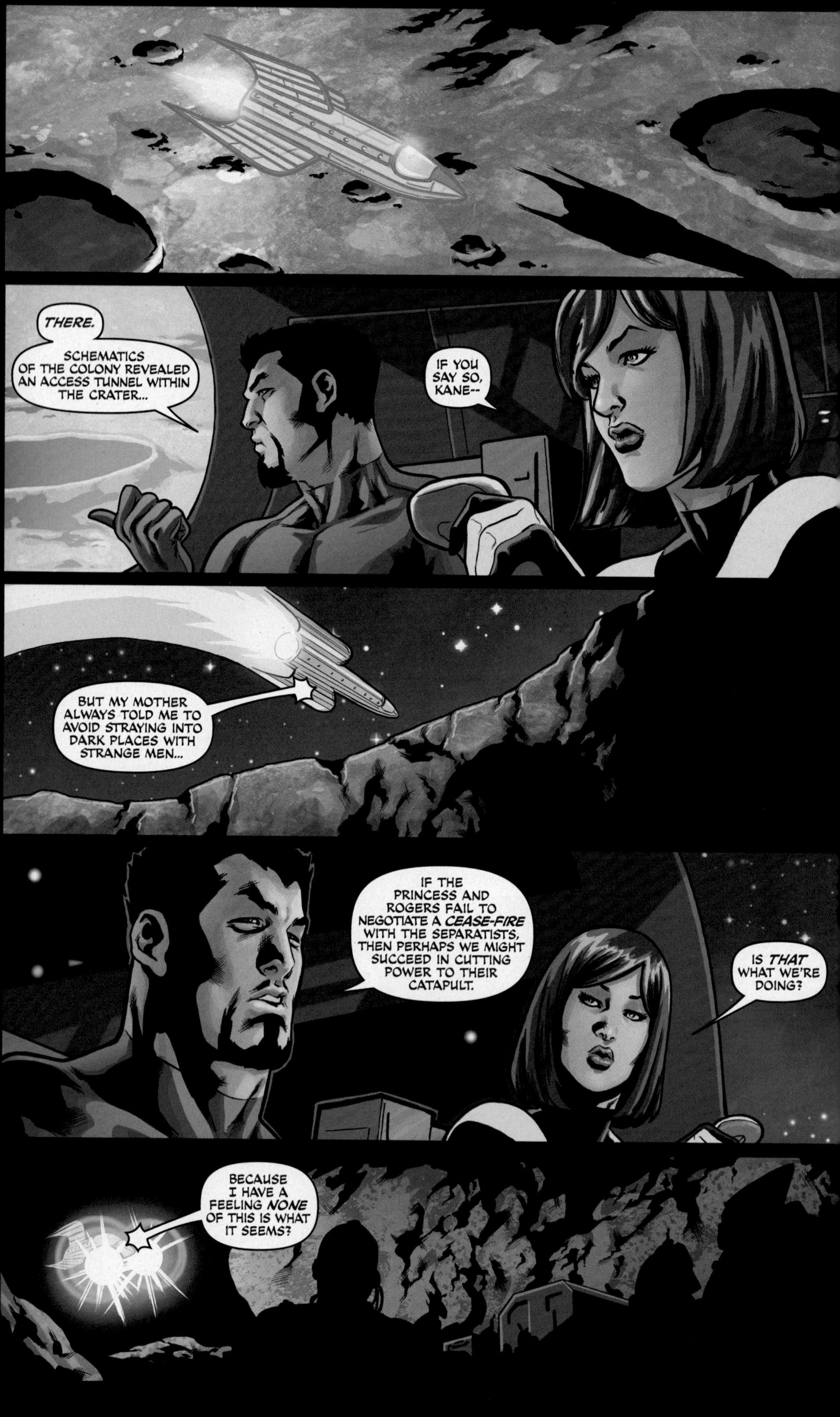
THERE.
SCHEMATICS OF THE COLONY REVEALED AN ACCESS TUNNEL WITHIN THE CRATER...
IF YOU SAY SO, KANE--
BUT MY MOTHER ALWAYS TOLD ME TO AVOID STRAYING INTO DARK PLACES WITH STRANGE MEN...
IF THE PRINCESS AND ROGERS FAIL TO NEGOTIATE A CEASE-FIRE WITH THE SEPARATISTS, THEN PERHAPS WE MIGHT SUCCEED IN CUTTING POWER TO THEIR CATAPULT.
IS THAT WHAT WE'RE DOING?
BECAUSE I HAVE A FEELING NONE OF THIS IS WHAT IT SEEMS?

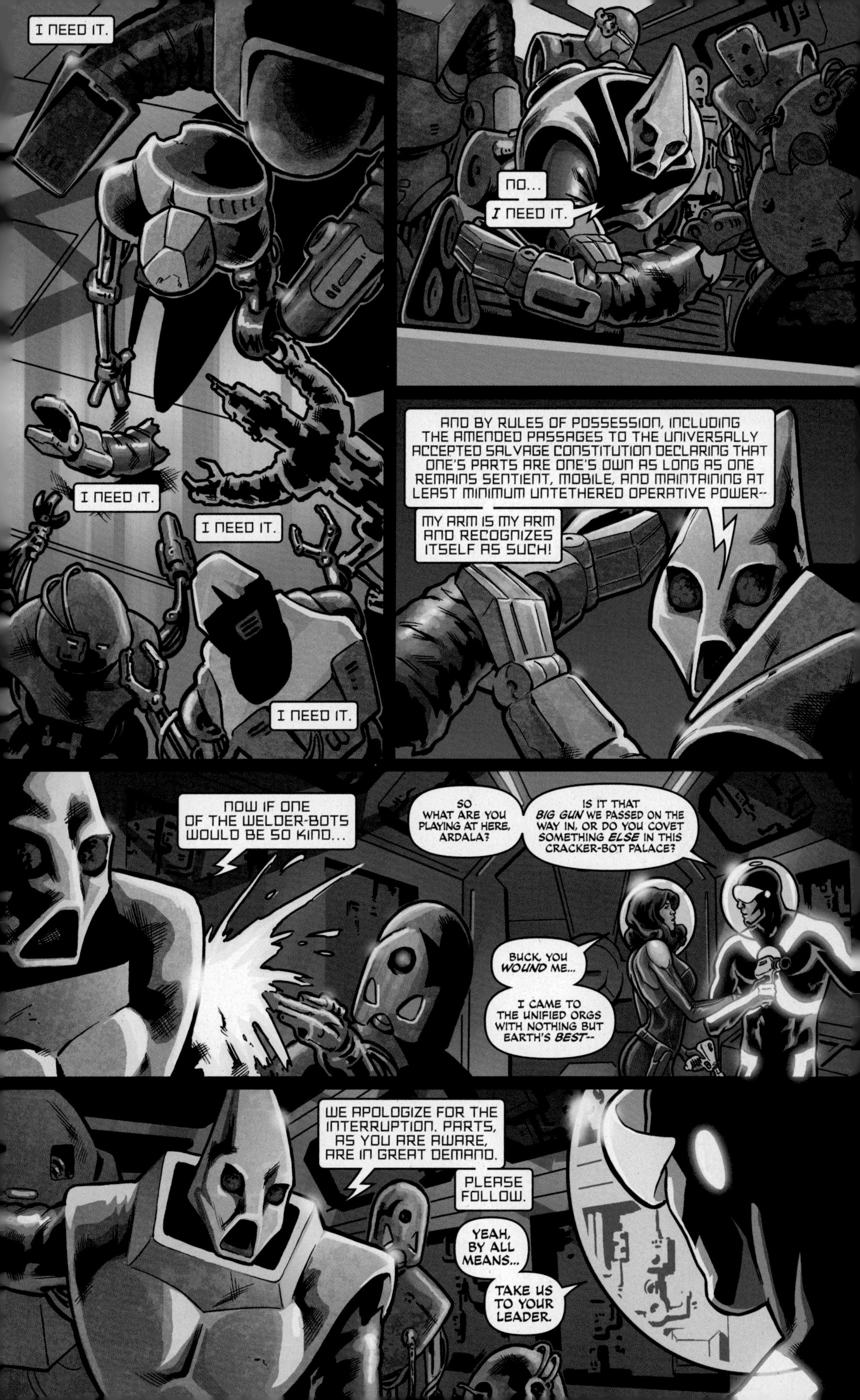
I NEED IT.
NO...
I NEED IT.
I NEED IT.
I NEED IT.
I NEED IT.
AND BY RULES OF POSSESSION, INCLUDING THE AMENDED PASSAGES TO THE UNIVERSALLY ACCEPTED SALVAGE CONSTITUTION DECLARING THAT ONE'S PARTS ARE ONE'S OWN AS LONG AS ONE REMAINS SENTIENT, MOBILE, AND MAINTAINING AT LEAST MINIMUM UNTETHERED OPERATIVE POWER--
MY ARM IS MY ARM AND RECOGNIZES ITSELF AS SUCH!
NOW IF ONE OF THE WELDER-BOTS WOULD BE SO KIND...
SO WHAT ARE YOU PLAYING AT HERE, ARDALA?
IS IT THAT *BIG GUN* WE PASSED ON THE WAY IN, OR DO YOU COVET SOMETHING *ELSE* IN THIS CRACKER-BOT PALACE?
BUCK, YOU *WOUND* ME...
I CAME TO THE UNIFIED ORGS WITH NOTHING BUT EARTH'S *BEST*--
WE APOLOGIZE FOR THE INTERRUPTION. PARTS, AS YOU ARE AWARE, ARE IN GREAT DEMAND.
PLEASE FOLLOW.
YEAH, BY ALL MEANS...
TAKE US TO YOUR LEADER.

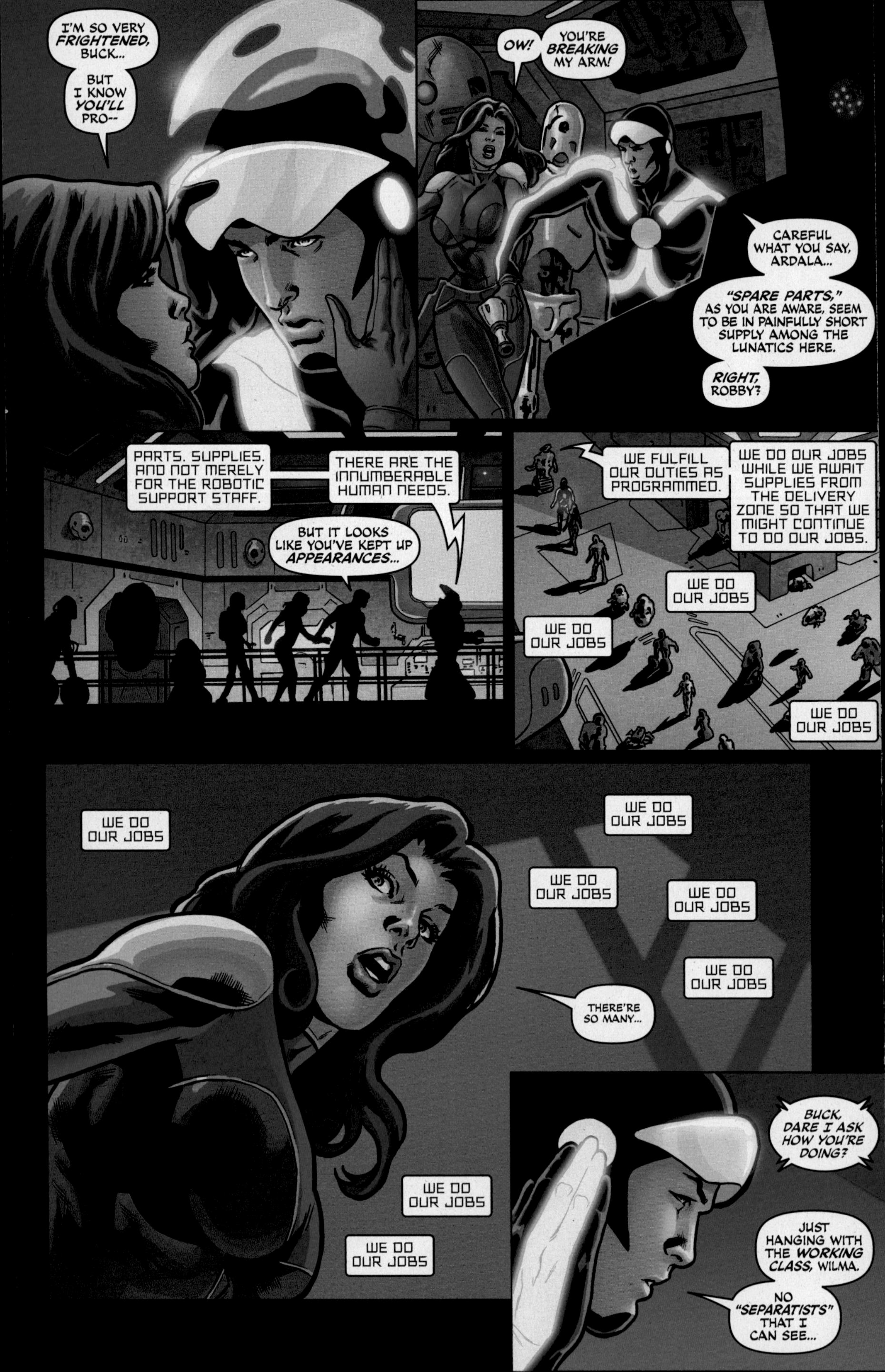
I'M SO VERY FRIGHTENED, BUCK...
BUT I KNOW YOU'LL PRO--
OW!
YOU'RE BREAKING MY ARM!
CAREFUL WHAT YOU SAY, ARDALA...
"SPARE PARTS," AS YOU ARE AWARE, SEEM TO BE IN PAINFULLY SHORT SUPPLY AMONG THE LUNATICS HERE.
RIGHT, ROBBY?
PARTS. SUPPLIES. AND NOT MERELY FOR THE ROBOTIC SUPPORT STAFF.
THERE ARE THE INNUMBERABLE HUMAN NEEDS.
BUT IT LOOKS LIKE YOU'VE KEPT UP APPEARANCES...
WE FULFILL OUR DUTIES AS PROGRAMMED.
WE DO OUR JOBS WHILE WE AWAIT SUPPLIES FROM THE DELIVERY ZONE SO THAT WE MIGHT CONTINUE TO DO OUR JOBS.
WE DO OUR JOBS
WE DO OUR JOBS
WE DO OUR JOBS
WE DO OUR JOBS
WE DO OUR JOBS
WE DO OUR JOBS
WE DO OUR JOBS
WE DO OUR JOBS
THERE'RE SO MANY...
WE DO OUR JOBS
WE DO OUR JOBS
BUCK, DARE I ASK HOW YOU'RE DOING?
JUST HANGING WITH THE WORKING CLASS, WILMA.
NO "SEPARATISTS" THAT I CAN SEE...

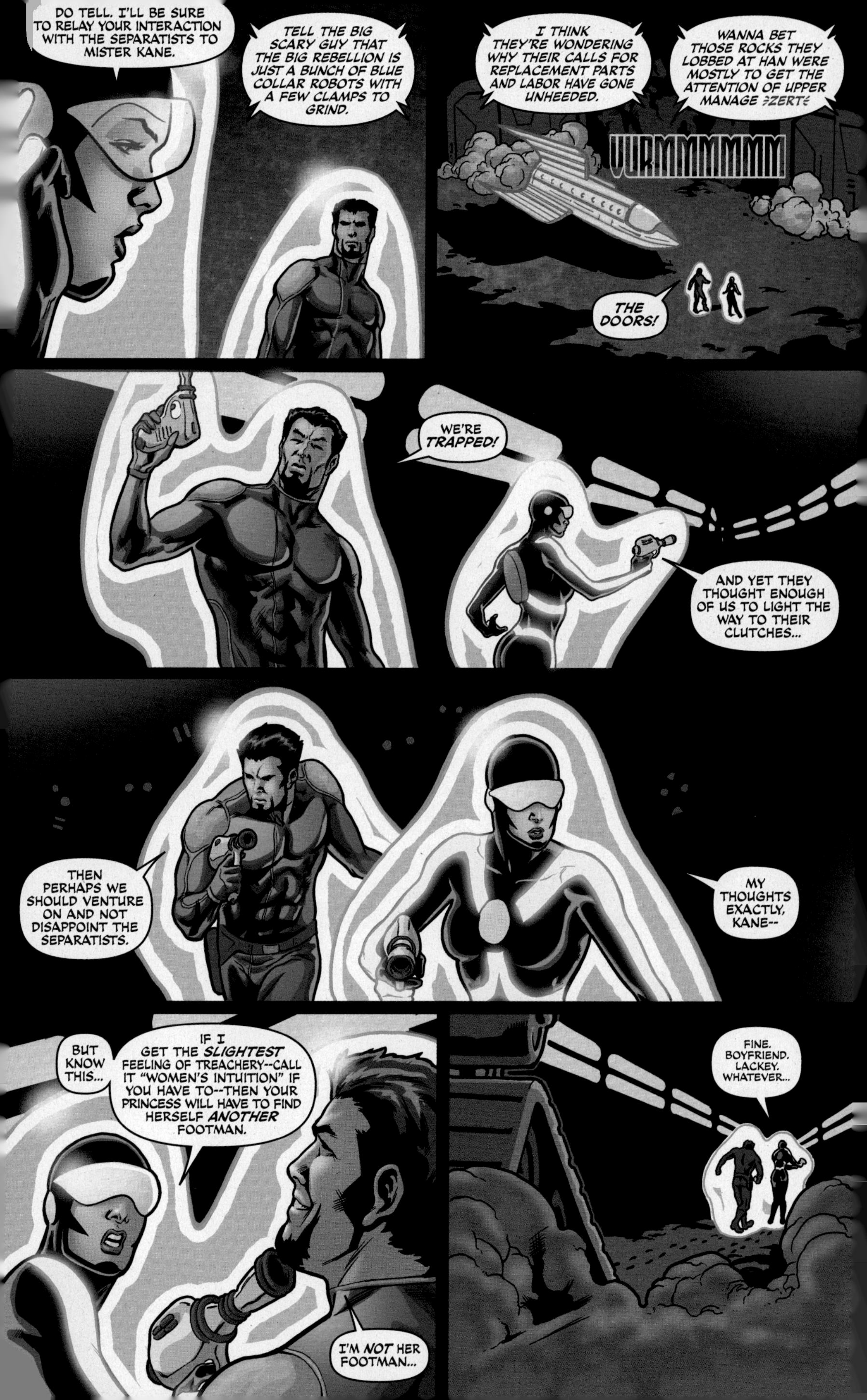

DO TELL. I'LL BE SURE TO RELAY YOUR INTERACTION WITH THE SEPARATISTS TO MISTER KANE.
TELL THE BIG SCARY GUY THAT THE BIG REBELLION IS JUST A BUNCH OF BLUE COLLAR ROBOTS WITH A FEW CLAMPS TO GRIND.
I THINK THEY'RE WONDERING WHY THEIR CALLS FOR REPLACEMENT PARTS AND LABOR HAVE GONE UNHEEDED.
WANNA BET THOSE ROCKS THEY LOBBED AT HAN WERE MOSTLY TO GET THE ATTENTION OF UPPER MANAGE ≈ZERT≈
VURMMMMMMM
THE DOORS!
WE'RE TRAPPED!
AND YET THEY THOUGHT ENOUGH OF US TO LIGHT THE WAY TO THEIR CLUTCHES...
THEN PERHAPS WE SHOULD VENTURE ON AND NOT DISAPPOINT THE SEPARATISTS.
MY THOUGHTS EXACTLY, KANE--
BUT KNOW THIS...
IF I GET THE SLIGHTEST FEELING OF TREACHERY--CALL IT "WOMEN'S INTUITION" IF YOU HAVE TO--THEN YOUR PRINCESS WILL HAVE TO FIND HERSELF ANOTHER FOOTMAN.
I'M NOT HER FOOTMAN...
FINE. BOYFRIEND. LACKEY. WHATEVER...

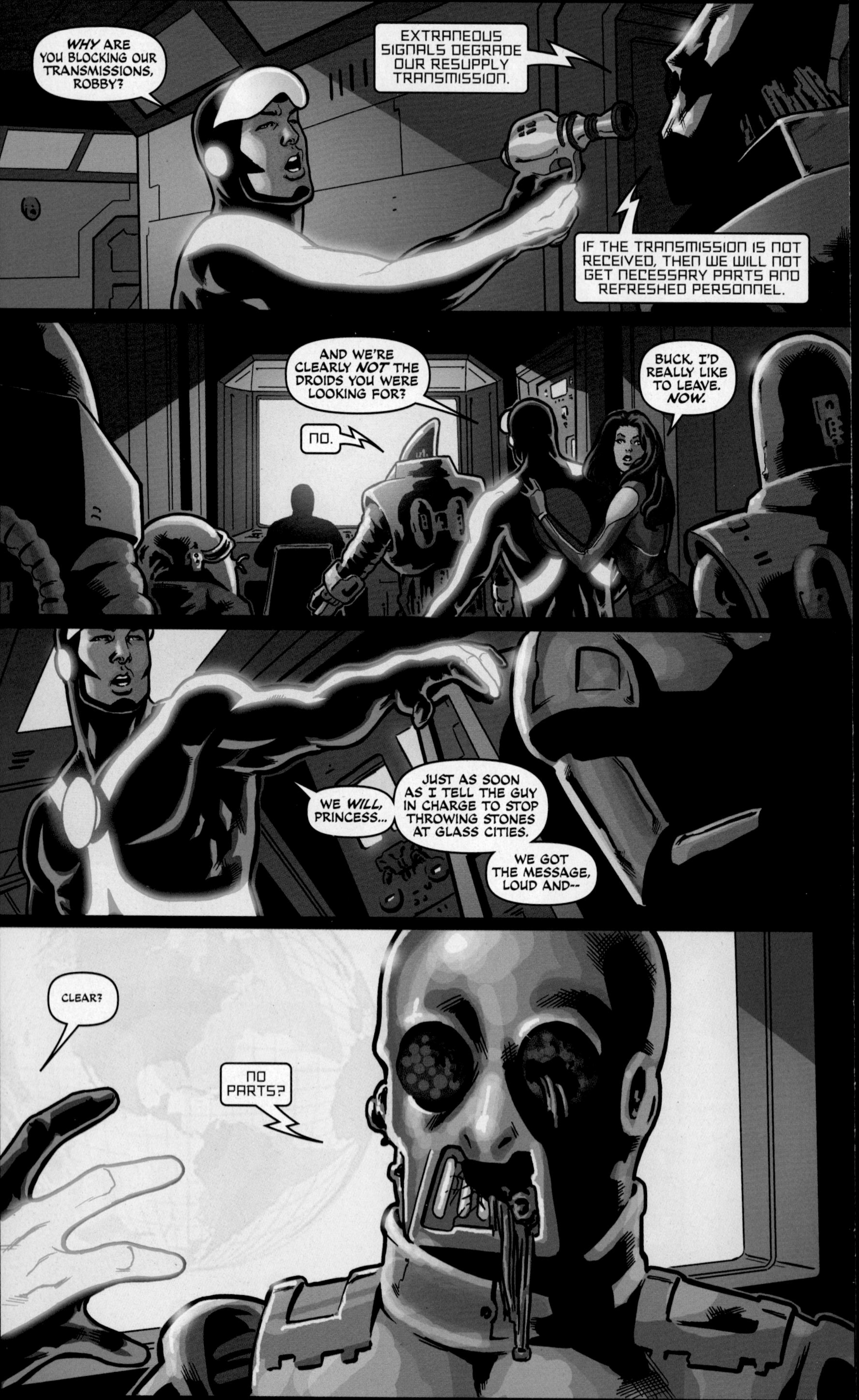
WHY ARE YOU BLOCKING OUR TRANSMISSIONS, ROBBY?
EXTRANEOUS SIGNALS DEGRADE OUR RESUPPLY TRANSMISSION.
IF THE TRANSMISSION IS NOT RECEIVED, THEN WE WILL NOT GET NECESSARY PARTS AND REFRESHED PERSONNEL.
AND WE'RE CLEARLY NOT THE DROIDS YOU WERE LOOKING FOR?
NO.
BUCK, I'D REALLY LIKE TO LEAVE. NOW.
WE WILL, PRINCESS...
JUST AS SOON AS I TELL THE GUY IN CHARGE TO STOP THROWING STONES AT GLASS CITIES.
WE GOT THE MESSAGE, LOUD AND--
CLEAR?
NO PARTS?

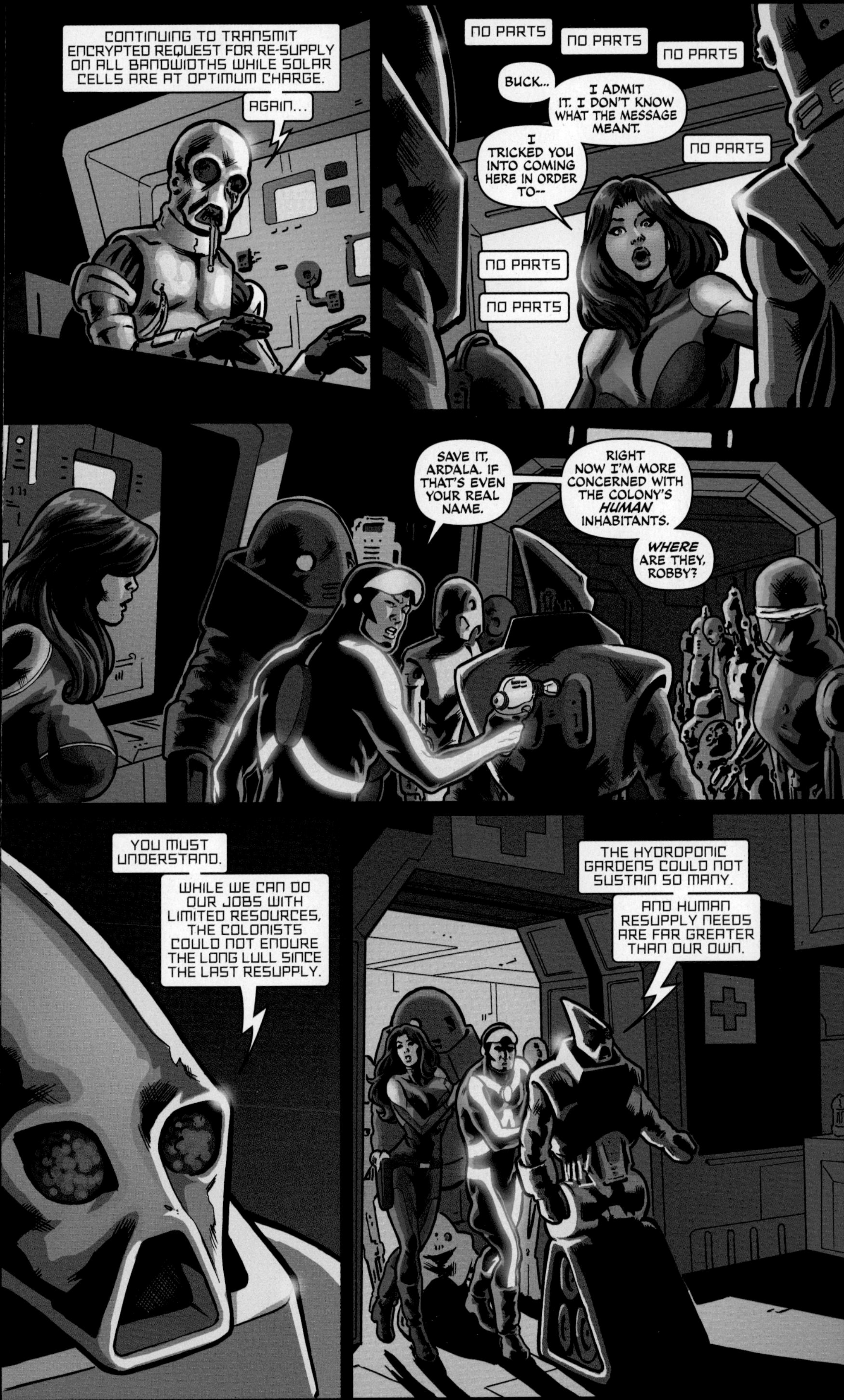
CONTINUING TO TRANSMIT ENCRYPTED REQUEST FOR RE-SUPPLY ON ALL BANDWIDTHS WHILE SOLAR CELLS ARE AT OPTIMUM CHARGE.
AGAIN...
NO PARTS
NO PARTS
NO PARTS
BUCK...
I ADMIT IT. I DON'T KNOW WHAT THE MESSAGE MEANT.
I TRICKED YOU INTO COMING HERE IN ORDER TO--
NO PARTS
NO PARTS
NO PARTS
SAVE IT, ARDALA. IF THAT'S EVEN YOUR REAL NAME.
RIGHT NOW I'M MORE CONCERNED WITH THE COLONY'S *HUMAN* INHABITANTS.
WHERE ARE THEY, ROBBY?
YOU MUST UNDERSTAND.
WHILE WE CAN DO OUR JOBS WITH LIMITED RESOURCES, THE COLONISTS COULD NOT ENDURE THE LONG LULL SINCE THE LAST RESUPPLY.
THE HYDROPONIC GARDENS COULD NOT SUSTAIN SO MANY.
AND HUMAN RESUPPLY NEEDS ARE FAR GREATER THAN OUR OWN.

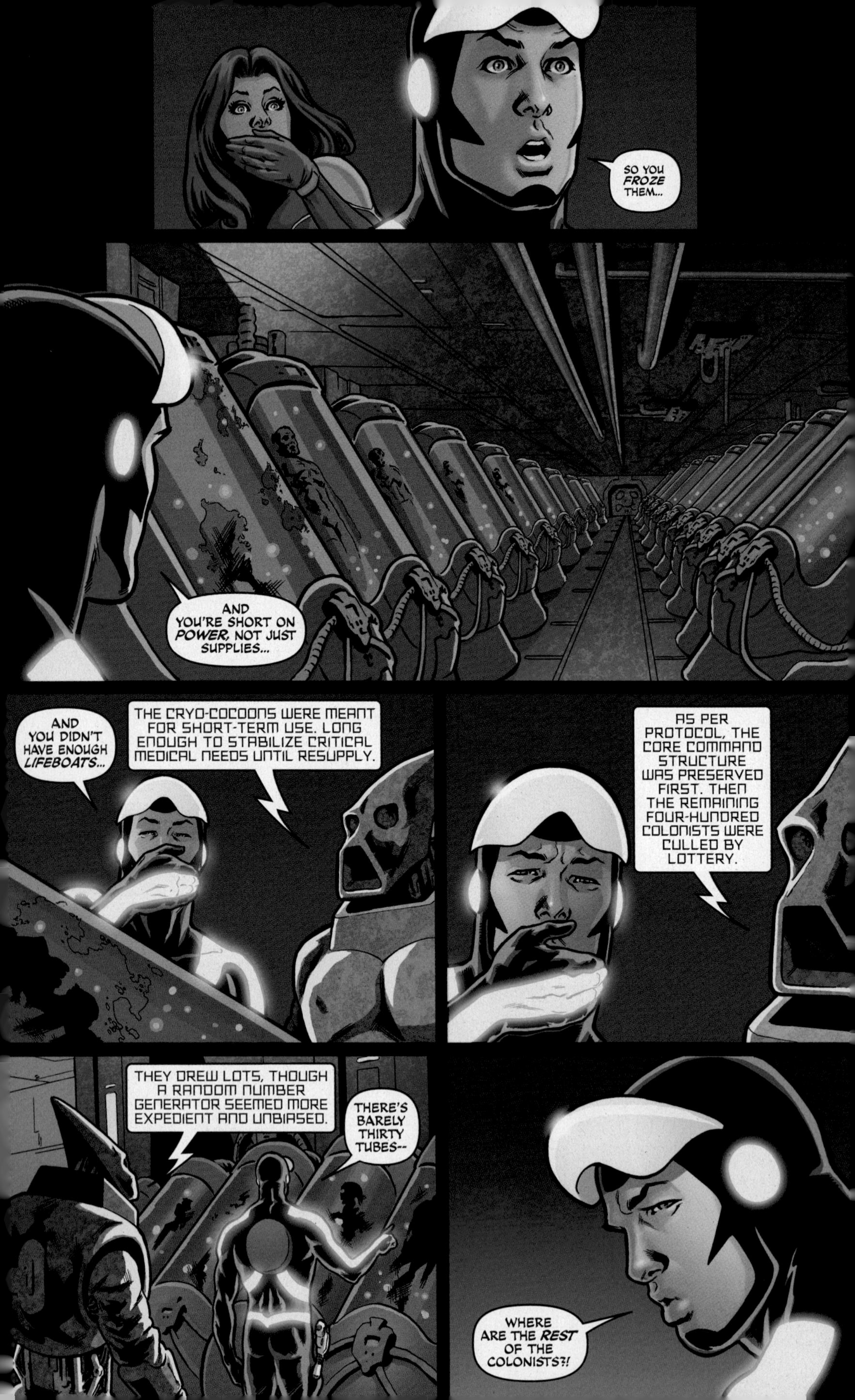
SO YOU FROZE THEM...
AND YOU'RE SHORT ON POWER, NOT JUST SUPPLIES...
AND YOU DIDN'T HAVE ENOUGH LIFEBOATS...
THE CRYO-COCOONS WERE MEANT FOR SHORT-TERM USE. LONG ENOUGH TO STABILIZE CRITICAL MEDICAL NEEDS UNTIL RESUPPLY.
AS PER PROTOCOL, THE CORE COMMAND STRUCTURE WAS PRESERVED FIRST. THEN THE REMAINING FOUR-HUNDRED COLONISTS WERE CULLED BY LOTTERY.
THEY DREW LOTS, THOUGH A RANDOM NUMBER GENERATOR SEEMED MORE EXPEDIENT AND UNBIASED.
THERE'S BARELY THIRTY TUBES--
WHERE ARE THE REST OF THE COLONISTS?!

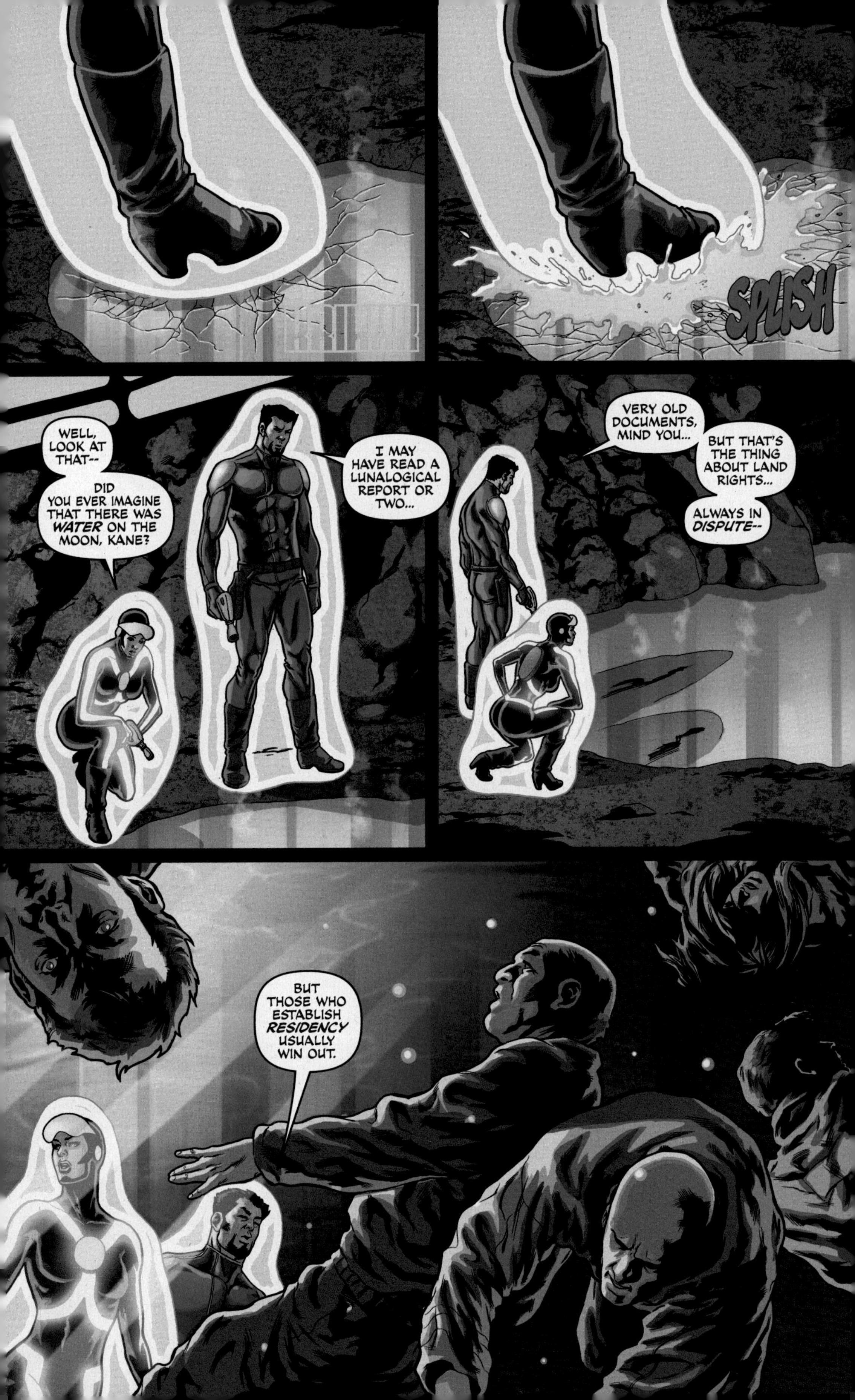
SPLISH
WELL, LOOK AT THAT--
DID YOU EVER IMAGINE THAT THERE WAS WATER ON THE MOON, KANE?
I MAY HAVE READ A LUNALOGICAL REPORT OR TWO...
VERY OLD DOCUMENTS, MIND YOU...
BUT THAT'S THE THING ABOUT LAND RIGHTS...
ALWAYS IN DISPUTE--
BUT THOSE WHO ESTABLISH RESIDENCY USUALLY WIN OUT.

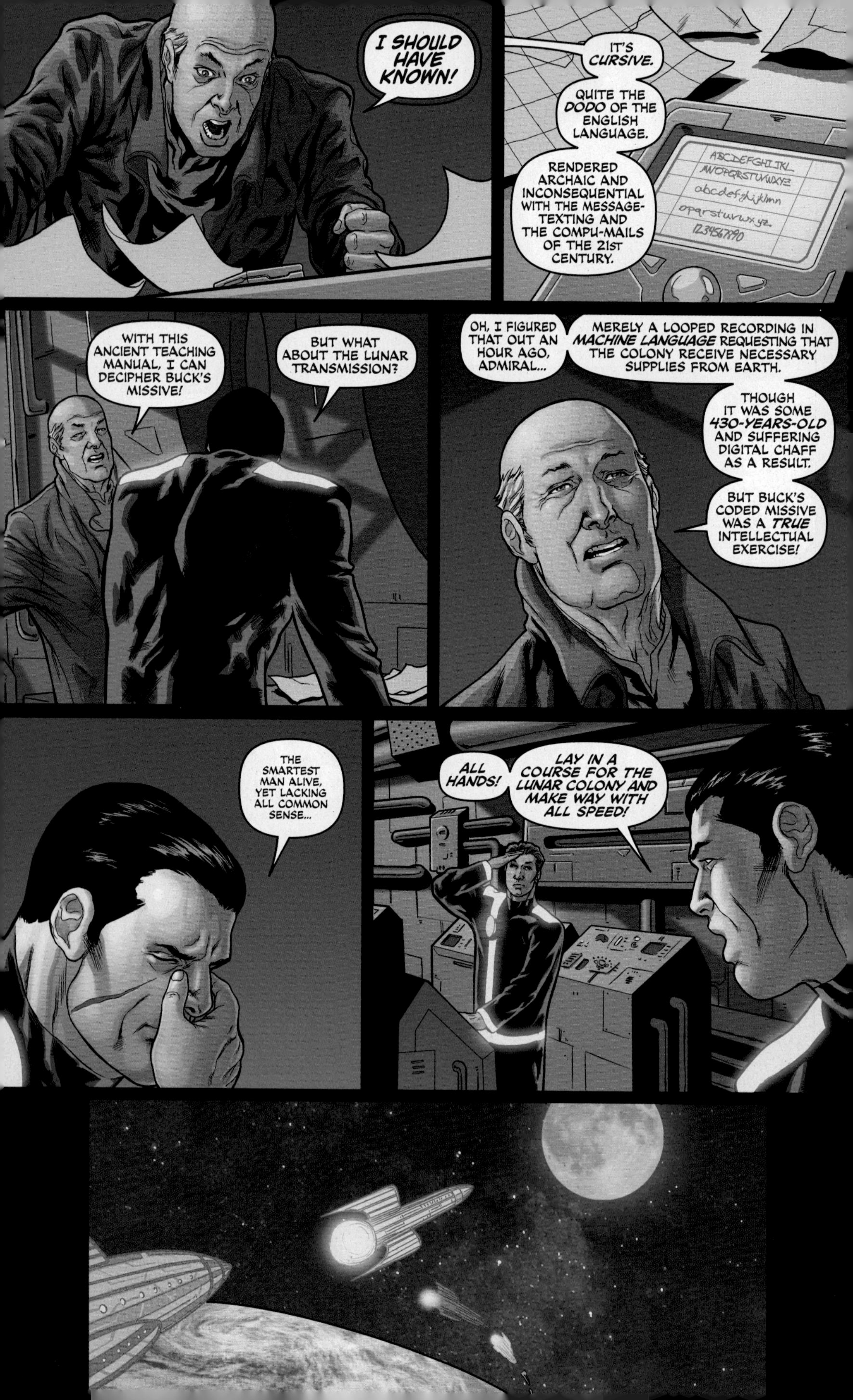
I SHOULD HAVE KNOWN!
IT'S CURSIVE.
QUITE THE DODO OF THE ENGLISH LANGUAGE.
RENDERED ARCHAIC AND INCONSEQUENTIAL WITH THE MESSAGE-TEXTING AND THE COMPU-MAILS OF THE 21ST CENTURY.
ABCDEFGHIJKL
MNOPQRSTUVWXYZ
abcdefghijklmn
opqrstuvwxyz
1234567890
WITH THIS ANCIENT TEACHING MANUAL, I CAN DECIPHER BUCK'S MISSIVE!
BUT WHAT ABOUT THE LUNAR TRANSMISSION?
OH, I FIGURED THAT OUT AN HOUR AGO, ADMIRAL...
MERELY A LOOPED RECORDING IN MACHINE LANGUAGE REQUESTING THAT THE COLONY RECEIVE NECESSARY SUPPLIES FROM EARTH.
THOUGH IT WAS SOME 430-YEARS-OLD AND SUFFERING DIGITAL CHAFF AS A RESULT.
BUT BUCK'S CODED MISSIVE WAS A TRUE INTELLECTUAL EXERCISE!
THE SMARTEST MAN ALIVE, YET LACKING ALL COMMON SENSE...
ALL HANDS!
LAY IN A COURSE FOR THE LUNAR COLONY AND MAKE WAY WITH ALL SPEED!

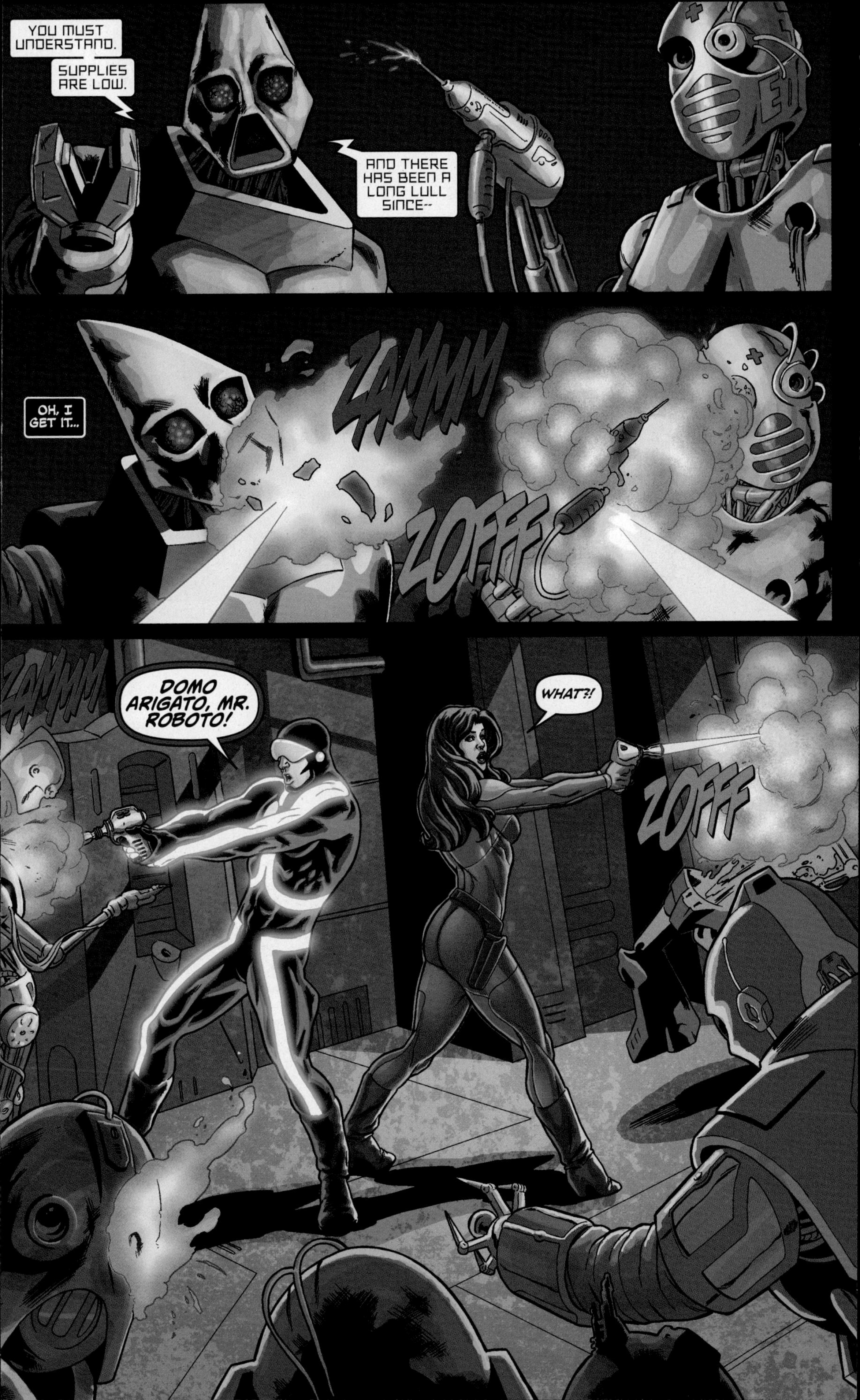
YOU MUST UNDERSTAND.
SUPPLIES ARE LOW.
AND THERE HAS BEEN A LONG LULL SINCE--
OH, I GET IT...
ZAMMM
ZOFFF
ZAMMM
DOMO ARIGATO, MR. ROBOTO!
WHAT?!
ZOFFF

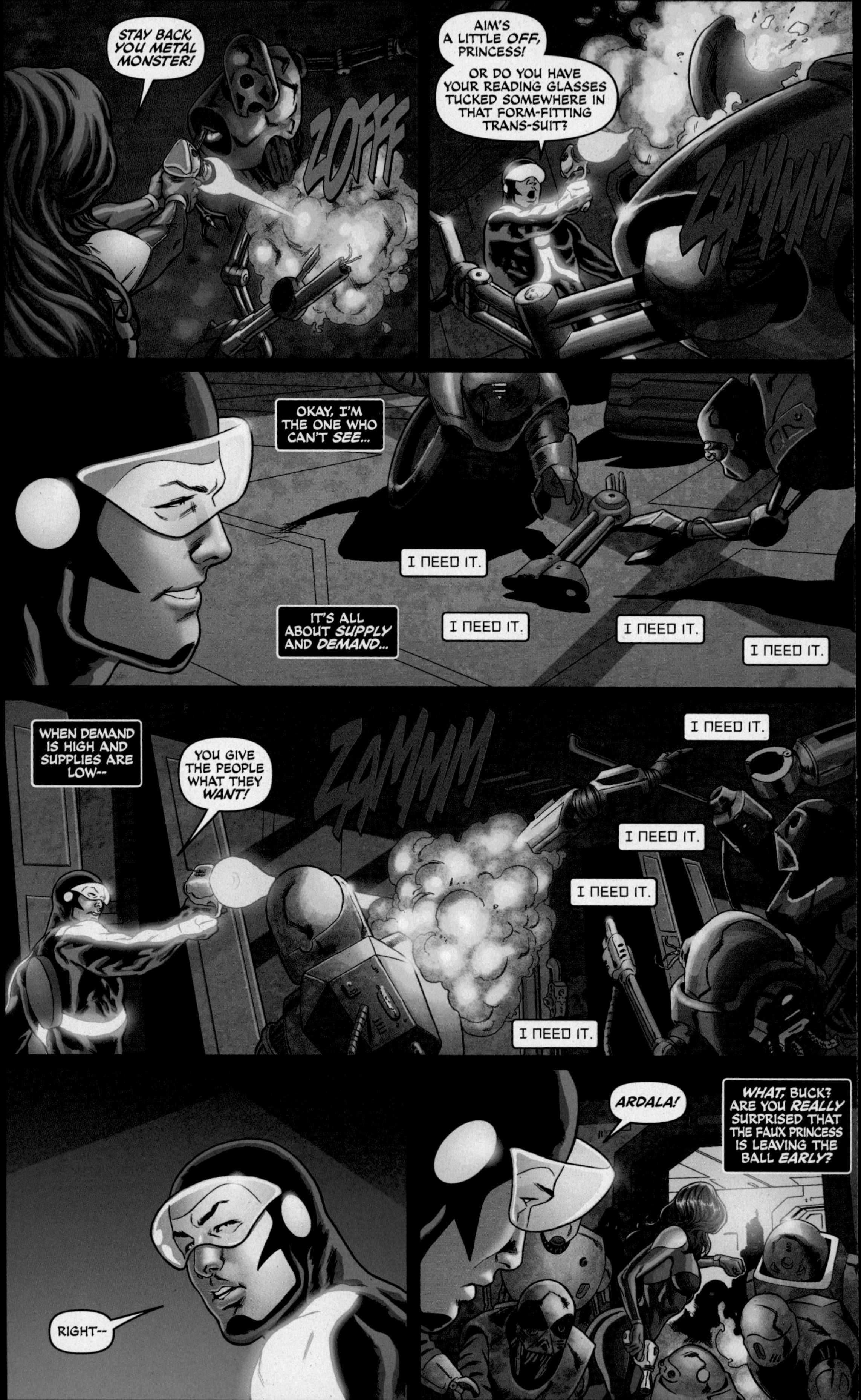

STAY BACK, YOU METAL MONSTER!
ZOFFF
AIM'S A LITTLE OFF, PRINCESS!
OR DO YOU HAVE YOUR READING GLASSES TUCKED SOMEWHERE IN THAT FORM-FITTING TRANS-SUIT?
ZAMMM
OKAY, I'M THE ONE WHO CAN'T SEE...
I NEED IT.
IT'S ALL ABOUT SUPPLY AND DEMAND...
I NEED IT.
I NEED IT.
I NEED IT.
WHEN DEMAND IS HIGH AND SUPPLIES ARE LOW--
YOU GIVE THE PEOPLE WHAT THEY WANT!
ZAMMM
I NEED IT.
I NEED IT.
I NEED IT.
I NEED IT.
RIGHT--
ARDALA!
WHAT, BUCK? ARE YOU REALLY SURPRISED THAT THE FAUX PRINCESS IS LEAVING THE BALL EARLY?

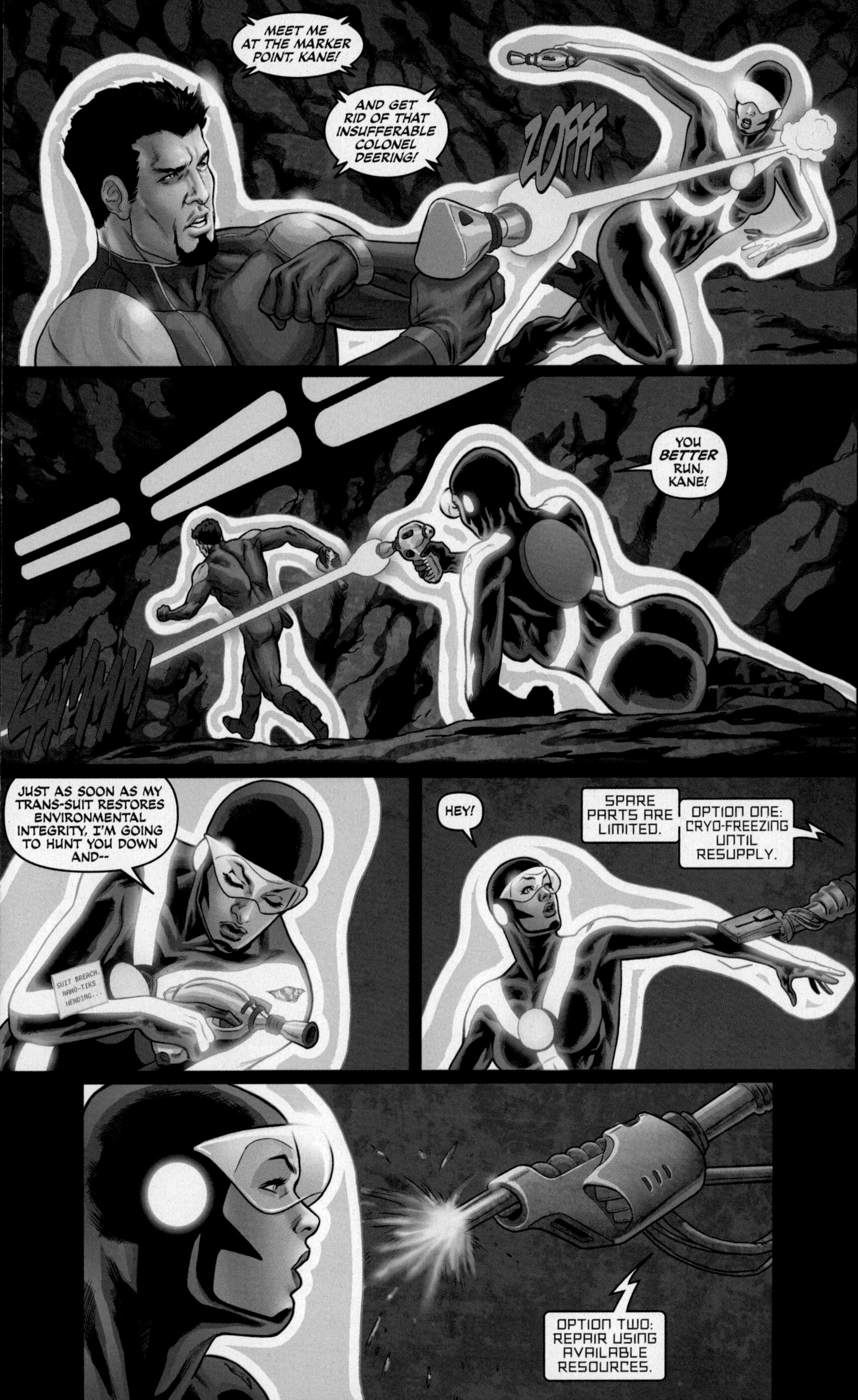
MEET ME AT THE MARKER POINT, KANE!
AND GET RID OF THAT INSUFFERABLE COLONEL DEERING!
ZOFFF
YOU BETTER RUN, KANE!
ZAMMM
JUST AS SOON AS MY TRANS-SUIT RESTORES ENVIRONMENTAL INTEGRITY, I'M GOING TO HUNT YOU DOWN AND--
SUIT BREACH. NANO-TIKS MENDING...
HEY!
SPARE PARTS ARE LIMITED.
OPTION ONE: CRYO-FREEZING UNTIL RESUPPLY.
OPTION TWO: REPAIR USING AVAILABLE RESOURCES.

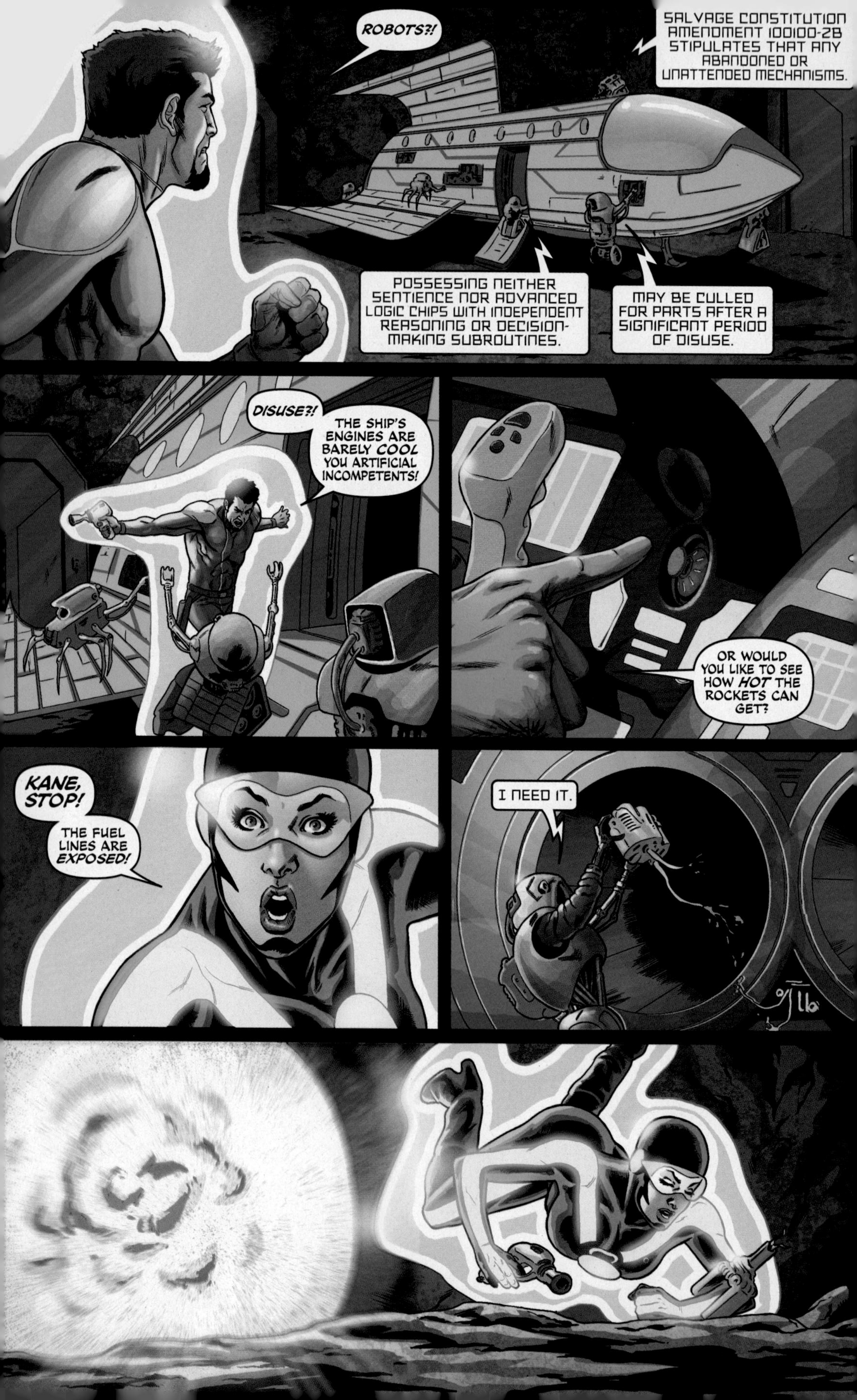
ROBOTS?!
SALVAGE CONSTITUTION AMENDMENT 100100-2B STIPULATES THAT ANY ABANDONED OR UNATTENDED MECHANISMS.
POSSESSING NEITHER SENTIENCE NOR ADVANCED LOGIC CHIPS WITH INDEPENDENT REASONING OR DECISION-MAKING SUBROUTINES.
MAY BE CULLED FOR PARTS AFTER A SIGNIFICANT PERIOD OF DISUSE.
DISUSE?!
THE SHIP'S ENGINES ARE BARELY COOL YOU ARTIFICIAL INCOMPETENTS!
OR WOULD YOU LIKE TO SEE HOW HOT THE ROCKETS CAN GET?
KANE, STOP!
THE FUEL LINES ARE EXPOSED!
I NEED IT.

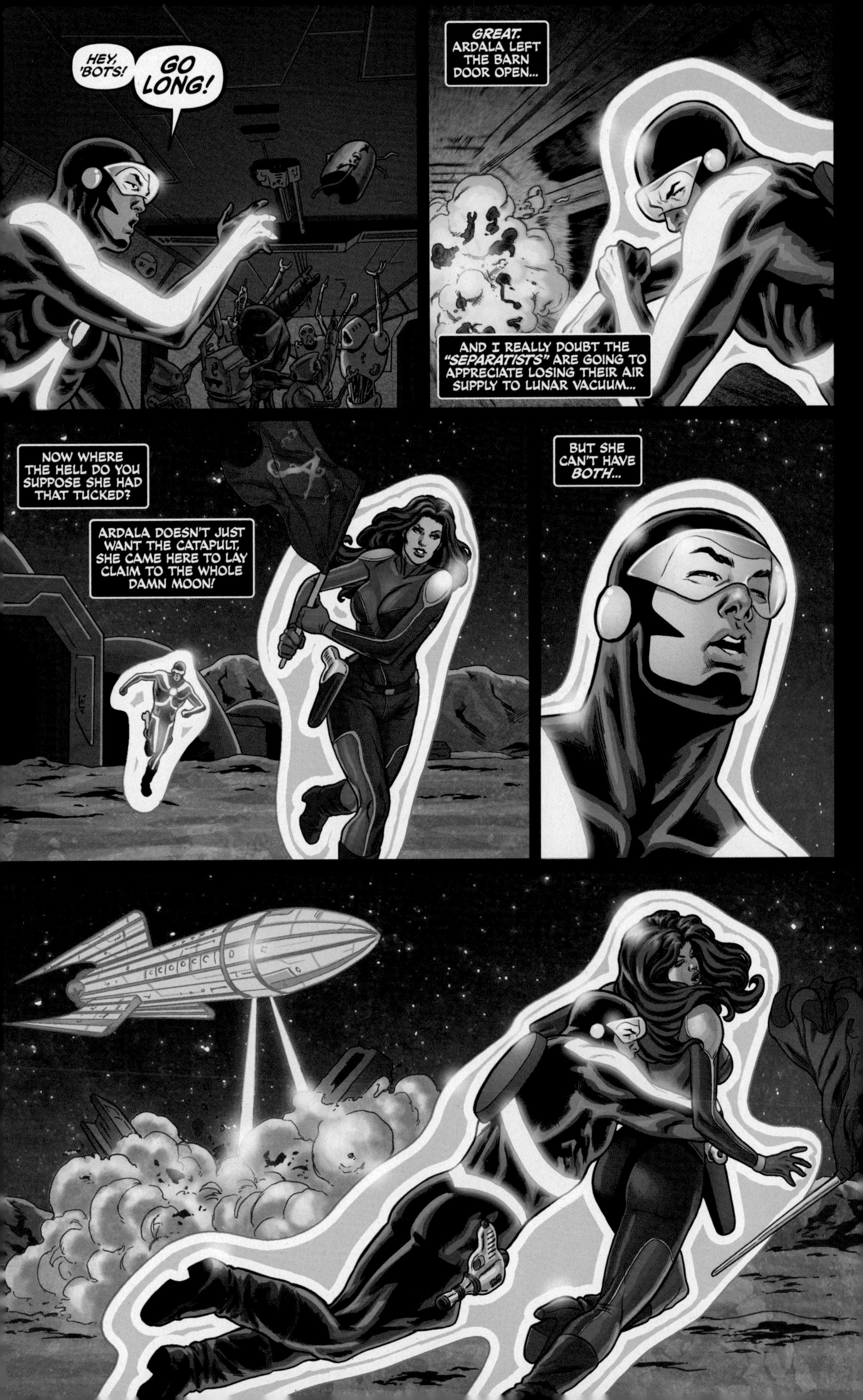
HEY, 'BOTS!
GO LONG!
GREAT. ARDALA LEFT THE BARN DOOR OPEN...
AND I REALLY DOUBT THE "SEPARATISTS" ARE GOING TO APPRECIATE LOSING THEIR AIR SUPPLY TO LUNAR VACUUM...
NOW WHERE THE HELL DO YOU SUPPOSE SHE HAD THAT TUCKED?
ARDALA DOESN'T JUST WANT THE CATAPULT, SHE CAME HERE TO LAY CLAIM TO THE WHOLE DAMN MOON!
BUT SHE CAN'T HAVE BOTH...

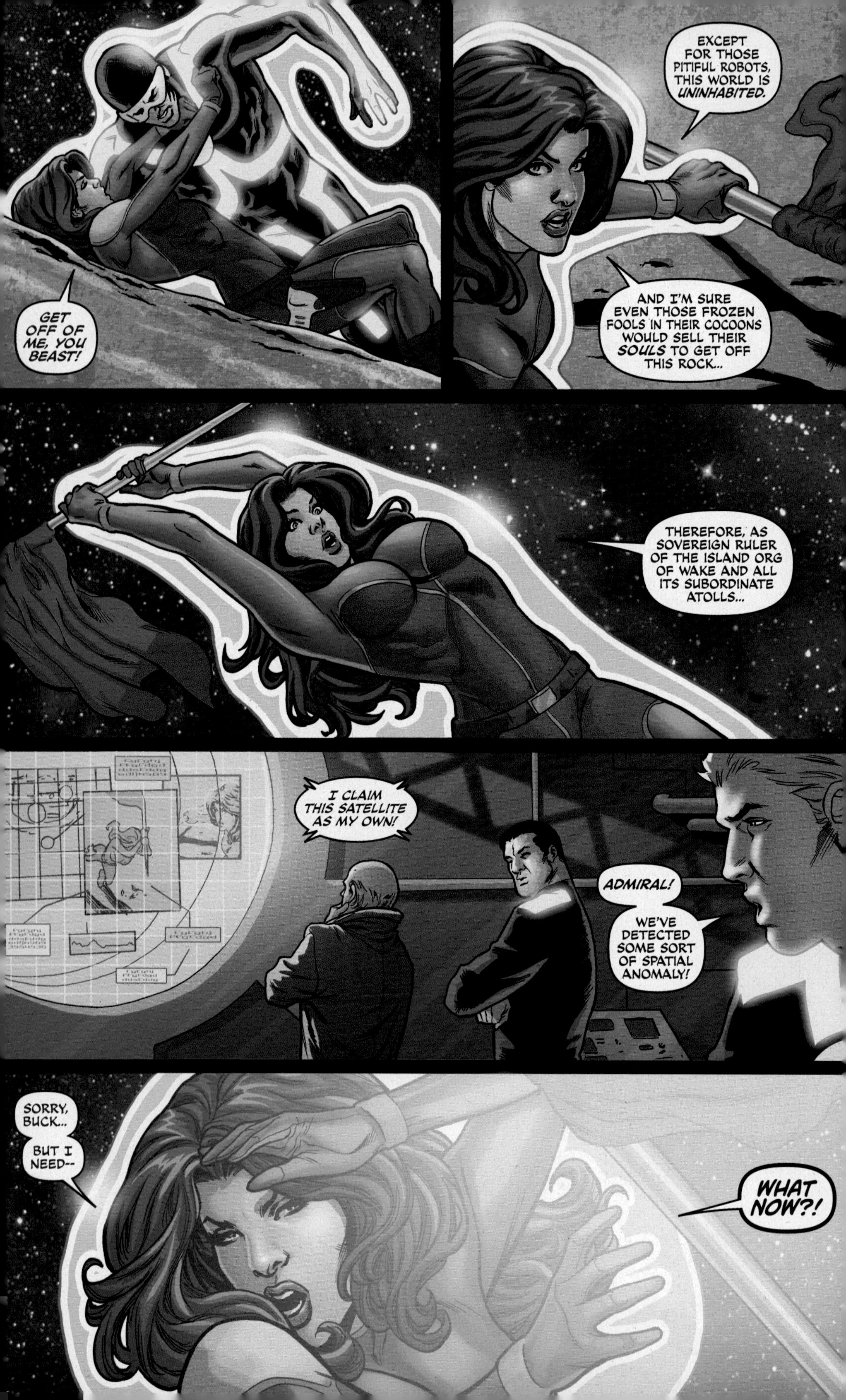
GET OFF OF ME, YOU BEAST!
EXCEPT FOR THOSE PITIFUL ROBOTS, THIS WORLD IS UNINHABITED.
AND I'M SURE EVEN THOSE FROZEN FOOLS IN THEIR COCOONS WOULD SELL THEIR SOULS TO GET OFF THIS ROCK...
THEREFORE, AS SOVEREIGN RULER OF THE ISLAND ORG OF WAKE AND ALL ITS SUBORDINATE ATOLLS...
I CLAIM THIS SATELLITE AS MY OWN!
ADMIRAL!
WE'VE DETECTED SOME SORT OF SPATIAL ANOMALY!
SORRY, BUCK...
BUT I NEED--
WHAT NOW?!

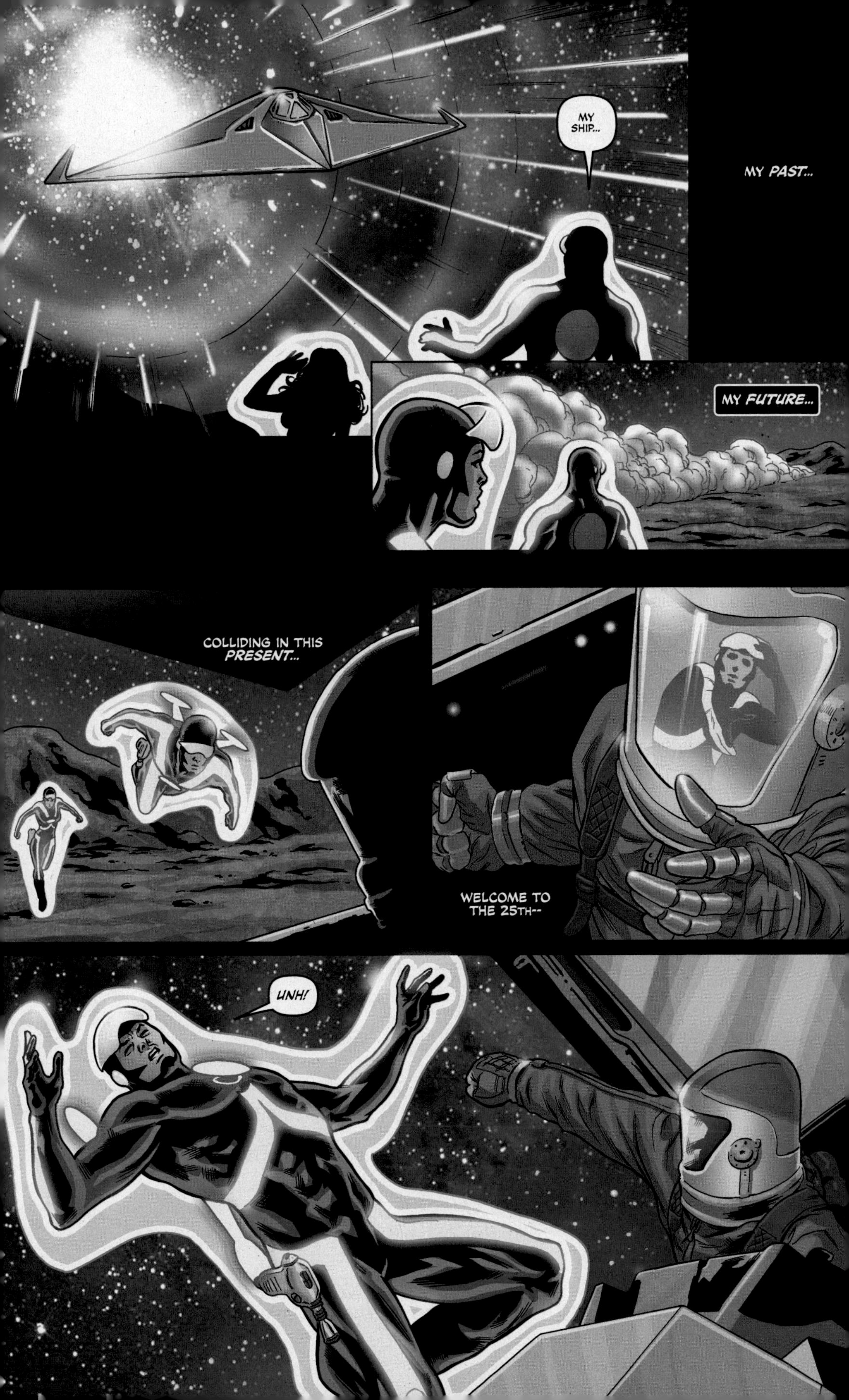
MY SHIP...
MY PAST...
MY FUTURE...
COLLIDING IN THIS PRESENT...
WELCOME TO THE 25TH--
UNH!

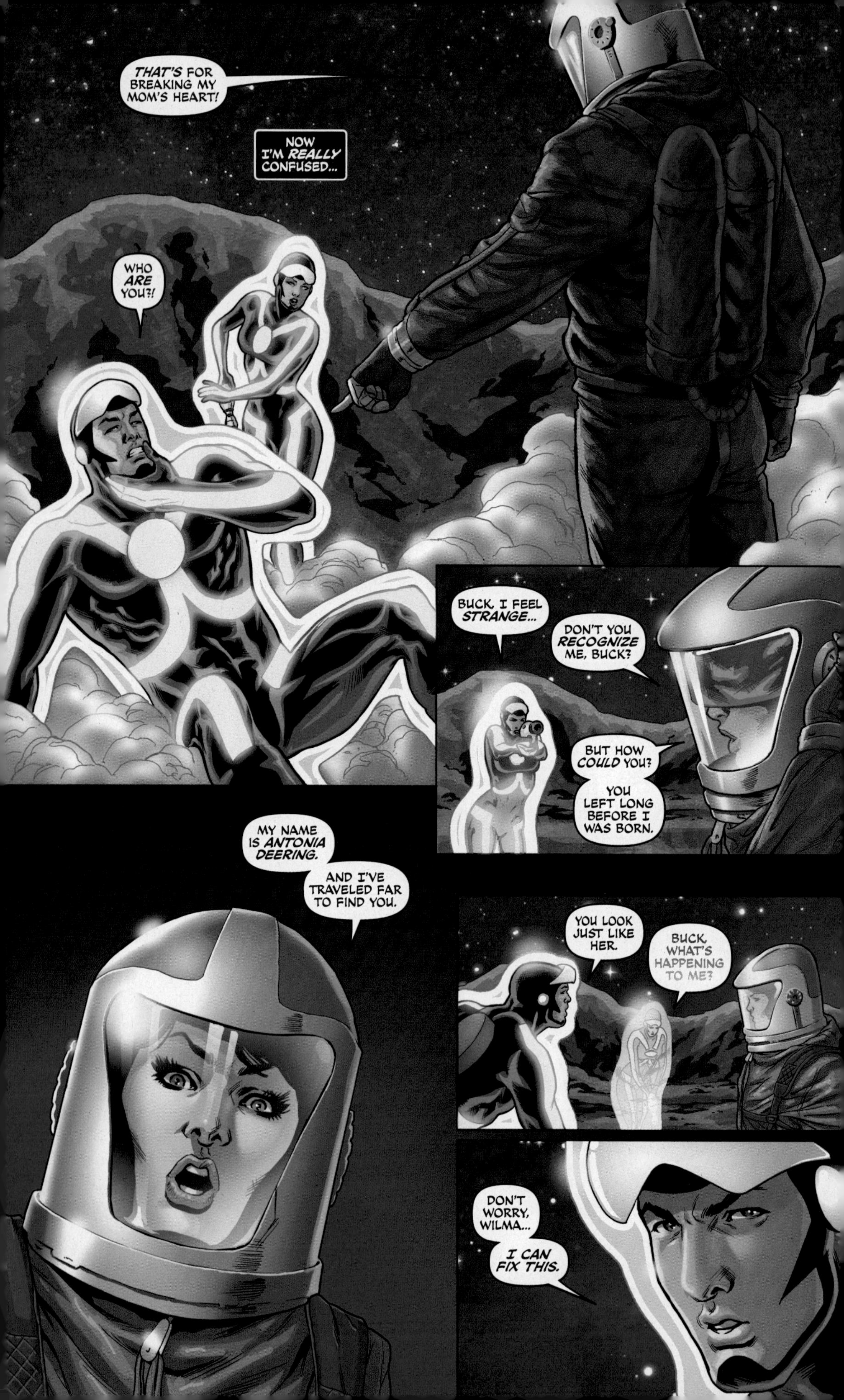
THAT'S FOR BREAKING MY MOM'S HEART!
NOW I'M REALLY CONFUSED...
WHO ARE YOU?!
BUCK, I FEEL STRANGE...
DON'T YOU RECOGNIZE ME, BUCK?
BUT HOW COULD YOU?
YOU LEFT LONG BEFORE I WAS BORN.
MY NAME IS ANTONIA DEERING.
AND I'VE TRAVELED FAR TO FIND YOU.
YOU LOOK JUST LIKE HER.
BUCK, WHAT'S HAPPENING TO ME?
DON'T WORRY, WILMA...
I CAN FIX THIS.

BUCK ROGERS®
WILL RETURN!

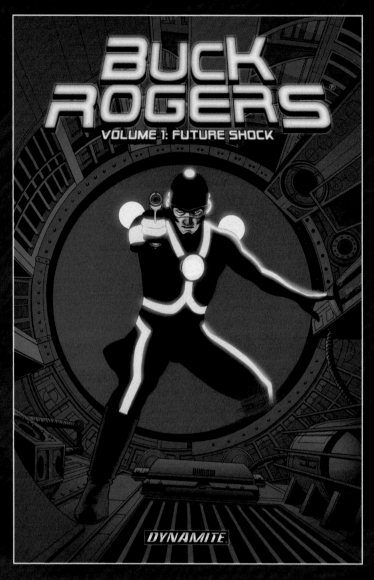

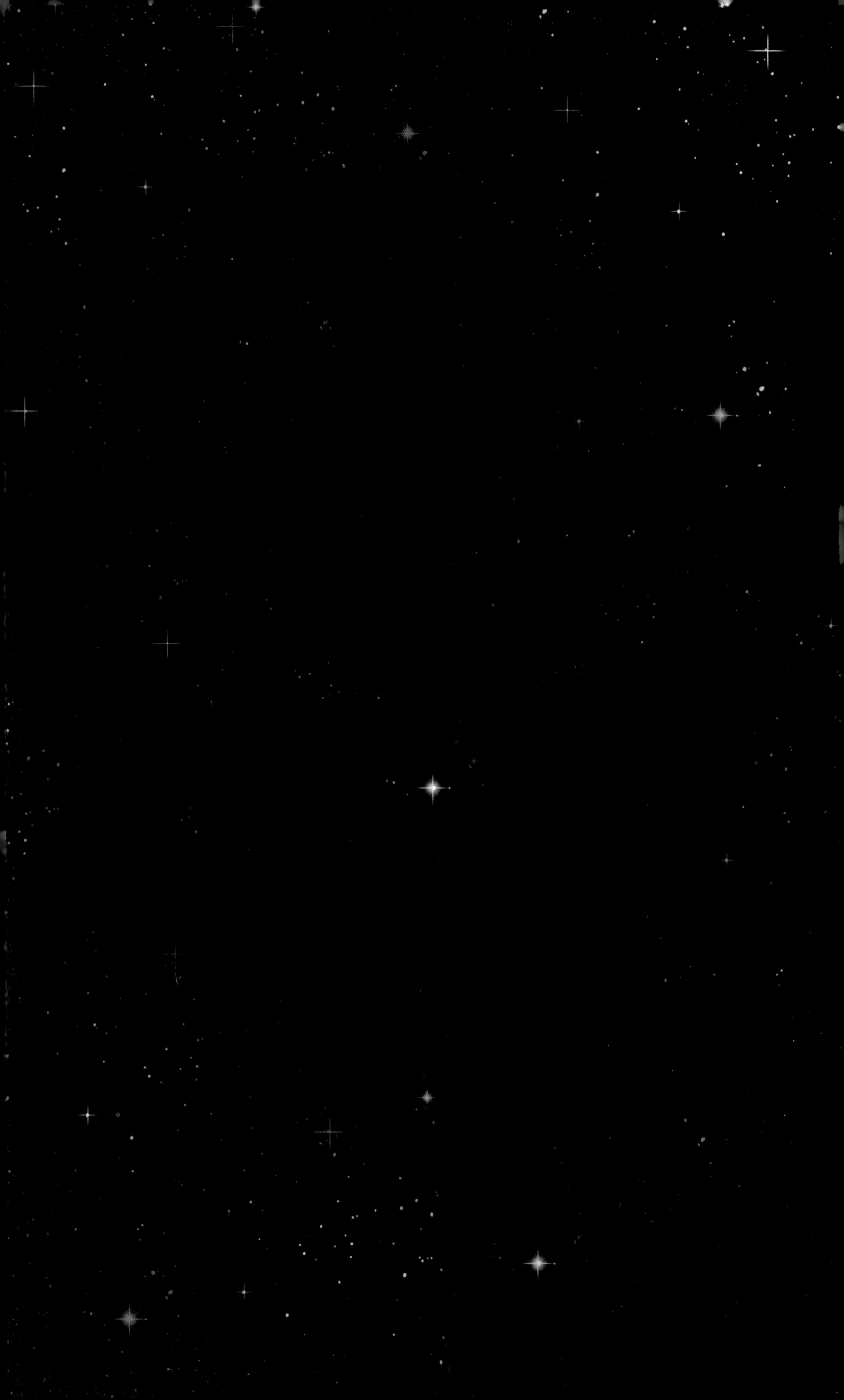